Conversations with Classic Film Stars

Conversations with Classic Film Stars

Interviews from Hollywood's Golden Era

JAMES BAWDEN
and
RON MILLER

Scholarly publisher for the Commonwealth,
serving Bellarmine University, Berea College, Centre College of Kentucky, Eastern Kentucky University, The Filson Historical Society, Georgetown College, Kentucky Historical Society, Kentucky State University, Morehead State University, Murray State University, Northern Kentucky University, Transylvania University, University of Kentucky, University of Louisville, and Western Kentucky University.

Editorial and Sales Offices: The University Press of Kentucky
663 South Limestone Street, Lexington, Kentucky 40508-4008
www.kentuckypress.com

Library of Congress Cataloging-in-Publication Data

Names: Bawden, James, interviewer, editor. | Miller, Ron, 1939– interviewer, editor.
Title: Conversations with classic film stars : interviews from Hollywood's golden era / James Bawden and Ron Miller.
Description: Lexington, Kentucky : University Press of Kentucky, 2016. | Includes index.
Identifiers: LCCN 2015041242| ISBN 9780813167107 (hardcover : alk. paper) | ISBN 9780813167121 (pdf) | ISBN 9780813167114 (epub)
Subjects: LCSH: Motion picture actors and actresses—United States—Interviews. | Motion pictures—United States—History—20th century.
Classification: LCC PN1998.2 .C614 2016 | DDC 791.4302/80922—dc23
LC record available at http://lccn.loc.gov/2015041242

This book is printed on acid-free paper meeting the requirements of the American National Standard for Permanence in Paper for Printed Library Materials.

Manufactured in the United States of America.

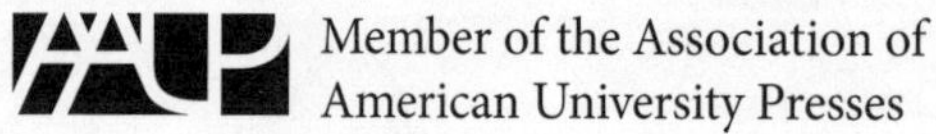

In memory of my parents, Maisie and Russell Bawden,
who never imagined my childhood obsession with movies
would result in an adult career as a newspaper TV critic.
—James Bawden

To my wife, Darla, who shares my love of classic movies;
and my loyal siblings: Barbara Childers of Colleyville, Texas,
and Norman of Minden, Nevada, who paid my way to a showing
of *Samson and Delilah* in 1950 and has never let me forget it.
—Ron Miller

Contents

IV. The Queens of the Bs

V. The Singing Cowboys

VI. A Giant of Comedy

VII. Four Very Special Stars

Introduction

Ron Miller

When my coauthor, James Bawden, and I retired from our regular jobs as television columnists, we possessed a treasure trove of rare interviews with some of the greatest stars of Hollywood's golden years, collected over more than half a century. Reviewing what we had in our inventory, we realized most of these performers were now gone and that the conversations we had with them should be part of their luminous legacy as icons of film history. That's when we first began to envision combining our interviews for a book that would preserve them for generations of film lovers as a valuable work of oral history.

Our notion, using our original tape recordings and written notes, was to re-create the atmosphere of the interviews, describing the conditions under which we met and talked with the stars. These are not reprints of the articles as they originally appeared. We have presented the interviews in a format that expands and enhances them beyond their original presentation in newspapers and magazines. In every case, they've been expanded and updated, covering what took place in each actor's life after we talked.

All the interviews included in this book were conducted face-to-face; we have not included press conferences that we attended with the stars. In a few cases, both of us had done separate interviews with the same stars, so we have merged those encounters to enrich the overall content while retaining our separate comments on how our individual chats took place.

From the start, we knew we wanted to do this book together because we share a love of classic movies and knew that our approach is basically the same: to accurately reflect the personality of the star and to encourage him or her to take us behind the scenes for the real story of how they made their great films.

We sincerely believe that the stars of Hollywood's golden era were a different breed. Most came into movies while the so-called studio system held sway. In the golden age of the 1930s, 1940s, and early 1950s, movie stars were groomed carefully by the studios. Some actors had already established public personas if they came from Broadway, radio, or the music business. Irene Dunne, for instance, had starred on Broadway and Gene Autry was a singing star on radio. But most were retrained by their studios, which put them into a variety of roles in B movies or in smaller parts in A movies, a reliable way to discover if they had the appeal to become leading actors.

Actors of the golden age had to be pretty versatile if they hoped to survive. The studio might put you on a horse to see if you could handle the lead in a western. Or it might have you sing or dance to see if you could carry a role in a musical. Jane Wyman, for instance, worked in lots of silly comedies and musicals before she was deemed ready for the dramatic roles that made her a major star in *The Lost Weekend* and *Johnny Belinda*. Joan Fontaine was given a showcase role as Fred Astaire's dancing partner in a musical, though she would gain fame as a dramatic actress. And so on. Of course, when the studio finally figured out the groove it deemed right for an actor, that often meant the actor was typecast, perhaps having to risk suspension for a chance to rise out of that studio-determined persona.

In our chats with these stars, you can learn a lot about the old studio system by reading between the lines, picking up on their common frustration with the conduct of their careers under studio rule. Austrian Luise Rainer, for instance, rebelled against the trivial roles she was given by MGM even after winning back-to-back Academy Awards. When her marriage also began to fall apart, she left Hollywood for good and virtually retired from movies.

However, they weren't all miserable—and you'll sense that, too, as you listen to them talk to us in their own words, not the words put into their mouths by studio publicists.

As the 1950s wore on, the pervasive new competition from television, the antitrust rulings that forced studios to sell their movie theaters, the rising influence of powerful talent agencies, and the growing strength of the craft unions fostered an economic crisis for the studios, forcing them to jettison most of the exclusive star contracts they had held for a generation.

In putting this collection together, we have for the most part chosen wide-ranging interviews that give us a picture of the star's whole career.

But we've also included some that, although less comprehensive, offer some rare insight into a star's life.

We also highlight some character actors who almost always played supporting parts in movies and seldom saw their names above the film's title. The great Chinese American actor Keye Luke's memories throw an important light on the experiences of ethnic minorities during Hollywood's golden age. We wanted also to celebrate the rich contributions of beloved character players like Margaret Hamilton, the unforgettable Wicked Witch of the West in the Land of Oz as well as the talents of B players like Audrey Totter and Marie Windsor, whose work is praised even more today than it was in their working years.

James and I have been friends and colleagues for more than forty years, though we come from different nations and wrote for quite different newspapers. But we share a deep love of movies and a respect for the great creative people who combine their diverse talents to make them. We hope you will enjoy these samplings from our combined archives of memories. Perhaps they will enrich your own memories of these truly great performers.

I

The Silent Era

Jackie Coogan

Interview by Ron Miller

The greatest and most memorable of the silent movie child stars was surely Jackie Coogan. Charlie Chaplin discovered him performing onstage at the Orpheum Theater in Los Angeles. Noticing the boy was a natural-born mimic, Chaplin cast him—at age five—in a small part in *A Day's Pleasure* (1919). The boy glowed on camera, so Chaplin put him into his 1921 feature film *The Kid* and Jackie became an overnight sensation in one of Chaplin's biggest hits.

Director Frank Lloyd quickly capitalized on Coogan's international fame, casting him in the title role of *Oliver Twist* in 1922. As Coogan's winsome appeal continued to grow, he eventually became the centerpiece of a whole new Hollywood approach to child stardom. He became the first child star to get the full product-marketing treatment: dolls, figurines, whistles, recordings, and even a brand of peanut butter bore his image, usually wearing a large cap and a sad-eyed expression. The marketing boom for Shirley Temple a decade later was modeled on the Coogan experience.

Coogan also revolutionized legal treatment of the earnings of child stars. After he discovered that his mother and stepfather had usurped most of his earnings—an estimated $4 million, worth about $50 million in today's dollars—the then twenty-four-year-old successfully sued them. He got only $126,000, all that remained from his parents' spending spree, but the court case led to passage of the California Child Actors Bill, now commonly known as "the Coogan act," which requires that a child actor's employer must set aside 15 percent of his or her earnings in a trust account. The bill also set standards for work-hour limitations and required schooling for child actors.

Once he grew out of the juvenile phase of his career, Coogan saw his popularity fade; he was no longer a headliner by the late 1930s. Coogan

Jackie Coogan with Charles Chaplin in *The Kid* (1921). Courtesy of Thames Television.

attended the University of Southern California and then Santa Clara University, but did not do well and never received a degree. In 1935, when Coogan was twenty, he barely survived a horrendous car crash near San Diego that killed his father and his good friend the child actor Junior Durkin.

With his acting career stalled, Coogan enlisted in the U.S. Army in 1941, before the attack on Pearl Harbor. He transferred to the Army Air Force after the United States entered World War II and became a glider pilot. With the First Air Commando Group, he flew British troops on raids behind Japanese lines during the fighting in Burma.

After the war, Coogan resumed his acting career, this time mostly in the new world of television. He landed the role of Stoney Crockett in the 1952–1953 series *Cowboy G-Men* and appeared in a number of other TV roles, but he is best remembered by baby boomers as Uncle Fester, the ghoulishly funny character he played in ABC's *The Addams Family* from 1964 to 1966. He appeared in many small roles in movies, including Elvis Presley's *Girl Happy* (1965) and John Wayne's *Cahill, U.S. Marshal* (1973). His final screen appearance in a movie was in 1984's *The Prey*.

Setting the Scene

My chat with Jackie Coogan took place in April 1968 while he was playing the role of Boss Finley in a production of Tennessee Williams's *Sweet Bird of Youth* in the round at Circle Star Theater in San Carlos, California. I joined him in his dressing room and we talked between his turns onstage with costar Shelley Winters. Our time was limited because he was doing his own makeup, which he did quietly and expertly while we talked.

Coogan was then a little heavy and had a receding hairline. He was dressed in a bathrobe over a pair of polka-dot shorts. His face had a good many furrows and creases, but it still retained the look of that sad-eyed little boy adopted by Chaplin's Little Tramp in *The Kid*. He was warm and friendly and often seemed to speak of the famous child star as if he had been someone else whom Coogan just happened to know.

In the middle of our chat, Shelley Winters came into Coogan's dressing room, heavily made up for her role as a dissipated former movie star, and remarked to me, "So, you're interviewing him? Well, that's good. He's a hell of an actor!" I thought that assessment, coming from the two-time Academy Award–winning actress, was a pretty good testament to Coogan's enduring star quality.

The Interview

Miller: The author Irvin S. Cobb once described you as "the blithest spirit that ever gave unending joy to countless millions." How did it feel to be adored by "countless millions"?

COOGAN [*chuckling*]: Maybe that's why Lloyds of London insured me for $250,000 whenever I went on a trip. Stars were different then. There was no television, no radio. When a star showed up, the people turned out to see him—by the thousands.

MILLER: When you became a star, movies were silent, so there was no language barrier and people all over the world could see and appreciate what you did on-screen. As a little boy, did you realize you were world famous?

COOGAN: When I was around nine, I was taken on a trip to Europe. It wasn't like a normal kid's trip to Europe. I met heads of state. I was "received" by royalty. I exchanged photos with Benito Mussolini. I kissed the pope's ring. Everywhere I went, I was mobbed by fans. I can remember being in a car in Paris when the mob nearly killed me. They picked up the whole car with us in it and paraded us down the street on their shoulders.

MILLER: What about back home in America? Could you go out and do things in public that a regular kid could do?

COOGAN: Once I made the mistake of going shopping with my mother. People recognized me and right away there was a huge group of people all over us. We finally had to be rescued by the police.

MILLER: How did this all begin? How young were you when you made your show business debut?

COOGAN: My parents were in show business, and I made my movie debut at eighteen months of age in an unbilled part in a picture called *Skinner's Baby*. I was still an infant. My dad [John Henry "Jack" Coogan] was a dancer, and I'd gone onstage with him many times.

MILLER: The legend is that you were dancing the shimmy onstage at the Orpheum in L.A. when Charlie Chaplin, who was in the audience, saw you and thought he detected a special appeal in you. In fact, in his autobiography, Chaplin said your mugging to the audience might have been obnoxious in another child, but that you were "charming and the audience thoroughly enjoyed it." I guess that was your lucky day because his decision to build *The Kid* around you made you a star overnight. How do you remember him?

COOGAN: Chaplin was very nice to me. He would just sit down with me and say what he wanted me to do and I'd do it. If Chaplin didn't feel right about filming, he just wouldn't film and I'd go play ball.

MILLER: After *The Kid*, you did a lot of famous juvenile parts in films like *Peck's Bad Boy* and *Oliver Twist*, but you also did a lot of popular pictures that are forgotten today.

COOGAN: They made some crazy stuff. When I got my first haircut, it made headlines—and MGM made a movie about it, *Johnny Get Your Hair Cut* [1927].

MILLER: When the talkies arrived, you were older, but were still appearing in some classic kid stories, like *Tom Sawyer* [1930] and *Huckleberry Finn* [1931]. Then the roles stopped coming so regularly. How did you feel when you realized you weren't as "hot" as you'd been as a little boy?

COOGAN: There was nothing to be sorry about. I had as complete a life as any boy could have had. I was never bitter about it.

MILLER: I know you had a terrible ordeal in 1935 with the auto crash.

COOGAN: My father, my best friend, and two of my dad's friends were returning from a dove hunt in Mexico when our car was forced over a cliff by another car near San Diego. I was the only survivor.

MILLER: As if that weren't enough, you then turned twenty-one and learned that your mother and her new husband had used up almost all the money you had made in the movies.

COOGAN: They even cut off my $6.25 a week allowance. I sued and finally collected what was left. It gave me a serious distrust of "jurisprudence and politics."

MILLER: How are things for you today?

COOGAN: I have four children from my four marriages and a horde of good memories. I'm financially stable, and my wife and I live permanently in Palm Springs. I've got damned little hair left, but I've been letting what's left of it grow out for this role. I've put on some weight, so some people might mistake me for an out-of-work sumo wrestler.

MILLER: I think you're well regarded as a very good character actor these days.

COOGAN: I'm probably only known by people old enough to remember *The Kid* or all those kids who watched *The Addams Family*. That's all right. I'm happy doing these character parts. I won't say I can do anything that comes my way, but I could never quit this business. When I lay off, I get way too jumpy.

Jackie Coogan (*second from left*) as Uncle Fester in the 1977 TV special *Halloween with the Addams Family.* Also shown: Carolyn Jones (*left*) as Morticia, Ted Cassidy (*third from left*) as Lurch, and John Astin as Gomez. Courtesy of NBC.

Afterword

Jackie Coogan was married four times—first to Betty Grable (1937-1939) before she became a major star. His fourth marriage—to Dorothea "Dodie" Hanson—was the lasting one, from 1953 until Coogan's death from a heart attack in 1984. The greatest child star of the silent era is honored with a star on Hollywood's Walk of Fame on Vine Street near Hollywood Boulevard.

Gloria Swanson

Interview by James Bawden

If there is one actress who personifies the silent movie leading lady, it would be Gloria Swanson. She was certainly one of the great stars of that era—first as a comedienne, then as a fine dramatic actress. She was also celebrated for her beauty. As if that were not enough, she also had a fine singing voice. But today Swanson is mostly remembered for her amazing comeback performance in Billy Wilder's 1950 *Sunset Blvd.,* in which she played Norma Desmond, a mentally unstable former silent movie star still living in her own glittering past.

Swanson had a stormy love life, which included an adulterous affair with Joseph Kennedy, father of the future president. Kennedy bought a movie studio to give Swanson a new showcase and helped finance her ill-fated final silent film, the notorious *Queen Kelly* (1928), directed by Erich von Stroheim. It was a financial fiasco, savaged by censors and barely seen anywhere as talkies dominated America's movie theaters.

Nominated for Academy Awards in both the 1920s and the 1950s, Swanson represents the greatest glory of the silent era and, as Norma Desmond, its darkest vision.

Setting the Scene

Gloria Swanson had always been a movie puzzle to me. Sure, I'd seen her in *Sunset Blvd.* Who hadn't? But when it came to the hundred or so silent movies she'd made, beginning in 1915, I simply drew a blank. Where was I going to see any of them shown? Then one night in 1972, CBC-TV showed 1934's *Music in the Air,* her last really successful movie before her initial fame faded. It was an operetta in which she and John Boles were like a luminous preview of the future pairing of Jeanette MacDonald and Nelson Eddy. I was impressed.

Gloria Swanson in *Airport 1975* (1974). Courtesy of Universal Pictures.

So when the invitation came in the spring of 1974 to interview Gloria Swanson before a scheduled TV appearance on the Canadian series *The Great Debate,* I jumped at the chance.

The Interview

SWANSON: Dear heart, fashionably tardy, I see. You have arrived four minutes and twenty seconds late. But do not despair. The young like to be fashionably late these days, or so I am told. But not me! I am forever punctual. If I had been fashionably late my first day at the studios, Charlie Chaplin would have given my job to somebody else. But I have more pressing problems, as you can see! Here I am in a supposedly grade-one hotel suite, and look for yourself! The ignominy of it all! No full-length mirror! No chandelier! Must I rough it? Must I?

BAWDEN: The elevator stuck.

SWANSON: No doubt! No doubt! Excuses! The last time I was in your Toronto, I was onstage in *Butterflies Are Free* (1970). You saw it? And you adored me? Now you are talking sense. But one night I was desperately sick. Did I make excuses? No! I went out there with a tummy ache and I performed with a temperature of 101 and only the standing ovation at the end made that evening of excruciating pain seem to be worthwhile.

Now you sit over there and I'll sit full profile for your darling little photographer and I'll place a long-stemmed red rose at my chin. Can I switch to white? Never, sir! Never! Now you may begin your questions. Don't look so scared. I assure you I do not have a freshly killed corpse floating head down in the bathtub!

BAWDEN: Why are you back in Toronto for one night?

SWANSON: To appear on the series *The Great Debate*, hosted by Pierre Berton. It will make for grand TV. I'll defend the undefendable—namely, we should all eat organically.

BAWDEN: Does it bother you to be so closely identified with *Sunset Blvd.*?

SWANSON: Ah, you cut to the chase! Yes and no. I was [as] completely unlike Norma Desmond as one could hope to be. I wasn't living in a destitute mansion. I had a chic townhome in New York City and several companies, including a line of cosmetics, dress patterns, and a radio show. I was doing live TV in those days and touring in plays. Billy Wilder had first tried to get Mary Pickford, but she was so wealthy why would she do it? He told me Garbo sent the script back without comment, so to fix her he added a nasty line about her that stayed in. They had to paint lines on my face, you know, and I insisted on an extravagant wardrobe. I don't think Billy truly likes women. Oh, we had great clashes on that set.

BAWDEN: But you were back at Paramount.

SWANSON: That's when the lines got blurred. And Billy added Cecil B. DeMille [to play himself in the movie], who'd given me my first bursts of stardom. And C. B. insisted on calling me "young fellow," which is what he really did in real life. They added [to the cast] such relics as Buster Keaton and Anna Q. Nilsson, and who could tell where reality ended and illusion began? The shots of Norma at her peak came from *Queen Kelly*, which Erich von Stroheim directed me in in 1928. And he was playing my former husband here. Who wouldn't be confused?

BAWDEN: I understand Bill Holden was a last-minute addition.

SWANSON: Right! It was always going to be Monty Clift, but he was having an affair with Libby Holman at the time and it was too close for comfort, I'm afraid. Monty quit two weeks before filming. Bill was a Paramount contractor but he wasn't as young as the character Joe was supposed to be. Bill was thirty-four by then. The shoot was fast and economical. We used a real house but not actually on Sunset Boulevard. I got second billing because Bill was supposed to be this big sexy star. And that was that. I think it's Billy's best film and I think I have a lot to do with that!

BAWDEN: Do you remember Oscar night?

SWANSON: Not much because that night I was starring on Broadway in a revival of *Twentieth Century* with José Ferrer, who was also nominated. He won, lucky man, for *Cyrano de Bergerac*. I lost to Judy Holliday [for *Born Yesterday*], and we were all sitting in New York waiting for the announcements and at midnight all I wanted to do was go home to sleep. I told Judy, "Oh, my dear, you have all the time in the world." But she didn't. She was never nominated again and she died of cancer in 1965. I was told Bette [Davis, who was nominated for *All about Eve*] and I had almost tied in votes, and Judy had squeaked forward with only a few more votes to take it.

BAWDEN: Did that typecast you?

SWANSON: No. I worked where I wanted. Paramount dared offer me another film where I was the mother of a teenaged girl, but I turned it down! Can you imagine! And Joan Fontaine did it [*Darling, How Could You?*] instead. I finally did one for Warners that was ghastly. Blah! Called *Three for Bedroom C*. And nobody saw it. I couldn't even sit through it.

BAWDEN: These days you're identified with health foods.

SWANSON: Think what you've just said. All foods should be healthy. As a child I ate hard rock candy, not the terrible soft junk they give out these days. We ate meat without any of the things they inject in cows and chickens these days. Bread tasted like bread. Now everything is refined, teens are fat, people have heart attacks at thirty-nine. Does that make me nuts?

BAWDEN: I only meant to say—

SWANSON: Please be quiet. I'm trying to tell you my life story and you are interrupting me. I was going to tell you when I met the warden of Alcatraz and I offered to send my bean sprouts diet guaranteed to cure criminality out of the most dastardly mass murderer. I visited the prison commissary and the smell of that gunk they were giving the convicts gave me a headache. He politely declined my services and there still are criminals among us.

BAWDEN: Have you ever been sick?

SWANSON: In the thirties I was told I had a tumor down there. I met with a surgeon who was puffy faced and sweating and his hands trembled. He said he wanted to cut through my rectum to get at the growth. I stood and shouted, "Physician, heal thyself!" and I simply fled. A pure bean sprouts diet cured me in months and the tumor shrank and disappeared. I rest my case.

BAWDEN: Did you always want to be a movie star?

SWANSON: No, I wanted to be successful at whatever I was doing. If I'd been a ribbon clerk in a department store, I would have been the best. When I was a little girl, the nickelodeons were quite disreputable. It was the genius of Adolph Zukor [founder of Paramount] who tried to legitimize the business by building those gorgeous palaces and promoting movies that the family could see or ones appealing to women. He really was promoting consumerism, although I doubt he knew it. Mr. Zukor—like Goldwyn, Harry Cohn, Louis Mayer—was an immigrant Jew who was painfully aware of his shortcomings and above all craved respectability. But he never was a producer himself. He always referred to movies as "product." His company made the movies and exhibited them in his theaters. He invented block booking.

BAWDEN: Did he make you a star?

SWANSON: No, the public did. They saw something in me. He saw the lineups to my movies and signed me for more. It was C. B. DeMille, who wasn't Jewish or an immigrant, who built me up in racy movies like *Male and Female* and *Why Change Your Wife?* He was a Victorian prude. He loved to show sin first, so he could show the repentance. That and the outlandish fashions and the beautiful sets pulled them in. Audiences gasped

Gloria Swanson with Rudolph Valentino in *Beyond the Rocks* (1922). Harry Purvis collection.

when I was shown in a huge bathtub, presumably nude, but the water had been heavily colored. That was considered very daring, I can tell you. I look at those pictures now and see a chubby teenager. I don't recognize her as me.

BAWDEN: Did you like yourself and Rudolph Valentino in *Beyond the Rocks* [1922]?

SWANSON: It's a missing [lost] film. But, yes, I did like him—a very shy, miserable young man. He surrounded himself with tough women who bossed him around. Paramount built him up as the sheik, but the papers made fun of his masculinity. He took it personally and developed ulcers. But his quality came from his astigmatism. He was blind as a bat. He would not have survived sound with that effeminate voice and mannerisms.

BAWDEN: Director Alan Dwan, born right here in Toronto, says you got too big for your britches when you moved to United Artists.

SWANSON: He said that? He's right. I wanted to be my own boss, so I left Mr. Zukor and I made pictures for UA. *The Loves of Sunya* [1927] was just awful. *Sadie Thompson* [1928] was a hit, but the censors really made us change the story line around and we couldn't use the original title, *Rain.* And *Queen Kelly* with its brothel scenes—really! I finally phoned Joe Kennedy, who was my financier, and he stopped production and we released it only in Europe. Talkies arrived around that time. It almost broke me, that one.

BAWDEN: In *The Trespasser* [1929] you sang up a storm.

SWANSON [*singing*]: "Love, your magic spell is everywhere. Yet I feel you but you are not there!" See, I still remember. A huge hit. Mother love stuff. If I'd stuck with that formula, I could have sailed through the Depression. But I was typed as a twenties symbol, although I usually lived in New York and made my Paramount [films] mostly at Astoria Studios [in New York]. After the crash, the banks stopped lending us money and I was in trouble and so were Doug Fairbanks, Mary Pickford, Sam Goldwyn—the whole UA crowd.

BAWDEN: Didn't Irving Thalberg at MGM offer you a contract?

SWANSON: Yes! But he had a heart attack soon after I arrived and never truly recuperated. I was on salary for a year, but no pictures ensued. So I went to Harry Cohn at Columbia with a [script for a] tearjerker and he yells, "A girl with a brain tumor? Swanson, yer slipping!" It eventually was sold to Warners and became *Dark Victory,* Bette Davis's biggest moneymaker! I went to Fox and made *Music in the Air,* where I warbled up a storm. The Met phoned with an offer, but I wanted to stick with movies. Then Fox was sold and I was out in the cold again.

BAWDEN: You left town?

SWANSON: No, Hollywood left me. I was considered old stuff. I moved to New York, started my cosmetics firm, a line of clothing. I was always working. I tried once more with that dog-awful comedy [*Father Takes a*

Wife in 1941]. But I was second billed to Adolphe Menjou! Me! The director [Jack Hively] came from Pomona. It was awful.

Bawden: Do you ever see Mary Pickford?

Swanson: No one sees her! She's locked herself up in Pickfair. She telephones old friends from time to time. Not me! We had a parting of the ways in the thirties. Over United Artists. I'm not saying Mary cooked the books, but she drove others away with her financial diddlings. Walt Disney left. David Selznick left. Even Goldwyn had to. And she said I'd said things about her, and this was simply not true. So I sent her a copy of her own book, *Why Not Try God.* Hint, hint. But she always seemed so angry fame had left her. Serves her right. She bought up all her old movies and nobody saw them for twenty-five years. Why be angry that Doug Fairbanks left her forty years ago? Why?

Bawden: Was there any old silent star who actually went crazy like Norma Desmond?

Swanson: Well, Mae Murray used to board the Hollywood Boulevard bus and she'd sing strains from *The Merry Widow* just to make sure passengers knew who she was. And she'd go into the Academy Awards library and ask for her picture file and start shredding the photos she hated until she was asked to leave. But crazy? Well, Mae went into Larry Edmunds bookshop and asked, "Do you have any pictures of that fabulous actress Mae Murray?" And the clerk said, without batting an eye, "Sorry, Miss Murray, we have nothing new from the last time you asked." They were scared she'd start autographing them all.

Bawden: Do you go to screenings at the Museum of Modern Art?

Swanson: You mean of my old silents—those that are left? No! I'm not crackers yet. A lot of strange young men attend and swoon appropriately, but I assure you I'm not camp. Not yet anyhow.

Bawden: Didn't they want you to take over from Katharine Hepburn on Broadway in *Coco*?

Swanson: Oh, yes! I went to a matinee and saw Kate swanning about and thought she was just awful. Imagine a woman who loves to dress in men's slacks cast as a great French designer! And the audience went wild! But the producers knew when she left attendance would slip. So they invited me on board, but at half her salary. And I said I could guarantee that attendance would rise, not fall—because, after all, I have always set fashion and not followed it. But they refused, so I walked, and they went after Claudette Colbert and offered the same deal. She said no and they

Gloria Swanson is ready for her close-up in *Sunset Blvd.* (1950). Courtesy of Paramount Pictures.

finally hired Danielle Darrieux, who really is French but she's unknown outside her homeland, and it all predictably failed. The moral is this: one must spend money to make it. And neither Claudette nor I come cheap.

BAWDEN: Didn't you once write a note to Greta Garbo?

SWANSON: You've done your homework! Yes! I invited her to the League of Former Movie Stars. I'm the president! She'd moved to New York City after the war and people were always seeing her walking about town. I mean, if she really wanted to be alone, why New York at all? I invited her around and said I'd give her lessons on remaining a movie star without ever actually making movies. She never replied. I'm sure she got it; I dropped it off at her apartment block. We could have worked together.

BAWDEN: You once sang a song from *Sunset Boulevard,* the musical, on *The Tonight Show,* but nothing more came of it.

SWANSON: I sang the one song written for it. Around 1966. The producers had a deal with Paramount, which owns the rights. Billy Wilder was furious, but it makes sense. A musical about a silent movie star! What fun! So I phoned up Johnny Carson and he was enthusiastic and he let me do it, but nothing more happened. Nobody would put up the required advance. They twice remade it live on TV, you know, with Mary Astor and Miriam Hopkins. Poor things, they must have needed the money.

BAWDEN: Why not a sequel? Norma is finally released from the funny farm and plots her next career move on TV in a sitcom?

SWANSON: Seriously? No, you are going too far. Carol Burnett wanted me to parody it on her show, but I can't and won't make fun of this woman. So I did my Chaplin imitation and it really went over big. It was sweet revenge on Charlie, who had hired me for my first job in 1916, and then said I'd never make it in pictures. The audience roared with applause.

BAWDEN: I loved you in the TV movie *Killer Bees* [1974].

SWANSON: So you're the one. Wait a minute—you actually liked it! Why?

BAWDEN: Well, your Swedish accent was perfect . . .

SWANSON: Dear heart, it was a German accent. How dare you? How do you dare? But as long as you liked it—well, you are forgiven. I played Madame Von Bohlen and I was told my costars would be Kate Jackson, Edward Albert, and John Getz, none of whom I'd ever heard of. I'd heard of Craig Stevens and that was about it. He asked why I was doing "a piece of crap like this"? And I shrugged. There's good and bad in everything. The ratings went sky high. It was the closest thing I've ever done to a horror film. They made it in nineteen days, about the same speed as I'd make one of my silent Paramounts.

BAWDEN: And then I've just caught the trailer for the upcoming *Airport 1975* [1974].

SWANSON: Universal phoned and said they wanted me to play one of filmdom's greatest stars. I angrily retorted, "*One?*" And the name given her was preposterous. I said, "I shall simply play myself," so they allowed me to rewrite all my lines. Director Jack Smight kidded me and said on the set, "Gloria, do you also want to direct yourself, too?" And I said, "Oh, no, you've got to earn your salary. Just point me in the camera's direction and I'll take it from here."

These disasters are big business these days. On my first day I bumped into Myrna Loy and was stunned. Her skin was like parchment. I ordered her to eat nothing but bean sprouts and chamomile tea for a week and brought over a large jar of my own ointment, and in a week those lines as big as the Grand Canyon vanished. She was ever so grateful. Sid Caesar asked for some, too, but he was beyond saving, and anyways I was running low on the precious stuff. I told Chuck Heston this was going to be his most arduous assignment and he said, "No, that would be parting the Red Sea." We sat for weeks in a scale model of an airplane and for verisimilitude they even wanted to serve us airport food on trays. Which is when I rebelled and placed an urgent call to Chasen's for organic delicacies, which were promptly delivered, and Mr. Smight signed on the dotted line, as well he should have.

BAWDEN: Future plans?

SWANSON: To go on being Gloria Swanson. It's my life's work. To keep busy and never feel angry about the past. Because the past is dead. I shall continue my fight for decent food. Maybe I'll date Frankie Avalon. Maybe I'll write my memoirs. But everything I'll attempt will be with a certain style. Now I must prepare for my TV triumph. Even with C. B. gone, I'm still getting ready for my next close-up.

Afterword

Swanson won *The Great Debate* with a spirited defense of organic foods. The poor professor she was debating didn't have a chance. She was immediately whisked out the door to the waiting stretch limousine. As it moved off into the dark, the window opened and a white glove stained with organic blueberries was spotted waving good-bye.

Gloria Swanson was married six times. Her first husband (1916–1919) was actor Wallace Beery. Her second, Herbert Somborn (1919–1922) founded the Brown Derby restaurant. Her third was a French count, Henri de la Falaise (1924–1931). Her fourth was Michael Farmer and her fifth was George William Davey. Though she had a long love affair with Joseph Kennedy, she could not marry him because he already had a wife and nine children. Still, he financed many of her last films in the silent era. Her sixth and last husband was health food writer William Duffy (1976–1983).

Swanson died from a heart attack in 1983 at age eighty-four in New York City. She'd been partying the night before, still loudly proclaiming her status as one of moviedom's greatest screen goddesses.

II

The Leading Men

Ralph Bellamy

Interview by James Bawden

Ralph Bellamy was the complete actor. A leading man in his films of the 1930s, he was even more effective in secondary or supporting roles, where his expertise as a character player really came through. He made more than one hundred films, starred frequently on TV, and had a distinguished Broadway career, earning both Tony and New York Drama Critics awards. He was a founder of the Screen Actors Guild and a four-term president of Actors Equity.

Though he played many memorable roles, he is probably best remembered as the screen's most convincing portrayer of Franklin D. Roosevelt, playing the president on Broadway in *Sunrise at Campobello,* then in the film version, and in the TV miniseries *The Winds of War* (1983) and *War and Remembrance* (1988–1989).

Setting the Scene

If I had to name an actor's actor, I'd certainly pick Ralph Bellamy. I became a fan early, watching him in everything from grade B melodramatics to screwball comedy on TV's *Late Show.* He seemed to be in every other TV movie made in the 1970s. And he appeared to do it all with such ease.

I first met him by chance on the set of a TV movie, 1978's *The Clone Master,* at Paramount in Hollywood, and we talked at length. He invited me to call him when I was in L.A., and we met again in 1983 at his home high in the Hollywood Hills. Then in 1988 we enjoyed high tea at his hotel in Toronto while he was making the movie *The Good Mother.*

The Interview

Bawden: How did you get started in acting and eventually into the movies?

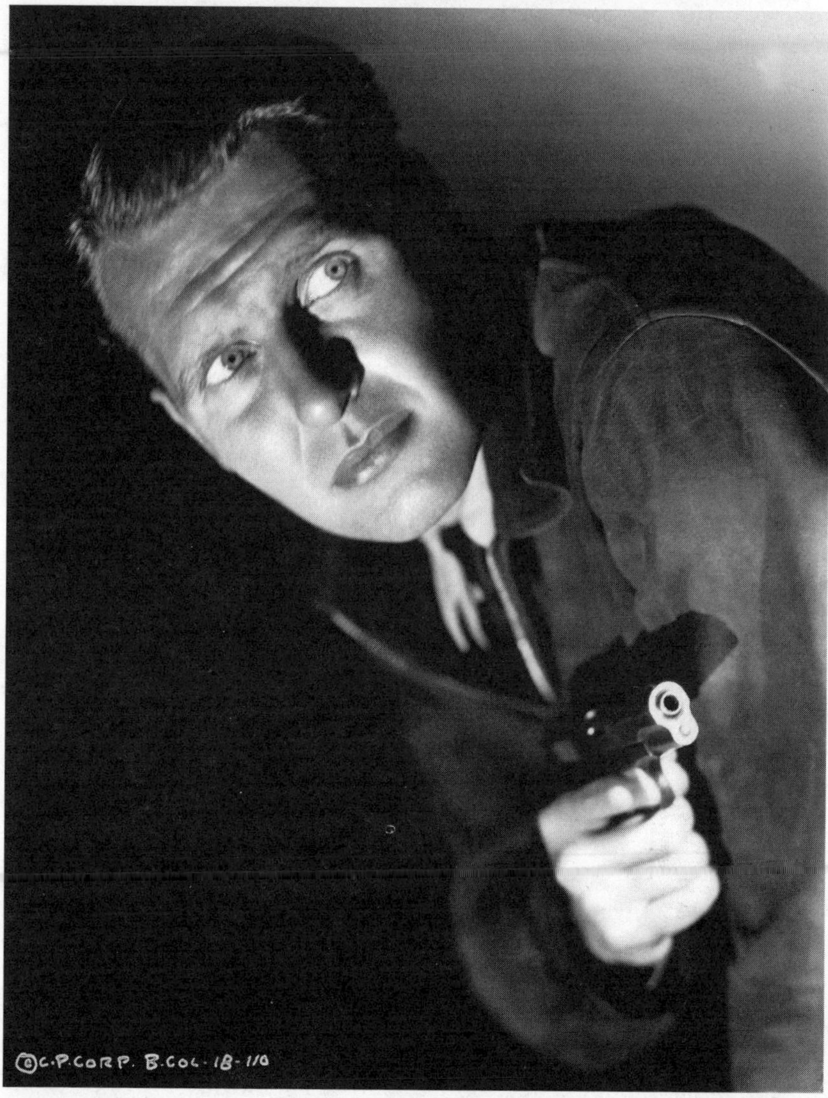

Ralph Bellamy, circa 1937. Courtesy of Columbia Pictures.

BELLAMY: I was born in Chicago [in 1904]. My dad was an advertising executive. I was president of the Drama Club in high school. I guess I always wanted to act. I started out in bit parts in road shows out of Chicago. Eventually, in my twenties, I founded my own repertory theater—the Ralph Bellamy Players—and toured in Nashville and Evanston and Des Moines. We'd be alternating two plays at night, and in the day we'd be learning a new play for the next week. We played in all kinds of theaters, and for me it was the chance to understand modulation, stillness, how to listen, which is the actor's most important work.

When talkies came along, our company disbanded. I made my Broadway debut in 1929. I was a mean bastard of a bootlegger. Even Broadway was crumbling after the crash, so I came west in 1931, like so many other stage actors.

BAWDEN: Your first film, *The Secret Six* [1931], starred Clark Gable and Jean Harlow?

BELLAMY: It was my first movie but I wasn't the star and neither were Clark and Jean. We were all given plum parts as sort of instant screen tests by MGM. And all three of us got $650 a week and thought we were in heaven. Lewis Stone and Wallace Beery were the stars. But as the movie progressed, Johnny Mack Brown's leading man part was whittled down and key scenes given to Gable. Johnny has a southern accent that limited his range. And Jean, who was red-hot sex on wheels, had her part built up, too. I tried watching it on TV recently and it's very crude.

But Irving Thalberg [MGM's production chief] thought Harlow would soar and finally bought out her contract from Howard Hughes, and he was the one who determined Clark would go to the top. At the time, Clark looked like Jack Dempsey. MGM tried gluing his ears back but it didn't work. He had what's called animal magnetism.

Anyway, after filming completed, I'm down in a shady bar swilling down illegal liquor and in comes Clark. He told me he figured he only had a couple of years in the biz before he was found out and he wanted to salt away as much dough as possible.

BAWDEN: Then you made a second movie for MGM, *West of Broadway* [1931].

BELLAMY: MGM did not know what to do with [former silent movie star] Jack Gilbert. He'd signed a six-film contract at $300,000 a film, and they had to pay him off even if they couldn't use him. Just a grand guy in person. And the stories about his voice are bogus. He had a lovely light Irish tenor. But the dialogue they'd given him in his first talkie was just plain stupid: "I love you" said over and over again. It was the way he overacted in silent style that ruined him, not his voice!

So MGM tried to get him to leave. They'd call up at 3 a.m. and order him to report to the studio. Failure to do so would result in dismissal. But Jack showed up, and one night jumped in a frigid swimming pool a dozen times as ordered by the director. Then they told him there was no film in the camera and to go home. I hated that and told Mr. Mayer off at length in his office. And he merely said I'd never work again at MGM, and I never did until 1968.

BAWDEN: You got work elsewhere?

BELLAMY: I got a deal at Fox, another at Columbia. Harry Cohn [head of Columbia] loved to tweak Mayer. Both were very crude guys, but the difference is Harry knew he was crude. He'd belch in the screening room and then laugh. If a picture seemed overlong, he'd shout, "My bum itches!" Stuff like that. Ran a very tight studio. It was the cheapest and located in Gower Gulch. And yes, he had sweeties among the chorines, but so did Mayer. I did a couple of quickies that made piles of dough and I asked for double the salary for my next one and he closed his office door and whispered, "Just don't tell Jack Holt," who made quickies like I did but was some twenty years older.

BAWDEN: Let me ask you about a B you made at Columbia as an example. Let me pick *Parole Girl* [1933]. How fast was it made and how much were you paid?

BELLAMY: They all were shot in two weeks or less—ten to twelve working days since we worked Saturdays in those days. For the men, you had to supply your own wardrobe, so I accumulated a variety of suits, coats, shoes, etc. Also I had to bring my own makeup kit. The women got stuff from the wardrobe department, but nothing was ever made specifically for them. Eddie Cline was the director here—a terrific guy. He shot at breakneck speed. Sometimes he used multiple cameras. He didn't shoot as on an A picture: establishing shot, middle shots, then close-ups. He only shot what he needed. Mae Clarke was the leading lady and she was a theater veteran, too, and worked quickly and efficiently. On an Irene Dunne vehicle, they'd take an hour just to light her close up. Not here. The others included Marie Prevost, Hale Hamilton, Ferdinand Gottschalk. Never actually saw that one.

I made eleven movies in 1933—I was busy! I'd say I maybe got $1,500 tops for it, perhaps a little less. Then it was on to the next B.

BAWDEN: Why do you think *Wild Girl* [1932] was important in your career?

BELLAMY: Because I met Charlie Farrell, who was the star. And we got together and founded the Racquet Club, which is still in operation. I was always founding stuff in those days. I was one of the founding fathers of the Screen Actors Guild, which did not entirely endear me to the big studio heads.

Bawden: But you also did A movies.

Bellamy: But not as the lead. That same year I made *Picture Snatcher* [1933] at Warners with my pal Jimmy Cagney. We were part of the so-called Irish mafia that included Pat O'Brien, Spencer Tracy, Frank Jenks. Jimmy played an ex-con who becomes a photographer for a tabloid. Today they call them paparazzi.

The girls were Patricia Ellis, who was all of sixteen, and Alice White, and [Cagney] got to kick and shove them around with glee. One scene we had a fight and I rearranged his mug, broke his nose and teeth. He forgot to duck, I guess. I also did *The Narrow Corner* with Doug Fairbanks Jr. at WB [Warner Bros.] the same year. It was a South Sea Islands thing based on a Somerset Maugham story. We shot at Catalina and used a lot of back projection that seems so phony these days. Alfred Green shot it and much of the script was written by Darryl Zanuck, who was head of WB production at the time.

Bawden: Another A was the Katharine Hepburn film *Spitfire* [1934].

Bellamy: What a stinker that was! Great Kate was a mountain girl named Trigger who somehow had acquired a Bryn Mawr accent. Bob Young was an engineer who is building a dam and has a romance with her. She doesn't know he's married. We shot in Hemet, California, both rural and hilly, and John Cromwell directed. The original male lead was Joel McCrea, but Hepburn had him dismissed, I don't know why. Anyhow, it's Saturday night on the last day of the shoot and Great Kate tells Cromwell her contract is over at the stroke of midnight. A contingent of RKO execs arrive and they go into a barn with her and she emerges, but it's now 1 a.m. on Sunday. Says she'll finish the last scene of the picture and when I asked why, from her gingham dress pocket she pulls a check made out for an additional $10,000. Pretty smart for a mountain lass, I must say.

Bawden: Why did *The Wedding Night* [1935] turn out so poorly?

Bellamy: It was called all over town "Goldwyn's Folly." Every studio tried to import a central European actress to vie with Garbo and Dietrich. C. B. DeMille had Franciscka Gaal, Universal had Elisabeth Bergner. There was Gwilli Andre. Warners had Lil Dagover. Sam Goldwyn's choice was Anna Sten, fairly beautiful, a grand actress. But she had no heart, she had no soul. The public just wouldn't accept her. That mystical bond with the audience just wasn't there. Nothing Sam could do could force her on

Americans. He made three expensive flops. Gary Cooper was the big name and even Coop couldn't bring in customers. You see, the public makes a star, and not the producer. MGM tried with Luise Rainer, who won two Oscars, but the public never warmed to her. And eventually Sam just gave up on Miss Sten.

BAWDEN: The same year you made the delightful screwball comedy *Hands across the Table* [1935]. Describe Carole Lombard.

BELLAMY: An angel in terms of screwball comedy. She did not have perfect features, you know. There was a big scar on her cheek, the result of a car crash as a child. But on the set, she was one of the gang. She sat with the crew between takes. No movie star airs for her. She always played jokes on all of us, like placing a squawk cushion on my wheelchair seat. One day she comes to me and asked why Freddie MacMurray didn't make a pass at her. I said he was in a happy marriage, which floored her. She'd just gotten out of an abusive relationship with Bill Powell, so she didn't know what a happy marriage was. Most days we laughed ourselves silly and that camaraderie really showed in the film.

BAWDEN: You got your only Oscar nomination for *The Awful Truth* [1937]. How did this come about?

BELLAMY: It started out as just another assignment from Columbia. The script was sent to me and I was told what clothes to bring. The character at that stage was a stodgy Englishman. Then new scripts arrived—three—from Mary McCall, Dwight Taylor, and finally Dorothy Parker. All were discarded by our director, Leo McCarey. I'd be reunited with Irene Dunne, who I first worked with in the drama *This Man Is Mine* [1934]. It became one of my favorite pictures. And Cary Grant I'd never met.

The story was constantly being reworked by Leo McCarey—who, by the way, was a complete clone of Cary. Only Cary then took some of Leo's characteristics and interpolated them into his character. For days we'd sit around swapping stories and Cary, who is so disciplined, finally went to Cohn and said if Harry let him go he'd do two pictures for free. The first day Leo asked if I could sing. I said no, so he had me sing "Home on the Range" while Irene very shakily played the piano. It still gets a laugh when shown today. The result was serendipitous. Irene and I got Oscar nominations; Cary had a new career as *the* light comedy actor of his day. I wish all assignments could be as wonderful as this one turned out to be.

BAWDEN: Not many directors could improvise.

BELLAMY: One who couldn't was Greg LaCava, who was on a downward spiral when Irene and I joined him for *Lady in a Jam* [1942]. He decided he'd do a McCarey and here we were stuck in Phoenix in blazingly hot weather. We shot a few bits from a script that was awful, then Greg disappeared for weeks with a writer and Greg's psychiatrist. Irene lost her serenity and trashed her trailer—and remember, there was no air-conditioning in those days. And *Lady in a Jam* was so awful Greg only did one more movie before retiring to Malibu, where he spent his last years shooting seagulls from his balcony window.

BAWDEN: What about *His Girl Friday* [1940]?

BELLAMY: Cary just asked for me, and Howard Hawks readily agreed. It was a variant on my *Awful Truth* character. This is the fastest-talked movie of all time. The lines just fly. Look at all those reporters in the prison scenes, veteran theater actors all: Gene Lockhart, Porter Hall, Regis Toomey, Ernest Truex. All highly competitive. For variety and comparison, Howard told me to talk ever so slow as a dimwit would. I savored every line while those characters chattered all around me. Roz Russell got so frightened at Cary's glibness she told me she'd hired a gag writer on the side to interpolate bits for her. I first saw it complete with a preview audience. At one point Cary, asked to describe my character, ad-libbed as "He's like that actor in movies, Ralph Bellamy," and there was this roar of laughter and I jumped out of my seat!

BAWDEN: You had a lock on these characters.

BELLAMY: In *Brother Orchid* [1940] I was a dim chauffeur who was an amateur ornithologist. In one scene where I'm driving in a convertible with Eddie Robinson and Ann Sothern in the back, I'm supposed to imitate all these bird tweets. We did the scene against a transparency, then Eddie rushes to the director, Lloyd Bacon, and barks, "Ralph is interpolating bird whistles not in the script. He's trying to steal the scene with these tweets." We all dissolved in laughter but Eddie was dead serious.

BAWDEN: You were serious in a series of Ellery Queen mysteries.

BELLAMY: I did four of them: *Ellery Queen, Master Detective; Ellery Queen's Penthouse Mystery; Ellery Queen and the Perfect Crime; Ellery Queen and the Murder Ring.* Made them for Columbia as Bs with Margaret Lindsay, who was an old pal, and Charlie Grapewin as my dad. Jimmy Hogan directed the last three I did but they became ordinary. I asked for more money and they replaced me with William Gargan. In the first, Marsha Hunt was one of the suspects, I remember, and Michael Whalen and Ann Shoemaker were there. And I loved doing them, although shooting was very fast. Kurt Neumann directed the first one, but I forget why he was replaced.

BAWDEN: You knew Errol Flynn well?

BELLAMY: A darling. Couldn't or wouldn't take himself seriously. And he drank like there was no tomorrow. Had a bum ticker from the malaria he'd picked up in Australia. Also a spot of TB. Tried to enlist but flunked his medical, so he drank some more. Knew he wouldn't live into old age. He really had a ball in *Footsteps in the Dark* [1941]. He was so glad to be out of swashbucklers. In *Dive Bomber* [1941] all the color shots of Pearl Harbor were shot only months before the Japanese attack. It made a fortune because war was coming by the time it got released.

BAWDEN: I want to ask you about *The Wolf Man* [1941].

BELLAMY: I already know the question. What the hell happened to Warren William? He gets second billing. I get third, but he disappears from the picture early on. The reason: Warren was quite the drinker, even boasted he could outlast John Barrymore. So he went on a bender and never came back to the set. We just worked around him.

Craziest thing about that movie—that the diminutive Claude Rains is the father of hulking Lon Chaney Jr. The sets were impressive. They even built a small woods on a soundstage, and the special effects when Lon turns into the wolf took days of stop-action work. I asked Maria Ouspenskaya [the great Russian actress] why she was doing dreck like this and she answered, "Same as you. American bucks." Curt Siodmak wrote it and he was always around and George Waggner directed. He should have had a long movie career, but wound up doing TV stuff.

BAWDEN: Then came *The Ghost of Frankenstein* [1942].

BELLAMY: Ugh. It sort of picked up the story from *Son of Frankenstein* [1939]. Lon Chaney Jr. was the monster this time and he really resented that. Cedric Hardwicke was Ludwig Frankenstein, Lionel Atwill was the doctor, Bela Lugosi was Ygor, and Evelyn Ankers, a wonderfully sensitive British lady, was Elsa Frankenstein. The damned dumb director was Erle C. Kenton, complete with whip and an air of pomposity. On one scene he was going on giving Evelyn directions: "Elsa, your father was killed by the monster, your husband dragged off by Ygor. Now what I want from you is one clear emotion—that you're fed up with it all." At which moment Sir Cedric lay on the floor howling with laughter and he couldn't stop for some time. And forever afterwards at Hollywood parties I'd see him and he'd shout, "Fed up with it all?"

BAWDEN: The story goes that you were in producer Mark Hellinger's office and saw on a secretary's desk a script with a note about you.

BELLAMY: It said something like, "A wonderfully comic creation, this character dumb as a doornail, clumsy, frightfully daft—perfect Ralph Bellamy part!" At which I got up, walked out, walked out of Warners, and rang my agent to say I was being typecast and I needed a Broadway part right away. And he delivered. Within days it was announced I'd be going back to Broadway in a new play, *Tomorrow the World* [1943]. And I left Hollywood two years later and I was away for fifteen years with just one picture, 1955's *The Court-martial of Billy Mitchell* in all that time. I never missed it. And I don't think Hollywood missed me.

BAWDEN: So you decided to go back to Broadway?

BELLAMY: Luckily, I picked a huge hit. *Tomorrow the World* opened in 1943 and ran over a year. I had a wonderful costar in Shirley Booth, Arnaud D'Usseau and James Gow wrote it, and Elliott Nugent directed and we opened at the Ethel Barrymore. It was all about a little blond boy who is on the last boat out of Nazi Germany before war is declared, and it turns out he's already been turned into a Nazi. Little Skippy Homeier was the boy, and when they made the movie he was eighteen months older and no longer quite as effective. He then retired to finish high school but then came back in adult parts, but always as a villain.

BAWDEN: An even bigger hit was *State of the Union.*

BELLAMY: We opened in 1945. Opening night at the Hudson there was this huge cheering. It was a political play by Howard Lindsay and Russell Crouse, who'd done the monster hit *Life with Father.* Leland Hayward packaged it all up and Bretaigne Windust directed it. We had quite the cast: Margalo Gillmore, Ruth Hussey as my wife, Myron McCormick, Minor Watson. It was about a captain of industry who is fed up with the mess in Washington. Later on Kay Francis replaced Ruth and we even toured in it. Spence Tracy got the movie part, but the film directed by Frank Capra was a big messy thing. Our version ran 765 times and I did it for years.

BAWDEN: Then came *Detective Story* [1949)]

BELLAMY: It ran over 580 times. Opened in March 1949, closed in August 1950, and only because the summer heat that year was horrendous. It was the perfect play, really. I loved our cast: Jean Adair from *Arsenic and Old Lace;* Ed Binns, his first detective part; Lee Grant, who repeated her dazzling turn in the film; Horace McMahon. A lot of these wonderful people repeated their work in the 1951 film, but I was replaced by Kirk Douglas. Reason? Box office. Sidney Kingsley directed his own play. How can one argue with the playwright, I ask you? We started at the Hudson, transferring to the Broadhurst, and road companies played everywhere.

BAWDEN: Then came your role as Franklin D. Roosevelt in *Sunrise at Campobello,* which I understand is your favorite.

BELLAMY: It's the reason I'm still active today. I wasn't in such great shape by then, but I had to play in a chair every night, so I got a great physical instructor in. We had to work on my arm and back muscles. FDR had great biceps, he had to drag himself around. My neck muscles grew. I no longer had backaches. And I've continued that regimen ever since.

BAWDEN: What was it like opening night?

BELLAMY: We opened [in] January 1958. Opening night I took a peek through the stage curtain and the entire contingent of New Dealers were sitting in the first few rows. I nearly had a heart attack. I mean, you have to remember FDR had been dead fourteen years. That's not a whole lot of time. But Mrs. Roosevelt was sitting right there and the "children," now all grown up. Mary Fickett was Eleanor, Anne Seymour was Mrs. Sara Delano Roosevelt, a young pup by the name of James Earl Jones was there. Crowds cheered. It was something special in my acting life. We played 556 performances at the Cort, always to the same rapturous reaction. I got the Tony Award as best actor, which pleased me to no end.

BAWDEN: But you told me you hated the movie version.

BELLAMY: I overplayed to the rafters. We had Vince Donohue do the movie as well as the play, and he had precious little movie experience. I took one look at the finished product and it was awful. There's no modulation. We're all shouting our lines, except Greer Garson, who came in as Eleanor and she's perfect. She was the only one nominated for an Oscar. I certainly did not deserve one. But I got a whole new career playing FDR. He's been very good for my bank account. And I always thought there was more than a little rich, ripe ham in him.

BAWDEN: Explain to me how you could do eight performances a week *and* do a live TV series for CBS all at the same time.

BELLAMY: It's back to the routine I'd done in repertory. And also I was quite a bit younger. From 1949 through 1953, we played the half-hour detective saga [*Man against Crime*] on CBS, and that meant live from Grand Central studios. In 1952 we switched to film, which made things easier for me. One night while I was on in *Detective Story,* I finished the broadcast exactly at 9 p.m. They'd hold the curtain another fifteen minutes while I cabbed it over to the theater, and I'd just stroll on without makeup. But that night a drunk hit the cab and I had to run for the last few blocks. Dripping with perspiration, I raced in, staggered onstage, and gave what was called my best-ever performance.

The filmed shows were made at the old Edison studios in the Bronx. CBS cancelled us in 1953, and we then ran on two separate networks, NBC and DuMont, exactly at the same time, Sundays at 10:30. When I took a vacation in 1951, Robert Preston came on as my brother Pat and kept things going. I loved doing it!

BAWDEN: I have the VHS copy of you and Bill Shatner costarring in *The Defenders* live in 1957 on CBS's *Studio One* series, but when the weekly series started, you and Bill had been replaced. So what happened?

BELLAMY: Why, I was a bad boy. It took CBS almost three years to decide to do it as a series, and then they wanted to film it in California. They were phasing out live drama. I simply asked for too much dough, and I think Bill's movie career had heated up. So E. G. Marshall and Bob Reed replaced us and that's that.

I just continued on TV elsewhere. In 1962, I was asked to replace Wendell Corey in the medical series *The Eleventh Hour.* I did about thirty of those, and then I tried to get on every drama show around. I wanted it all.

BAWDEN: How did you get the choice part of Dr. Sapirstein in *Rosemary's Baby* [1968]?

BELLAMY: Oh, the little man wanted me—[director] Roman Polanski. Very dwarfish creature with a high giggle. After a take, he wouldn't say, "Cut." One would just hear a "Tee hee hee." He used a lot of veterans: Patsy Kelly, Elisha Cook Jr., Maurice Evans, Ruth Gordon, Sidney Blackmer. I knew most of them from way back when. Roman presented everything in [such] a calm, matter-of-fact way that the creeping terror just builds. It's sheer genius on his part. It's a very quiet movie where a door creaking can unnerve one. There's a lot of dark comedy in there, too. He was a very careful director—explained everything, multiple takes, very demanding, very appreciative when one got it right. Loved to talk old movies with me.

BAWDEN: Then he offered you another role which you turned down?

BELLAMY: Oh, yes, phoned me up when he was starting work on *Chinatown* [1974]. Told me he wanted me for Noah Cross. I'd be the stern old man who had raped his own daughter, had the illegitimate child and . . .

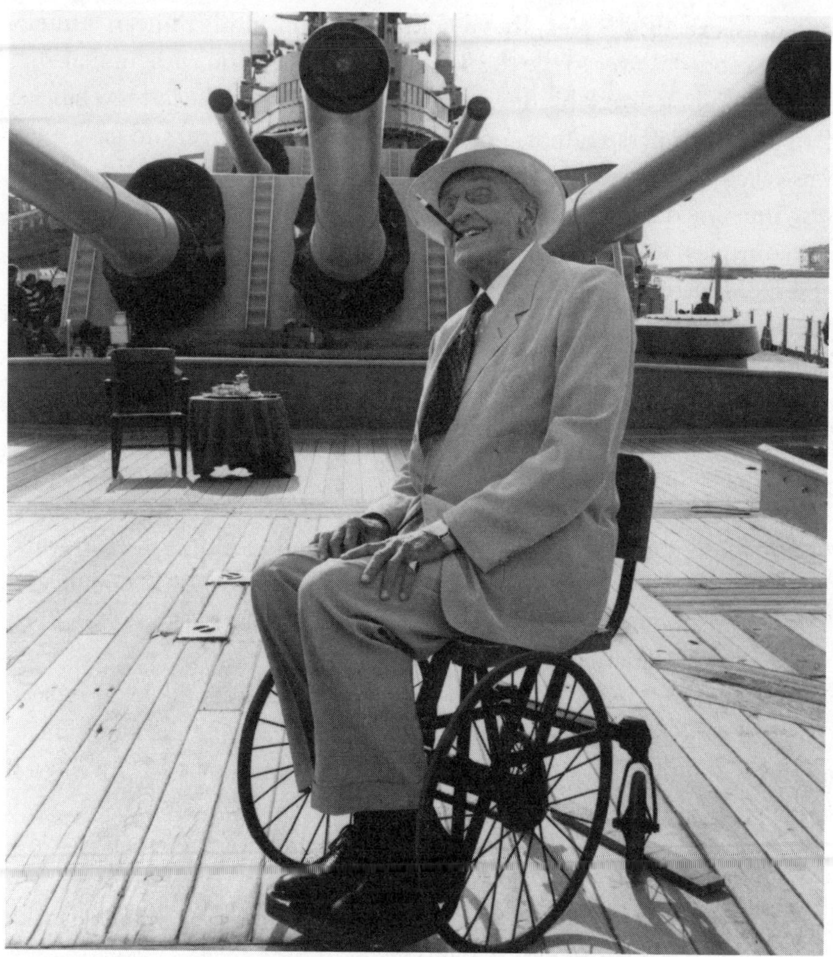

Ralph Bellamy as Franklin Delano Roosevelt in TV's *War and Remembrance* (1988). Courtesy of ABC.

And I said, "Whoa! Wait a minute!" And that was that. It may be a brilliant movie, but I still had to look at my wife across the breakfast table every morning and I had grown children. And Roman said I was afraid of being evil. But that's not the case at all! Johnny Huston did it, but I don't think he should have. So I got the little man mad at me and that was that.

BAWDEN: You had another big hit with *Trading Places* [1983].

BELLAMY: Went in for costume rehearsals and Ray Milland, chosen as my brother Mortimer Duke, was having difficulties. Finally he had to bow out just before filming and they got in Don Ameche. The script was choice.

First morning in the makeup trailer, I said, "Why, this is my seventy-second movie." And Don answers, "Why, this is my fifty-sixth." And Eddie Murphy looks embarrassed and says, "Boys, this is my first. Ever." It broke everybody up, and the movie became my biggest-ever hit.

[Years later, in 1988, we talked again over lunch in Toronto while he was filming *The Good Mother.*]

BAWDEN: As usual, you've been busy.

BELLAMY: I got to play FDR again in *The Winds of War.* That was challenging. And I'm back at it in *War and Remembrance,* which comes on next season. I'm still doing my FDR exercises every morning. Then they asked me to join *Hotel* [1985–1986] as Uncle Jake Cabot. Had a grand reunion with Anne Baxter, who I'd last worked with on *Guest in the House* in 1944. She bade me good-bye one weekend and went back to New York City and died there of a stroke right on the street. I'm also doing the mystery movies titled *Christine Cromwell* with Jackie Smith, a great beauty.

And here I am in Toronto, my first time here since selling war bonds in 1944. My mother, who was Canadian born, asked me to get her some maple leaves and it was fall, so we got some red ones and pressed them on wax paper and preserved them for her. This part is small but dandy and I'm getting to know and love Teresa Wright, the latest in a long line of wonderful leading ladies. And I just know I'll continue for a little bit longer at least.

Afterword

Ralph Bellamy, eighty-seven, died in a Santa Monica hospital of a lung ailment on November 29, 1991.

Rory Calhoun

Interview by Ron Miller

Rory Calhoun was always tinged with a bad-boy reputation in Hollywood because rumors about his criminal youth dogged him most of his professional life. As a result, even the many heroic roles he landed in westerns and dramas were usually men with an element of danger about them. Though he was a handsome, well-built man in his younger years, he seemed more at home playing gamblers or reformed outlaws and seldom took the role of white-hatted action hero as did other leading men of his time.

Born Francis Timothy McCown, he had no acting ambitions of any kind as a young man. A high school dropout, he progressed from petty thievery in his teens to armed robbery. He was sentenced to the California Youth Authority reformatory, but busted out and became a fugitive. He was caught after stealing a car and crossing a state line, which earned him a three-year federal prison term in Springfield, Missouri. When he finished his time there, he was arrested on other pending charges and sent to San Quentin State Prison in California. He was finally paroled and decided to clean up his life and make a new start.

While riding horseback one day in the Hollywood Hills, he met actor Alan Ladd. They struck up an acquaintance and Ladd asked his wife, talent agent Sue Carol, to see if she could get the rugged, good-looking young man any parts in movies. That led to small parts in several films of the early 1940s, and the erstwhile criminal started learning the acting business. He soon attracted the attention of top Hollywood producer David O. Selznick, who put him under contract. Talent agent Henry Willson gave him a new screen name: Rory Calhoun.

His rise to stardom didn't happen overnight. In many of the pictures he worked in from his debut in 1944 he didn't even earn screen credit. (One of his showier roles was as heavyweight boxer "Gentleman Jim" Cor-

Rory Calhoun, circa 1965. Courtesy of Screen Gems.

bett in the 1945 film *The Great John L.,* in which he was billed as Frank McCown.)

His breakthrough role came in the hit film about singer Jane Froman's life, *With a Song in My Heart* (1952), in which Calhoun played the young airman who saves Froman (Susan Hayward) after their plane crashes during World War II, then later marries her. The studio, 20th Century-Fox, afterward gave him a big buildup, putting him in with some of the brightest stars on the lot, including Marilyn Monroe in *How to Marry a Millionaire* (1953) and *River of No Return* (1954).

By the mid-1950s, Calhoun had moved up to prominent roles in westerns at other studios, mainly B pictures like *Dawn at Socorro* (1954), *Four Guns to the Border* (1954), and *Utah Blaine* (1957), becoming firmly established as a leading man in action roles. He also tackled a variety of roles in TV, including a dramatic turn in Alfred Hitchcock's *Suspicion* series, and in 1958 he landed his own western series, *The Texan* on CBS, which ran for two seasons.

As westerns faded from the scene, Calhoun worked for a few years in European action films, then returned to the United Sates to appear mainly in episodic television. By the 1980s, Calhoun had aged into supporting character roles in films and television, but he still enjoyed some showcase parts—especially his leading role in the 1980 horror film *Motel Hell*, in which he played a deranged farmer who traps highway motorists and chops them up to make the sausages he sells to tourists. Two other films that gave the aging Calhoun a rich role were *Angel* (1984), in which he played a wacky Hollywood Boulevard western weirdo named Kit Carson, and its 1985 sequel, *Avenging Angel*. Also during that period, Calhoun spent four years playing the role of Judge Judson Tyler in the CBS daytime serial *Capitol*.

In his twilight years, Calhoun had a running battle with the tabloids, which reported he was dying of prostate cancer. They had feasted on him throughout much of his career, constantly digging up his criminal past and dwelling on the charges made by ex-wife Lita Baron in their divorce case that he was a serial womanizer. (Superstar Betty Grable, his love interest in *How to Marry a Millionaire*, was one of the women Baron named.) He was the father of five daughters—three with Lita Baron, one with second wife Sue Rhodes, and one with a woman who won a paternity suit against him.

Setting the Scene

I grew up with a special appreciation of Rory Calhoun because he spent much of his youth in my hometown, Santa Cruz, California, and went to some of the same schools before he dropped out. I remember digging his clip file out of the "morgue" of the *Santa Cruz Sentinel*, where I worked in the first few years of my newspaper career, and finding some accounts of his behavior as a "juvenile delinquent." That only enhanced my interest in an actor I already thought was pretty impressive on the screen—and I saw most of his films because I was a big fan of westerns.

I finally met him in the summer of 1983 when I was covering the TV and movie business in the Los Angeles area. CBS, promoting its new daytime soap opera, *Capitol,* offered a chat with one of its stars—Rory Calhoun. Over lunch, I found him to be a very good-natured "regular guy" who had a great sense of humor, especially about himself. He had gray hair and quite a few wrinkles in his handsome face, but he looked pretty darn good for a man who had just turned sixty-one.

I guess we hit it off pretty well because Calhoun asked if I would like to go with him that evening to a screening of *Angel* before it was released to theaters. I met him at the screening room and together we watched him give one of his best performances in years.

The Interview

MILLER: What kind of a childhood did you have? I know that your father was a gambler who died when you were less than a year old and you lived with your mother and stepfather after that.

CALHOUN: In those days, the early 1930s, people were very transient. We moved from Los Angeles to San Diego to El Centro to Marysville to Santa Cruz.

MILLER: What did your family do for a living?

CALHOUN: Stole, mostly [*laughs*]. My mother was a waitress. My uncle was an underwater welder. The people in my family went where the work was. They were just ordinary working people.

MILLER: So you were a working-class kid who grew up in mostly small towns like Santa Cruz. What did you think about Hollywood back then?

CALHOUN: That was a whole other world. All the glamour, the big cars, and all that stuff. That was fairyland.

MILLER: I know that your youthful flirtation with crime and your time behind bars came back to haunt you once you were a well-known actor and the tabloids went after you. How did all that finally come out?

CALHOUN: I'd had a few phone calls from guys I did a little time with. I never avoided them, but we got in a few scrapes here and there because they wanted to blackmail me. So we'd have a punch-out. I was in my late twenties and I didn't fear anybody, but I decided it was time to do something about it and come out with the story. But how and where to do it was the problem. I decided *Redbook* magazine was the place to do a gentle exposé of my past. We were ready to do that when *Confidential* magazine contacted me. They said they had the whole story, pictures and everything, so did I want to talk to them. I said, "You're goddamn right I do!" So I did, and what it turned out to be was a success story about how I changed my life.

MILLER: Does your past still haunt you today?

CALHOUN: Today it doesn't mean anything in our society. It doesn't really hurt you unless you murdered somebody, which I never did. The whole philosophy has changed. Man has become much more permissive. In those days, it was Mama and apple pie. There were certain things you didn't do that are now common. If you were the "bad boy" in town, nobody wanted to talk to you. Now they want to know how you're doing.

MILLER: Is the story about running into Alan Ladd on a riding trail true?

CALHOUN: Yes. I met him on the bridle trail early one morning. I was working in a lumberyard then. He asked me to lunch and I met Sue Carol, his wife and agent, who took me over to Fox the next day. I did a scene from *Heaven with a Barbed Wire Fence,* and next thing I knew I was under contract.

MILLER: That was in 1944 and they put you into a musical with Perry Como called *Something for the Boys.* What do you remember about that?

CALHOUN: I didn't say anything in that picture. I just hung around.

MILLER: You followed that up with an unaccredited part as "soldier in a truck" in *Sunday Dinner for a Soldier* [1944] with Anne Baxter and John Hodiak.

CALHOUN: That was my first speaking part. Oh, I had a hell of a line in that: "Gee, does she have a sister?" They left it in. I wasn't on the cutting room floor.

MILLER: You did manage to get a showcase scene in *The Great John L.,* playing "Gentleman Jim" Corbett, who took the world heavyweight boxing title from John L. Sullivan [Greg McClure].

CALHOUN: I only had that one big scene where I was dancing around the ring, beating the hell out of John L. Sullivan. I think I had one line where, after I beat him, he tells me to take care of the championship and I say, "I'll do that, Mr. Sullivan!" But I had a lot of action shots.

MILLER: Did they tell you they figured you as a certain "type" on-screen?

Calhoun: They never really told me anything. I made a couple of other pictures where I was in automobiles or just walking around in the big city. But nobody remembers much about those.

Miller: What did you think was going to happen after those first couple of little parts in pictures? Did you think you were on your way to stardom?

Calhoun: It didn't really matter to me. I didn't care what happened because I could go back to the lumberyard. I was making more money selling redwood than I was under my movie contract. I didn't know anything about acting. The only acting I'd ever done was in front of my creditors or a judge. For me, it was a lark. I had a seven-year contract, but Fox had a six-month option and they dropped me after the first year. Said I had no talent.

Miller: So what happened then?

Calhoun: David Selznick picked me up and put me under contract to him for five years.

Miller: Some actors loved Selznick, but others hated being under one of his exclusive contracts because he often didn't find anything for them to be in. Your take on him?

Calhoun: I have a deep affection for the man. He never put me in any of his pictures, but he never did anything bad to me. He helped me constantly. I was with him for five years and when he closed his studio, he negotiated a new contract for me back at Fox and got me eight times the money I'd been making.

Miller: While you were with him, he loaned you out for one of the best pictures you made in your early years—*The Red House* [1947] with Edward G. Robinson and Judith Anderson.

Calhoun: That really got me started. That was my first big thrill in movies. I don't think I'll ever feel quite like that again unless I do something unlikely, like win an Academy Award or something.

Miller: What was it like to be a young actor with no training working with an old pro like Edward G. Robinson?

Calhoun: He was magnificent. Two of us made a test for that part. The other guy was a better actor than me at the time. It was Robert Horton. He did a better test, too, but Robinson wanted me for some reason. He knew I really couldn't handle it, so every night while we were on location he would bring me up to his suite of rooms with his wife and he'd go over my scenes with me. He believed in helping young people along. He also knew that the better I was, the better it was for the picture. I try to do the same. I don't impose myself on the young actors today, but if I see the opportunity to help them make it better, I do it. I think I owe it to them because it was done for me.

MILLER: Finally, people began to notice you after *The Red House.* What was that like?

CALHOUN: For about the first two years, if somebody came up to me and asked for an autograph, I was in shock. I still didn't grasp the idea since I'd been doing nothing but little bits and stuff. I mean, I still drove a wrecking truck at night.

MILLER: How did you really learn to act when you were getting just these little parts?

CALHOUN: Selznick was a wise man. He made me the "king of the tests." If he heard they needed somebody to do a test with somebody for a role, he'd send me over. I would test almost every week with some big star—Ingrid Bergman, Jennifer Jones, Gregory Peck, Joe Cotten. He gave me experience that way—working with these competent professional people! I would never have had a chance to work with that caliber of actor or actress if it hadn't been for that.

I was in thick with Selznick, though I was still at arm's length. I sort of did a lot of legwork for him. Like, he'd call me at 11:30 at night and tell me to set him up with a table for twelve at the Mocambo and that he wanted me to be there. He kept me visible and, for me, it really worked well.

MILLER: Did you ever see a part in one of his films that you really wanted but didn't get?

CALHOUN: I've lost a lot of parts, but I think the only one that ever got to me was in his *The Paradine Case* [1948]. I'd just finished *The Red House,* which was a heavy part, but he brought in Louis Jourdan from France to play the gatekeeper in *The Paradine Case.* I felt I really was ready for that, but he wanted Jourdan. Louis did a hell of a job on it. Selznick was trying to build a stable of the best people in Hollywood.

MILLER: He loaned you out to Warner Bros., which put you in *That Hagen Girl* [1947] opposite Shirley Temple in one of her first grown-up roles. And you also got to work with Ronald Reagan in that film. Your memories?

CALHOUN: Selznick must have blackmailed them or something—but anyway, I got the part. I didn't have much to do in it. Reagan was pretty political, even back then. He sent me a nice letter on my birthday. It went right into my scrapbook.

Rory Calhoun comes on to Marilyn Monroe in 1954's *River of No Return.* Courtesy of 20th Century-Fox.

Miller: Once you were back at Fox, you really started to get career momentum after your romantic role opposite Susan Hayward in *With a Song in My Heart.* How was she to work with?

Calhoun: She was marvelous—a real pro. God, what a pleasure to work with that lady!

Miller: And of course the studio put you into two of its big CinemaScope pictures with Marilyn Monroe—*How to Marry a Millionaire* and *River of No Return.* Your memory of Marilyn?

Calhoun: She was a phenomenon that I doubt like hell this town will ever see the likes of again. There have been a lot of people trying to copy her one way or another—and to me, they're third stringers.

Miller: In *River of No Return,* you lost her to Robert Mitchum. Like you, he's an actor who had his hard times in the tabloids. What do you think of him?

Calhoun: He's one of the greatest guys you'll ever meet in your whole life. I'm very fond of Bob. He's a hell of a guy. I guess we could have swapped roles [in that picture], but he was right for that and I was right for what I was doing because I was more greasy, more slick. Well, let's face it: that's where it is. I had this shitty look. That's what they wanted and that's what I gave 'em. There wasn't a hell of a lot of effort involved.

MILLER: Did you have a hard time getting truly romantic roles?

CALHOUN: I'm uncomfortable with it. I guess that's a bridge I haven't crossed over. I never felt really comfortable kissing a girl in front of eighty people. I'm self-conscious about that. I like to kiss girls—don't misunderstand me. But you're always thinking some guy up on the catwalk is thinking, "Hell, I can do it better than him!" And he probably can.

MILLER: So you're more comfortable playing heavies?

CALHOUN: They're a ball. It's fun to growl, snarl, and look wicked. They're fun to do. It's a game.

MILLER: When nothing big seemed to be happening anymore at Fox, you left and went to Universal, where you started getting leading roles in their westerns.

CALHOUN: Fox tried to pull a slick one on me, to keep me on another year for the same salary. But I'd already been over to Universal and they told me that if I could ever get out of my Fox contract, they'd like to use me. So I said no to the deal with no raise and Fox didn't pick up my option and I went to Universal, where I did five pictures in the first year. I worked so much I was cross-eyed.

MILLER: Then you began to make pictures in Italy.

CALHOUN: They were civilized in their filmmaking. You went to work at 11 in the morning. You block out a scene and then you break for lunch for three hours from 1 to 4. You go back and work until 10, then go home, shower, put on some clothes, and have dinner at a sidewalk café at 11:30 at night. And I was being paid for it, too.

MILLER: And you also began to work a lot more in television.

CALHOUN: I wanted to try another medium. I was scared to death of the stage. I'd tried a couple of plays and hated it. I did a lot for Dick Powell's *Four Star Theater* in those days. I was on a search for knowledge and decided this wasn't a bad business to be in.

MILLER: Now you've gone from starring in your own TV series—*The Texan*—to being a member of a daytime drama ensemble in *Capitol*. What's that like?

CALHOUN: They're kind of easy on me. I do an average of a show and a half a week. Some weeks I don't work and some others I do three shows.

Rory Calhoun as the Hollywood "cowboy" known as Kit Carson in *Avenging Angel* (1985). Courtesy of New World Pictures.

It's not that consuming—and they give me time off. [Producer] John Conboy is good about that. If you have something to do, he'll shoot around you. I think this is probably the greatest continuing experience I've ever had. If it ends tomorrow, I'll be richer from having gone through it.

MILLER: But your movie career now finds you playing much more character-driven roles, not all of them leading parts. Was that hard to accept?

CALHOUN: There's a point you have to come to realize after awhile. It hit me sometime after my mid- or late forties. You say to yourself: "Hey, I'm no longer the heartthrob." You're gonna get gray hair unless you dye it, and you're going to get a bunch of wrinkles. So you'd better be prepared to make a transition and be happy about playing a little older part like I'm doing now.

MILLER: How did you like starring in a horror movie like *Motel Hell*?

CALHOUN: I had a ball doing that. Hey, I made sausage out of nice little people!

MILLER: And now you're playing a character in *Angel* that seems to make fun of the western heroes you used to play.

CALHOUN: Yes, I'm a character they call Kit Carson, who's one of the Hollywood Boulevard people. They wanted Slim Pickens for the part, but he wasn't available, so they came to me. He wears a fringed jacket, a big white hat, and a long gray wig and a moustache. He carries two pistols, boots and spurs, and walks up and down Hollywood Boulevard talking about yesteryear—Tom Mix, William S. Hart, and all that stuff—giving people autographs whether they want them or not. But in the end I shoot the villain who's trying to kill the girl [Donna Wilkes]. And I shoot him in old-time western style in an alleyway with the light behind me. What's not to like?

MILLER: How would you sum up your career today?

CALHOUN: I've been up and down like a yo-yo many times, but I've always worked. I have to tell you, I was probably the most naïve son of a bitch this town ever saw. I really don't know how they ever tolerated me.

Afterword

Rory Calhoun died on April 28, 1999, from emphysema and diabetes. He was seventy-six. Calhoun's last screen appearance was in an episode of TV's *Tales from the Crypt* in 1993. He has two stars on Hollywood's Walk of Fame, one for his movie work and the other for his TV roles.

Joseph Cotten

Interview by James Bawden

Joseph Cotten made a very auspicious screen debut in 1941 in the film most often acclaimed as the greatest-ever American movie: Orson Welles's *Citizen Kane*. The talented stage and radio actor went on to become a leading man in scores of important films, including a number of renowned classics, among them *Shadow of a Doubt* (1943), *Gaslight* (1944), *Since You Went Away* (1944), *Duel in the Sun* (1946), *The Farmer's Daughter* (1947), and *The Third Man* (1949).

Cotten worked into the 1980s, even after he had slipped from leading roles to character parts. Though he appeared in quite a few uninspired productions late in life, his legacy on film is one of the richest of any actor of Hollywood's golden age.

Setting the Scene

The first time Orson Welles's *The Magnificent Ambersons* was shown on Canadian TV in 1960, I stayed up half the night to watch it. Though it wasn't easy for me to get up the following morning for my eighth-grade class, it was an experience I had to get used to because Welles's *Citizen Kane,* another "must-see" movie, ran not long afterward on late-night TV. Those two classic films made me appreciate the particular talents of Joseph Cotten, who starred in the two Welles masterpieces. But then I also saw him in *Gaslight, Portrait of Jennie, Since You Went Away,* and *I'll Be Seeing You* in rapid succession on late-night TV. In fact, I don't think I actually saw Joseph Cotten on the big screen of a movie theater until 1964, when *Hush . . . Hush, Sweet Charlotte* opened.

The following year, I saw Cotten in person at a matinee performance of the short-lived play *Calculated Risk,* costarring his wife, Patricia Medina,

Joseph Cotten, circa 1961. James Bawden collection.

at the Royal Alexandra. That confirmed one fact in my mind: he was a masterful theater actor as well as one of Hollywood's most versatile leading men, capable of playing romantic leads (*The Farmer's Daughter*), villains (*Shadow of a Doubt*), or heroes (*The Third Man*) with equal success.

Fifteen years later, in 1980, I wrote my final article for the *Hamilton*

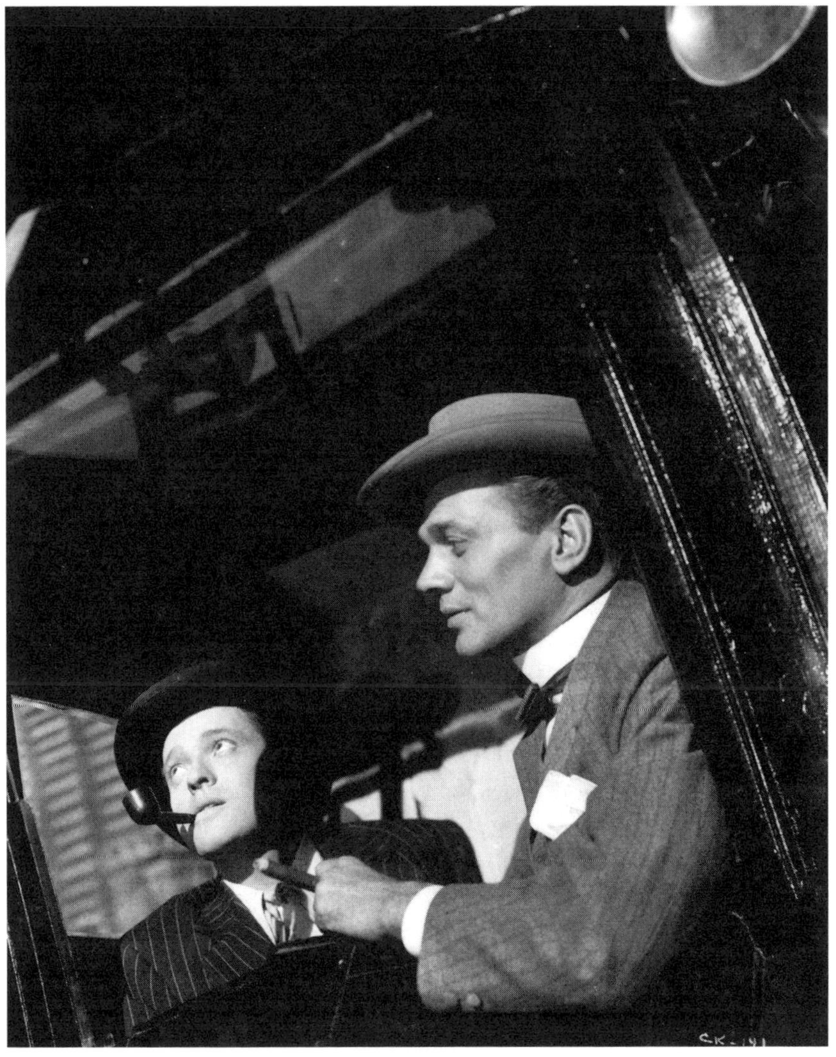

Joseph Cotten (*right*) with Orson Welles in *Citizen Kane* (1941). Courtesy of RKO Radio Pictures.

Spectator before moving on to the *Toronto Star.* It was a profile of Cotten, based on my interview with him at his Beverly Hills apartment. I remember how that afternoon stretched into the evening as the then seventy-five-year-old Cotten chatted on about his lengthy career as Hollywood's most dependable leading man.

The Interview

BAWDEN: Did you always think of a life in movies?

COTTEN: Never! My parents were well-to-do southerners. I grew up in Petersburg, Virginia. I was born there in 1905, the oldest of three brothers. But I always wanted to act—of course, onstage and not in the flickers. I studied acting at the School of Expression in Washington, but no offers came. So I moved to Miami and was the freelance drama critic for the *Washington Herald* from 1926 to 1928. I had other side jobs to keep me going while I acted in amateur stock. By 1930, I'd made my Broadway debut, but right then the Depression killed off Broadway as a viable option, so I tried to get as many radio gigs as possible. I'd married in 1931 and I felt any experience was all right.

BAWDEN: Don't you think it strange you made your movie debut in probably the best American movie of all time . . . *Citizen Kane* [1941]?

COTTEN: But I didn't. It was my second movie.

BAWDEN: So what was your first then?

COTTEN: *The Philadelphia Story.* I can see your eyebrows lifting. I'm not in the MGM movie that was released. But I'm in the first one MGM made. Let me explain. Metro bought the rights [to the play] from Katharine Hepburn and decided to film it several times right through and edit that into a movie version. So they rented out our Broadway theater for two performances, had an invited audience, and the cameras rolled. That way they could get an understanding of how the story flowed. And it made for a better final movie with Hepburn, [Cary] Grant, and [James] Stewart because much of the dialogue was cut down by Don Stewart and he also completely eliminated the role of Tracy's brother. I was C. K. Dexter Haven, replaced by a guy named Cary Grant. And Van Heflin was the reporter replaced by Jimmy Stewart. The photographer, Liz Imbrie, was Shirley Booth, replaced by Ruth Hussey. MGM told me my version is still somewhere in the vaults, but legally cannot be shown.

BAWDEN: How did you meet Orson Welles?

COTTEN: It was about time. I was "only" thirty-five! I'd originally met Orson Welles in the midthirties when CBS had a producer on Madison Avenue, Knowles Entrekin, and I was in his office with Orson, and Orson dumped his pipe into the wastepaper basket and set it on fire. Now that's one way of getting known. He was a boy of twenty-one or twenty-two. I had started going to auditions for radio shows in New York and met him while he was also auditioning. Days later we were rehearsing a play for *School of the Air* and the line "barrels and barrels of pith" caused me, Orson, and fellow actor Ray Collins to continually double up in laughter, And Knowles became very red-faced with anger and almost, but not quite, fired us.

But when Orson founded the Mercury Theater in 1937, he asked for me to come on board. His first production was a modern-dress version of *Julius Caesar,* mounted for $5,000. I'd been in such flops as *Jezebel* with Miriam Hopkins and *The Postman Always Rings Twice* with Dick Barthelmess. Orson saw me in both, told me I'd never be a good actor, but with my curly hair I'd have to get by as a star.

BAWDEN: Did you get to play in *Citizen Kane* through your connection with Welles then?

COTTEN: No, I was brought out to Hollywood by my agent, Leland Hayward, and trotted around to the studios, all of whom turned me down. I was at RKO, so I dropped in to say hi to Orson and he hired me on the spot as Jededia Leland. The name was a combination of Jed Harris and Leland Hayward. Ray Collins, Everett Sloane, Paul Stewart, and George Coulouris had already been set. The script was still being written by Orson and Herman Mankiewicz out at the Mankiewicz home. Orson said he'd already wasted six months on a script for *Heart of Darkness* that RKO turned down.

BAWDEN: But when did shooting begin?

COTTEN: In August 1940. I just hung around for weeks, not even getting paid, listening to the fantastic stories Orson and Herman were dreaming up. I was in a wheelchair in my first scene as an old man. I hadn't seen a finished script until one was presented to me at 7 p.m. I was told to report to make up at 4 a.m. for a rubber mask to be applied. I'd already had an assortment of wigs made for me. At 9 a.m., the buzzers sounded and Orson was in a wheelchair, too, after spraining an ankle at tennis. We went out to a sanitarium; I'm an old senile coot reminiscing about the glory days. *Citizen Kane* had begun! Gregg Toland [the cinematographer] said to start the cameras and that was that.

BAWDEN: Did anybody know they were doing a film that would be hailed as the best ever made in America?

COTTEN: Nope. Certainly not me. That first day we shot until 6:30 the next morning. Then it was all junked because my wig wasn't right. Orson would say, "This is what I want to achieve here," and Gregg would nod and go off and make magic or Herman would trot to a corner to cook up a rewrite. It cost well under $1 million, less than budget. Completely on time. What Orson hadn't reckoned on was the enormous power of the Hearst press, which refused all ads for the picture. [The film's main character is a thinly disguised portrait of newspaper baron William Randolph Hearst.] So people across the country did not know it was ever on.

RKO told me it would open at the Radio City Music Hall. It didn't. Hearst phoned the Rockefellers, who owned the theater, and the offer was withdrawn. For years after, any movie I was in, the Hearst papers would "forget" to mention me in the reviews. We got nine nominations, but on Oscar night the audience booed mere mention of the title. It got one award—for best original screenplay. *Citizen Kane* ended up losing money for RKO. It broke Orson's spirit. But in an odd way it made me, and I just kept on going even when Orson couldn't take it anymore.

BAWDEN: Some people think Welles's follow-up film, *The Magnificent Ambersons* [1942], was an even better picture.

COTTEN: We thought that when we were making it. It was more expensive to make and the costumes were expensive. Much of the house was built as a fully working house. I mean, walls wouldn't move out so our cinematographer, Stanley Cortez, had a hell of a challenge lighting scenes. One problem: it had no stars to entice patrons into the theater. We shot it very quickly, as I recall. I loved my part. Dolores Costello was so beautiful it was easy imagining I was in love with her. Orson wrote the script in two weeks using great gobs of dialogue from the book.

When Anne Baxter came from Fox [to play] Lucy, she was accompanied by a guardian [because she was legally a minor]. It was Frank Lloyd Wright, her grandfather, the great architect. Orson showed him the footage already shot and Frank said, "Magnificent architecture. Story so-so."

For the scenes in winter, we shot in an icehouse so you could see our breath. And, yes, it is true—Agnes Moorehead's hysterical scene on the stairs was shot a number of different ways, all believable. Aggie is that kind of actress, you see.

We were shooting on December 7, 1941, Pearl Harbor day. That's what killed us: American war anxiety. Suddenly the problems of a turn-of-the-century family in Indianapolis became completely irrelevant. The first preview was before a bunch of louts expecting a Hopalong Cassidy western. Instead they got this strange film without titles at the beginning and an unseen narrator. They hollered back at the picture and the RKO [brass] heard about it and ordered it be cut down to eighty minutes. Bob Wise, our editor, stretched it to eighty-eight minutes, but at least forty minutes was lost. And the picture tanked with the public. Orson's short reign as a golden boy was over.

BAWDEN: Didn't you write the screenplay for his next film, *Journey into Fear*?

COTTEN: I used so little of the plot the novelist, Eric Ambler, later thanked me, saying he could sell the story again for another movie. By this time Orson was in love with Dolores Del Rio [the film's leading lady]. The adjective "orchidaceous" applies to her. Being the world's most beautiful woman made her quite childlike about everything. She lived in a house straight out of Omar Khayyám. It was the last Mercury production. RKO hated it so. [The studio took Welles off the picture, which was finished by Norman Foster.] I thought it was made too fast because Orson wanted to get out of RKO as quickly as possible. And he got his wish.

BAWDEN: How did David Selznick pick you up?

COTTEN: Blame my agent. Leland shopped me around town. David seemed mildly interested, so I went out to meet him at his Culver City office. Parts of the sets from *Gone with the Wind* were up all over the lot. I later met him at the swimming pool at the Beverly Wilshire Hotel. David liked to operate out in the open so people could see him. He'd produced two Oscar-winning movies in a row, *Gone with the Wind* and *Rebecca,* and then went into this three-year funk. Didn't make a single movie, but he had all these hot stars under contract—Joan Fontaine and Ingrid Bergman and was about to hire Jennifer Jones and Shirley Temple.

BAWDEN: First impressions?

COTTEN: A bulky, ugly man. Warts all over the place, bulbous nose, glasses that didn't suit him. Talked a mile a minute. But he made a grand pitch for me. I told Leland I'd sign and it changed my career. In typical Selznick fashion, he had me making two movies at once: *Gaslight* for MGM with Ingrid Bergman and *Since You Went Away* right up the street, for him, with Claudette Colbert. When I'd tell him how tiring it all was, he'd slip me some Benzedrine, which I definitely would not take. I realized he thrived under the pressure of deadlines. Anything less and he'd become positively lethargic. And also he was beginning to fall for Jennifer in a way that surprised and disturbed her. After all, she was married to Robert Walker at the time.

BAWDEN: *Gaslight* is one of your most memorable films.

Joseph Cotten (*left*) with Charles Boyer and Ingrid Bergman in 1944's *Gaslight*. Courtesy of MGM.

COTTEN: Well, Ingrid, Charles Boyer, and even teenager Angela Lansbury all got Oscar nominations, and Ingrid even won. But not me. Where did I go wrong? For starters, we all trooped off to the screening room to watch the 1940 original, which MGM had bought and then suppressed. My part really didn't exist in that. It was played by a very old actor and he was a retired detective who was running some kind of bicycle repair shop, as I recall. And it was very obvious from the beginning the husband was planning to kill the wife. George Cukor [who directed the MGM remake] insisted on a more nuanced interpretation.

MGM never did anything by half measures. A complete Victorian house was constructed—and, in fact, a whole row of them—for Thornton Square. That set on the back lot was there for the next twenty-five years. I made parts of a 1951 movie, *The Man with a Cloak,* on the same set.

I met and truly fell for Ingrid on a completely nonromantic level. We've been buddies ever since and now she is so very sick. [Bergman died in 1982, just over a year after I talked with Cotten.] Charles [Boyer] was a master actor; I believe his is the film's best performance. My part was the third wheel. I could be away up the street making another film and not be missed.

BAWDEN: And what do you think of *Since You Went Away*?

COTTEN: A Herculean achievement. After *Gone with the Wind*, David could never make just a good little movie. It had to be gargantuan. I'd been warned about Claudette Colbert—how she wanted all the sets to be constructed to show off her left side. When I asked her, she giggled and assured me her right side wasn't the dark side of the moon. A tiny person, so methodical. She left me amazed at her understanding of the film process. John Cromwell was the nominal director, but David was always lurking in the background. We shot and shot. Claudette's two daughters were played by Jennifer Jones and Shirley Temple, in a comeback part at the ripe old age of fifteen. We had a lot of fun on the set because filming never seemed to stop. Or should I say some of us had fun. Jenny's marriage to Robert Walker was falling apart even as they had to film romantic scenes where they were supposed to be falling in love. I'm a naval officer who comes and goes. There was a slight whiff of romance but nothing more. Today the characters would all be heaving away in bed. We thought we were finished several times and then David would recall everyone for additional scenes. Prints were about to be delivered when he ordered Claudette back again to shoot new scenes with Nazimova [the great Russian actress Alla Nazimova, who played a Polish immigrant in the film]. She told me since she was hired on a week-to-week basis that she made a fortune for it. And it was a big hit, a three-hour black-and-white saga of a family on the home front.

BAWDEN: Around this time you got to kick Hollywood gossip columnist Hedda Hopper in the butt.

COTTEN: Well, somebody had to do it. I was then making a Deanna Durbin picture at Universal, a little something called *Hers to Hold* [1943]. And my wife and I were in San Francisco for the weekend. When we got back to L.A. it was after midnight, and since I had a 7 a.m. call I decided to proceed to the studio and sleep a few hours there in my dressing room. What I didn't know was Deanna had decided on doing the same thing in her gargantuan dressing room on the other side of the lot. I never knew she was there until I read an item in Hedda Hopper's column blasting me and hinting we were having a clandestine affair. Obviously, a security guard had sold Hedda the item. But it angered me, got my wife upset, and

Joseph Cotten (*left*) as the villain of Alfred Hitchcock's *Shadow of a Doubt* (1943), shown with Teresa Wright and Macdonald Carey. Courtesy of Universal Pictures.

later at a party I saw Hedda bending over to pick something up and I let her have it. She toppled and I walked away singing. Well, a lot later Hedda comes up to me at another party and says, "Joseph, I had that coming to me," and she just walks away, but with her head turned just in case I try for a repeat.

BAWDEN: How did you and Alfred Hitchcock get to Universal for *Shadow of a Doubt*? You both were under exclusive contract to Selznick.

COTTEN: It was part of a deal engineered by Selznick, a two-for-the-price-of-one fire sale. Hitch still says it's his best U.S. picture because it is grounded in reality. Every shot was made in Santa Rosa except for a scene on the veranda. I still think Teresa Wright marvelous in it. We had a grand cast of characters. Pat Collinge was my older sister, married to Henry Travers, and Hume Cronyn was the mama's boy living next door, who was always trying to fashion a perfect murder scenario. The malt shop actually existed; so did the library where young Charley [Teresa Wright] runs one night just as it is closing. After that, I played a lot of disturbed young men, often guys in uniform. I blame Hitch—I still do—for discovering my murderous side.

BAWDEN: You say *I'll Be Seeing You* [1944] was your most profitable war picture?

COTTEN: Oh, yes. Made for David's B unit, Vanguard Pictures. He wanted nothing to do with it, telling young producer Dore Schary, "Make it or don't make it, I couldn't give a damn." So Dore made it at breakneck speed. No retakes! No memos! Ginger Rogers was a girl out of jail on a Christmas pass, and I was a disillusioned war veteran slipping into insanity. We meet, we date. I meet her relatives, played by Spring Byington, Shirley Temple, and Tom Tully. It worked for the females in the audience. Add a big song hit and David had huge profits from a film because for once production costs had been so low.

BAWDEN: You also play a disturbed soldier in *Love Letters* [1945].

COTTEN: Paramount borrowed Jennifer [Jones] and me for it. Watching it on TV recently, it seems so unreal. I mean, the art director's concept of England, all thatched cottages and winding lanes. Jennifer was beautiful in it, ethereal even. She practically made one believe in it, and she got her third Oscar nomination in a row. It was a huge hit for Paramount and David then put us together in our third picture as costars.

BAWDEN: That would be *Duel in the Sun.*

COTTEN: Or "Lust in the Dust," as one critic said. It ran on and on, the filming. I got the offer from David in the form of a telegram while I was at the Fairmont in San Francisco. I shouted at the bellhop to slip it under the door, but he said it was too big. Too big! It seemed like a small telephone directory! But David's memos always did run on a bit. Of course, I had to take the part—I was under contract. I hated being the good son, Jesse; I wanted to be the bad one, but Greg Peck was hotter at the box office than I was. So I made do. Filming dragged on and on, depending on David's whims. [Director] King Vidor finally walked away in disgust, and Josef von Sternberg took over for a bit. Then King returned. We shot vast amounts of stuff that was never used. One night at [a] campfire out on the lone prairie, David said if he were starting *Gone with the Wind* today—in 1946—he would use Greg Peck as Rhett, Jennifer as Scarlett, me as Ashley, and Dorothy McGuire as Melanie. *Gone with the Wind* seemed like another time, but it was only seven years old and already Clark [Gable] was off at war or just getting back, and Leslie Howard had died in a plane crash. David was clearly thinking of it when he started this one.

BAWDEN: Then you squired Loretta Young in *The Farmer's Daughter,* which won her an Oscar as the Swedish American farm girl who ends up running for Congress.

COTTEN: I loved working with Ethel Barrymore [who played a major supporting role]. Very coquettish. Those black eyes would stare at me if I made a goof and had to have a retake. David bought it for Ingrid Bergman, but after *The Bells of St. Mary's,* she said, "No more Swedes." So Loretta came in and was every bit as movie savvy as Claudette. We shot it fast, and it was considered this fragile little comedy. But Loretta won over some tough opposition because our picture affirmed American values. It was very positive. It never hurt to be the leading man in that kind of situation.

BAWDEN: When did you make *The Third Man* in Vienna?

COTTEN: In 1948. Cold months. The city really was as divided as Berlin, you know, into four zones of occupation. Do you know what starvation looks like? I found out that winter. Most of the early locations were night exteriors. But there was a problem—the electrical system was unreliable and many nights we had to give up, and I'd crawl into my hotel bed simply shivering. It was made by a master director, Carol Reed. I thought Orson [Welles, who acted in the film] might act up and he tried on occasion, but Carol was the soul of patience and he really knew what he was doing. I drank a lot of coffee laced with bourbon on those shoots in cobblestone squares. The condition of the people was pathetic. Orson isn't in much of the early scenes. We're chasing him through the darkened streets until he just pops up. The Ferris wheel sequence contains the only bit of dialogue he was allowed to interpolate, when he says the Italians under the Borgias had warfare, terror, poisonings—and they produced the Renaissance. By contrast, the Swiss had six hundred years of democracy and what resulted? The cuckoo clock.

What I remember is the smell of the sewers, which were constructed in the nineteenth century. It really and truly stank. A lot of fine sewer men were down there and we became great friends. They'd been working underground for up to thirty years and they said they couldn't smell anything. Anyhow, thirty years later, I was back in Vienna and a newspaper asked me to return to the sewers for a photo opportunity. I agreed and was greeted with elation by all my old friends still down there. And it still stank as bad as ever.

I spent a lot of time with the great Italian beauty Alida Valli. David

[Selznick] had "discovered" her, but the movies she made for him—like *The Paradine Case*—were not star-making parts.

One night we were sitting around a saloon in Vienna and Carol hears the zither being performed and on the spot he hired the player, Anton Karas, to do the score and it really made the picture, it really did. [Karas's "Third Man Theme" also became a top pop music sensation.]

And now about the famous ending in the cemetery where Valli at Harry's grave walks right past Holly Martins (that's me) and into the distance. Carol started the day without an ending. He made that up on the spot and it's wonderful. I'm in the foreground waiting patiently for her to walk into my arms and it never happens. She walks right past me and out of my life.

BAWDEN: Bette Davis says *Beyond the Forest* [1949] is her worst movie.

COTTEN: Oh, I've made far worse. It should never have been made. Jack Warner was trying to fire Bette but refused to just release her. He wanted to drive her out. And she wasn't going unless he paid her off. So there was this impasse and we made this dreadful film. I had to do it because David had sold my services to Jack. If I backed out, David, who was already bankrupt, might suffer even more. Today it is considered camp but it was hell making it.

BAWDEN: You were back with Hitchcock in *Under Capricorn* [1949].

COTTEN: Filmed in London's Elstree Studios, but [it was supposed to be] Australia in the nineteenth century. Hitch's first after leaving Selznick and setting up shop on his own back in Britain. A hell of a challenge for actors. In *Rope* [1948] and this one, Hitch decided to eschew editing and the takes could last up to ten minutes while we walked around and walls were removed on cue and all we had to do was remember our lines and our cues. Hitch used a lot of Irish actors from the Abbey Theatre because this was all about convicts down under. Hitch has rightly disowned *Under Capricorn* ever since. It was a huge flop, his biggest-ever mistake. And I never again was asked to be in one of his movies.

BAWDEN: How long was *Portrait of Jennie* [1949] in production?

COTTEN: Off and on for almost a year, most of 1948. [Director] Bill Dieterle did a good job in catering to David's whims, but even Bill could get angry at the number of memos received. Finally, he shouted at David, "Why don't you direct it yourself?" David was stunned—"No, you are doing a great job"—and walked back to his office to write another memo. Joe August could only get the effects David needed by using the lenses he'd used shooting William S. Hart pictures thirty years earlier—the glow that always seemed to encompass Jennie. We shot the winter scenes for days in Central Park and then David says to Bill, "If it looks bad, we can always fake it back in the studio." The looks Bill gave were truly terrifying. You see, David was in one of his manic states.

It's really a very tiny piece, all about time traveling. It was David's love poem for Jennifer. She's so real as the young girl Ethan first meets in Central Park. It should have been a mood piece. But costs mounted as David added all sorts of scenes that were not necessary and many were later jettisoned. Jennifer got more nervous as filming progressed. He really dominated her by this time. Then he added the huge storm at the end and the picture bankrupted him. The public stayed away. He had overproduced the whole damned thing.

BAWDEN: Then what happened?

COTTEN: He sold off the studio lot, all unused properties. He disbanded his family of actors, selling our contracts all over the place. He only produced one more picture in his life. He was a spent force, destroyed by his obsessions about Jennifer.

BAWDEN: People say your fifties movies were not as good as the forties ones.

COTTEN [*snappish*]: I know that! *September Affair* [1950] is pretty good. Joan Fontaine and I survive a plane crash and decide we'll desert our families and live together. Very romantic. It should have been in color but the cameras were too bulky to be transported around Italy. *The Man with a Cloak* [1951] has me as Edgar Allan Poe investigating a possible murder in 1850s New York City. Silly stuff. My only film with Barbara Stanwyck. I was embarrassed I got first billing because MGM was trying to punish her for some transgression. Little Leslie Caron was the ingenue and she cried throughout the shooting. I mean, to go from *An American in Paris* to this! Blah!

BAWDEN: But you were Marilyn Monroe's husband in *Niagara* [1953].

COTTEN: Another murderous ex-soldier type. I never met a girl as introverted as Marilyn. The whole fame explosion had just set in and whenever we filmed on location at Niagara Falls, great crowds gathered to see her. She couldn't cope, retreated into her shell.

Director Henry Hathaway was a tough taskmaster at the best of times. He got so exasperated with Marilyn and her Russian [acting] coach he finally banned the woman from the set. I tried to keep her distracted. At night there'd always be a party in my hotel suite, but she'd look in, say hi, and then go off with her instructress. We'd wait for hours for her to show up. Hathaway started shooting the rehearsals as backup and found she was less mannered there and actually used some of the footage.

I asked her about the nude photograph and she said, dead serious, "But I had the radio on." I'm glad I knew her before the troubles enveloped her and destroyed her. I want to remember that superb girlish laughter when I told her an off-color joke. One day Hathaway shouts at her and she yelled back, "After paying for my own wardrobe, my coach, my assistant, and God knows who else I barely have enough left over to pay my shrink!" And the crowd watching applauded her!

BAWDEN: You went into TV.

COTTEN: Still did movies, but many were ones I wouldn't have gone to see. But yes, I "did" television. I tried live TV in 1954—*State of the Union,* directed by John Frankenheimer, with Maggie Sullavan and Nina Foch. Maggie couldn't remember a thing in rehearsals, but when that red light went on she was word perfect and I was a bundle of nerves. We had just finished a tour of *Sabrina Fair* around that time. She desperately wanted to get the movie, but Audrey Hepburn got it, so she phoned [the film's director] Billy Wilder to ask why and he said very brutally, "Because she's nineteen years younger."

But I kept returning to TV. For a half-hour play the pay was very good, about $2,500. Hell, it paid the bills, of which I had many. Jane Wyman and Loretta Young and Hitch and June Allyson gave me work on their anthologies; I was a regular on *G.E. Theater.* I had my own show called *On Trial.* I always worked.

BAWDEN: But you had a big part in *Hush . . . Hush, Sweet Charlotte.*

COTTEN: It was old home week. Bette [Davis] said, "I have to kill you in this one, Joseph!" I said, "Go ahead and try! I may kill you instead." We did exteriors in Louisiana and then Joan Crawford, who was first billed, got sick and was in the hospital. [Director] Bob Aldrich tried to replace her with Vivien Leigh, who cabled, "I could just about stand to be in a southern plantation at 5 a.m. with Miss Crawford. But never with Miss Davis!" The nerve! So Bob got on a plane to Switzerland to entice Olivia de Havilland back, and she was quite good as the evil cousin. And there was Cecil Kellaway from *Portrait of Jennie* and Aggie Moorehead from *Citizen Kane.* It was old home week.

BAWDEN: How did you get to do *A Delicate Balance* [1973]?

COTTEN: Well, Kath Hepburn had promised we'd work again in 1940 after I lost out the movie version of *Philadelphia Story* to some unknown named Cary Grant. And it took her only thirty-three years to fulfill that pledge. It was shot in London to save money and the director, Tony Richardson, first assembled us in the house in north London that sort of looked like a typical American home.

We sat around a table—Kath in her slacks, Paul Scofield, Kim Stanley, Lee Remick, Betsy Blair, who played my wife. And we read the play for four days and just talked. Then Kim stands up and shouts, "Let's improvise here!" And she starts screaming and writhing around the floor, to our shared astonishment. That night Kate and Paul gave Tony an ultimatum: either she goes or we go. So Kim went. And they flew that great Canadian actress Kate Reid in from Toronto on a day's notice, and in her first scene she just steals it from Kath by neat underplaying. Can't tell you what it was all about. Beats me. But I thought my character is supposed to be another part of Paul, so I dressed exactly like him right down to the tie and it was a small success in the market. But very satisfying to do.

BAWDEN: Then you made a disaster movie, *Airport '77* [1977].

COTTEN: Well, many of those movies around then were disasters. This one was actually designed to be a disaster. I spent weeks in the water with Olivia de Havilland and Jimmy Stewart. They'd once planned on marriage but never made a picture together. To my shock it was a huge success. When NBC bought it for TV they called back Lee Grant and Christopher Lee to do additional scenes to pad out the length and paid them huge amounts. But no way would you get me back into a wet suit. Never!

BAWDEN: Talk about the film you've just finished.

COTTEN: Titled *Heaven's Gate*, it's a Selznick-type mammoth production that goes on and on, and everyone seems to be in it: Kris Kristofferson, Chris Walken, John Hurt. My part is described as a cameo, meaning I was paid a lot of money and do very little. I'm the reverend doctor seen in the pulpit at Oxford University. I'm told the film is now down to 219 minutes from a five-hour rough draft, which was rather Selznickian in length. So we'll just have to see. Meanwhile, I've been signed for a TV film, *Churchill and the Generals*, and they want me for *The Love Boat*, not a bad year's work for this seventy-five-year-old.

Afterword

In fact, 1981 was Cotten's last year as a working actor. He suffered a stroke in the shower and spent several years in rehabilitation before he could speak again. He wrote a funny memoir, *Vanity Will Get You Somewhere* (1987). He died of cancer in Westwood, California, on February 6, 1994, aged eighty-eight.

Kirk Douglas

Interview by Ron Miller

He was the son of a Jewish immigrant from the old Russian empire, and he grew up in poverty in America, speaking Yiddish and answering to the name Izzy Demsky. But he became the legendary film actor Kirk Douglas, whose vivid portrayals enriched the motion picture screen from his debut in 1946 into the twenty-first century.

Douglas came along in the final days of the major studio system, and he was one of the first box office stars to take charge of his own destiny by becoming involved in the production and marketing of the films in which he appeared.

He was a vital force in such classics as *Out of the Past* (1947), *Champion* (1949), *Detective Story* (1951), *Ace in the Hole* (1951), *The Bad and the Beautiful* (1952), and *Lust for Life* (1956). He formed his own company, Bryna, and made such major films as *Paths of Glory* (1957), *Spartacus* (1960), *Lonely Are the Brave* (1962), and *Seven Days in May* (1964).

Along the way, he distinguished himself in a number of westerns, including *The Big Sky* (1952), *Man without a Star* (1955), *Gunfight at the O.K. Corral* (1957), and *The War Wagon* (1967), while also tackling several action roles in historical period pictures like *20,000 Leagues under the Sea* (1954), *Ulysses* (1955), and *The Vikings* (1958).

Douglas began his career on the stage, and he returned to the stage in 1963 as the producer and star of *One Flew over the Cuckoo's Nest,* based on the Ken Kesey novel. When he was unable to convince any film studio to star him in a movie version of the play, he turned it over to his actor son, Michael Douglas, who, with his dad's help, got it produced. The film starred Jack Nicholson and won five Academy Awards, including Best Picture, Best Actor (for Nicholson), and Best Actress (Louise Fletcher).

Kirk Douglas in a western mood. Ron Miller collection.

Renowned for his support of liberal causes, Douglas is often credited with helping break down the dreaded Hollywood anti-Communist "blacklist" by hiring blacklisted writer Dalton Trumbo to write the screenplay for *Spartacus*. Twice married, he's the father of four sons, including Oscar- and Emmy-winner Michael Douglas.

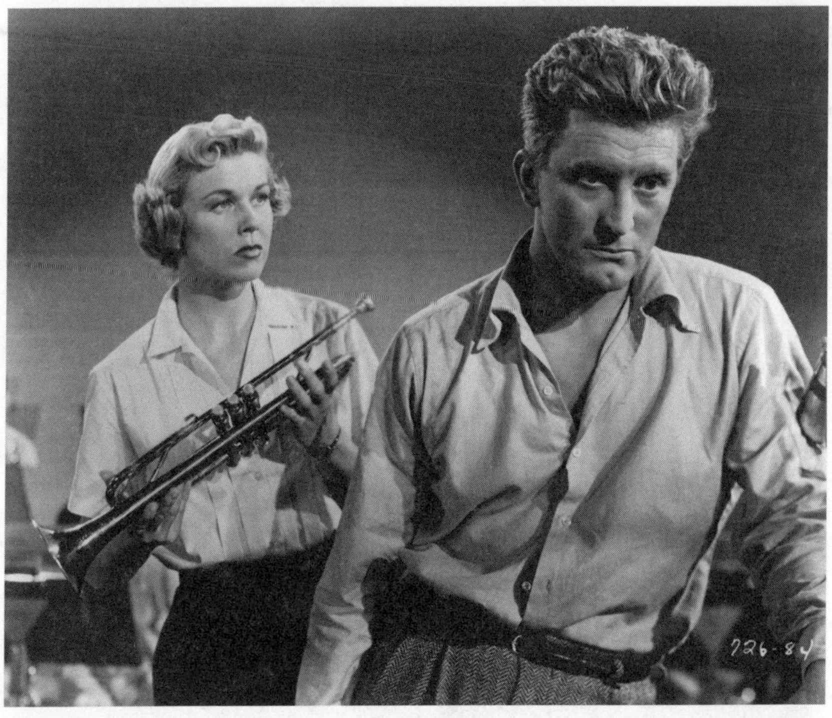

Doris Day comforts Kirk Douglas as the ambitious jazz musician of 1950's *Young Man with a Horn.* Courtesy of Warner Bros.

Setting the Scene

My interview with Kirk Douglas was arranged in conjunction with his appearance in the 1984 HBO TV western movie *Draw!* in which he costarred with James Coburn. Though sixty-seven at the time of our chat, Douglas was in peak physical condition—fresh from the gym, wearing his workout clothes. He was as vital as I'd ever seen him on the screen, which meant he was very vital indeed.

The Interview

MILLER: I think the first time I saw you in a western was in *Along the Great Divide* [1951]—and now you're back on horseback in *Draw!* more than thirty years later.

DOUGLAS: I love westerns! I haven't made a lot of them, but I sure

Kirk Douglas as Vincent van Gogh in *Lust for Life* (1956). Courtesy of MGM.

enjoyed them. They haven't been making many of them anymore, but I know from my trips around the world that people still enjoy them. You know, some people think the Wild West lasted for a couple hundred years, but it only lasted about twenty-five to thirty years, and yet people all over the world identify that spirit with Americans, which I think it a great compliment to us since not that many countries have that pioneering spirit.

MILLER: And in 1984, your contribution to the western was remembered when they inducted you into the Cowboy Hall of Fame in Oklahoma City. How did you feel about that?

DOUGLAS: You know, I went there with a lot of cynicism, but I must say I was very impressed. At one point, I was standing there in front of a giant oil portrait of John Wayne, who always stood for the best of the western, and yet most times I've represented the worst of the West in my roles. But they appreciated me because they have nothing against a sense of humor.

MILLER: Speaking of John Wayne, you made several pictures together and yet he always was a hero of the political right wing while you stood for the left. How did the two of you get along?

DOUGLAS: There's a famous story about that. When I played van Gogh in *Lust for Life,* we had a private showing of it and John Wayne was there. We had a little supper party and Wayne had a few drinks. Afterward, he motioned to me to go out on the veranda with him and he berated me! He said, "How the hell could you play a goddamn character like that?" And I said, "What do you mean? I'm an actor. He's a fascinating character." And Wayne said, "No, no. We should never play those kind of weak, sniveling characters. I don't ever want to see you in a part like that again! They have no dignity!"

As far as I'm concerned, I have always believed it's important for an actor to know the difference between make-believe and reality. So I've never hesitated to kid myself if the part calls for it. I find characters with a little evil in them much more interesting to play than the good guy. I'd rather play Doc Holliday than Wyatt Earp.

MILLER: Obviously, John Wayne thought you were messing with your heroic image while you were just playing a rich character. Did that kind of difference of opinion make it hard for you to work together?

DOUGLAS: Wayne and I made four movies together. Politically, we were completely apart. We might have dinner together once during the making of a picture. Yet he'd call me and suggest we make a picture together. We had a respect for each other. The fact that you start a picture where everybody loves each other doesn't mean you're going to wind up making a good movie.

Kirk Douglas (*left*) teams up with John Wayne against the bad guys in 1967's *The War Wagon.* Courtesy of Batjac Productions, Universal Pictures, and TV station KBHK, San Francisco.

Miller: I'm of the opinion that you were always respected as an actor because you were willing to take chances with your image and play some unsavory characters that you made unforgettable. In fact, didn't you help start the whole trend toward antiheroes in movies?

Douglas: I suppose I played one of the first antiheroes in *Champion.* I don't think virtue is that photogenic.

Miller: My favorite among your films of that type is *Ace in the Hole,* which some people know as *The Big Carnival.* But it wasn't a big hit for you. Was that because [the character] was a corrupt journalist who wanted to see a man remain trapped in a cave so he could prolong the front-page story he was covering?

Douglas: *Ace in the Hole* is a good example. That was one of the best pictures [director] Billy Wilder ever made, but it was never as successful in the U.S. as it was in the rest of the world. I blame you guys for that. You guys who come with your pencils and do interviews and criticize movie stars. You're a little sensitive about the portrayal of an unscrupulous reporter. I love that character with all the dark side of him. When I play a man with a weak character, I look for where he's strong. That character wasn't all bad. When he realized he'd gone too far, he was desperate. He tried to get the guy out of the cave. But it was too late. It was human nature. There are a lot of people like that. He wanted to succeed, to come back and be the top journalist again. But in the audience's mind, he was still a shit because of what he'd done. I like being an actor and I don't mind playing someone the audience doesn't like. I'm not worried about image.

MILLER: But doesn't the viewer have to care about the person you're playing?

DOUGLAS: I don't know if they have to care. I'm only concerned if they're interested in me. I don't care if you love me or hate me, but don't be indifferent to me. That to me is the worst thing.

MILLER: You've worked with every kind of movie director and you don't have a reputation for getting into disputes with them, but you are known for demanding a collaborative atmosphere on the set. Explain that.

DOUGLAS: I've worked with [Joseph] Mankiewicz, [Howard] Hawks, [Elia] Kazan, [William] Wyler, [Billy] Wilder. I've been very fortunate. All of them work differently. I've even directed a couple of pictures, so I have respect for the work. But no matter what anyone says, it's a collaborative art form. No matter how much one person is a binding force, it's still a collaboration. I think the problem today is that we've been contaminated by the European concept of the auteur system. I've had movies where I bought the book, developed the script, and cast the whole picture, but then the director walks in and says, "It must be a John Smith film!" I think sometimes we emphasize that too much.

MILLER: Though you've avoided big hassles with your directors, you've had a few disputes with studio managements, haven't you?

DOUGLAS: Let me give you an example of that: *Lonely Are the Brave.* You need the proper selling of a picture like that. I thought Universal just threw it away. They didn't give it a chance. They took it out of circulation. Then there were all those great reviews and people said, "Where's the picture?" Their ego prevented them from making a different campaign for the picture. The longer I'm in this business, the more amazed I am that a movie can be made, good or bad.

MILLER: You've taken lots of chances in your career, but I imagine one of your greatest frustrations was not being able to play McMurphy on the big screen in *One Flew over the Cuckoo's Nest* after acquiring the rights to the book from Ken Kesey and playing the part on the stage in New York.

DOUGLAS: It was way ahead of its time. When I took it to Broadway, the critics didn't know what to make of it. The audience loved it, but it didn't do very well. I tried for nearly twelve years to make it as a movie. I took it to every studio. But they wouldn't do it, even with a limited budget. Finally, I went into partnership with my son, Michael, and we were able to find somebody outside of the industry to put up the money and we made a little picture that I never predicted would be a hit. So it did over $200 million! Nobody knows what will really be successful.

MILLER: What do you think of Michael as a producer?

DOUGLAS: I told him, "Michael, you're the kind of producer I'd like to work with because you give everything to the other person even when you're in the movie." He did that in *Romancing the Stone* [1984]. He focused all the attention on the girl [Kathleen Turner]. I haven't been that generous. I've been a producer, but I find a product like *Spartacus* or *The Vikings* or *Seven Days in May* or *Paths of Glory* and somehow there always seems to be a good part for me.

MILLER: So many of your most memorable performances came in films like *Paths of Glory* and *Lonely Are the Brave,* which were not big box office performers.

DOUGLAS: Well, I've made millions and millions of dollars for studios. A few of those have dribbled down to me. But boy, before they've dribbled down to me, the studios have made a fortune! I told Michael that *Romancing the Stone* is his most important picture because it's entertaining and it's making a fortune for the studio. I've always placed a very high emphasis on entertainment. I can afford to say this because I've also made a lot of pictures that were socially significant. One of my pet peeves is directors who only want to make significant pictures. If you have significance in a picture, it should be secondary. It's there for those who can see it. A person doesn't go to a movie to learn something. He goes to forget his problems. You have to make an exciting movie that, hopefully, will entertain them.

MILLER: Why did you go to Australia to make, of all things, an Australian western?

DOUGLAS: I thought they were making some good pictures down there and I'd never played a dual role before and thought it would be interesting. So I went there and made *The Man from Snowy River* [1982] and it became the most successful movie in Australian history. It came here and made a lot of money, too, but I don't think they gave it the kind of campaign it should have had. When Fox took it over [for the U.S. market], I had an argument with them over it. I was willing to do a lot of things for nothing to help bring the picture to the attention of the public, but they wouldn't go for it.

MILLER: As for taking chances on offbeat films, there you were at age sixty-four, rolling around in the nude with Farrah Fawcett in an outer space saga called *Saturn 3* [1980].

DOUGLAS: Don't knock it if you haven't tried it.

MILLER: You've worked with lots of young actors lately. What do you think of the new breed?

DOUGLAS: I resent it when I hear some of these young actors say they won't sell a picture. I've always felt that's part of my responsibility—to help getting people to see a movie. Funny thing is I don't even remember any of these young guys' names. I want to spank them.

MILLER: Is it true that they tried to get you to do a small part in *Against All Odds,* the remake of your classic film *Out of the Past,* like they did with Jane Greer?

DOUGLAS: Yes. They wanted me in the picture. It was supposed to be a kind of homage. I looked at it in a professional way. Though Taylor Hackford is a terrific director, it just wasn't a part that was that exciting. That's all.

MILLER: You look to me to be in superb physical shape. Is fitness a major issue with you?

DOUGLAS: Michael once asked me what was the most important thing that an actor needs. I didn't even hesitate. I said, "Vitality." If you don't have energy, vital good health, you can't do it. I'm not an ascetic about it, but I work out. I don't spend hours at it. Yesterday I played tennis. Today I'm going to Ray Stark's ranch and ride a bit. I've always been active. And the movies I've done? Some of those have been real workouts!

MILLER: When you look in the mirror today, do you see the same Kirk Douglas?

DOUGLAS: You mean, do I ever look in the mirror and say I'm not the guy I was back in 1952? The answer is no. I am still the same guy. I can still do all the things I could do in 1952, except I can't do them as often.

Afterword

In 1996, Douglas suffered a severe stroke that since has limited his ability to speak, but he has continued to act and in 2003 appeared with two of his sons, his grandson, and his ex-wife in the film *It Runs in the Family.*

Douglas never won an Academy Award in competition, despite several nominations, but in 1996 he received an honorary Oscar for his contributions in fifty years on film.

Melvyn Douglas

Interview by James Bawden

Melvyn Douglas was a stage-trained actor who became one of the busiest, most reliable Hollywood leading men in the 1930s. He specialized in sophisticated characters and was often teamed with such popular female stars as Greta Garbo, Irene Dunne, and Joan Crawford.

In the 1940s, Douglas became deeply involved in liberal causes and Democratic Party politics. He was married to former stage and screen star Helen Gahagan (*She,* 1935), who became a member of the U.S. Congress, representing Beverly Hills, and was branded a "pinko" with pro-Communist leanings by Richard Nixon when he successfully ran against her for the U.S. Senate.

Douglas's movie career waned in the late 1940s, but he became one of the first Hollywood stars to pursue a career in television, starring in the DuMont network detective series *Steve Randall* (1952), which later moved to CBS. He also briefly hosted the DuMont game show *Blind Date* (1953) and several episodes of CBS's western series *Frontier Justice.*

Still later, Douglas reemerged as one of the screen's most cherished character actors, winning Supporting Actor Oscars for *Hud* (1963) and *Being There* (1979). He won a Tony Award for his leading role in the Broadway play *The Best Man* (1960) and an Emmy for his 1967 TV role in the acclaimed drama *Do Not Go Gentle into That Good Night.*

Despite his persona as a well-educated man, Douglas did not even finish high school. Born Melvyn Edouard Hesselberg in Macon, Georgia, he was the son of concert pianist Gregory Hesselberg and Lena Priscilla Shackelford, a descendant of the original *Mayflower* settlers and the granddaughter of Civil War general George Shackelford.

Douglas had a brief first marriage to Rosalind Hightower, an artist, with whom he fathered a son, Melvyn Gregory Hesselberg, whose own daughter is the actress Illeana Douglas. Douglas met Helen Gahagan in

Melvyn Douglas, circa 1938. Courtesy of Columbia Pictures.

1930 when the two costarred in the Broadway hit *Tonight or Never.* They were married until her death in 1980.

Setting the Scene

I first interviewed a seemingly frail Melvyn Douglas in his dressing room and back at his hotel in Toronto when he was costarring in the 1976 CBC-

TV movie *A Gift to Last* opposite Gordon Pinsent. Affable and endearing, Douglas joked, "I'm the last of my generation who can still stand up!" Yet a second supporting Oscar for 1979's *Being There* was just around the corner. We met again in Toronto in 1980 when he was promoting his role in *Tell Me a Riddle* and we chatted until he excused himself for his afternoon nap.

The Interview

BAWDEN: How did you get to Hollywood?

DOUGLAS: On the train! [*chuckling*]. I think you mean why would I want to go there? Economics, my dear boy. Needed a job. Half the Broadway theaters were closed because of the Depression. I'd been lucky in a long run of *Tonight or Never* and I'd just wed my leading lady, Helen Gahagan, on my thirtieth birthday. Now I needed to make some money, and when Sam Goldwyn bought the movie rights, he offered me a contract for the princely sum of $900 weekly—far more than I got on Broadway. I asked Helen, she said yes, and off we went.

BAWDEN: Had you ever thought about the movies before doing the 1931 film version of *Tonight or Never*?

DOUGLAS: Never! I was very much into the theatah! But my leading lady in the film, Gloria Swanson, told me to sit tight and make money and then go back [to the stage]. I didn't really return until some two decades later. The movie didn't interest many of her fans, I'm afraid. Sam told me it laid a big egg.

BAWDEN: So what happened?

DOUGLAS: There was nothing for me, so Goldwyn loaned me out to RKO to replace Adolphe Menjou in a movie called *Prestige* [1932] with Ann Harding. This was the one Ann begged RKO to let her buy the negative and destroy it because she feared it was so bad. No, I'm not kidding. It was set in a French prison in Indochina, all sorts of lashings and illicit love. And another bomb.

BAWDEN: Around this time you made *As You Desire Me* [1932] with Greta Garbo.

DOUGLAS: MGM had six weeks left in her contract. She said she was returning to Sweden and had set a definite date as her contract was ending. They had to shoot it very fast and needed a certain type of leading man and didn't have one handy. Our director was a veteran—George Fitzmaurice—

who explained, "Garbo may not recognize you ever!" She was that icy and distant. Many scenes had already been shot with her and Erich von Stroheim. She looked fabulous in a blond wig, I thought. There was no small talk between scenes. Huge curtains were set up so nobody could observe except the director, who had a peephole, and the cameraman, who had a hole cut through the cloth. It made dough because of Garbo. I tried to watch once on TV and fell over laughing. In one scene I hear she has returned to my estates, so I'm riding fast and the speed was exaggerated and I'm suddenly in a Keystone Kops chase!

BAWDEN: From Garbo to *The Vampire Bat* [1933]?

DOUGLAS: I did whatever Goldwyn told me to do. We shot it in a few weeks and it's horrid, but this is the film everybody tells me they've seen recently on TV because it's now in the public domain. Then I did *Nagana* [1933], where I'm fighting tropical diseases and the lure of Tala Birell, who was a sort of pseudo Garbo. Then Sam simply dropped my contract and advised me to seek employment back on Broadway.

BAWDEN: You were saved by *Counsellor-at-Law* [1933]?

DOUGLAS: A brilliant film directed by Willie Wyler and starring the ravaged Jack Barrymore. He's mesmerizing, even if he was half drunk all the time. We all protected Jack as Willie would shoot for hours before getting that perfect take. I saw this one recently and it's about as good as Hollywood can get. At that time.

BAWDEN: You did go back east.

DOUGLAS: I was always working but I had young kids and a wife and she was often on tour herself. I signed an RKO deal and made a dandy B—*Dangerous Corner* [1934], from the J. B. Priestley play. It's a sort of what-might-have-happened plot and the play is still revived. Helen, as you know, made her only film around that time—*She*—and she still gets kidded for it.

BAWDEN: Then they teamed you with Claudette Colbert?

DOUGLAS: There was *The Gentle Sex* [1931], *She Married Her Boss* [1935], *I Met Him in Paris* [1938]. I complemented her, made her seem funny and important. It was a big job. I had no pretensions. And Claudette was an ace technician. Between takes she'd be chatting about the latest lens with the cameraman. Greg LaCava directed *She Married Her Boss,* so it's very funny in stretches.

Then I did *Annie Oakley* [1935] with Barbara Stanwyck, and I got too big for my britches and opened in a new play, *Tapestry in Gray,* on Broadway and we lasted two weeks.

BAWDEN: You went back to L.A. with a double contract with Columbia and MGM. How did that work?

DOUGLAS: I went to Columbia for *The Lone Wolf Returns* [1936], and Harry Cohn offered me a full contract. The thing with Harry is he knew he was a slob and loved playing the role with bad English, occasional fluffing. But he also wanted Columbia to become a major player. My second Columbia was *And So They Were Married* [1936] with Mary Astor. Then MGM borrowed me for the Joan Crawford opus *The Gorgeous Hussy* [1936]. I was John Randolph, Lionel Barrymore was Andrew Jackson, and it was crackers as far as history went.

I was very naughty one day. I'd watch in amazement as Joan would arrive with a long retinue of servants, hairdressers, maids, personal assistants, even her chauffeur. So next day I asked my brother, my chauffeur, and whoever else I could dig up, and we went in in a single line. Joan was not amused and I got chewed out by director Clarence Brown, who told me he was having enough problems with Joan before this calumny!

BAWDEN: So you went back to Columbia and Irene Dunne in *Theodora Goes Wild* [1936]?

DOUGLAS: Irene had endured a string of weepers and now they were testing her in comedy for the first time. I told her to remain in character and she'd get her laughs simply because in person she was so prim and proper. It was a revelation. She got an Oscar nomination and a new career. MGM then bought part of my contract because Louis B. Mayer said it was cheaper than paying huge salaries to Columbia every time I was wanted. I was seen as a sort of stand-in for Bill Powell whenever he wasn't available.

BAWDEN: What happened when both studios wanted you at the same time?

DOUGLAS: They sat down at the start of each year and mapped it out. I could do a Columbia film like *Women of Glamour* [1937] in two to three weeks. Then I'd go to MGM for *Captains Courageous* [1937] and that would take two to three months. I much preferred Columbia because it was all light and breezy. But those MGMers kept my name up there.

BAWDEN: Explain what billing meant in those days.

DOUGLAS: Well, Freddie Bartholomew had first billing in *Captains Courageous* and that drove Spencer Tracy mad. I was fourth billed—couldn't have cared less. Joan Crawford once explained to me she was over Clark Gable and Bill Powell but under Norma Shearer. Powell was under

Melvyn Douglas with Greta Garbo in 1939's *Ninotchka.* Courtesy of MGM.

Jean Harlow but above Bob Montgomery and Myrna Loy. Are you still with me? After he won two Oscars, Spence said that henceforth he'd only take first billing and he kept that promise after *Boom Town* [1940], where he was second to Gable but still over Colbert. When MGM tried to give Gable first billing over Crawford in *Strange Cargo* [1940], she kicked up quite a stink because it would suggest she was failing.

Bawden: What did you think of the Crawford picture *The Shining Hour* [1938]?

Douglas: Typical of MGM to buy a hit British play, transfer the geography to Wisconsin, and turn it into a Joan Crawford weepie. We had a great director [Frank Borzage] and he could do nothing with it. It just did not make much sense anymore. The surprise was Joan and Margaret Sullavan got on very well together, so much so that Joan decided she had better adopt some children to compete with Maggie's children.

Bawden: How did you get to costar with Garbo again in *Ninotchka* [1939]?

Douglas: [Director Ernst] Lubitsch wanted me. Had first borrowed me from Columbia in '37 for *Angel* with Marlene Dietrich. Later told me it was a mistake. She's married to genteel Herbert Marshall, and he said her lover needed to be the Clark Gable type. I was too sophisticated. It was a flop because of this, I was told.

Marlene was totally taken with Garbo, her biggest rival. Kept asking me what was she like. How was I to know? I'd only acted with her. [Marlene] called her "that peasant." And later, when I made *Ninotchka,* I found Greta was equally enchanted with [Marlene], although they never actually met.

Lubitsch was overjoyed to see me and hired me immediately over MGM's protests. They'd wanted Bill Powell. It was a very long shoot. Greta never understood comedy, which was the point of the movie. The humor in her humorlessness. In between takes, Ina Claire tried to show her how to tap dance. "Not with my clodhoppers," Garbo said. Now that was funny. That scene in the restaurant where she laughs? She mimed it expertly, but there was no sound. They had to dub in her laugh later. How about that for special effects?

Bawden: That movie made you red hot.

Douglas: It also typecast me. I was only up for sophisticated comedies for years after. At Columbia I did *Too Many Husbands* [1940] with Jean Arthur and Fred MacMurray on loan from Paramount. We all felt we were being very clever here—too clever by half. Then a similar movie called *My Favorite Wife* with Irene Dunne and Cary Grant beat us to the box office. When ours was released, it tanked. The critics said it had all been done before. Then at Columbia I made *He Stayed for Breakfast* [1941], only this time I'm the Communist. And I was opposite lovely Loretta Young, who truly did not understand comedy.

Bawden: You once said you wanted to apologize for closing down the careers of both Greta Garbo and Norma Shearer within the same year.

Douglas: I can't accept all the blame. First there was *Two-Faced Woman* [1941], Garbo's last-ever film. It wasn't that bad. Carole Lombard would have been sweet in it. The irony is this was the real Garbo. She was very athletic, took sunbaths in her backyard as the neighbors gawked, ate health foods, and never dressed up. But after Pearl Harbor, this kind of thing was so very out of date. The censors made us go back and shoot a scene on the telephone where I emphasize I know it's her impersonating a nonexistent twin. But there was a similar plot in *The Chocolate Soldier* [1941] with Nelson Eddy and the censors did not balk at all.

Norma's movie [*We Were Dancing,* 1942] was just plain flat. Without [her husband, the late MGM production chief Irving] Thalberg to guide her, she turned down *Gone with the Wind, Pride and Prejudice,* and *Mrs. Miniver.* For this! George Cukor directed both, so why not blame him? I'd finally advanced to the point I could be accepted as Shearer's costar and then this!

Bawden: Why did Garbo retire?

Douglas: She never did. MGM had cut her pay to $125,000 a picture and wanted another cut for the next one. She thought she'd just stop until the European conflict ended, but by that time she had lost all confidence. And frankly, she wasn't wanted anymore. During the war there was this backlash against her. How dare she refuse to wash dishes at the Hollywood Canteen? MGM gave *Madame Curie* [1943], which had been bought for her, to Greer Garson. Lubitsch wanted her for his Catherine the Great movie, *A Royal Scandal* [1945], at Fox, but [studio boss] Darryl Zanuck said Garbo was too expensive and used Tallulah Bankhead instead. She just slipped away and never came back. She has remained a great star by not making movies.

Bawden: You left too?

Douglas: I made an even worse comedy called *Three Hearts for Julia* [1943] with Ann Sothern. It was truly awful. I was needed elsewhere, but I also just had to escape the MGM mill. Mayer shouted how dare I desert the ship—and for what? Only my country! When I returned I tried to break my contract, but MGM's lawyers threatened to blackball me and I staggered back as the reluctant third star of *Sea of Grass* [1947], a horrid western shot entirely within studio walls. Spencer Tracy refused to go on location, so they went out and photographed all that grass blowing in the wind and we acted before plates [projected images] of that.

It symbolized all that was wrong with the old Hollywood. Spence was so stout he needed a little ladder to get onto his horse. Kate Hepburn swanned around in beautiful gowns no western woman would have worn. They brought in Elia Kazan and he was beside himself as director. He was a Method man, but Spence and Kate were these two great unreachable stars and they'd do everything their own way. I was watching Spence in a scene when Kate whispered, "Oh, Mel, he's yar, that's what he is." [She'd been using the word *yar* for all kinds of situations ever since she uttered it on-screen in *The Philadelphia Story.*] I wanted to say, "No, Kate, he's just too fat!"

I finished up at Metro with *The Great Sinner*, which was made in '47 but kept back for MGM's twenty-fifth anniversary [in 1949]. There wasn't a single thing Russian about this. Greg Peck knew he was trapped in this stinker. So did Ava Gardner. Ethel Barrymore's eyebrows would arch each time [director] Bob Siodmak gave her instructions. It was so empty and deservedly flopped.

BAWDEN: Your wife, meanwhile, ran for the U.S. Senate. I think this hampered your acting career in Hollywood.

DOUGLAS: She'd represented Beverly Hills in the House. In 1950 she ran against an unknown Richard M. Nixon. But Helen failed by a very small margin because President Truman refused to campaign for her. Truman thought she was a bit soft on the issue of the Communist menace in Europe. Helen insisted she was not. As far as dirty tricks go, the Republicans had pamphlets printed up in pink. The charge of being a "pink lady" was actually first used by a Republican opponent in the primary. And picked up by Nixon. Helen got back at him: she coined the phrase *Tricky Dick*.

BAWDEN: You left L.A. in 1950?

DOUGLAS: I never made any movies 1951 to 1962. No offers. I wanted to restart my stage career and I succeeded. Best damned job I ever had was replacing Paul Muni in *Inherit the Wind* in 1956 and the sheer joy of passing it back to him when he recovered from cancer. Never thought either of us would get the movie roles, but it was terribly done. Both [Spencer Tracy] and [Fredric] March were one-dimensional. Finally, in 1965, Ed Begley and I did a TV version that has the real verve of the original play. Ed did it onstage, too. It's a play you have to work on over many months to truly understand its meaning.

During breaks I'd do live TV, which I absolutely loved. The best of these was on *Playhouse 90* in 1958 where I played Stalin in *The Plot to Kill Stalin*. Everybody talked about it the next day. The Kremlin was so incensed they kicked out CBS's man in Moscow. Delbert Mann directed it brilliantly. I later watched a kinescope. I loved it; it was terrific.

BAWDEN: How did it feel to finally win an Oscar for *Hud*?

DOUGLAS: Horrible! I felt awful. I mean, I got second billing in the cast. Supporting player? Hardly. I accepted that category because I was told Paul Newman and I would divide the votes. Well, I won and he did not and the movie after all is all about him. And Pat Neal won, too. And photographer Jimmy Howe. And Paul, who is the best of his generation, just

Melvyn Douglas (*center*) with Brandon de Wilde (*left*) and Paul Newman in *Hud.* Douglas won the 1963 Best Supporting Actor Academy Award for his performance. Courtesy of Paramount TV.

walked away empty-handed. But it gave me momentum and I went on to make *The Americanization of Emily* [1964], which I adore. And then *I Never Sang for My Father* [1970]. I couldn't do it onstage because I frankly thought my heart might not hold up. But [in the film] I had Gene Hackman as the son, a great actor who really tested me.

BAWDEN: You're still at it.

DOUGLAS [*chuckling*]: Barely. They gave me another Oscar for *Being There.* I think it's because I'm still standing. I'm one liberal the Hollywood conservatives can't get away from. *Being There* was quite a workout. I can't believe Peter Sellers has already left us.

I loved working with [director] Lee Grant in *Tell Me a Riddle* [1980]. She treated me and Lila Kedrova beautifully. We had catnaps during the afternoon—much needed at my age.

Now I've got another one, *Ghost Story,* quickly coming up. I'm the kid in the cast, you know. Besides me, there's Fred Astaire, Douglas Fairbanks Jr., and John Houseman. I steal it all with a terrific death scene. I told

Melvyn Douglas (*right*) was one of four aged stars who played leading roles in the haunting 1981 thriller *Ghost Story.* The others (*from left*): Douglas Fairbanks Jr., Fred Astaire, and John Houseman. Courtesy of Universal Pictures and HBO.

Douglas, "Stand back! I'm about to act. I'm going to steal this one by expiring." Actually, it's just a dress rehearsal for what surely will soon come. Life once again imitating art.

Afterword

Melvyn Douglas died from heart disease on August 4, 1981. He was eighty.

Douglas Fairbanks Jr.

Interview by James Bawden

Major stardom for a second-generation actor is never an easy thing to accomplish since it's human nature always to compare the "copy" to the original. But Douglas Fairbanks Jr. managed not only to reach major stardom in Hollywood but to remain a star throughout his long career.

Born in 1909 to silent screen swashbuckler Douglas Fairbanks and his first wife, Anna Beth Sully, Fairbanks Jr. overcame a youthful tendency to be overweight and honed himself into a tall, handsome, and commanding screen presence by the 1930s.

Though Fairbanks Jr. early established himself as both a fine dramatic actor and one capable of light comic and romantic roles, he also proved he could step into the same type of dashing physical role his father had played in silent films. In fact, some of those roles—especially in *The Prisoner of Zenda* (1937), *Gunga Din* (1939), and *Sinbad the Sailor* (1947)—suggested he might even have been his dad's equal if he had decided to take his career in that direction.

Fairbanks Jr. was married three times—first to Joan Crawford, from whom he was divorced in 1933; then to Mary Lee Hartford, ex-wife of Huntington Hartford, from 1939 until her death in 1978; and finally to Vera Lee Shelton, a merchandiser with QVC, Inc., in 1991.

During World War II, Fairbanks Jr. enlisted and served as a lieutenant commander in the navy, assigned first to the commando operations of Lord Mountbatten's unit in the United Kingdom. He helped develop a special unit of beach-landing forces that served to dupe the enemy into thinking a major invasion was taking place. For his efforts, he received the Navy Legion of Merit and similar medals from several Allied nations.

Douglas Fairbanks Jr. with Helena Carter in *The Fighting O'Flynn* (1949). Courtesy of MCA-TV.

Setting the Scene

I first interviewed Douglas Fairbanks Jr. over lunch in 1970 when I was a very jittery summer student, interning at the *Toronto Globe and Mail.* At one point Fairbanks put his hand on my shoulder and said, "I order you to stop shaking! Your questions are just fine." (Fairbanks was in Toronto to promote construction of a new condominium called the Fairbanks, but construction never began on the project.)

We met again in 1984 when he was promoting other properties, and he shared his reminiscences with me during a long afternoon in his hotel suite. He professed to remember me, but I chalked that up to his fine manners.

In 1998, a few years before his death, I talked with him again on the phone for more than an hour. He was preparing to return to Toronto to introduce a new print of Chaplin's *The Gold Rush* (1925) to the Toronto Film Society. Toronto film director Norman Jewison (*In the Heat of the Night,* 1967) had asked him to host the event because Fairbanks had played on the set of the Chaplin film as a gawky teenager.

The Interview

BAWDEN: You now live and work out of New York City. Any chance of bumping into your most famous costar?

FAIRBANKS: You mean the great Garbo? It's funny, but I thought she passed me on Fifth Avenue last spring and I know she was in town at the time. But say it was her and say she recognized me. What would we have to talk about? A silent movie made more than four decades ago?

BAWDEN: Your 1928 classic *A Woman of Affairs*?

FAIRBANKS [*chuckling*]: It really was my first big part. And Garbo could play the English socialite, particularly in a silent world. At that time she spoke English very haltingly. I saw it recently, newly rescored, and I think I'm pretty terrific in it. After all, I was only nineteen and she was an old woman of twenty-two to twenty-three.

It's strange that all the history books say Jack Gilbert [Garbo's lover and frequent silent movie costar] was destroyed by the coming of sound, but he was destroyed by Garbo. She's the dominating force in the film. He was relegated to a secondary part even though he was making the astounding sum of $6,000 a week—equivalent to a cool million today, I would think.

I got my first good notices, but the raves went to Johnny Mack Brown [Garbo's leading man in the film], based on his incredible good looks. He was one big victim of sound. His Alabam' accent quickly made him hard to cast in anything but westerns.

Douglas Fairbanks Jr., with his first wife, Joan Crawford, in 1928. James Bawden collection.

BAWDEN: You started in movies at age fourteen?

FAIRBANKS: It was for a film called *Stephen Steps Out* and I was terribly chubby. Did it for the money. When my parents separated, it was hardly amicable, and Mother and I needed to eat. Movie companies were willing to exploit my famous name. I really didn't understand that at the time. So *A Woman of Affairs* was a new beginning for me.

BAWDEN: In her autobiography, *A Portrait of Joan,* your first wife, Joan Crawford, says how much your father liked her and how your stepmother, Mary Pickford, looked down on her.

FAIRBANKS: She got it backwards. Dad—or "Pete," as I always called him—took pity on her. She came from the poorest circumstances. Mary recognized herself in Joan. Mary went out of her way to make Joan feel acceptable at Pickfair. We'd go there every Sunday afternoon and Joan complained how dull it was. She and Clara Bow were the two rival Jazz Age babies. Joan was terribly competitive. She never knew her father. She washed tables at the boarding school where her mother worked. Later she was a taxi dancer and danced with escorts for 10¢. MGM's Louis Mayer saw something inside her that appealed to all women—I think it must have been her vulnerability—and he kept her going in bits for several years until she hit it big.

BAWDEN: Tell me about your father and stepmom.

FAIRBANKS: The first time I saw Mary was in 1919 and she was queen of the world. I mean the biggest star today can't come close. And this is because silents were a universal phenomenon. She went on a trip to Russia in 1923 and was mobbed—all her films were playing illegally in bad prints. To be one of the first movie stars was to entrance the world. Everybody assumed she was that spunky little girl, but in reality she was a shrewd businesswoman. At ten or eleven, I was already taller than she was. Those curls, the cute little dresses—she was a doll come to life. And impish and grinning. Who could not have loved her? We became fast friends, still are.

Pete was equally famous and going on his sets was such a thrill. I'd always be playing tennis with Charlie Chaplin. Bill Hart played cowboys and Indians with me. I watched Pickfair being built. I played on the sets of *Zorro* and took a magic carpet ride with Pete for sheer fun. And now it has all faded to dust. Except the films, which Mary at one point threatened to burn. When they married, she lost her British citizenship. She was born in Toronto and was a citizen of the British Empire and when the Canadian government gave it back to her recently, she sobbed with joy. Today [1970] she's wafer thin, very doddery, tired all the time. She doesn't want the world to see that the glad girl has now become a very old woman. And who can blame her?

BAWDEN: You and Crawford were the great lovebirds of the final years of silents.

FAIRBANKS: She was petrified of crowds. At premieres she'd be sweating right through her dresses. She assumed with talkies she'd disappear, just as Bow faded fast. But her voice matched her screen personality. She was all career, still is. On our honeymoon I took her to Europe and she hated every minute of it except when we'd head for the local MGM distribution office where she could do some publicity. She was four years older than I was. It was her experience that attracted me to her, I'm guessing. She never thought I was trying hard enough. I was. It was just my way not to get overly eager. We were on all the movie magazines. It strengthened my personal popularity. And we did a few movies at MGM together as an official couple: *Our Dancing Daughters* [1928], *Our Modern Maidens* [1929]. I wasn't the star, but the boy she could hang on to and share the farewell kiss at the fade-out.

BAWDEN: Fairbanks Sr. and Pickford did not long survive in the sound era.

FAIRBANKS: Pete hated talkies, just hated them. Because the cameras were hidden in these booths, it meant they could not move. And he hated just standing there and saying lines. Also, he was over forty and it showed. He was no longer the lithe young man of 1915. It was his decision to star with Mary in *Taming of the Shrew* [1929] and he almost got away with it. He'd spent so many years onstage, the dialogue didn't bother him. But he hated to rehearse. Mary was apprehensive about the project and it shows. She's kittenish throughout, but the film did make dough because they'd never been together in a movie.

Then she made *Coquette* [1928] and got an Oscar, although I thought the film was awful. She was thirty-six to thirty-seven by then, and the little girl characters she'd once played were now beyond her reach. And she made some mistakes. *Secrets* she started in 1930, abandoned, then finished in 1933, and it got released during FDR's Bank Holiday, so nobody had money to go to the pictures. And Pete made *Reaching for the Moon* [1931] and cut all the songs before release, when musicals suddenly died.

He was fooling around. She finally heard about it and there was this separation. She told me she woke up one morning at Pickfair, looked out the window, and saw Pete sitting on the diving board by the pool. And he was sobbing. He realized he'd lost it all.

BAWDEN: How did you wind up at Warners under contract?

FAIRBANKS: I was making up to seven pictures a year, all over the map. Then Jack Barrymore invited me to costar in his next Warners picture, *Moby Dick* [1930], a remake of *The Sea Beast* [1926], which he'd made only a few years before. I was on the lot to make a test and Darryl Zanuck, head of production, saw me and offered me the second lead in *The Dawn Patrol*

Douglas Fairbanks Jr. (*left*) with Edward G. Robinson in *Little Caesar* (1930). Courtesy of Warner Bros.

[1930]. Dick Barthelmess was the star. He became a wonderful friend. He was tops at the box office right then, making $4,000 a week, which was a huge salary. And I tested with an English accent, got it, and had to tell Jack I wasn't going to be in *Moby Dick.* Our version [of *The Dawn Patrol*] is never seen on TV. Teddy Goulding remade it in 1938 with Errol Flynn and David Niven in my part. That's the one on TV. It's so inferior. They used all the aerial shots from the original, just stuck them in—and it shows.

Leslie Howard saw it and offered me a big part in *Outward Bound* [1930]. It was about a shipload of passengers who finally figure out they're dead and being shipped to the hereafter. Alfred Lunt had played it onstage with Leslie in support. For the movie, he took Lunt's part and I got his. I never saw all of it. It gave me the creeps. Still does, just thinking about it. It was a prestige picture, never made a cent. I think it is more frightening than *Dracula.* And Warners remade it in 1944 with John Garfield as *Between Two Worlds.* And it flopped again.

Bawden: Then came *Little Caesar* [1930]. Were you under contract by then?

FAIRBANKS: No. It put me over the top and Jack Warner finally offered me a big deal. I told my agent to go back and ask for cast and script approval, which Jack only granted to Barthelmess. And Jack agreed, much to my surprise. It was all because of *Little Caesar,* which was such a hit. When I first met Eddie Robinson in wardrobe I couldn't figure out how this diminutive, balding little man, so meek in person, was going to be this lout. It was his sheer acting genius. And director Mervyn LeRoy was only thirty-one himself. He used all kinds of innovations. The camera actually moved! And here I was as a gigolo, all slicked-down hair. Not a big part, but it made people sit up and notice.

BAWDEN: Your films were up and down in quality at Warner Bros.

FAIRBANKS: Tell me about it. After *Little Caesar,* I did *Chances* [1931] and it was a hit. Then came *Union Depot* [1932], a big picture. I remember being directed by Al Green on it, but the credits say Bill Dieterle. On many of these films the directors would change back and forth. Then, because I owed Warners some weeks' work and could speak French, Jack had me in *L'athlete incomplet* [1932], which ran only in France. They had yet to figure out dubbing, so foreign versions of films were shot at the same time.

So my career went up and down. When Bette Davis had to choose a scene from her worst-ever film . . . she chose *Parachute Jumper,* which we made in 1933. And she was right—it was awful.

BAWDEN: Why were you costarred so often with Loretta Young?

FAIRBANKS: Gretch [her nickname] was a wild young thing, still a teenager. She looked so beautiful and she always had a new beau—some, like Spence Tracy, were married! We did *I Like Your Nerve* [1931]. We did *The Life of Jimmy Dolan* [1933]. If she wasn't available, I'd get Mary Brian or Ann Dvorak. Jack always kept us very busy when he had product that had to be moved. New pictures were released every week.

Then I did *Captured!* [1933] with Leslie Howard and it was a big hit. On that one Leslie got a bit too friendly with a script girl and I had to bail him out with a $500 loan so she could get a "procedure." His wife never knew about it, although I think she always suspected he was screwing around.

BAWDEN: You worked with Crawford, Davis, Hepburn, Dunne. Compare them.

FAIRBANKS: All very frightening to me. Davis took every scene seriously. Joan was very work oriented. Dunne had the most talent. On *Morning Glory* [1933] I watched as Great Kate [Katharine Hepburn] snatched every scene away from me—very greedily. She played up to me and I took the bait. One night I was driving her home and made the pass, but she said she had an early call and sweetly kissed goodnight. I was about a block away with engine trouble when I looked up and saw her running out of her home and sprinting for another car—Leland Hayward's. But you know Adolphe Menjou [who played producer Louis Easton in the movie] did not like to be taken for granted. On the set. He accused her of scene stealing and there were some ugly moments.

BAWDEN: Why did you leave Warners in 1934?

FAIRBANKS: In 1932–1933 the Depression was at its height, and Jack ordered everybody to take a 50 percent pay cut. Then six months later executives got their pay restored, but Jack refused to look after the crews and the talent. Zanuck left the lot in disgust and formed his own company—Twentieth Century. Others, like Barthelmess and [Ruth] Chatterton, decided to stay. Loretta left with Zanuck, as did Connie Bennett. I had a job offer with Alex Korda in London and I also quit.

BAWDEN: That would be *The Rise of Catherine the Great* [1934].

FAIRBANKS: I was amazed at getting the part of crazy Peter. Opposite Elisabeth Bergner, who was to be directed by her husband, Paul Czimmer. I asked Korda why he chose me and he said he needed a name. Paul had wanted Joseph Schildkraut, but Alex said there would be too many Europeans in the cast! So I studied like hell. Had wonderful moments with Flora Robson and that greatest of actors Sir Gerald DuMaurier. And somehow I pulled it off. [Marlene] Dietrich's version [*The Scarlet Empress*] came out months later and lost it at the box office.

BAWDEN: But you stayed in London.

FAIRBANKS: Oh, no, on the basis of the Catherine film, [Ernst] Lubitsch hired me for the film version of Noël Coward's *Design for Living*. But I contracted pleurisy en route and was nursed back to health by my mother in New York. Gary Cooper got my part. I did a stinker of a potboiler called *Success at Any Price* opposite Colleen Moore and then I did *Mimi* [1935] in London opposite Gertrude Lawrence. There wasn't a bigger stage star at the time, but she wasn't photogenic. Had a big, crooked nose, eyes weren't right. Onstage she was a mesmerizer even when singing off-key. Films brought her down a notch. She never made a successful movie. I fell completely in love. We had a time of it, but ultimately her high living threatened to bankrupt both of us.

BAWDEN: Some of your British films of that period I've never seen.

FAIRBANKS: What! You've never seen *The Amateur Gentleman* [1936] with Elissa Landi? Or *Accused* [1936] with Dolores Del Rio? I was in a rut. Then a telegram came from David Selznick offering me the small but choice part of Rupert of Hentzau in *The Prisoner of Zenda.* I consulted Pete and he said, "Take it. It's the best part going. Played it for years on the road." And I did and it got me back to Hollywood. Ronald [Colman] and I were strutting around in our Ruritanian uniforms in wardrobe and I asked Mary Astor who was the sexier. And she said, "That guy over there—Ray Massey. He can put his boots under my bed any time of the week." Ronnie was so insulted he stormed off the set!

BAWDEN: Then you tried comedy.

FAIRBANKS: I had the best teacher around: Miss Irene Dunne. The picture was *The Joy of Living* [1938], and she could do it all—singing, comedy, both in this one picture, and she was a wow. Never got an Oscar despite her five nominations. No AFI Award [the American Film Institute's Life Achievement Award], but in 1989 the Kennedy Center [the annual Kennedy Center Honors] bestowed recognition and I was asked, as one of her few extant leading men, to introduce her segment. When Bonita Granville went to her fabulous home to tell her of the honor, Irene broke down and wept. She just assumed she'd been forgotten. We got her to the White House in a wheelchair; I was so shattered because she'd failed that badly. The Reagans were devastated at her condition. But that was as far as she got. Her daughter had to rush her to the hospital. The long flight from L.A. had so weakened her. She had the honor, but couldn't receive it in person. When I saw her slumped over, all bent over with a widow's humpback, I just wanted to cry.

But all great favorites age. The last time I saw my darling Mary [Pickford], her arms were shrunken. She was as thin as a bird, and she could only say, "My . . . my."

BAWDEN: You made three other comedies that year.

FAIRBANKS: *The Rage of Paris* was designed by Universal to show off their new French find, Danielle Darrieux. Fox had just introduced Simone Simon, and Danny was far better a looker and actress. But she loathed L.A. and took the first opportunity to return to France, where she got trapped during the war and had a nasty time of it.

Having Wonderful Time was all Ginger Rogers's movie. She was riding high by then. Red Skelton used his bit in it to get an MGM contract. And I was in one of little Janet Gaynor's last movies, *The Young in Heart.* She was all of thirty-two but no longer the box office sensation she'd been a year before. As the little old lady, David Selznick auditioned every old doll around. We even tested with the legendary Maude Adams, who then decided celluloid was not for her. Janet said David had offered her Melanie in *Gone with the Wind,* but she would only take it with first billing. That's the way superstars thought in those days.

BAWDEN: *Gunga Din* was your biggest-ever hit.

FAIRBANKS: I was first offered [the role of] Cutter by [director] Howard Hawks and I accepted. That would be at the end of 1938. Then he sheepishly phoned back and said would I exchange for the role of Ballantine, and I think that suited me better. Cutter went to Cary Grant. It was very loosely based on Kipling. Very loosely! We filmed exteriors at Alabama Hills and Lone Pine, Sherwood Forest, Venice for the canals, Death Valley—all in California. Never went near India. And just before filming started, RKO dumped Howard for George Stevens. Receipts for Howard's *Bringing Up Baby* were coming in, and it had bombed at the box office. But George was even more of a fastidious director. He took far more time than Howard would.

I always thought it was strange that just as the empire was fading Hollywood began embracing it with these kinds of films. Yes, it was considered racist even then. But just try to turn away when you're watching. It has a rhythm all its own. People today say it should have been shot in color, but RKO couldn't afford that. And [Ted] Turner, you know, tried a colorized version and it's a horror. No, *Gunga Din* is not politically correct. But it never was! That last line, "You're a better man than I am, Gunga Din"—it still gets to me when I see it. *Gunga Din* was my sole masterpiece among all the hundred or so films I made.

BAWDEN: Joan Fontaine, who was your heroine, told me about watching you and Marlene Dietrich go off to a gala and thinking you two were Hollywood's most glamorous couple.

FAIRBANKS: About Marlene: I was in love with her. Marlene was in love with Marlene. It lasted for about two years. My role was that of the grateful admirer. 'Nuff said . . .

BAWDEN: You were now doing action films.

FAIRBANKS: As long as Pete was alive, I never would have dared. His sudden death made it okay. I was saluting him, don't you see? I did *The Sun Never Sets* [1939]. Wonderful cast: Basil Rathbone, Lionel Atwill, Melville Cooper, Sir C. Aubrey Smith. First day Aub walks up and says, "Rotten title. It already has set!" and walks away! Rowland Lee directed, wonderful talent. Did nothing at the b.o. [box office] because Americans were realizing we'd soon be at war. By "we" I mean both the U.S. and the British Empire.

Rulers of the Sea [1939] was another slice of British history. They brought over Margaret Lockwood, who made one other movie with Shirley Temple, and then she left because she was wanted back home. Cary Grant declined, but many, like David Niven, went and even Madeleine Carroll chose to go home. This one was a very boring story about the first steamer to make the transatlantic run. Very static. Lost a bundle.

BAWDEN: But you continued this theme in 1940: *Green Hell, Safari*.

FAIRBANKS: *Green Hell* was hell. Every cliché of the jungle was trotted out. Joanie Bennett says it remains her worst movie. I remember George Sanders saying he held his nose every time he had to read a line. The director was Jimmy Whale, who'd just lost it. He didn't care about it at all. Saw this on the *Late Show* once and I couldn't stop laughing, but maybe I should have been crying?

Safari was better. Anything after *Green Hell* would have been better. It was another jungle thing, but this time I was a guide for Madeleine Carroll and her husband Tullio Carminati. Mad was the most beautiful costar I ever had. Sorry about that, you Garbo fans. Did you know they asked the real Beryl Markham to be in it as herself, and she said it was scarier than flying the Atlantic solo? You know, it all worked somehow. Eddie Griffith was Mad's favorite director. They made six films together, and Delmer Daves did the screenplay. It's beautifully photographed, not a bad movie at all.

BAWDEN: Then you produced and costarred in *Angels over Broadway* [1940].

FAIRBANKS: I got everything together, convinced Harry Cohn to bankroll us at Columbia. Ben Hecht did the screenplay and Lee Garmes and Ben directed it together. An enchanting character study, I think. We needed a cheap leading lady and took Rita Hayworth, who was under contract. We redressed her, regroomed her, and this was her first A picture. She even got the character's speech impediment down pat. Tommy Mitchell took a pay cut to do it; so did John Qualen. Cohn couldn't figure out what the film was all about but neither could we. Thanks to Lee, the photography glistens. Today it would be an art house film and Cohn ran it off on double bills, but it convinced me I should produce.

BAWDEN: Your last prewar film was *The Corsican Brothers* [1941].

FAIRBANKS: My salute to Pete. We got Ruth Warrick fresh. Akim Tamiroff was great; so was J. Carrol Naish. For good luck I plopped in H. B. Warner and William Farnum, who'd worked with Pete in stock. Seeing it today, the special effects could be better, but our budget was limited. So we concentrated on stunts. Fifteen years [later] Burt Lancaster comes up to me at a function and says can I still do that charge and I tried right then and there—to hop over a big chair—and tore my Achilles [tendon]. So there you have it. I studied swordplay for weeks before we shot, and the final swordfight is the best thing about this picture.

BAWDEN: Then you went to war.

FAIRBANKS: Enlisted. You can read all about it in that book on me [*Knight Errant,* the 1955 biography by Brian Connell]. When I got back everything had changed. Those guys who declined to fight, like John Wayne, were big stars. I wasn't forgotten but I was sidelined, now thirty-eight. And I wasn't the only one. Bob Montgomery and Mel Douglas never regained career momentum. And Jimmy Stewart just refused to return to MGM, and I don't blame him. He had to reinvent himself to come back as a bigger star.

It took me two years to find a property, and I picked *Sinbad the Sailor.* The sets and color were lavish, but Errol Flynn told me I'd made a big mistake because nobody was interested in swashbuckling, and I had to agree. Receipts were thin even with the lovely Maureen O'Hara as costar. But I was nothing if not stubborn. I turned right around and produced *The Exile* [1947], directed by the marvelous Max Ophuls. I kept him on a short leash and he delivered a print that was outstanding. We made money but not as much as expected.

I thought *That Lady in Ermine* [1948] would recoup everything for me. The great Ernst Lubitsch sent for me and talked it up and I signed. Me with Betty Grable, I wasn't so sure, but she's a guy's gal, very funny, very blowsy in a sexy way. I was looking forward to it until at the last moment Ernst had another heart attack. Zanuck put Otto Preminger in charge and he ruined everything. No sense of fun, no humor, everything light in the Samson Raphaelson script was squeezed out. Betty got touchy and our wonderful cast of Cesar Romero, Walter Abel, Reginald Gardiner would sit around for days while Otto confabbed with Ernst from his sickbed. It just wrecked my momentum, just wrecked it.

BAWDEN: You went to Britain to make *State Secret* [1950], one of your best-ever movies.

FAIRBANKS: As good as anything Hitchcock would do. And the reason is director-writer Sidney Gilliat, who'd cowritten *The Lady Vanishes* [1938]. Jack Hawkins, Glynis Johns, Herbert Lom—we made it special. I was a visiting American surgeon in a dictatorship—a situation much like *Crisis* with Cary Grant, made the same year. But Cary said, "Douglas, your picture was better." I thought I did my best work ever; Sidney really kept the pot boiling. But it wasn't properly advertised in the U.S. And then I made a stinker called *Mr. Drake's Duck* [1951], and I just left films for a long time, acting-wise, I mean.

BAWDEN: You started out on TV in 1950.

FAIRBANKS: For his first-ever spectacular, Bob Hope said, "I must have Bea Lillie and Doug Fairbanks." And he got us. Nobody had done live TV. We were all scared crazy when that red light went on. I did *Pulitzer Prize Playhouse* in 1950, too; Spring Byington and Mel Douglas were in it, too, but it was nerve-wracking, this live drama stuff.

BAWDEN: You were based in Britain by then?

FAIRBANKS: It was where my business interests were. I felt comfortable there. Then in 1953 I started producing *Douglas Fairbanks Jr. Presents.* We had five seasons, all filmed in Britain, total of 157 episodes. Some big-name directors were involved: Leslie Arliss, Terence Fisher, and we used top British actors. The lady I'm dining with tonight, Lois Maxwell, did some. So did Ron Randell, Christopher Lee, Renee Asherson, the Canadian actor Lee Patterson, Greta Gynt, even Sybil Thorndike. Oh, Ella Raines was in two episodes, Muriel Pavlow, Dulcie Gray, a little girl Luciana Paluzzi, who grew up to be a sex symbol. I did all the hiring and I did all the firing. It ran on both American and Canadian TV, too.

BAWDEN: You never acted on it?

FAIRBANKS: Didn't want to. When I produced *Chase a Crooked Shadow* [1958] everyone said to do a cameo. Everyone but me. Then I got coaxed back for two *United States Steel Hours* and a *DuPont Show of the Week,* all in 1962. And I did *Red Skelton* around then. Loved that one because it was taped. One day I answer the phone and it's Roz Russell offering me the male lead in a TV movie she's doing—*Crooked Hearts* [1972]—and Maureen O'Sullivan was in it, too. But Roz looked like a squirrel with those huge cheeks. She was taking cortisone for arthritis. Then I toured in *The Pleasure of His Company* [1970–1972], including stops in Toronto and Chicago, but I wouldn't take it to Broadway. And I did three episodes of

The Love Boat [1979–1981]. Cary Grant said, "Oh, Douglas, you are being very daring." But I had fun.

BAWDEN: Then a big part in *Ghost Story* [1981].

FAIRBANKS: Freddie Astaire, Mel Douglas, John Houseman, Pat Neal. We shivered collectively on those wintry exteriors. Fred joked that our collective ages must be nearly four hundred years! Mel had a wonderful death scene and snorted, "It's my dress rehearsal for the real thing." The story scared me. I still can't watch it on TV. It was a bit ghoulish contemplating how we'd all aged, but who doesn't get older? Mel said, "Haven't shivered so much since I kissed Garbo!" And Fred would get up and do a two-step to break the monotony of waiting to be called. I was glad my character died early. I told the rest of those boys I was off to my Florida pad. But to be in such a hit at my age, well, it was very rewarding. A nice way to end almost six decades in the business I've always adored.

Afterword

Douglas Fairbanks Jr. died at his Park Avenue apartment on May 7, 2000, aged ninety.

Glenn Ford

Interview by Ron Miller

Glenn Ford, a movie leading man for more than half a century, finally was taken seriously as an actor by critics in the 1950s, when he made a series of dramatic films dealing with social issues.

Born in Canada as Gwyllyn Samuel Newton Ford, he came to America with his parents in his childhood and became a naturalized U.S. citizen in 1939. He was a descendant, on his father's side, of Canada's first prime minister, Sir John A. Macdonald.

On-screen, Ford often seemed to hold his emotions rigidly in check. No matter how awful the situation became around the character he was playing, he seldom lost his cool. He seethed with anger, of course, and his forehead wrinkled with angst, but he generally held it back until time for the showdown. Even then, he often looked rather uncomfortable getting emotional. As schoolteacher Richard Dadier in *The Blackboard Jungle* (1955), he mumbled and grumbled as those high school hoodlums gave him the business in the classroom. Most of us couldn't hold it in like that. We'd have grabbed the sullen and dangerous Vic Morrow by the forelock the first time he called us "Daddy-O" and tried to run his greasy head through the pencil sharpener. But, no, not Glenn Ford. He held it in until showdown time.

Before that—in the 1940s—Ford was groomed as a romantic leading man, often paired with the sexiest screen goddesses, especially his good friend Rita Hayworth, who scorched the screen in *Gilda* (1946) but wound up in Ford's comforting arms.

In real life, Ford also associated with several beautiful women, marrying and divorcing four times—the first time to MGM's leggy dancing star Eleanor Powell, the mother of his only child, son Peter. He also was known to have had quite a few relationships with other women, including Marilyn Monroe and Hope Lange, in between his marriages.

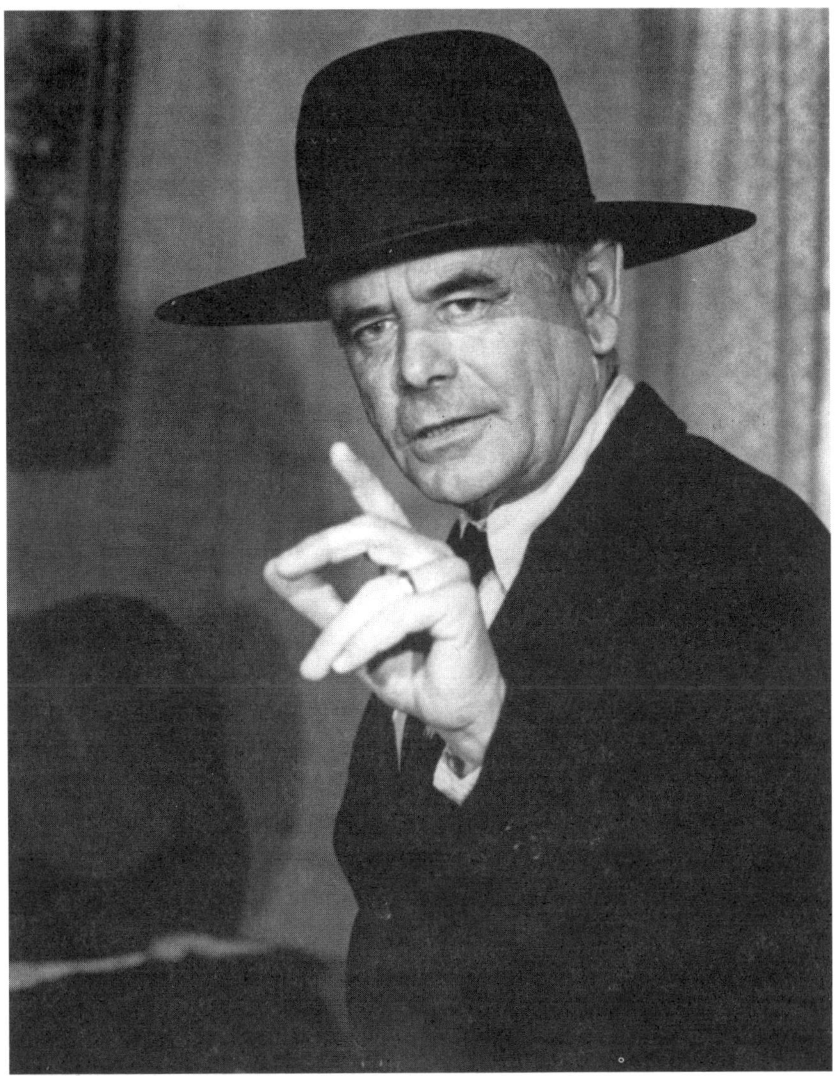

Glenn Ford as a small-town preacher in the 1974 TV movie *The Greatest Gift*, which was the pilot for his 1975 TV series, *The Family Holvak*. Courtesy of Universal Television and NBC.

Director Frank Capra, who was not a big fan of Ford, once said the actor "has been in more pictures than the President's bodyguards." Ford claimed to have been in more than 250 movies and TV shows. Among his many great films are dozens of memorable westerns, some very good ones. He starred in *Texas* (1941) with a young William Holden. Ford usually

Glenn Ford with Bette Davis in the 1946 thriller *A Stolen Life.* Courtesy of Warner Bros. and UA-TV.

played the hero, but he was an unforgettable villain in Delmer Daves's *3:10 to Yuma* (1957), the original version of what many consider one of the all-time great westerns. Ford was inducted into the Western Performers Hall of Fame in 1978.

Ford performed often on television in the 1970s, starring in *Cade's County,* a modern-day western series, for CBS (1971–1972) and later in *The Family Holvak* (1975–1976), in which he played a preacher in a family drama set in the Depression years. He also was one of the stars of two TV miniseries—*Once an Eagle* (1976–1977) and *The Sacketts* (1979). He was scheduled to star in the cable TV series *African Skies* [1992-1994] when he fell ill; he was replaced by Robert Mitchum.

Setting the Scene

Ford's tenure as a leading man in movies was pretty well over when I met him in 1978. He was then starring in *Evening in Byzantium,* a TV drama on the ad hoc Operation Prime Time TV network. My wife and I met him for dinner at an upscale restaurant in San Francisco. He was with third wife Cynthia Hayward, who was about thirty-five years younger than the sixty-two-year-old Ford. Joining us were the TV station publicist and her husband.

Before the Fords arrived, the press agent advised us to "fasten our seat belts" because we might be in for a tantrum or two. The bumpiness she anticipated was because Ford was furious about an item that had appeared that morning in Herb Caen's column in the *San Francisco Chronicle* revealing that Ford had demanded that the restaurant management provide him with a bottle of his favorite Russian vodka frozen in a block of ice.

Well, Ford had made the request, all right, but he didn't want anybody but the publicist and the restaurant to know about it. That sort of demand sounded pretty autocratic, as I'm sure he knew, and he hated to have it exposed in a column that everybody in the San Francisco Bay Area read every morning. "He'll pretend he didn't do it," the press agent said. "You watch."

Sure enough, when the Fords arrived, the headwaiter hurried over, wheeling a cart bearing a bottle of Russian vodka frozen in a block of ice. With an elegant flourish, he presented the "special order" and asked if he should open it now. The look Ford gave the poor guy could have frozen him into a block of ice as well. But after Ford chewed the fellow out for his "mistake," he relented and let the man serve the vodka.

The incident demonstrated a streak of autocratic behavior that Ford was known for among many who worked with him over the years. And again I cite Capra, who directed Ford in *Pocketful of Miracles* (1961)—and had so much trouble with Ford that he never directed another movie after that experience. In his autobiography, *The Name above the Title* (1971), Capra said Ford constantly made unreasonable demands, requiring the director to hire Ford's personal makeup man, wardrobe man, chauffeur, publicity man, and still photographer. Ford also insisted that all clothes he wore in the picture must be tailor-made and become Ford's personal property—at no cost to him. He demanded first choice on taking possession of furniture and props used in the film. Capra further claimed that Ford forced him to fire Oscar winner Shirley Jones, who was signed as his love interest in the film, and instead hire Ford's current girlfriend, Hope Lange. Capra wanted Ford replaced, but the studio wouldn't go for it—Ford got his way.

Capra confirmed that all his stories about Ford were true during an interview I conducted with him when his book came out. He added that it cost him $75,000 to get Shirley Jones out of the film, and Ford's reaction was that it wasn't his problem.

During our interview that fateful night, I asked Ford about the rift with Capra. He sighed a few times and said he probably shouldn't have pushed so hard with the great director.

To be honest, though, Glenn Ford was very nice to me the night of our interview after his outburst over the frozen vodka. He warmed up when my questions turned away from the TV project toward his movie work. He seemed to love to talk about his studio days. Either that or his ice-cold vodka was having a therapeutic effect on him.

Ultimately, I enjoyed the evening. But my overall impression was that Glenn Ford was a self-conscious man despite his fame. He wore dark glasses and spoke in a low tone that was close to a whisper. He veered away sharply from any questions about his screen persona because, he said, he'd never read anything about his screen presence that he thought really fit.

Capra wrote Ford off as a garden-variety actor. As much as I admire Capra, I don't think that's a fair assessment. Ford left behind a great many vivid performances, and I still enjoy seeing them as much as I did the first time.

The Interview

MILLER: You were still Gwyllyn Ford when you began to attract attention as a theater actor in the late 1930s. How did you become Glenn Ford?

FORD: I was signed to a contract at Columbia Pictures in 1939 and [studio boss] Harry Cohn called me to his office. He said a name change was necessary, so he looked out the window, saw the street sign for Gower Avenue, and said, "We'll call you John Gower."

MILLER: And you said what?

FORD: I said, "No way, Mr. Cohn. No way!" I was prepared to forget about Columbia and go back to the stage. I picked my own name from my dad's hometown in Quebec: Glenford.

MILLER: I've heard some horror stories about actors who didn't do what Harry Cohn wanted them to do. How did you get along with him?

FORD: It seems chic for everybody to say something bad about Harry Cohn. I resent it because he was what the industry is all about. If you had a weakness, he found it and used it against you. He respected me because I wasn't afraid of him.

MILLER: In your early days at Columbia, it seemed like they didn't really know what to do with you. I mean, you went from a silly comedy like *Blondie Plays Cupid* [1940] into a western action picture like *Texas* [1941] and then a war picture like *Flight Lieutenant* [1942]. What was going on?

FORD: You didn't question it when they assigned you a role. They made you do sometimes a whole feature in one week. You had to work all day and all night. That was the advantage of being a contract player in those days. You learned to be a professional.

MILLER: But you quickly became a leading man, and by *The Adventures of Martin Eden* in 1942, you were the title character in a major studio production. What was your ticket? Was it the "boyish charm" the fan magazines always talked about?

FORD: Boyish charm? Jeez, that's disgusting! Shit, man, I've been in three wars! Boyish charm? I was never what you call good looking. I was never an Arrow Collar man.

MILLER: Well, let's not go there then. I guess we can both agree that by 1946 and *Gilda,* you had arrived as a movie star. But I've read that you did not get along with your director, Charles Vidor. What's the story there?

FORD: One day he started berating the extras and it made me so mad that I walked off the set and wouldn't return until Vidor apologized to them. It took a couple of hours, but he finally did it and the soundman recorded his apology to the extras for me, so I went back to work.

MILLER: Then Harry Cohn and Vidor got into a legal dispute and, knowing that you and Vidor didn't get along, he assigned Vidor to direct your next picture?

FORD: It ended up with me getting my direction relayed through the assistant director. Harry wanted to break Charles—and he did. He couldn't take it and quit after two weeks. Later, though, we became good friends.

MILLER: You and Rita Hayworth were the most valuable of Columbia stars and *Gilda* made you this amazing romantic team. Your impressions of her?

FORD: I love the woman. She lives next door to me, you know. [At this point, Ford went silent and an anguished look crossed his face.] I worry about her. There used to be lights on over there, late at night, every night. Now I don't see them.[Again, Ford became silent and his wife, Cynthia, tried to explain how close the Fords were to Rita Hayworth, how they

Glenn Ford with Rita Hayworth in *Gilda* (1946). Courtesy of Columbia Pictures.

often went places together. With a wary glance at her husband, she said Glenn and Rita were "like brother and sister."]

Not like brother and sister! I love the woman. Cynthia understands.

[Ford went on to say that recently he had found Rita unconscious on the floor of her home and had to call a doctor. She was then beginning to suffer from the ravages of Alzheimer's disease. She lived another nine years, but had been retired from acting for six years prior to my interview with Ford.]

Miller: You made some great films with Rita, but I've heard that you thought your 1948 film with her, *The Loves of Carmen,* was the worst movie you ever made.

Ford: The only mistake Harry Cohn ever made was casting me in that film. I was the most ludicrous Don José you could imagine in the world. But he was sold on the idea that anything Rita and I did would make money.

Miller: Not long after that, you made what I consider one of your all-time best films, *The Big Heat* [1953], but it was directed by Fritz Lang, and I've heard some fine actors tell me he was a nightmare. Your opinion?

FORD: We made two pictures together—*The Big Heat* and *Human Desire* [1954]—and we remained pals. I'd heard the same thing about him, so I laid it on the line from the beginning. I told him, "Fritz, don't fuck with me. I know your reputation, so don't try it with me. I don't take that kind of shit." He said, "Yeah?" But from then on he liked me.

MILLER: I think many critics really sat up and noticed you as a fine actor for the first time after seeing you in *Blackboard Jungle.* Was that a turning point in your career?

FORD: It was and it was because of the director, Richard Brooks. He changed my whole conception of what acting is about. Brooks taught me truth in acting. He shook me up and told me: "Don't care how you look. Just be real."

MILLER: You've been incredibly busy on the big screen and now on television for your entire career. You star in a TV drama like *Evening in Byzantium* and you play a cameo role as Clark Kent's adoptive father in *Superman* and then you go into a western TV miniseries like *The Sacketts.* What's the secret?

FORD: I've never been pigeonholed as an actor. They don't think of me as just one kind of character.

MILLER: What do you do when you're not working in a project?

FORD: We travel a lot and I have a lot of hobbies—gardening, raising cattle, horseback riding, winemaking, gourmet cooking. I enjoy life.

MILLER: I know you're proud of many things you've done, but you don't like to sum yourself up. Why is that?

FORD: I never feel like I've done a good job. I always know I can do better. If I ever feel satisfied, that's when I'll be in real trouble.

Afterword

Ford suffered a series of strokes in his later years and died at age ninety in 2006.

Cary Grant

Interview by James Bawden

If you ask movie fans to draw up a list of legendary leading men in the history of the movies, you can be sure Cary Grant's name will be right near the top of everyone's list. Though he didn't collect a lot of awards in his thirty-four years in movies—his only Academy Award was a 1969 "special" Oscar "for his unique mastery of the art of screen acting"—Grant was the quintessential Hollywood leading man, a handsome and debonair fellow who was as impressive in action roles as he was in romantic love stories, as convincing in serious dramatic parts as he was in flat-out comedy roles. And his appeal to female moviegoers seemed eternal—he was still in demand to play romantic leads when he made his last film at the age of sixty-two.

Cary Grant had come a long way from his days as a British-born acrobat named Archie Leach. He had scaled the heights of stardom in America but was known all over the world. He had evolved into an international symbol of style and grace.

Setting the Scene

In the last twenty years of his life, Grant seldom gave interviews, and he never got around to writing an autobiography. Most reporters didn't even bother to ask for a chance to talk with him since the odds were so heavy against him ever saying yes.

Yet on August 8, 1980, at a time when I was writing about television for the *Hamilton (Ont.) Spectator,* I received a surprising telephone call at my apartment from a publicist for the Fabergé perfume company, asking if I would join Mr. Grant for high tea at 2 p.m. sharp. I knew Grant was now a spokesman for Fabergé. He was in Toronto for the grand opening of the company's new Canadian plant and had patiently answered all questions

Cary Grant. James Bawden collection.

the day before at a mass press conference. It didn't seem likely he'd want to do an interview, too. "Well, he does and you can ask him why," the publicist said as she rang off.

And so at noon I was barreling down the Queen Elizabeth highway toward Toronto with photographer Bob Chambers. We lost our way but luckily got there just in time. No sooner had we assembled our gear in the plush Fabergé boardroom than Grant arrived. "Hello, James," he said, "I'm Cary Grant."

"Y-y-yes, you are," I answered hesitantly as a gigantic silver tea tray was wheeled in with a rich assortment of tea cakes, buns, tarts, pies, and enough plates and saucers for an assembly of twenty or so. I was awed at meeting one of the biggest-ever Hollywood stars—and he really looked the part in his stylish black Armani suit and a handsome blue tie, which he said was knotted in the fashion taught him by the Duke of Windsor!

The only other person present was his publicist, Barbara.

The Interview

BAWDEN: I can't believe you wanted to talk to the *Hamilton Spectator* separately.

GRANT: Well, I do. I like to return favors. In 1923, when I was a teenager appearing in vaudeville with Bob Pender's acrobats, I passed through Hamilton on the vaudeville circuit. And I got my first-ever review when the *Spectator* said, "Archie Leach is ever so agile." And I came back to Hamilton with Pender every season through the early twenties. We'd do a week in Toronto, then a split week of Hamilton and London [Ontario], then on to Detroit. I was five years on that circuit. It got me used to crowds and appearing in public. It made me. And I remember my first-ever review came out the week before Canadian Thanksgiving, which was in October, I believe.

BAWDEN: Seeing the way people behave around you, is it still fun being Cary Grant?

GRANT: I don't like to disappoint people. Because he's a completely made-up character and I'm playing a part. It's a part I've been playing a long time, but no way am I really Cary Grant. A friend told me once, "I always wanted to be Cary Grant." And I said, "So did I." In my mind's eye, I'm just a vaudevillian named Archie Leach. When somebody yells "Archie" on the street I'll look up. I don't look up if somebody calls "Cary." So I think Cary Grant has done wonders for my life and I always want to give him his due.

BAWDEN: But you don't always dress like this?

GRANT: At home it's jeans or slacks. Once, when my daughter was little, I had to go to the chemist's late at night for a prescription to be filled. It was a rush and I was wearing jeans and the woman cashier looked at me askance and said, "Oh, Mr. Grant—how could you?" I got her message. I'd disappointed her and I guess I apologized.

BAWDEN: Do you remember your reply when *Encyclopaedia Britannica* telegraphed you for information?

GRANT: The telegram read, "How old Cary Grant?" And I telegraphed back, "Old Cary Grant fine. How you?" My last batch of movies, I was being reviewed for how old I looked instead of how good or bad the movie was.

BAWDEN: I understand you gave William Holden terse information when he was starting in movies.

GRANT: Bill was twenty-two and we were introduced on the set of *Only Angels Have Wings* [1939]. He was visiting and had just signed with Columbia. And he asked for career [advice], so I told him, "Get a good tan." He's been thanking me ever since.

BAWDEN: You're as famous for the movies you didn't make as for the movies you made.

GRANT: Strangest-ever request came from old C. B. DeMille, who asked me if I wanted to test for Samson in *Samson and Delilah* [1949]. And I said, "Only if I could wear my dinner jacket." Billy Wilder was serious when he asked me to do *Sabrina* [1954], and I turned him down. I'd heard he didn't like actors very much and I'd already worked with enough of those kind of directors to last a lifetime. Humphrey Bogart did the picture and he looks very unhappy all the way through.

I dithered about playing Norman Maine in *A Star Is Born* [1954]. It was a part I think I could have done. But Freddie March had aced the part in the original [1937] version, and Judy Garland had the key part and she seemed difficult to work with and I couldn't make up my mind. Jimmy Mason did a grand job and said how hard a chore it was waiting day after day to see if Judy would appear.

It's true I turned down *Bridge on the River Kwai* [1957] for *The Pride and the Passion* [1957]. I did it to work with Marlon Brando and then he quit just before we started and was replaced by Frank Sinatra. I think I could have done *Kwai,* although not perhaps quite as brilliantly as Alec Guinness.

BAWDEN: You also turned down *My Fair Lady* [1964].

GRANT: It was Rex Harrison's part. He'd done it on Broadway. And I was sorely tempted. Jack Warner offered me $1 million plus a piece of the action. And the costars were to be Audrey Hepburn and Jimmy Cagney.

When Jimmy refused to come out of retirement, I had my reason for not signing. I knew there would be a backlash, and Audrey felt it [because she took the part Julie Andrews had played opposite Harrison on Broadway.] I told Jack, "Not only will I not do it, but if you don't use Rex I even won't go to see it."

BAWDEN: What was your life like in vaudeville?

GRANT: As tough as anything. We'd work up to six performances a day and go on the all-night train to the next destination. Had to sleep in the coach car. Three or four of us would bunk in a single room. Meals were cans of beans heated on radiators. You'd wash clothes in the bathtub. I was a stilt walker. That was my specialty. But I also performed in comedy skits. When the troupe returned to England, I decided to stay [behind]. There was more promise of jobs in the U.S. and Canada.

BAWDEN: It was a lonely life?

GRANT: On the night trains, I'd look into the windows of the houses along the way and see people living ordinary lives. That was my goal. To live in my own home.

BAWDEN: How did you support yourself later on?

GRANT: I painted and sold neckties with a young chap who became the designer Orry Kelly. I was a bogus mind reader in another vaudeville act. All the time I was auditioning for legitimate plays and finally I was scouted and signed by Arthur Hammerstein for Oscar Hammerstein II's operetta *Golden Dawn* [1937]. It opened on Broadway the same night as another musical, a little something called *Show Boat.* I made friends with George Brent, who was a chorus boy in it.

And then I had another singing part in *Boom Boom* [1929], which starred a lovely newcomer—Jeanette MacDonald. We both got Paramount screen tests. She was hired right away and I was told, "Your neck is too thick." It ruined my image of myself for a long time.

BAWDEN: You wanted to be a Broadway star at the time?

GRANT: That's it. I sang operetta in St. Louis after that and then had a drama part in a play starring Fay Wray called *Nikki* [1931]. My character's name was Cary Lockwood. But I was still billed as Archie Leach.

BAWDEN: Why did you then go to L.A.?

GRANT: Fay suggested it. Broadway was dead because of the Depression. At first the only work I could get was helping young actresses get through their screen tests. Then the director Marion Gering saw me—or rather the back of my head—and gave me another test. Paramount reluctantly signed me to a five-year deal, but I had a boardroom meeting about my name. I took "Cary" from the play I'd been in and the studio took "Grant" after the U.S. president. Right then the rage was for short names: George Brent, Bette Davis. A Richard Barthelmess was the kind of name to be avoided.

BAWDEN: How did you get your first break?

GRANT: The brass quickly put me into *This Is the Night* [1932] with Roland Young and gave me a pay raise to $450 a week. I watched the initial rushes and sank in fear. My face was as white as a ghost. All the actors wore tons of thick makeup and even had lipstick. I was petrified. I was twenty-eight and didn't know who I was. So I pretended to be Noël Coward for years after.

BAWDEN: Do you recognize yourself watching these movies today?

GRANT: Not at all. I was desperate to succeed. But I couldn't act at all. But the Paramount publicity machine blasted into high gear. I got all the parts Gary Cooper turned down. I even was in a Coop picture called *The Devil and the Deep* [1932]. I have a few lines at a bar.

BAWDEN: You got top billing in *Hot Saturday* [1932], which I just saw, but you had only a few scenes.

GRANT: The leading lady was Nancy Carroll, but she was fading fast. So they promoted me to billing above her, which was embarrassing. A feisty Irish girl, she always brawled with management. But everybody brawled with management. Clara Bow walked out around that time. Fredric March left as soon as he could and so did Cooper. The stance of the studio was to keep one working at any cost. I'd get a new script and if I balked I'd instantly be on suspension, which meant I wasn't being paid anything.

BAWDEN: But Mae West says she spotted you on the back lot and gave you your first big break.

GRANT: *She Done Him Wrong* [1933] was my eighth picture. And the exposure was tremendous. When I first met her, I was astonished how tiny she was, barely five feet. And not at all svelte. She had a flabby belly which always wiggled when she walked. She talked badly. Not dirty. I mean when she was called to set she'd yell, "I ain't ready!" That kind of bad. She was actually a prude. Innuendo was her game and not explicitness.

BAWDEN: She stacked her movies with handsome young men.

GRANT: Right. I was window dressing. Gilbert Roland was in it and she ogled him all the time. But everyone saw it. The movie was my first smash and later that year I made a second film with her [1933's *I'm No Angel*], which I think is better. But when strict censorship came in, her day was over. What she said needed that touch of suggestiveness.

BAWDEN: Did you have any choice over films?

GRANT: No. Paramount was determined to build me up as a rather serious young man. Who was I to object? Only a few of those movies are watchable. In *Blonde Venus* [1932] I was the cad after Marlene Dietrich. The director, Josef von Sternberg, yelled at her all the time. I was a male mannequin. *Thirty-Day Princess* [1934] starred Sylvia Sidney and is quite lovely. The same idea was used in *Roman Holiday* [1953], you know. But *Born to Be Bad* [1934], which I made on loan to Fox, was sheer awfulness. I was a pig farmer and Loretta Young a hard-boiled single mother. Jean Harlow just refused to do it. None of these could be called a Cary Grant film.

Wings in the Dark [1935] was a challenge because I was a blind flyer, but it was a Myrna Loy vehicle most of all. Friends told me that *Last Outpost* [1935] wasn't that bad, but it was. Paramount took all the outtakes from *Lives of a Bengal Lancer* [1935] and used these for the action sequences.

BAWDEN: Then you made the film that changed your life.

GRANT: It was *Sylvia Scarlett* [1935] and RKO bought my rights for seven weeks. [Director] George Cukor said he saw something behind my smoothness. I had a Cockney accent and was a real character, not a lounge lizard at all. I loved the part and George helped me unwind. It was a Kate Hepburn vehicle, but I got noticed. I wasn't just a nice young man with good teeth any longer.

BAWDEN: So you gave your notice?

GRANT: I turned down $1 million for a contract renewal from Paramount. I looked around and made deals with Columbia and RKO, which were smaller studios. I figured I could squeeze one picture out of each studio every year and be able to pick and choose my roles. I was one of the very first to freelance. Others saw what I was doing and tried to copy it.

BAWDEN: It seems only a few directors were able to create the Cary Grant character for you.

GRANT: Right. George Cukor with *Sylvia Scarlett, Holiday* [1938], and *The Philadelphia Story* [1940]. Then Leo McCarey with *The Awful Truth* [1937] and *My Favorite Wife* [1940]. Then Howard Hawks with *Bringing Up Baby* [1939], *Only Angels Have Wings,* and *His Girl Friday* [1940]. Then

Cary Grant with Katharine Hepburn in *The Philadelphia Story* (1940). Courtesy of MGM and TV station KTVU of Oakland, CA.

George Stevens with *Gunga Din* [1939] and *Talk of the Town* [1942]. I signed for *Gunga Din* because Hawks was going to direct it and then RKO fired him after *Baby* lost money. George Stevens was even slower and it wound up costing over $2 million—and lost money the first time out. And five years after leaving Paramount I was up to $200,000 a picture.

BAWDEN: I felt you should have killed Joan Fontaine in *Suspicion* [1941]. She was such a complaining person.

GRANT: That was the intention. We shot the whole picture that way. Then the RKO president saw the rough cut and came running onto the soundstage claiming, "You can't have Cary Grant as a killer!" So he forced Hitch [director Alfred Hitchcock] to film an alternate ending. Originally, I post the letter she's written to her parents after killing her. And she tells them her suspicions, so I don't get off. But Joan won the Oscar anyway, although she never thanked me for helping her.

BAWDEN: Favorite leading ladies?

GRANT: Four with Hepburn, but only the last, *The Philadelphia Story*, was successful at all. A real character. She'll try anything. I taught her acrobatics and she even does a turn in *Holiday.* She was always standing on my shoulders and heaving into a rolling fall. In *Bringing Up Baby,* we had the sweetest leopard to work with, very adorable, always purring when petted. When they substituted the nasty leopard, Kate got scratched up. So in the scene when she's dragging the leopard into the police station, they double-printed the leopard in later. Look closely and you'll see the strands of rope don't match.

In the final scene, we had one chance at doing it on top of the dinosaur skeleton or somebody could get hurt. I trained Kate myself. She was fearless. There was no mattress on the floor. I had her let me grab her, not by her hands because her arms would pop out of the sockets. I grabbed her by her wrists and we're up there tossing back and forth as the skeleton crashes. Scariest thing I'd ever done, but Kate said it was wonderful and talked about deserting acting for acrobatics!

I tried to get out of *Philadelphia Story* because my part was small. So in the movie version Hepburn doesn't have a brother. I got all those lines. But it still didn't flow. On the last day of shooting, Cukor came up with the visual gag that opens the movie: Dexter is moving out and she comes behind him and breaks all his golf clubs over her knee. Then I push her violently backwards, using her face to push her away. Of course, there was a mattress out of camera range, but most big stars would have hollered. On the second take Kate merely said, "Push harder, if you like."

Of the four stars—Hepburn, Jimmy Stewart, Ruth Hussey all got Oscar nominations and Jimmy won. How do you think that made me feel?

BAWDEN: How about Jean Arthur?

GRANT: We just never got along. In *Only Angels Have Wings,* she gave Hawks a real rough ride. Resisted all directing hints, claimed I was mugging. In *Talk of the Town,* it was more of the same, including hysterics when I thought she was overdoing it in one big scene. When [director Frank] Capra offered us *A Woman of Distinction* [in 1950], Jean said, "With anybody but Cary." She only made one more movie [*Shane,* 1953] and then it just got too much for her. [Capra never made the film, but it was made by another director without Grant or Jean Arthur.]

BAWDEN: Irene Dunne?

GRANT: Three pictures. Wish we'd done ten more. In *Penny Serenade* [1941], that was the last time I took second billing. For the first and only time I cried on camera and when Irene saw it in the morning rushes next day she said, "That's your Oscar." Well, I did get my first nomination.

Cary Grant and Ingrid Bergman in Alfred Hitchcock's *Notorious* (1946). Courtesy of Selznick International and Viacom TV.

On *The Awful Truth* we just clicked. She'd been a weepie star and comedy was strange to her. She'd do a bit and whisper to me, "Funny?" She was the sweetest smelling of my leading ladies and such a lady. If one of the crew cussed, she'd blush. She claims she was out shopping at Bullock's for a present for her husband and the saleslady said, "I don't think Mr. Grant would like that." In the minds of the public, we were married. Reunions became impossible because we both liked first billing. It's ladies first in rowboats but not in movies, I'm afraid. But I still see her at the races and she still smells wonderful, although it's not Fabergé.

BAWDEN: Carole Lombard?

GRANT: Three pictures with her and nary a comedy. I just think that's strange. We were always meaning to reunite and then she was gone from our midst. Claudette Colbert was also at Paramount but I wasn't considered big enough to be paired with her. She's the one who got away.

BAWDEN: Marilyn Monroe?

GRANT: Hawks says it's wonderful we knew and worked with Marilyn

Cary Grant with Deborah Kerr in *An Affair to Remember* (1957). Courtesy of 20th Century-Fox.

before she got difficult. Because she was so winning and adorable in *Monkey Business* [1952]. When I drink that youth serum and I'm acting like a teenager, Marilyn really got into it. I'm diving off the high board and she's giggling and waving me on. Years later she asked me to costar in something called *The Billionaire*. It was a comedy and she said her husband Arthur Miller was reworking it. Arthur Miller a comedy writer? I ran away and so did Greg Peck, and the completed film, *Let's Make Love* [1960], showed she'd become all blurry and distant. It was sad.

BAWDEN: You retired for several years.

GRANT: In the early fifties my films were dull: *Crisis* [1950], *People Will Talk* [1951], *Dream Wife* [1953]. I just gave up for awhile. Nobody wanted me. It was all Method actors. And I don't look right in a torn T-shirt. They asked that wonderful actor Basil Rathbone why he wasn't working anymore and he said, "I blame it all on that Marlon Brando." And that's the way I felt, too. Then Hitch phones and offers me *To Catch a Thief* [1955] with Grace Kelly and things started looking up.

Bawden: You had your biggest-ever hit with *An Affair to Remember* [1957].

Grant: It still makes money. I know because I have a percentage and the checks keep arriving every six months.

The only time I played myself was in *None but the Lonely Heart* [1944], and nobody wanted to see the real me. So I put Archie Leach away and went back to being Cary Grant.

Bawden: With Hitchcock, you made my favorite Cary Grant movie, *North by Northwest* [1959].

Grant: The writer, Ernie Lehman, did it as a tribute to all the Hitch films. There was the mysterious blonde. After Grace [Kelly] retired, we got Eva Marie Saint, who is perfect. There's the chase, the McGuffin, the suave stranger played by James Mason. Hitch shot all the Mt. Rushmore close-ups in a gigantic MGM soundstage. He has such a sense of humor. There we were dangling up there and he calls a tea break! And he wanted me to cower inside Lincoln's nose and then sneeze. The crop-dusting scene took only a day to complete because it was so meticulously planned. The pilot had radio contact with Hitch and it went so smoothly. It was my most physical scene since *Gunga Din*.

My mother in that movie was Jessie Royce Landis. She was Grace's mother in *To Catch a Thief*. She was a year older than me. When somebody later asked her why she no longer made movies, she said, "I guess Cary Grant no longer needs a mother."

Bawden: You once said you wanted total control over your pictures.

Grant: And I got it when I started my own company with Stanley Donen. All these films made big profits and still bring in money today. On *Indiscreet* [1958], we got Ingrid Bergman after her Oscar win. It was her first-ever comedy and she just glows. The story is about two mature people falling in love, nothing more. But by the time of *Charade* [1963], I felt at fifty-nine I was too old to chase the girl any longer. So Stanley fixed the script and Audrey Hepburn chases me. Ingrid saw it and said Audrey was too old for me. She suggested Jane Fonda would be my next costar, but that never happened.

Bawden: Do you consider yourself retired these days?

Grant: Well, it's true I don't act anymore. Haven't since *Walk, Don't Run* [1966]. For years afterward I kept offices at Universal but nothing interested me. Then I quietly disbanded the team and went home. I'm on the board of directors of Fabergé and MGM. I have a company that looks after the movies I own. I do exercise every day, but it's mild stretching. I gave up stilt walking a long time ago. No nicotine and no caffeine keep me feeling young. In the afternoon, if I'm home, I'll slip out to the back patio to catch the last rays of sunshine in the afternoon. Tan from a bottle looks awful.

People keep telling me I've had such an interesting time of it. But I remember all those stomach disturbances that afflicted me every time I started a new picture. I was an idiot until I was forty, all wrapped up in my own ego. I loosened up somewhat when I took LSD under controlled conditions. I do try to keep in contact with the people I worked with.

And, speaking as Archie Leach, I'm not ungrateful for all that being Cary Grant has done for me.

Afterword

Cary Grant was married five times: to actress Virginia Cherrill, Charlie Chaplin's leading lady in *City Lights,* from 1934 to 1936; to heiress Barbara Hutton from 1943 to 1945; to actress Betsy Drake from 1949 to 1962; to actress Dyan Cannon, the mother of his only child, daughter Jennifer, from 1965 to 1968; and to publicist Barbara Harris from 1981 until his death.

Grant died in Davenport, Iowa, on November 29, 1986, aged eighty-two, as he was preparing another appearance in the one-man show *An Evening with Cary Grant.*

Van Johnson

Interview by James Bawden

Van Johnson seemed unlikely ever to become a big star at a major studio. He was a tall, freckle-faced former chorus boy with reddish curly hair and a sort of boyish look that didn't exactly say "leading man" in an era of macho men and debonair ladies' men. But Johnson, who was ineligible for military service because of an injury, loomed large in a Hollywood bereft of most of its regular leading men during World War II. What's more, the camera loved him and his charm just flew off the screen, dazzling female moviegoers. He was merchandised as a "boy next door" type.

Extremely popular at MGM, where he stayed for most of his early career, he eventually proved amazingly versatile, costarring—and dancing—with Gene Kelly in *Brigadoon* in 1954, then playing a solid dramatic role the same year in Columbia's *The Caine Mutiny.*

Though his career lost much momentum after the studio system dissolved and MGM dropped him, Johnson continued to work for other studios, in TV, and on the road in stage productions.

His biographers have reported that Johnson was homosexual and that his one marriage was arranged by the studio to quell rumors about his sexual preference.

Setting the Scene

When Van Johnson walked into the hotel restaurant, heads turned. It was the summer of 1987 and he was a splendidly preserved seventy-two-year-old wearing full pancake makeup. The onetime big MGM movie star was in Toronto to film an episode of the *Alfred Hitchcock Presents* TV series, a revival of the original series, and I was joining him for lunch and a *Toronto Star* interview.

Van Johnson. Courtesy of MGM.

He sat down, smiled, and said, "I never met Rock Hudson." The reference to Hudson, who had died a few years earlier from AIDS-related illness, was an obvious warning to stay away from questions about Johnson's sexual preference. I honored his implicit request.

The Interview

BAWDEN: Do you remember your first day at MGM?

JOHNSON: Well, I came out to the coast to do *Too Many Girls* [1940] and wound up with only a few lines. RKO dropped me and I went back to Broadway in 1940 for *Pal Joey* and on one of the few nights that Gene Kelly was sick, I stood in for him. Jack Warner was in the audience and he signed me. My only Warners picture was *Murder in the Big House* [1942] with Faye Emerson, and it was a ripe stinker. Jack fired me. Lucy Ball, who I met on *Too Many Girls,* tipped MGM scout Billy Grady I was available. I tested and started a year contract at $75 a week. When I got big at MGM, Jack rereleased *Murder* and it finally made back its costs.

BAWDEN: You were lucky many of MGM's biggest male stars were fighting in the war.

JOHNSON: Of course I knew that. MGM always had battalions of replacements waiting in the wings in case a star got too uppity. James Craig looked just like a young Clark Gable, so he got a lot of work. John Carroll just went from picture to picture and so did John Hodiak. I was part of a group of "boys next door" and this included Tom Drake, Marshall Thompson, and Robert Walker. As a matter of fact, I was signed by Vincente Minnelli, who saw me on the back lot, for *Meet Me in St. Louis.* But there was a scheduling clash and Tom Drake took over. Bobby Walker and I were both in *Madame Curie* [1943], so Mr. Mayer [studio head Louis B. Mayer] could look us over.

BAWDEN: But you were the soldier next door, you made so many war pictures.

JOHNSON: All from the safety of the back lot. Because of my injury, I was passed over for real duty. MGM had a room filled with service uniforms, all for me. I did *Thirty Seconds over Tokyo* [1944], *A Guy Named Joe* [1943], *High Barbaree* [1947], *Battleground* [1949], so on and so forth. I always seemed to be in uniform.

BAWDEN: One story about you from those days said you liked MGM so much you never wanted to go home.

JOHNSON: When [silent screen star] Colleen Moore visited the lot, I just had to see her. She was a favorite when I was watching silent pictures as a kid. At MGM I'd have a haircut in the MGM barbershop, research my next role at the MGM library. It was a walled city with everything right there. When I got a star dressing room with the other male players, I vowed never to relinquish it. I felt right at home. But I never ate in the MGM commissary. I brown-bagged it, so I'd sit in my dressing room and go over the lines for the next scene.

BAWDEN: Your first big picture was going to be *A Guy Named Joe,* but you almost got replaced after that accident.

JOHNSON: I was blindsided by a swerving car—the driver was drunk—and lay there while two sets of ambulances argued over the jurisdiction. Had to have a silver plate put in my head, which ruined me for army service. When I came back, MGM insisted I do a bit in *Madame Curie.* I knew what that was about. They wanted to see if my scar would show on-screen. Spence Tracy had refused to go back to work on *Joe* without me, so I owe a lot to him. Just to confuse things, they had also started up *The White Cliffs of Dover* [1944], so I was making two films at the same time and so was Irene Dunne. I had a very small part in *Dover* and I also did *Three Men in White* [1944] and *Between Two Women* [1944]—two *Dr. Gillespie* programmers—before the decision was made to try me out as a feature star as opposed to a promising newcomer.

BAWDEN: Talk about working with Clark Gable.

JOHNSON: On *Command Decision* [1947], Gable wasn't the same after he came back from the war. He'd do a scene and stroll out the door and hide out in his dressing room. Perfectly nice guy. No star temperament. At 5:30, he left the set no matter what. Sam Wood was our crusty director and he kept things humming along. The cast was as big as a telephone directory: Walter Pidgeon, John Hodiak, Brian Donlevy, Charlie Bickford. No women at all. On Broadway it was a hit, but the decision was made not to show the actual aerial attack. I just think the audience felt cheated but Sam ordered the cameras to remain inside the bunker for claustrophobic effect. But audiences just wanted the action. The only shots of the planes are in the opening credits. What followed seemed anticlimactic to a lot of people.

BAWDEN: You became expert at the care and feeding of a big group of female stars.

JOHNSON: I only worked with Ava Gardner in one of those *Dr. Gillespie* B movies. Oh, she was in *A Guy Named Joe,* but it was a walk-on. I was eighteen years younger than Irene Dunne, but audiences accepted that. But there was nothing with [Greer] Garson after *Madame Curie.* Here's something for you: MGM in 1943 wanted me to report for the next Greta Garbo picture, which was going to be a remake of *Flesh and the Devil—*

Van Johnson in a romantic scene with Janet Leigh (in her film debut) from the 1947 *Romance of Rosy Ridge*. Courtesy of MGM.

and I'd be her much-younger lover. She looked at the script and said, "I tank I go home now," and she never came back to acting.

BAWDEN: You were frequently teamed with June Allyson and Esther Williams.

JOHNSON: With Esther Williams, it was time for the tank. I was an okay swimmer, but days in that water and I felt like a prune. But who is kidding who? Nobody was looking at me anyway. The titles were similar: *Easy to Wed* [1946], *Easy to Love* [1953]. Women loved that stuff. Esther had more female fans than male. MGM had a policy of encouraging teams. *Easy to Wed* was a remake of an old Bill Powell–Myrna Loy film, *Libeled Lady*.

But I was more of a team with June Allyson. We started with *Two Girls and a Sailor* [1944], and Mr. Mayer said he was testing both June and Gloria DeHaven. He wanted to see which one audiences preferred. Gloria was prettier and had a better voice, but females preferred June's spunkiness, so he promoted her and let Gloria drift away. June was my soul mate. She was married to Dick Powell, but she confided everything to me.

They tried me, too, with Janet Leigh: *The Romance of Rosy Ridge*

[1947], *Confidentially Connie* [1953]. I did two very bad movies with Liz Taylor, *The Big Hangover* [1950] and *The Last Time I Saw Paris* [1954]. The idea was to keep making these programmers. MGM didn't make B films, but these were programmers with pretensions.

BAWDEN: Wasn't *Romance of Rosy Ridge* Leigh's first picture?

JOHNSON: She had never acted anywhere except in screen tests. Norma Shearer saw her photograph on her father's desk. He managed ski resorts. But just to be on the safe side, they had an accomplished actress standing by if Janet failed. That would have been Beverly Tyler. Janet was so inexperienced we were off on location and I caught her washing out her own clothes at night in preparation for next morning's scene. I gently told her they had [wardrobe] people for that. She was completely natural, so winning. MGM felt they had a real big star in the making, and they were right.

Five years later that whole studio setup started collapsing. I watched it crumble from within.

BAWDEN: Is it true you watched Gable leave the studio?

JOHNSON: They had given him notice. He was considered too expensive at $6,000 a week. I was in the Thalberg building with the little girl [Sandy Descher] from *The Last Time I Saw Paris,* and we watched from an upstairs window as Gable drove his convertible right around that loop. Then he stood up and saluted and drove away and with him went the studio's glory. Of course, they'd already fired the old man, Mr. Mayer. What was left was Metro-Goldwyn-Schary [Mayer's successor Dore Schary], and that wasn't much of anything.

BAWDEN: Margaret Hamilton once told me you suffered a crisis of confidence on the set of *State of the Union* [1948].

JOHNSON: She told you that? Well, it's absolutely true. I was going around saying, "What am I doing in a movie with Kate Hepburn, Spencer Tracy, Lewis Stone?" Felt I was out of my depth. One day I was saying all this and more to Frank Capra, our director, and he bellowed, "Van, you are here because I specifically asked for you. I've just been watching the dailies with Kate and she is complaining you stole that last scene from her with a bit of underacting. Do you understand what I'm saying?" What he was saying was continue being Van Johnson and stop mouthing off about it.

BAWDEN: Why did MGM pictures turn so rancid in the 1950s?

JOHNSON: They started lending me out, so I knew trouble was brewing. I didn't mind being with Loretta Young in *Mother Was a Freshman* [1949], although we couldn't swear in front of Loretta. Back at MGM we had conferences about the slide. The actors were told we were getting too old. And this was kind of true. My fans were now married and living in their new suburban homes. Why should they come into the increasingly scary downtowns to watch me trying to play a young kid when I was nearing forty? In *Remains to Be Seen* [1953], my last with June, I was thirty-seven and she was thirty-eight, and we're so very cute it was sickening.

BAWDEN: But you still made good pictures occasionally. *Battleground* is a terrific war movie.

JOHNSON: For ten days we were marched in battalion formation all over the Metro back lot. The director was Wild Bill Wellman and he said he wanted to make a war picture that looked completely real. Bob Pirosh, the writer, had served and said everything he put in the script he'd seen in action. We ate the grub of soldiers, we were forbidden to take baths or use makeup. It got too much for Bob Taylor and he stormed off in disgust, to be replaced by Johnny Hodiak. The Ardennes footage looked completely authentic, but it was shot out at the Metro ranch and on the back lot. Mr. Mayer hated it, but it got six Oscar nominations, and the rift between Mayer and Schary was out in the open.

BAWDEN: I also like *The Caine Mutiny* [1954].

JOHNSON: I sat for weeks in that courtroom and watched the back of Humphrey Bogart's head, and he was magnificent. Tracy could not have done that part because he wanted to be loved by audiences. [Director] Eddie Dmytryk delivered a cut that was an hour longer than the released film. When I saw it, the running time was slightly over three hours and it was terrific. Harry Cohn [studio boss at Columbia Pictures] ordered it cut to the bone so theaters could have an extra play a day. The longer version was amazing—the one you've seen is pretty good but not great. They say the director's cut no longer exists, which is a real shame.

Back at Metro I did *Brigadoon* [1954] and the dancing was great, the songs magnificent, but to save dollars they shot it inside a soundstage with painted backdrops and audiences stayed away. They were seeing better stuff on live TV and it was free.

BAWDEN: You're fine in *Brigadoon,* but your pictures were becoming routine.

JOHNSON: They shot all of *The Last Time I Saw Paris* on the back lot and it looked it. They couldn't get away with that anymore and I was lousy. I was also lousy in *The End of the Affair* [1955]—so much was cut to appease the censor. Then I was back at Metro making *Slander* [1956] and next door Elvis Presley was shooting *Jailhouse Rock.* Nobody was visiting us, but there were crowds next door. So I walked over and watched and I could see Elvis mouthing to an assistant, "Is that Van Johnson?" So I waved and he waved and I walked back to my lonely set and I just knew the gig was over.

BAWDEN: You almost did the TV series *The Untouchables.*

JOHNSON: My wife, Evie, said I had to ask for two payments because the pilot was going to be two hours extended over two time slots on *Desilu Playhouse.* So she phones [producer] Desi [Arnaz] the night before filming starts and he hollers and gets Bob Stack. And I did *The Music Man* on the London stage instead. Years later at an L.A. party, Bob comes up and asks me if I ever regretted turning down *The Untouchables.* And I say, "Bob, I got to sing '76 Trombones' [in *The Music Man*] for an entire year, so the answer is no."

BAWDEN: In the 1960s, they say, you invented dinner theater.

JOHNSON: My fans now sported blue hair. So I'd go out every season in an old play—preferably with music—and we'd cut it down to ninety minutes, give them a big meal with wine, and they had a night of it. The dinner would be at 6 and at 7:30 the play would begin because they couldn't be up that late anymore, considering their ages. And I'd answer questions about my career and we'd all be home and in bed by 11. And pretty soon all the older stars were at it. Gene Kelly even watched me from behind the curtains for a week before he went out on his first dinner circuit tour. I always wear my red socks and the theater is usually filled.

Then I started doing Italian crime flicks. I'd say my lines in English, but I met the guy who dubbed me and I gave him pointers. After I finish this TV job with Rory Calhoun I'll be going to New Zealand with Kathryn Grayson. The object is to keep going just as long as I can.

Afterword

Van Johnson spent his final year under hospice care at an assisted living facility in Nyack, New York. He died of natural causes on December 12, 2008. He was ninety-two.

III

The Leading Ladies

Anne Baxter

Interview by James Bawden and Ron Miller

Anne Baxter was a prodigious acting talent from a prestige-heavy family—her grandfather was America's leading architect, Frank Lloyd Wright—and always seemed destined for greatness. She began acting at age eleven and went on to study with Russian actress Maria Ouspenskaya and America's Stella Adler. She made her Broadway debut in *Seen, but Not Heard* in her early teens and her movie debut at seventeen. While still a teen, she worked with Orson Welles in his 1942 masterpiece *The Magnificent Ambersons.*

Baxter will always be remembered as the conniving Eve Harrington in the 1950 *All about Eve,* for which she was nominated for a Best Actress Oscar, but she already had won a 1946 Supporting Actress Oscar as the sad alcoholic in *The Razor's Edge.*

Baxter also wrote a best-selling memoir, *Intermission: A True Story* (1976), which detailed her unsuccessful attempt to live in the Australian outback with second husband, Randolph Galt.

In her sixties, Baxter replaced Bette Davis in the role of the hotel-owning matron in TV's *Hotel* series and made no appearances in feature films after that.

Setting the Scene

Both of us conducted separate interviews with Anne Baxter over the years. We have combined them for this presentation, but offer our individual memories of the circumstances of those interviews.

Bawden: I first interviewed Anne Baxter during a long afternoon in 1974 at the Century Plaza Hotel in Southern California's Century City. Then I interviewed her again in the late 1970s when she was making a TV movie, *Nero Wolfe,* that took years to actually get on the network schedule.

Anne Baxter, a teen newcomer to Hollywood in 1940. Photo by Frank Powolny; courtesy of 20th Century-Fox.

(The film's star, Thayer David, had died.) When she was promoting her book *Intermission* in Toronto, we met again. And I visited her on the set of *Hotel* a year before her unexpected death.

Miller: I had a long interview with Baxter in a chic West Hollywood restaurant in 1983. While filming episodes of *Hotel,* she was living in a nearby apartment and had walked to the interview, which was done without a network publicist present at her request. She was radiant, the picture of health. In those days, she was commuting by air weekly to her permanent home in Connecticut. She struck me as industrious and involved, a woman who probably found it hard to ever completely relax. But she was very engaging and extremely nice. I'll never forget her brisk, purposeful stride as she headed back to her apartment after we'd said our good-byes. She looked like a very vigorous woman with a long life ahead of her.

The Interview

BAWDEN: Let's go back to your first film, *Twenty Mule Team* [1940].

BAXTER: Oh, let's not. I'd been on the stage since I was fifteen in New York. My teacher was that old sourpuss Maria Ouspenskaya. Then in 1938 David Selznick asked me, along with Montgomery Clift, to read for *Tom Sawyer.* Monty had bad acne right then. David had me open my mouth and examined my teeth like I was a prize horse. And both of us flunked our tests.

Two years later David asked me again to come out and read for *Rebecca* and [the film's director] Alfred Hitchcock said I had made the best test but the lead at that time was going to be Ronald Colman and he was thirty-one years older. That would make the story seem to be one of robbing the cradle, so I lost again. But the test went the rounds and I had definite offers from MGM and Fox. I simply chose Fox because it was for more money. My parents were worried until it was arranged I'd room with a family friend, Nigel Bruce, and his wife. They were very strict, which is what I needed.

Then MGM asked to borrow me for *Twenty Mule Team,* a Wally Beery western, after Ann Rutherford was too busy, and I made my debut there. Wally Beery had very busy hands and Marjorie Rambeau said she'd protect me—and she did, very nicely. Stepped right in and would snort, "Back off, you old sea horse!" Acting with him was impossible. He'd paraphrase everything and told me to "jump right in when I stop talking."

MILLER: You were so young then. What did you look like in 1940?

BAXTER: I had a body like a mini Mack truck and a face that looked like it was storing nuts for the winter. I was very naïve. I had been very well brought up and I was very well educated. I was precocious, I'm sure.

MILLER: Is it true that you actually were fired from the Broadway cast of *The Philadelphia Story* before you went to Hollywood?

BAXTER: Yes. I was fourteen and was already too busty to play an eleven-year-old.

MILLER: Even if you were pretty well developed for a young girl, it seems a testament to your acting ability that Hitchcock even considered you for the leading lady in *Rebecca*. Tell me about the audition.

BAXTER: They had me in a rubber girdle, laced up practically under my bosom. My knees were knocking. It was awful.

BAWDEN: After your debut at Fox, you were in one of John Barrymore's last films, *The Great Profile* [1940]. Legend has it he was pretty well juiced in his final films. How did that go?

BAXTER: I was the stock ingenue. Did my first take with him and I was flailing away and Barrymore turned to director Walter Lang and said, "Does she have to swim?" He was in terrible shape. In the morning, he was so wasted that his man would have to carry him in and set him down in an easy chair. Then he'd pour Barrymore a Coke. No response. Then he'd shake in some rum flavoring and this great actor would suddenly spring to life. Amazing. Once we were waiting for a take and I asked him why he read his lines from chalkboards. Couldn't he remember his lines? And he stood up and recited a Hamlet soliloquy. He never made a pass at me, but it was hard going for our resident vamp, Mary Beth Hughes. She bent over once to fix her stockings and he instantly leapt up to pinch her behind. If you'd asked the public of the day the greatest actor, they would have instantly responded, "John Barrymore."

MILLER: You say you were pretty naïve back then, but can you give me an example?

BAXTER: Well, Walter Lang rushed over to apologize to me once when Barrymore cut loose with a barrage of foul language, but I didn't even know he was swearing. The way I was raised, I didn't even hear a four-letter word until I was eighteen. I mean that.

Here's another example: I was autographing photos of me for fans once and my mother looked over my shoulder with a stricken look on her face and said, "What are you writing?" So I told her: "Good luck always, Anne Baxter." Then she told me, "Your 'L' looks just like an 'F,' and that's a very dirty word!" But the truth is I'd never heard that word before and hadn't a clue what it meant.

MILLER: What did Fox have in mind for you? Did they see you as a romantic lead? A girl next door?

BAXTER: I wasn't pretty enough to be used for cutesy parts. At my very best, I was attractive. I was not a face, so I never got into that rut. I was also constantly dieting to get rid of my baby fat. I was having a hard time with that and think I probably had a mild case of bulimia.

MILLER: Explain that.

BAXTER: I became a foodaholic. I loved rhubarb pies. There used to be this little place on Ventura Boulevard that made wonderful rhubarb pies. I'd buy one, drive my car onto a side road, eat the whole thing, and then spit it back into the box. I'd buy whole containers of ice cream and spit it into the disposal. It was disgusting!

BAWDEN: How did you get the lead in Jean Renoir's *Swamp Water* [1941]?

BAXTER: I read for Renoir, the great French director, and he had to choose a studio girl, so he chose me.

MILLER: I imagine it helped that you spoke fluent French.

BAXTER: That, too.

BAWDEN: How did you get along with Renoir?

BAXTER: Adored him, but he was a lost soul. Kept saying, "They don't make films here like we do in France, n'est-ce pas?" For one thing he had a pesty producer in Irving Pichel, who usually directed. He reported back to [studio boss Darryl F.] Zanuck every day on the number of minutes Jean had gotten, the number of takes, the constant tea and coffee breaks.

The movie may have been set in the Okefenokee Swamp, but all the second unit had already been done. [It was mostly filmed on the studio back lot, but a second camera crew shot some footage from the real swamp, which was interpolated into the film.] We filmed indoors on a studio stage with a re-created swamp. Jean could only clasp his arms and look horrified. He was limited in camera angles because of the transparency screens—a movement of inches and the screens would be exposed. And his English was learned from books. In conversations, he was terrible. One day he told a little girl extra to "Make some water." He meant get her dress damp because she'd just been pulled from the swamp. Her mother was horrified, thinking he'd asked her to tinkle—and slapped his face.

I mean, he had Walter Brennan and Walter Huston running loose and just daring him to try and tone down their outrageous mugging. Then Ward Bond and Guinn Williams would wrestle to break the tension. I was on my own, frantically overdoing it, and I got bad notices that stung me.

BAWDEN: When did you know you'd been loaned to RKO for *The Magnificent Ambersons*?

BAXTER: When it went out as a press release. It was a straight trade: Fox got Vic Mature, I think, and he subsequently joined the studio full-time. I'd talked with and tested for Orson Welles, but he said his heart was set on Jeanne Crain, who he'd met in the RKO commissary. Jeanne was prettier than I was but hadn't acted as yet. RKO studio head George Schaefer made the call, much to Orson's displeasure. His days as the studio golden boy ended when *Citizen Kane* failed to return a profit.

By the time I arrived, those huge sets were up—the main house was a fully functioning house built on a soundstage—everything worked, including the gas lighting. But the walls couldn't be moved to accommodate cinematographer Stanley Cortez. No wonder he stormed around all the time.

It was a reunion with Joe Cotten, who played my father and was perfectly cast. We'd been in the tryouts of *The Philadelphia Story* in 1939 when Kate Hepburn had me fired because she charged I was getting big laughs. Joe had made it a point to come to my dressing room and assure me I had a future.

Dolores Costello was so motherly to me. I couldn't believe she'd once been married to John Barrymore. She was so demure. And I had Tim Holt as my suitor, George, cast right to type. He was that way offstage.

I was nineteen at the time, new to this game. I remember we shot scenes in an icehouse so our breath would be visible. That impressed me.

I wasn't around when Agnes Moorehead tried the scene on the staircase five different ways and each way worked. To his credit Orson always asked us for acting solutions, to try something a different way. And yes, he did make the obligatory pass at me and I made the obligatory refusal.

I saw a print in a screening room at RKO that was very long—maybe almost two hours—and it seemed draggy to me. But Orson had left on his next film adventure to Brazil when the studio head ordered Bob Wise to cut it down to 88 minutes and ship it out. I think it's a great film, but how it would have run at 120 minutes I'm not sure—that was too long for most features in those days.

BAWDEN: In the war years you always seemed to play the girl left behind.

BAXTER: Over and over. I did get to Paramount again on loan for *Five Graves to Cairo* [1943], where Erich von Stroheim up and told me I'd be perfect for a sound remake of *Greed!* Sounds crazy—and it was—but I believed everything he said. Once he was in bed for a scene and he asked me, "How are my little babies doing?" He meant his protuberant tummy and breasts and that just broke me up. But back at Fox I did *Crash Dive* [1943], *Sunday Dinner for a Soldier* [1944], *The Sullivans* [1944]. I was getting almost as much mail as Betty Grable. I was our boys' idealized girl next door.

MILLER: Somewhere along the way, actor John Hodiak came into your life.

BAXTER: I was just leaving Alfred Hitchcock's house and John was just coming in. He was about to star in Hitch's *Lifeboat* [1944]. I took one look at him and that was the end of me. Then we made a picture together and fell in love. [The two were married and had a daughter, Katrina. They later divorced, and Hodiak died in 1955. Baxter generally spoke of him with great affection.]

BAWDEN: Making *The Razor's Edge* [1946] was a big step up for you, and it won you an Academy Award. How did it come about?

BAXTER: I read in the trades Bonita Granville was up for Sophie and I went into Zanuck's office and complained. I never did that before and boy, he was surprised. I appealed to him purely in terms of economics. I was under contract, [so] he'd have to pay me anyway. Bonita was freelance; she'd be expensive. Finally, he said go over and see the director, Eddie Goulding. [Zanuck said], "If he okays it, then I'll agree."

It was late at night when I went to Goulding's Beverly Wilshire penthouse suite. What luxury! A manservant led me into the library. I read a scene and the world-weary Goulding said I sounded fine. He told me he'd get me an Oscar. He said, "I did it for Mary Astor and *The Great Lie* was junk. This is great literature." On the studio floor Eddie would act out all the parts, much to the disgust of Herbert Marshall, who snorted and sneered.

MILLER: Why didn't Zanuck think you were right for the part from the start?

BAXTER: He thought I was a cold potato.

MILLER: You have this harrowing scene in the movie where you react to Tyrone Power breaking his engagement to you and it leads you to take your own life. How did you approach that?

BAXTER: I used my own memory of my grief. I was stricken by the death of my baby brother because I adored him. I relived that scene in the hospital. Very few times have I been so distraught at the end of a scene. I was in emotional tatters. When I saw the rushes, I knew it was real.

BAWDEN: Did you realize how important that role was going to be for you?

BAXTER: I wasn't on the set much. My part was truly supporting. I only had a few scenes to hit that mark. When I come out as drugged and boozy in France, I wanted the audience to be in complete shock. I think I got a compensation Oscar. Ty Power, the lead, wasn't even nominated. Clifton Webb was nominated in support and he was superb, but he lost to a nonactor, Harold Russell [the amputee veteran from *The Best Years of Our Lives*]. So, I figured the voters felt they had to give this film something. And so I got it. But I'd already won a Golden Globe, so I wasn't surprised at all.

MILLER: Did winning the Oscar change your career overnight?

BAXTER: Not really. It's like the Good Housekeeping seal of approval.

BAWDEN: Some publicity in advance of *Yellow Sky* [1948] mentioned Paulette Goddard would be Gregory Peck's costar. When was the change made?

BAXTER: The day after shooting started on the outskirts of Death Valley. Paulette did her costume fittings at the studio, arrived on location with the temperature 119 in the shade, and left on the next plane. Couldn't take it. Sometimes I wonder if our director, Wild Bill Wellman, had secretly planned her departure all along. I happened to be free, so I was sent over and the costumes fit me. The heat was a problem. All the makeup would run and end up as a big ball of goo on the end of my chin.

I loved that one because Greg Peck usually was so stolid in his pictures. Billy made him relax more than usual. He was playing an outlaw and I was shacked up in this ghost town with my pa and the outlaws are trying to smoke us out. Well, there's one line where I remark about his body odor and Greg tried to get it removed, saying it might undermine his box office appeal among girls. And Billy just chuckled and kept right on shooting.

BAWDEN: Wasn't it embarrassing making *Homecoming* [1948]?

BAXTER: You mean because I was married to John Hodiak in real life by then, yet in Clark Gable's arms during that picture as his wife? John stayed away during those scenes of domesticity. The film just was not believable. Gable and Lana Turner are doctor and nurse on the front lines and each night repair to separate tents? I think not. But the censor would not permit any hints of adultery. That was the Code in effect. And I was stuck on the home front and never wavered? Blah. It would have been far more realistic to confront the actual situations that had arisen. So the picture flopped. Big time.

BAWDEN: Then came two with Dan Dailey.

Anne Baxter (*center*) with Gary Merrill and Bette Davis in *All about Eve* (1950). Courtesy of Twentieth Century Fox Television.

BAXTER: Zanuck was trying to split up the Betty Grable–Dan Dailey partnership and get two big stars [because] the tandem had gotten very expensive. And Dan told me he wanted to break free, become his own star. But *You're My Everything* [1949] just didn't make it. It spoofed vaudeville and silent movies, but people couldn't have cared less. They did it so much better in *Singin' in the Rain,* I'm afraid.

Then we did *A Ticket to Tomahawk* [1950]; again, not much business, and Dan was shipped back to Betty. On that one I very well remember Marilyn Monroe as one of the chorus girls. She had dirty fingernails and always seemed so unkempt and then she just exploded in *Asphalt Jungle* [1950] and *All about Eve.* But here? Didn't even get billing.

BAWDEN: How did you get attached with *All about Eve*?

BAXTER: Well, it started with *A Letter to Four Wives.* I see that smile on your face. There was no such movie, right? Well, there was in [writer-director] Joe Mankiewicz's first draft, and I was the fourth wife. And Zanuck read the script and said, "Drop the last wife," which was my part. I vaguely remember I was a young mother concerned about getting her son into the right military college. [The film was released in 1949 as *A Letter to*

Three Wives.] And Joe came to me and was very apologetic and said he owed me one.

And that one was his next script, which was originally titled *Command Performance.* First cast was Claudette Colbert as Margo and then Zanuck insisted on Jeanne Crain as Eve because she had just had a huge hit in *Pinky* and got an Oscar nomination. Jeanne later withdrew because she found she was pregnant—again! And Joe then asked me. In the back of his mind, he said, Eve and Margo should resemble each other and Claudette and I both had these square faces. Next it was Claudette's turn to leave. She was filming the final scenes of the war drama *Three Came Home* and broke her back the last day of filming. So she needed three months of bed rest and we were starting rehearsals the next week.

Zanuck got on the blower and asked Bette Davis—late at night, I'm told. She was ready and she brought a different texture to Margo. At the beginning of the shoot, she had laryngitis—hence her hoarse voice, which she had to continue throughout shooting, but people assumed she was imitating Tallulah Bankhead.

Another thing: Joe wanted Ann Sothern as Karen, the playwright's wife, but *Letter* had made her hot again and she was back at MGM on a new two-picture deal, so Celeste Holm got it.

BAWDEN: Describe the shoot.

BAXTER: Not a single word was changed. The script was that beautifully written. And Bette and Gary Merrill really did fall in love, so they were usually off by themselves. We shot the San Francisco scenes first in Frisco, so the ending of the film was done before the beginning.

I can report George Sanders was twice as acerbic in person than on camera as Addison DeWitt. He was just plain nasty to poor Marilyn Monroe, who was always quaking in her boots. He'd pat her on her rump and say, "You almost got through that two-line speech, my dear. Shall we try again?" That confrontation between Eve and Addison in her hotel suite? We really went at each other, just as Eve says, "Champion to champion." And George did win the only acting Oscar after all, so he had to be terrific.

BAWDEN: Didn't Zanuck want you to be nominated as Best Supporting Actress?

BAXTER: Oh, yes, and he asked me, thinking I'd be tinkled pink. He said he could guarantee a win. But could he? Celeste Holm and Thelma Ritter both got nominations and split the vote, so Josephine Hull won. So how would I have won as the third nominee? I told him the movie was titled after my character. It wasn't called *All about Margo,* was it? So I refused. I got nominated and so did Bette as Best Actress and we split the vote and Judy Holliday got it. Bette was more than mildly upset, Zanuck more so. My career at Fox was over, although it took me awhile to realize that.

BAWDEN: Can you go into a little more detail?

BAXTER: I definitely was up for *David and Bathsheba* [1951] and the press ran with that story, but in the end Henry King picked Susan Hayward. Henry told me he couldn't see me as a biblical queen, which is what I became in *The Ten Commandments* [1956]. At one time I was up for *How to Marry a Millionaire* [1953] until [director] Nunnally Johnson picked Marilyn Monroe, as he should have. She had zoomed in popularity after *All about Eve.* But I turned blond for a screen test for him and I stayed blond for a bit. My agent, Henry Wilson, even had me smoking cigars for the sake of publicity!

BAWDEN: So *All about Eve* really didn't get you the career bounce you wanted at Fox?

BAXTER: I finally made *Follow the Sun* [1952], which was the story of golfer Ben Hogan, with Glenn Ford. I was the ever-loving wife. It was not popular. I also had a baby in there, remember. Then in 1953 I made a pretty poor Dale Robertson western, *The Outcasts of Poker Flat.* I'm getting my clothes selected in rehearsals and Miriam Hopkins comes up and pats me on the shoulder, saying, "My dear, both of us have survived Bette Davis!" And then I did a horrible so-called comedy with Macdonald Carey and Zachary Scott called *My Wife's Best Friend* [1952], and after one [segment] in *O'Henry's Full House* [1952], I voluntarily ended my twelve years at Fox. I simply asked for my walking papers and I got them in record time.

BAWDEN: You were once again a last-minute substitution in Alfred Hitchcock's *I Confess* [1953]?

BAXTER: Hitch had hired a Norwegian star, Anita Bjork, but when she arrived in Hollywood she confided in Jack Warner she was expecting. And Jack freaked out because that would have made her an illegitimate mother. So he fired her and told me to fly to Quebec City, where shooting had already commenced. Hitch was seething but there was nothing he could do, and I was never able to warm him up.

But he had bigger problems all rolled into Montgomery Clift. It had been fifteen years since we'd been in L.A. together, and Monty was now a fully fledged star. But he was also a Method actor and resisted most of Hitch's directions. In one bit as the priest he has to come out of the Château Frontenac hotel and walk across a courtyard. He's about to be arrested. And then he has to look up at the crowd looking down from the various windows. And Monty refused, saying, "My character wouldn't look up." Just plain refused, and the normally placid Hitch went crazy, just lost it. He finally ordered him, and Monty did it "under duress" and it's in the movie. And then there was the Russian dialogue coach Monty planted behind pillars in the church scenes, and after a take he'd look at her and not Hitch, and Hitch finally banished her from the set. And after all that turmoil, I think the film only half works. Something got lost along the way. Was it Hitch's sanity?

BAWDEN: Are you surprised your other Warner film of the time—*The Blue Gardenia* [1953]—is now considered a great film noir?

BAXTER: We only thought of it as a programmer. Ann Sothern quit movies after that for two TV series because she hated working with Fritz Lang. But he could get a lot out of the material and also he shot all over L.A., so the movie looks more expensive than it was. We made it in sixteen days. I think Ray[mond] Burr had a great heavy part. I mentioned that film to him decades later when I did an *Ironside* and he just growled.

BAWDEN: Then it was over to Universal for two pictures in 1955.

BAXTER: Universal-International was the kiss of death in those days. I took on *One Desire* [1955], which Lana Turner refused to do, but we made it right after *Magnificent Obsession* [1954], which turned Rock Hudson into a big star. He was going up and I was going down. Then I did a pretty bad remake of *The Spoilers* [1955] and that was that for me at Universal.

BAWDEN: How did you get the part of the pharaoh's wife in Cecil B. DeMille's *The Ten Commandments*?

BAXTER: DeMille asked me to come in. His office at Paramount was bursting with books, props, rolls of linens. I told him I'd have to wear an Egyptian false nose and he pounded the table. "No. Baxter, your Irish nose stays in this picture." He acted out my part and I kept nodding, and I walked out with the part. The soundstage sets were magnificent. It was all corny, sure, but DeMille knew it was corny—that's what he wanted, what he loved. I loved slinking around—really, this was silent film acting but with dialogue. No shading was permitted. "Louder! Better!" That's what DeMille roared at everybody. It was all too much for him, I'm afraid, and directing the desert scenes in the Sinai was so strenuous he had a heart attack. This one was the last film he directed. It's on TV every Easter. I advise sitting down with a big box of chocolates, a jug of white wine, and a loaf of freshly baked bread. I do it that way and I still love this last gasp of old Hollywood excessiveness.

MILLER: After your marriage to Hodiak came apart, you began a long relationship with publicist Russell Birdwell. Did he kind of take over your career after you left Fox?

BAXTER: I really had my adolescence at thirty. I got mad at all those beautiful glamour pusses who were getting the parts that I never seemed to be up for. Then Russell Birdwell came into my life. He saw a lot of potential in me. We fell in love with each other and he became my lover, my business manager, my everything. Nobody could get me on the phone. He filtered everything. I couldn't even see my family for two years.

MILLER: So he was really behind your drifting into all those low-budget pictures at Universal and United Artists. How bad did it get?

BAXTER: While I was making *Bedevilled* [1955] in France, Russell and I were still trying to keep our affair under wraps, so we spent most of our time when I wasn't on camera holed up in our hotel room. [Director] Mitch Leisen nosed it around that I was a lesbian and that's why I didn't go out at night. Talk about a smokescreen!

Then I did a picture called *The Come-on* in 1956, and Russell got me to forego my salary so they'd let him direct the picture. I finally felt a chill come over me. It was like a bell had finally rung. I knew this had been the peak of our relationship and it would be downhill from now on.

Paramount thought it would be great to reunite Charlton Heston and me in a fine western, *Three Violent People* [1957]. Then I did a British thriller, *Chase a Crooked Shadow* [1958], which Doug Fairbanks Jr. produced but few people in North America saw. By 1959 I was living in Australia and I did *Season of Passion,* which had been the play *Summer of the Seventeenth Doll.* John Mills, Angela Lansbury, Ernie Borgnine were the costars, and it wasn't very Australian at all, I guess.

BAWDEN: After your marriage to Randolph Galt, you lived in Australia in the early sixties but still got back every year to L.A. for a film.

BAXTER: *Cimarron* [1960] was this huge remake, and Glenn Ford and Maria Schell were ahead of me in the cast, but it tanked at the box office. Then I had fourth billing in *Walk on the Wild Side* [1962]. The bigger stars were Jane Fonda and Laurence Harvey, who positively loathed each other. I was thirty-nine by then—considered an older woman type! Barbara

Stanwyck was also in it as a whorehouse madam. To show she was playing a lesbian she wore a suit!

One day our leading man Harvey kept everybody waiting for hours after lunch and then lurched in quite inebriated. Barbara turned all guns on him, denouncing him for his unprofessionalism, and he burst into tears and ran to his dressing room. And he wouldn't come out for the rest of the afternoon. Don't blame him. Barbara would have socked it to him again if he dared appear.

BAWDEN: As your film career cooled down, you began to do more theater and television. Then there was the chance to star in *Applause,* the Broadway musical version of *All about Eve.*

BAXTER: When the stage musical came along, I was asked to play Margo [the Bette Davis role in the movie] to replace Betty [Lauren] Bacall, and I first thought it was gimmicky. But I can sing, or rather croak, and I wanted to do Broadway—and it turned out just fine. [Baxter starred in the show in 1971–1972.]

One matinee day Bette Davis phoned and said she was coming to check me out, and we got a chair placed for her right behind the curtain so she could watch without the audience watching her. After the curtain came down she said, "Baxter, you can still astonish me." And she left. Just like that.

On another occasion, she was in Chicago to receive the real Sarah Siddons Award and I popped out to give it to her. Get it? Eve giving Margo the award she'd first won. She looked hesitant when she saw me and then roared with laughter. She got it, she really got it.

BAWDEN: You gradually shifted to TV.

BAXTER: We all did. Had to. Movie work dried up. I did one of the first TV movies, *Stranger on the Run* [1967]. Hank Fonda was also in it—and we got that one done in nineteen days. Then came *Companions in Nightmare* [1968]. That one was twenty days—what a luxury! All the actors—Melvyn Douglas, Patrick O'Neal, Leslie Nielsen, Gig Young—were all veterans. We could handle this sort of schedule. Universal hired me as a stock company of one to "brighten up the schedule," as I was told, and I did all those Universal series: *Marcus Welby, The Challengers, Ironside, Columbo.* It was my busiest-ever period. But I absolutely refused to do a weekly series. I was asked to join *Marcus Welby* at the beginning, but I said no.

BAWDEN: Why not?

BAXTER: I was proud. I wanted to do theater, movies. I lived off TV movies as income. It was reunion month on *The Moneychangers* [1976]. I was back working with Kirk Douglas and Jean Peters from my Fox days. I replaced Lana Turner on one day's notice on one of them, *Little Mo* [1978]. Lana got pneumonia. Then I was in *East of Eden* [1981], which I liked.

BAWDEN: Now we come to *Hotel* [1983–1986].

BAXTER: I know what you're saying: Once again Eve was replacing Margo! Bette [Davis] did the pilot, had a stroke and mastectomy, and here we go again. At first it was only temporary until she got better, then the schedule was just too much for her to contemplate. She left but later said, with all the sex scenes, the title should be changed to *Motel.* So I did them and I love doing them because some weeks I'll be in only one scene so I can fly home to my new home in Connecticut.

I had a reunion with Ralph Bellamy. We last acted in *Guest in the House* [1944]. And Stewart Granger said he finally had me as leading lady. The one where Jane Wyatt plays an old school friend, that came out fine. We'd never met until our first scene together.

BAWDEN: Have you ever given any thought to retirement?

BAXTER: No [*laughing*]. I want to go on until they have to shoot me.

Afterword

Anne Baxter died suddenly in 1985 from a brain aneurysm. She was only sixty-two.

Joan Blondell

Interview by James Bawden

It's easy to understand why Joan Blondell became so popular in the 1930s: she was the personification of the Depression-era working girl—plucky, sassy, devoid of pretension, and with an upbeat attitude that was catching. And it didn't hurt that she was a good-looking blonde with a very curvaceous figure. As a result, Blondell starred in more movies at her studio—Warner Bros.—than any other actress of her era. The studio was known for producing movies characterized by brisk dialogue between tough guys and wisecracking women who matched them word for word, so Blondell was made to order.

Setting the Scene

In June 1972, I made arrangements to spend a day on the set of the new NBC detective series *Banyon*, starring Robert Forster and Joan Blondell. Forster declined to be interviewed, pleading a heavy work schedule, but I got to spend almost an entire day with one of my most favorite actresses. Joan Blondell turned out to be as great a "broad" as I could have imagined.

The Interview

BAWDEN: So how does it feel to be back at Warners after all those years away?

BLONDELL: Spooky! There's nobody left that I remember. Even the crews have changed. But the Burbank lot is still intact. Those Depression-era streets where we shot films like *Public Enemy* [1931] are intact, and since *Banyon* [1972–1973] is set in the thirties, it's the perfect studio to be filming.

BAWDEN: Do you remember your first day on the lot?

Joan Blondell, circa 1933. James Bawden collection.

BLONDELL: Oh, yes. April 9, 1930. I'd arrived along with Jimmy Cagney on the *Super Chief* from Chicago and we got off in Pasadena. A Warners car sped us to the Burbank lot and we met [studio boss] Jack Warner that day. He told Jimmy he'd never be a big star because he was short, had light hair, and his speech was too "New Yawk." But he said he might get supporting work. Then he complimented me on my jugs and said I was young and fresh, but warned me not to become loose in any way. My first paycheck was for $350 a week—that I remember.

I was way out on the lot a few weeks later and Darryl Zanuck came by in a limo, stopped, and rushed out with a long-term contract to sign. He'd been watching the dailies and said he thought I could be turned into a star. So I signed without even reading it!

BAWDEN: Your first picture was *Sinner's Holiday* [1930]?

BLONDELL: Jimmy and I had done it on Broadway, where it was titled *Penny Arcade.* Al Jolson saw it, bought the rights, then came backstage to tell us he'd sold it to Warners with the stipulation Jimmy and I should [be in it.] First thing, Jack changes the title, says it wasn't sexy enough! Then Jack said we weren't star material, so we played support to two Warners players he predicted would be going to the top: Grant Withers and Evelyn Knapp. Of course Jimmy stole every scene he was in.

The film took three weeks to shoot and was withheld for a spell, so I made another Warners flick called *The Office Wife* [1930], which starred Dorothy Mackaill and Lewis Stone. Lewis was a darling, but I thought he looked grandfatherly. It was actually released first. And I was on my way. By the way, I walked around in my undies a lot in that one and that embarrassed me. But I never had to show anything more than that, thankfully.

BAWDEN: The next year [1931] you made ten movies. How was that possible?

BLONDELL: By working up to fifteen hours a day, including Saturdays, until dawn appeared on Sunday. By taking every part offered because I was afraid of getting bumped. And this was the Depression and jobs were scarce out there. I made my first movie with Barbara Stanwyck, *Illicit.* And then we did another right after called *Night Nurse,* where we undress in our nursing assistant's bedroom and walk around in our lingerie, which was considered scandalous.

I did *Big Business Girl* with Loretta Young, who was only eighteen. And I made one of my most famous movies, *The Public Enemy.* Wild Bill Wellman directed it and a few days into the shoot he turns to Jimmy Cagney and says, "Now you're the lead, kid." He just switched actors around because Jimmy's charisma was so outstanding and Eddie Woods was more of a companion actor than a charismatic star.

Jean Harlow was on loan from Howard Hughes and she was ever so forward—or so I thought. One day Jimmy asks her how she got her nipples so taut before a take. She never wore a brassiere or panties. And she says, "I ice 'em!" Just like that.

I was "Mamie" and I was mostly involved with Woods as Matt. Jimmy and I were hardly a screen team at that point. The movie came out, and that grapefruit scene [Cagney pushes half a grapefruit in Mae Clarke's face during a breakfast sequence] had all the attention. It was only done as an afterthought after Jimmy figured an omelet just wouldn't work.

BAWDEN: But you and Cagney did become a team later that year with *Blonde Crazy*?

BLONDELL: Right. We just clicked. Jimmy once said I was the only one of his leading ladies he was ever in love with. And it's always been the same with me. Not romantically, mind you. But as pals, best buds. And we still talk on the phone all the time. He's still interested in what I'm doing. Roy Del Ruth directed this one for laughs. Jimmy was a con artist supreme. The first time I saw him dolled up as a bellhop I laughed out loud. We'd ad-lib furiously, to Roy's fury. In one scene I'm taking a bath and Jimmy comes in and, predictably, I hollered. "Move over!" he ad-libbed, which really caused the censor to twitch.

BAWDEN: In 1932 you were down to a mere nine movies. What caused that decline in productivity?

BLONDELL: I was headed for a nervous breakdown. And don't forget for five weeks I was over with Sam Goldwyn making *The Greeks Had a Word for Them*. The title of the play was *The Greeks Had a Word for It*, but the censors demanded a change. Nobody ever explained that to me because I still think it's dirty. I replaced Carole Lombard on short notice, who left suffering from abdominal pains. "Oh, Joanie, I had a botched abortion!" she later told me. I was up against Ina Claire, who was terribly condescending. "I'm from the theater," she told me, "and you, my dear, are from vaudeville." Ah, but I was twenty-two and she was forty and guess who lasted in movies and who didn't?

BAWDEN: Some of those 1932 pictures still work.

BLONDELL: *Union Depot* was Warners' answer to *Grand Hotel*. The railroad set was enormous and Warners usually stinted on sets. There was a huge cast that included Doug Fairbanks Jr. as a thief and I was a chorus girl. Al Green directed it in three weeks and the camera not only moved, it whizzed around that set. Then we moved over to the Warners lake and made much the same story as *Central Park*. We didn't get to New York but shot a lot of stuff in front of transparencies, and it showed. Then I was in *Three on a Match*—at the end director Mervyn LeRoy boldly predicted Ann Dvorak would be a big hit, I'd have a solid career, and Bette Davis would go nowhere. Bette hasn't spoken to him since.

BAWDEN: You were part of a rare female team.

BLONDELL: With Glenda [Farrell]. Warners first paired us in *Havana Widows* [1933] and we clicked. She'd ask me, "Who's Laurel? Who's Hardy?" We're both in the Pat O'Brien vehicle *I've Got Your Number* [1934], but I don't think we have scenes together. So we still were not considered a team. But *Havana Widows* was such a hit we did *Merry Wives of Reno* [1934] and *Kansas City Princess* [1934] and *Miss Pacific Fleet* [1935]. Oh, I forgot *Traveling Saleslady* [1935], *We're in the Money* [1935]. We were in *Gold Diggers of 1937* [1936] together, but not really as a team. The only other female comedy team was Zasu Pitts and Thelma Todd, but they only made shorts. I'd go home at night with my sides aching because she was that funny. I recently saw her in a Torchy Blaine movie on TV, and she was the whole show. Like most of us, she got rotten treatment from Warners. But she did rebound on live TV and we stayed close until her passing last year [1971]. I cried buckets, I can tell you.

BAWDEN: Why did Jack Warner drop you and Cagney as a team?

BLONDELL: He claimed that he could get two movies out of us at the same time instead of pairing us in one feature. He wasn't that big on teams. He'd put Bette Davis not with somebody her equal but with George Brent to save money. That's how he operated, an eye always on the cash flow. And let's face it, Jimmy became the biggest thing on the lot.

BAWDEN: What do you remember about those Busby Berkeley musicals?

BLONDELL: I remember I couldn't really sing so I sang-talked my part in "Remember My Forgotten Man" [a production number in the 1933 film *Gold Diggers of 1933*]. People still stop to ask about it. I think it took three to four days to shoot. The rehearsal in another stage took weeks; Buzz always had those designs on pieces of paper. The girls were housed dormitory-style in one gigantic soundstage with all their cots row after row. Buzz figured if he let them go home they wouldn't come back. Because on that number they tapped from 9 a.m. to midnight or until they dropped. I'm sure executives had their way with the easier ones. The pay was $7.50 a day and all one could eat and boy, there were herds of them lined up for every musical. Most were there to get husbands, and sometimes a star was

Joan Blondell (*left*) steps lively with Dick Powell and Ruby Keeler in the 1934 musical *Dames*. Courtesy of Warner Bros.

born. Toby Wing is one example. Buzz got away with murder. We see them naked in silhouette; underwater we see their crotches. That was before the Code, mind you.

"Forgotten Man" had a huge impact on the population. In other musicals, like *Footlight Parade* [1933], I was Jimmy's assistant and not in the numbers. In *Dames* [1934] I had this crazy number, "The Girl at the Ironing Board." It's where the underwear get up and dance. And that was all made up by Buzz because I was pregnant and showing.

BAWDEN: You kept on shooting?

BLONDELL: Certainly. It was my vaudeville training. When I was making *Back in Circulation* [1937], I was having terrible pains. The assistant director said it was my tight girdle. Then I fainted and was rushed to hospital. Appendicitis. Had I stayed much longer I'd have died, I was told. Shooting continued and they'd phone every day and ask me back. I was too weak. So they finally bribed the physician to charter an ambulance and they took me to Lookout Mountain and changed the script so the burst appendix became part of the story and they filmed that and were able to release the film on schedule. And because of my recuperation, I only made four movies that year.

BAWDEN: Sometimes you'd get loaned out.

BLONDELL: Walter Wanger borrowed me, Leslie Howard, and Humphrey Bogart for a comedy called *Stand In* [1937]. I never worked with Les at WB, although I can tell you he had very busy hands. This was done at the Goldwyn lot and Leslie was [playing] the mild-mannered head of a major studio. A lot more work went into it than the stuff I usually made at WB. Women had the hots for Leslie, I think it was his air of looking oddly distracted. He was actually Hungarian, you know.

Who would have known that out of the three of us Humphrey Bogart would be the biggest star? When they rereleased it a decade later, he got top billing and poor Leslie was dead in a wartime plane crash. I loved my part, a former child star who sees right through Hollywood. Tay Garnett directed it, and for his next, *Trade Winds* [1938], with Freddie March and Joan Bennett, he hired Ann Sothern as the fast-talking blonde when I was unavailable. And ever since I've been comically beefing that Ann stole my act. It always makes for good copy.

BAWDEN: There were some others.

BLONDELL: I was loaned to Columbia for *There's Always a Woman* [1938] with Mel Douglas, and we clicked as a couple. So Columbia put us right back to work in *The Amazing Mr. Williams* [1939], although I was Warners-free by then. The next time I saw him we were on set for *Advance to the Rear* [1964]. Around that time I did the Bing Crosby vehicle at Universal, *East Side of Heaven* [1939]. Bing did it while on vacation from Paramount and even brought along his favorite director, David Butler. I found Bing cool, standoffish, but completely professional. He said we had to rush to finish in four weeks. I said at Warners that would be considered leisurely.

Bawden: Why did you leave Warners?

Blondell: I was offered big dough to stay, but my husband [Dick Powell] was leaving and it would have been awkward. He didn't leave on warm terms. I was immediately offered a long termer with MGM but I turned it down because Dick had some rough years getting work. He definitely would have resented it. The film we made at Universal—*I Want a Divorce* [1940]—was prophetic, right? At one point he even took second billing to Abbott and Costello in 1941's *In the Navy.* Had I signed I might have gotten the *Maisie* movies, who knows?

But I did go to MGM occasionally. I did *Two Girls on Broadway* [1940] with a lovely new thing Metro was promoting to stardom—Lana Turner. I was in the all-girl thing *Cry Havoc* [1943] and, contrary to rumor, all the girls got on. I was crazy for Margaret Sullavan—such a talent, but persnickety. One clause in her contract said she didn't have to work during the rain and we stood around for hours one day until the clouds rolled by. When she died so strangely [in 1960], it really affected me.

And I did *Adventure* [1945], Clark Gable's return to MGM after war work. They gave me under-title billing, my first demotion in fifteen years. Clark was all worn out and to cast him in this very bad comedy was just crazy. Physically, he was ailing. He cried several times on set when people mentioned his dead wife [Carole Lombard]. He didn't click at all with Greer Garson, who told me he had bad breath, which she hated. They had zero chemistry. But the public flocked to it just to see him. But he so hated it, he didn't make another movie for two years.

Bawden: Do you know which movie of yours is most famous?

Blondell: Oh, *Topper Returns* [1941]. It was a hit but has grown on TV viewings because it is public domain. I laugh when I see it. I laugh at Eddie Anderson and Patsy Kelly and Billie Burke and Rollie Young. It's a send-up of all those dark house plots. I'm not that funny in it—I'm the ghost, after all.

Bawden: Did you ever feel you'd jumped into character parts too soon?

Blondell: Well, yes, I was thirty-three when I made *A Tree Grows in Brooklyn* [1945], and many leading ladies around town were considerably older. It was the first movie of Elia Kazan [as a director] and for Aunt Cissie he'd wanted Betty Grable, who took one look at this little squirt and passed. I mean, nobody knew who he was at that stage. So he asked me and I ran with this sensational part—although he never used me again. He was from the *theatah,* meaning he knew nothing about lighting, lenses, close-ups. All that was done for him by our ace cinematographer Leon Shamroy, who actually asked Zanuck for a codirecting credit. He was turned down. I remember great battles between Dorothy McGuire and Kazan. There were whispers Jimmy Dunn was drunk on the set but that was right in character and he did win a [Supporting Actor] Oscar. The movie made Kazan a hot commodity, but it made me a supporting character actress before my time.

BAWDEN: Then you gave your greatest performance in *Nightmare Alley* [1947] with Tyrone Power.

BLONDELL: I've seen that one on TV recently. And I can't figure how it got past the Hollywood censors. It's so raw and unnerving. Ty told me this one would mark his break from costume sagas, which he detested, and into truly serious acting. He'd been so outstanding in *The Razor's Edge* [1946] that Zanuck gave this one to him and it laid a mighty egg. All those female fans were sickened by its violence and crude sexuality. The director, Teddy Goulding, told me to play this dame as hard and blowsy as I could, but Helen Walker is even nastier as the psychiatrist who is secretly tape-recording her patients to blackmail them. The carny atmosphere was squalid, everyone was on the make. I remember the care [cinematographer] Lee Garmes took with the night photography. I do know the writer, Bill Gresham, later suicided. And that we all got great reviews and nobody came to see it because it was that scary.

BAWDEN: What do you remember of *For Heaven's Sake* [1950]?

BLONDELL: Oh, that one! We laughed ourselves silly. Clifton Webb was an angel come to help the faltering marriage of a Broadway couple, Joan Bennett and Bob Cummings. But he comes to earth disguised as a Texas oilman and he's clumping around in cowboy boots and says to me, "These high heels are killers!" Well, I'd laugh every time he said it for take after take. In one scene he plays a mean harp and it sounds like jazz. But the premise was so far out it wasn't popular and Clifton went back to his Belvedere character.

BAWDEN: You have said working with Spencer Tracy and Kate Hepburn in *The Desk Set* [1957] was a great experience.

BLONDELL: I was having a rough passage. Little work. One of those years I drank and drank on New Year's Eve and simply went to bed and slept it off. Then Great Kate phones me up and says she needs me for *Desk Set.* Why? We played librarians and the other one was a sexy, young number named Dina Merrill and Kate needed somebody in her own age group

Joan Blondell was reunited with her old Warner Bros. colleague Edward G. Robinson in 1965's *The Cincinnati Kid.* Courtesy of MGM and United Artists Television.

because she didn't want to look like an old crone. And I'd just stand around while Spence gave it to her and then she'd give it to him right back, and it was all so very sophisticated. Imagine a love story featuring two stars both over fifty!

BAWDEN: Then you made a movie with June Allyson, *The Opposite Sex* [1957].

BLONDELL: Oh, please, let's not go there!

BAWDEN: It was great seeing you reunited with Edward G. Robinson in *The Cincinnati Kid* [1965].

BLONDELL: The first day Eddie stumbles over and whispers, "I guess, Joan, I was a pretty big stinker back then?" And I say, "Eddie, bigger than you can imagine." And we both laugh. We had several great scenes director Norman Jewison cut because he said the film was overlong. Eddie suspected we blasted the nominal leads, Steve McQueen and Ann-Margret, outta the ballpark. But it got me a lot of other job offers. I'm used to that kind of treatment, I can tell you.

BAWDEN: You started out in TV very early but never tried a series until twenty years later. Why?

BLONDELL: Because I was stupid. I kept thinking that great big movie part was going to come along and instead my parts got smaller and smaller. I had my first live TV encounter on *Nash Airflyte Theatre* in 1951. It was a TV version of *Pot o' Gold* with Dane Clark and Bill Gaxton. That went without a hitch. All TV was then done in New York, and for that one we were in CBS studios atop Grand Central Station. Oh, two of the three live cameras blew during the live telecast so we all had to act to the only remaining camera and hoped it kept going until the conclusion. When that red light went out, I was awash in perspiration, I can tell you.

But I needed the money. In 1952 I did an episode of *Schlitz Playhouse* that was filmed in three days. Buddy Ebsen was also in it and Kathleen Freeman. And in 1953 CBS asked me to star in an episode of *Suspense* called "Vacancy for Death." Again it was live, but a half-hour show and Stephen Elliott and Dorothy Hart were also in it. I got a paycheck for $650 for the week and was glad to get it.

Then I did *Lux Video Theatre, Shower of Stars, Fireside Theatre.* I was big in TV. I did a *U.S. Steel Hour* in 1955 with a youngster named Joanne Woodward, who was all of twenty-four. So naïve, but brimming with talent. Two years later she had her Oscar [for *The Three Faces of Eve*]. I did a batch of *Playhouse 90s*—live from L.A., which means we did them at 6 p.m. to reach that 9 p.m. Eastern Time slot. *Child of Trouble* [1957] was the first, and it had Ricardo Montalban, Patty McCormack, Chester Morris. John Frankenheimer was the kid director on one of them, I remember that. Since these were all live I never saw them, you see.

Bawden: Eventually you did practically every TV series going.

Blondell: Yeah. *The Untouchables, The Barbara Stanwyck Show*—I said, "Missy, let's keep our clothes on in this one"—*The Dick Powell Show, Death Valley Days, The Real McCoys*—I had a running part as Aunt Win—*The Virginian, Wagon Train, Twilight Zone, Bonanza, Dr. Kildare, My Three Sons, Slattery's People, The Man from U.N.C.L.E, Petticoat Junction.* You want I should continue?

In 1965, Lucy Ball phones me up and says she wants me to replace Vivian Vance, who was retiring from *The Lucy Show,* and I said, "Sure." I'd heard from friends Lucy had become very dictatorial, but what the heck? We went back to the thirties and I loved her comical touches. I did two consecutive shows as a character called Joan Brenner. But Lucy was waspish, virtually directed her own shows, and she went after me but good after we had filmed the second one. Right in front of the crew, she screamed about this and that and I just turned and walked out and that was that. Ann Sothern said she'd had the same experience.

So I finally didn't get to my own series until *Here Come the Brides* in 1969. And the recognition factor was like *wow.* I'd walk down a street and kids would shout, "Hi, Lottie!" And we went for several years and fifty-one episodes and I learned to love being in a series. I had a new fan base. And now with *Banyon* as Peggy Revere, we're doing it all over again and who knows? And, yes, I will continue. I will prevail.

But. You know, when that time comes, I've got my epitaph all written out. The tombstone must read: "At Last I Get First Billing."

Afterword

At the end of a long day, Blondell and I went to her apartment complex, where we had dinner in the coffee shop. She asked for "gooey scrambled eggs," I remember. Then her assistant, Ted Morgan, drove me back to the Century Plaza Hotel. He told me she was recuperating from the flu, but would not have considered rescheduling an interview.

As it turned out, *Banyon* was cancelled at midseason. But Joan Blondell had one more comeback coming up: as the irrepressible waitress in the 1978 smash movie *Grease.* She made five TV guest appearances in 1979 before her death from leukemia on Christmas Day, 1979, aged seventy-three. She was a great trouper to the last.

Irene Dunne

Interview by James Bawden

Irene Dunne, the great singer and actress who became a Hollywood icon, once remarked that she "drifted into acting and drifted out." Happily, though, the drifting process took twenty-two years and included five nominations for the Best Actress Oscar and some of the most memorable films of Hollywood's golden age.

Dunne walked away from the movies in 1952, returning to performing only for a few television appearances, and began a new life devoted to charity and public service, much of it connected to her devout Catholicism. She was married only once—in 1930, to Dr. Francis Griffin, a marriage that lasted until his death in 1965.

Dunne did very few interviews after she stopped working in pictures and seldom talked for print about her years in show business.

Setting the Scene

Getting Irene Dunne to consent to an interview was difficult. When I first wrote to her in 1972, her secretary wrote back asking for clippings to make sure I was a legitimate columnist! Nothing came of it. Then, in 1974 in Los Angeles, I spoke to her brother, Charles, who passed on another request. This time Dunne quickly agreed.

I took a taxi to her swank Holmby Hills home, arriving at the agreed time of 1 p.m. She had given strict instructions that the interview could not take more than an hour, but she served tea and cookies and we wound up talking until it was dark outside. Then she sent me back to my hotel in a chauffeur-driven limousine.

After that pleasant start, we talked several more times on the phone over the next few years.

Irene Dunne, circa 1944. James Bawden collection.

The Interview

Bawden: How did you get from Broadway to Hollywood in 1930?

Dunne: Well, I'd been on Broadway starting in 1922 and then I did the road tours of musicals, passing through your city of Toronto in 1928, I believe it was. I'd always wanted a career at the Met, but I flunked two auditions. In those days they were looking for girls with far more sizable voices

Irene Dunne (*left*) in her first big role in *Cimarron,* the Oscar-winning Best Picture of 1930–1931. With her: Richard Dix and Nance O'Neill. Courtesy of RKO Radio Pictures.

than I possessed. At one audition I met another girl, Jeanette MacDonald, and she flunked, too. I guess Magnolia in *Show Boat* was my biggest moment, but by 1929–1930 musicals on Broadway and on the road were dead. Something called talkies had killed them off. Then along came the Depression and my agent suggested Hollywood. I'd never even thought of doing [movies], but I needed work, so I took an RKO offer. After all, it was for a musical. Can you believe it was all about singing Marines? But *Leathernecking* [1930] had production problems. By the time we finished, musicals were out of vogue. So every time I open my mouth in that one—plop!—the next scene comes up. They just snipped all the songs and the whole thing was excruciatingly bad.

I was packing in my dressing room when Richard Dix stuck his head in and asked me to test for Sabra in *Cimarron* [1931]. I got the part and I got a movie career out of it. I never thought it would last. I got an Oscar nomination and the movie won as Best Picture. All that helped get me a continuance of my RKO contract, but I was stuck for years in weepers. It's funny—I always had an enlarged memory of *Cimarron,* but I hadn't seen the darned thing since 1931. MGM bought it for a remake and suppressed the original and it didn't resurface until a few years ago at a retrospective of my films. I saw it and thought I was awfully hammy, but I'm guessing that was the style back then. But it no longer is one of my favorite films at all. Only the great land rush scene holds up.

BAWDEN: You suffered for your art.

DUNNE: Not my art! These films were big at the box office. RKO was a strange studio. I'd exchange scripts with Ann Harding and Connie Bennett. We three made the same stories over and over. On one vacation I went to Universal and suffered some more in *Back Street* [1933]. Then I suffered at MGM in *The Secret of Madame Blanche* [1933]. It was written by Frances Goodrich and Albert Hackett—can you believe it? They then wrote *The Thin Man!* Ours was a *Madame X* story line, all very tangled, but I got to sing some opera.

BAWDEN: What sort of a studio was RKO?

DUNNE: It was located in several different lots, parts of other studios that merged in 1931. RCA bought up FBO, which was owned by Jack Kennedy's father, Joe, plus the KAO theater chain [Keith-Albee-Orpheum] plus Pathé and Cecil DeMille's studio, and each had their own lots. I'd walk through a doorway in one scene and shoot the exterior one place and the interior at another location! One lot was right beside Paramount, another was in Culver City. It was all too confusing. The back lot was at Encino.

The economy had crashed, but RKO kept announcing movie chains they were buying up. *Cimarron* cost so much that it was listed as a loss until they rereleased it a few years later. Connie, Ann, and Helen Twelvetrees were all Pathé stars originally. [Bert] Wheeler and [Robert] Woolsey were the house comics. Joel McCrea, Ricardo Cortez, and Mary Astor were all under contract to RKO. Dix came over after Paramount dropped him because he was considered very expensive. I remember David O. Selznick arrived, just after *Cimarron* was released, to be the new production head. Great Kate Hepburn came on board as his first acquisition and just as he was leaving, David hired Fred Astaire and the modern musical was born. But in 1933 the company sank into receivership and I thought it best to leave as soon as I could. That was at the end of 1935.

BAWDEN: You just seemed to churn out your RKO weepers.

DUNNE: We'd do them in about three weeks—or eighteen days. We worked Saturdays. But a great director like Greg La Cava on *Symphony of Six Million* [1932] could get everything done with ease in that time frame.

Thirteen Women [1932] was so silly. Myrna Loy was an East Indian, vowing revenge on the sorority girls who had mistreated her as a student. She later said if she'd really killed me off she could have gotten all my juicy parts in the years ahead. And, you know, we never worked together again.

The Silver Cord [1933] is one of my missing films from the period. It was considered a hardheaded indictment of mother love. I liked making *This Man Is Mine* [1934] because I enjoyed acting with Clive Brook. He was very dissatisfied with Hollywood by then and preparing to leave. This kind of movie couldn't have been made a year later with the Code then in place. It was the end of that kind of weeper for awhile.

BAWDEN: Then you made *Magnificent Obsession* [1935] with Robert Taylor.

DUNNE: It was the best of the bunch, I agree. Universal got Bob Taylor on loan and groomed him and he became a big star off it, just as Rock Hudson did in the remake. John Stahl was the slowest of directors, but he got what he wanted.

BAWDEN: But tell me about the time you almost made a movie with Laurence Olivier.

DUNNE: Oh, that was in 1933 and Larry had just finished a film with Ann Harding at RKO and they kept him on for another with me. Then the reviews for the Harding movie came in and were devastating and the studio was being pounded by the Depression. The flats were up, we'd done costume and makeup changes, but RKO just cancelled it. The heads said it wouldn't make any money as projected so they killed it and lent Larry out to MGM for *Queen Christina* [1933], where Garbo asked he be dropped after five days of filming. And so he went home and became a very great actor. And that's how I almost worked with Larry Olivier.

BAWDEN: You were moving back into musicals.

DUNNE: Warners borrowed me for *Sweet Adeline* [1934]. I'm trying to remember who they gave up in return. Oh, yes, it was Bette Davis for *Of Human Bondage.* Our musical was quite sweet, with beautifully staged numbers, and I was a Jerome Kern girl in that one as I always was in movies. But the public just didn't buy it and it failed at the box office. Then back at RKO I made *Roberta* [1935] with Rogers and Astaire and Randy Scott as my leading man. Now that one was a roaring hit and I had some favorite songs including "Smoke Gets in Your Eyes." But MGM bought it for a remake and it was out of circulation for decades. It has resurfaced and they used it at a salute to me at the L.A. Film Festival and it's quite charming.

And now people can see it on TV. And one neighbor said, "Oh, Irene, you got billed above Astaire and Rogers. How did that happen?" And I said: "Why, yes, I used to be a big star, I really used to be." And RKO planned to reteam the three of us in *Follow the Fleet* [1936], but I'd flown the coop by then. My contract was up and I went bravely forth as a freelancer and never signed an exclusive long-term contract again. Harriet Hilliard replaced me in *Follow the Fleet.*

Bawden: How did that work?

Dunne: Well, at RKO, if I refused a part I went on suspension. It was Ronnie Colman who told me to take short-term nonexclusive contracts—he was at Fox and Selznick and MGM and got great parts that way. And Claudette [Colbert] had a Paramount deal that let her freelance one picture a year. So I signed with Columbia, Universal, Paramount, and I figured that way I'd get at least one good feature a year—and it worked for the next fifteen years. And when I turned down roles, as I frequently did, nobody could suspend me for months on end. And Cary Grant, Roz Russell, Charles Boyer—oh, a whole lot of us soon started working that way.

Bawden: You've said *Show Boat* [1936] was one of your favorite films.

Dunne: Well, I had played Magnolia for years in New York and on tour. The 1929 [first movie] version was terrible. They used a "new" score. "Junior" Laemmele, who was running Universal by then, had to make [her version, the first remake] by the end of 1936 or lose the rights, so we worked day and night on it. Yes, I do accept that I was at least ten years too old by then, but movie magic made me an ingenue once again. Our version [1936] had Paul Robeson and Helen Morgan from the original. But when they told me Jimmy Whale was to direct, I initially balked. He had done *Frankenstein* [1931]. It was sheer, exhausting fun making it, but the cost overrun was tremendous. Junior just fell in love with the material and couldn't stop pouring money into it and, while very popular, it just couldn't make back its costs. Junior lost control of the studio because of it. Only little Deanna Durbin saved the studio from completely folding. [Later] MGM got the rights and suppressed our version and announced [a new version] as a [Jeanette] MacDonald-[Nelson] Eddy vehicle, which wouldn't have worked. [MGM ultimately remade *Show Boat* in 1951 with Kathryn Grayson and Howard Keel.]

A couple of years ago they found a print [of Dunne's 1936 version] and made a new negative and showed it at a festival, and it really does hold up. It's one I'm very proud of.

BAWDEN: Your first comedy was *Theodora Goes Wild* [1936]?

DUNNE: Melvyn Douglas just got me through that. He'd say, "Take a pause, right there. A laugh is coming." Or, "Say that line quickly and toss it away." And [director] Richard Boleslawski could do everything. He'd done that Garbo thing [*The Painted Veil,* 1934] and then he did the one with Dietrich in color [*The Garden of Allah,* 1936]. He was horribly overweight, always a sandwich in his mouth. I'm not satisfied with *Theodora.* You can see my nervousness. I was trying too hard. I was learning that comedy is hardest of all. You can wind up just looking silly. But the comedy films are the ones that endure. *Theodora* was out of circulation for a long time. Columbia was trying to make it into a Broadway show with Carol Channing. I'm not kidding you. And, predictably, they just couldn't do it. Because by then, who cared if a girl wrote a risqué novel?

BAWDEN: The first time you worked with Cary Grant was on *The Awful Truth* [1937].

DUNNE: It was just an accident. Columbia bought up a lot of properties once owned by Pathé and this script was there. It had been a big Broadway comedy in the twenties with Roland Young. Then there was a 1929 movie with Ina Claire, which I've never seen. [Director] Leo McCarey convinced Harry Cohn at Columbia he could rework it and really, it still was a play. You can spot the acts, first at our house, then the sports club, then my apartment, and then Ralph Bellamy's. Simple sets. Few actors. Leo thought it would work well in the Depression—all those rich people having their own sets of troubles.

Cary had just started at Columbia and I'd never even met him before this. We just worked from the first moment. He's a generous actor. He can afford to be—any man that gorgeous—and who'd be watching little old me? He begged to get out of it and said he'd do pictures for free. Leo wouldn't let him go. And do you know, these two looked like one another. Cary became Leo and vice versa. But much of it was improvised on the set. I was playing—badly—on the piano "Home on the Range" and Ralph Bellamy was singing, also unevenly, and [studio head] Harry [Cohn] walks by, takes one look, and leaves, shaking his head. But it made me. It made Cary. Suddenly we're being hailed as the new funsters and it was all so strange.

BAWDEN: Talk to me about *High, Wide, and Handsome* [1937], which you say is among your favorite films.

DUNNE: Paramount took the *Show Boat* team [composers Oscar Hammerstein and Jerome Kern] and had them write a musical about the oil-drilling industry in Pennsylvania in 1859. It was a huge production, and just before we started, the studio bosses withdrew Technicolor and substituted black and white to save costs. And Gary Cooper suddenly left because he thought his part inferior to mine, which it was not. Randolph Scott came in at the last minute, but he lacked Coop's star qualities, as much as I love him as an actor. But years later the director, Rouben Mamoulian, told me at a party it was the precursor in his mind and Oscar's for *Oklahoma!* [1955]. Can you believe that? There were some wonderful songs, but not a one became a standard and that was a drawback. Somebody said audiences left the theater humming the scenery, which was very cruel but quite true. It didn't get people involved enough in its story. And that was the end for me as far as big musicals were concerned.

BAWDEN: Did you admire Charles Boyer?

DUNNE: Yes! He hated that French lover nonsense. Charles had a paunch and receding hairline, but on him it looked fine. *Love Affair* [1939] is an old story that worked because he was such a reticent actor. He'd never overdo anything. And it just all came together so smoothly. Every actress who worked with him—Jean Arthur, Loretta [Young], Garbo—he made us look so much better. Charles still jokes he'd always have to get his hair cut because the final clinch would have the girl kissing him in close-up and all you'd see of him was the back of his head. They had a recent screening and I went and loved it all over again, so I just had to phone Charles up and tell him how wonderful he was. And he said, "Oh, so you finally saw me!" I guess he was remarking how egotistical actresses are.

I immediately made a follow-up with Charles, *When Tomorrow Comes* [1939]. Some very nice moments, but it never came together quite like *Love Affair.* Barbara O'Neill as his deranged wife just stole her scenes. She looked so dangerous. But I didn't care; the story needed some pep and she provided that.

I got my fourth Oscar nomination for *Love Affair.* On Oscar night I didn't want to go—my poor little Terry up against Scarlett O'Hara? No contest. But I had to be a good sport. And Vivien [Leigh] deservedly won.

BAWDEN: How did *My Favorite Wife* [1940] come about?

DUNNE: Well, in those days sequels were not often done, and if they were, they bombed like *Son of Kong.* But people said Cary and I should continue with the characters in *The Awful Truth,* and that's exactly what

Irene Dunne in the classic 1941 tearjerker *Penny Serenade* with costars Edgar Buchanan (*left*) and Cary Grant. Courtesy of Columbia Pictures.

Leo McCarey did. We were all attached to RKO by this time so we couldn't use the original names, but let's face it, they were basically the same people. Only this time it was the story of Enoch Arden and I was Enoch—I'd been on a desert island for seven years with Randolph Scott. And I arrive home the day Cary had me declared legally dead and that frees him to marry Gail Patrick. Just as filming started, Leo was seriously hurt in a traffic accident and the prognosis was not favorable at first. So Garson Kanin stepped in and we all tried to put on our brave faces and get on with it. My favorite scene had Ellen taking a shy, meek shoe clerk—played wonderfully by Chester Clute—to visit husband Cary and try to persuade him this was the man she'd been on the island with. The conclusion was so close to *Awful Truth* I get them mixed up in my mind.

BAWDEN: Then came a third and final film with Grant—1941's *Penny Serenade.*

DUNNE: Back at Columbia. I went to a sneak preview and got into the theater after dark and heard a couple behind me say, "Oh, another Cary Grant–Irene Dunne comedy." Little did they know. By the halfway point both were blubbering. Oh, it was a four-hankie affair. I have a miscarriage in Japan, Cary has to cry when the judge tries to take away our adopted girl, then she dies. His crying scene was so magnificent I said, "Oh, he's going to win the Oscar." And he nearly did. He was also great that year in *Suspicion.* But I told him he'd never win. He made everything seem spontaneous, so easy. But that is fine acting when people think you're playing yourself. I found comedy hardest, drama less so, but what did I know? I never even got a nomination that year.

BAWDEN: And you never worked with Grant again.

DUNNE: It wasn't for want of trying. That was the last film in which he ever took second billing. And different ideas were submitted but we'd always be too busy. But it's strange. People thought of us as a team, you know. Around that time I was in Bullock's, getting a Christmas present for my husband and looking at dressing gowns, and the saleslady said, "Oh, I don't think that would fit Mr. Grant," and I didn't have the heart to correct her. People thought of us as a team and we only made these three movies in four years and then we unfortunately moved on.

BAWDEN: Ralph Bellamy once told me in *Lady in a Jam* [1942] you lost your legendary cool.

DUNNE: Can't a girl have at least one nervous breakdown on set? I'd done *Unfinished Business* [1941] for Greg La Cava and it had turned out half okay and I foolishly agreed to this one. He said he'd shoot it in the McCarey style—i.e., there was no real script. We'd improvise. We shot in Phoenix and it was very hot. There was no air-conditioning then. And I sweltered in my portable dressing room for ten weeks as Greg waited for inspiration and it never came and finally I just threw things around and it turned out to be a real disaster and Greg only made one more movie after that and it was five years later.

BAWDEN: You had trouble with Spencer Tracy on the set of *A Guy Named Joe* [1943].

DUNNE: He'd wanted Kate Hepburn for the part of the female flying ace, Dorinda. And [director] Vic Fleming had turned him down flat, saying she wasn't at all right for it. So when I showed up Spence was rude, brusque, and even made a pass at me. Me! And Vic said he'd settle down but it got worse and I called up [studio head] Mr. [Louis B.] Mayer and laid down the law. I said I thought MGM was a professional place.

He arranged to saunter over right at the moment of my biggest scene and afterwards Mr. Mayer turned to Vic and said very loudly, "If anybody goes, it will not be Irene." And Spence got all teary eyed and instantly cleaned up his act. And he was very good—I can't think of another actor who could have pulled it all off. He started coming to my dressing room for tea and telling me about the plight of his deaf son, John. And the picture was a huge success.

But Spence did one wonderful thing on the set. Van Johnson was injured badly in a traffic accident right outside the studio and ambulances from Culver City and L.A. battled over his crumpled body for the longest time before he got aid. MGM said they'd recast and Spence just refused to finish it without Van. When we finally did get to the concluding scenes, I was already making *The White Cliffs of Dover.* Playing two different parts on the same day for weeks on end was terribly confusing. I'd always lived my parts. I was not at all in a happy mood that year.

BAWDEN: What did you think of *The White Cliffs of Dover* [1944]?

DUNNE: Well, Roddy McDowall still calls me "Mother" to this day. It was a reverie, not at all realistic. I played a young American girl on a trip to England who marries into the British aristocracy. The funny thing is I recently got a letter from the Queen Mother's secretary asking me to be on a committee to preserve the real white cliffs. And I didn't have the heart to write back that our cliffs were in California because the real ones somehow seemed a tad diminutive. But we couldn't call the picture *White Cliffs of California,* could we?

So many of the British community were in this one: Gladys Cooper, Nigel Bruce, Sir C. Aubrey Smith. Everything was lavish—too lavish, if you ask me. But it was so well received in both nations as a morale booster for our side. Mr. Mayer told me only one MGM actress would get the Oscar nomination that year because of the crowded field and it would have to be Greer Garson for *Mrs. Parkington.*

BAWDEN: Actors always remember the parts they didn't get. What were some of the ones that got away?

DUNNE: Well, I had all but signed on the dotted line to make *Now, Voyager* [1942]. Hal Wallis at Warners sent me a script and then somebody slipped a mimeographed copy to Bette Davis, who hollered so loudly they gave it to her. And then there was *Lady in the Dark* [1942], which the director Mitch Leisen said to me that I'd be perfect as Jenny, but Ginger Rogers had first right of refusal and who would turn down a part like that?

And I remember Leo McCarey phoned and said if Ingrid Bergman turned down the part of the Swedish nun in *The Bells of St. Mary's* [1945], then I would get it. So I waited for quite a bit but Ingrid finally did it.

Of course, I also got parts others didn't want. Greta Garbo was the first choice for *I Remember Mama* and she sent back a note to RKO: "No mamas and no murderesses." She'd also turned down *The Paradine Case* concurrently.

BAWDEN: I'm not sure why you left MGM after only two big hits?

DUNNE: Louis B. Mayer asked me to see him and said, "Irene, here's your next part." And he sort of threw the script across his big table and the title was *The Thin Man Goes Home*. And I innocently asked, "But what part is there for me?" And he said I'd be the new Nora Charles since Myrna Loy had already left the studio for war work. And I argued forcefully that the series was precisely a hit because of the chemistry between those two big stars [Loy and William Powell]. And I flatly refused and that was it, MGM stopped offering me scripts.

So I went back to Columbia and did *Together Again* [1944]. The title says it all—Charles Boyer and I were a team in the minds of movie fans. And the slight comedy about a lady mayor commissioning a sculptor to do a statue of her late husband was an unexpected hit.

So Columbia bought *Over 21* [1945] for me. Ruth Gordon wrote it and starred on Broadway in it. My mistake was catching her on tour in L.A. and I aped her mannerisms and I was just awful. It just didn't jell, and Alexander Knox wasn't adept at comedy. Cary Grant would have made it work. It was about an overaged soldier and his wife who follows him to boot camp. So I thought, this is the perfect moment to retire.

BAWDEN: Instead you did *Anna and The King of Siam* [1946].

DUNNE: The script was just so unusual. I was a real-life English governess—Anna Leonowens—in Siam, and Rex Harrison came over from Britain and was excellent. We shot every scene on the back lot—one interior had a window with shots of Thailand back-projected. Rex Harrison had a separate throne than the one Yul Brynner later used [in *The King and I*, the 1956 musical remake]. John Cromwell shot it very acutely. A few missteps and it could have turned out flat indeed.

Then—can you imagine—I'm reading the *New York Times* in 1949 and they're announcing a Broadway musical of it. I was mighty angry, and I phoned Oscar Hammerstein up on the long distance and really gave it to him. "Hello? Oscar? You remember me, don't you? I toured for years in your *Show Boat* and made the movie and you thought I was just fine as Magnolia? Now this!"

But he explained Gertrude Lawrence had taken an option on the property and shopped it to him and Dick Rodgers as a star vehicle. So what could he do? I just don't think she had the voice for that. But later Oscar offered me the road tour for a year and I turned him down because I had a husband and growing daughter. I wouldn't want to leave them alone for a year.

BAWDEN: What do you think of *Life with Father* [1947]?

DUNNE: A very good piece of Americana but not the great film it could have been. It had been running on Broadway since 1939, and the expectations were just too high. Bill Powell was signed first and I initially refused. A billing problem again. So Jack Warner offered to give me billing in the newspaper ads every other day. Oh, the vanity of actors! And I rather liked doing it. Michael Curtiz with his bad accent didn't know the first thing about the period but it somehow all came together.

Did you know Mary Pickford had made a test of it as Vinnie? She's a good friend but hadn't acted in fourteen years and had no box office. Then Bette Davis made a test and Mike Curtiz said she hollered when he told her she was too strong. And we must have tested with dozens of little boys. I'd worked with Liz Taylor on *The White Cliffs of Dover* and she was this teeny thing. Three years later she was blossoming into a real beauty—and she knew it!

One anecdote: we all trooped down to Perc Westmore's one Saturday afternoon—he was on Hollywood Boulevard—to get our hair dyed red. The process in those days was very strong and just as the color was being mixed in they turned off the water mains for repairs. To keep that dye in our hair—it meant we'd soon go bald and there already was stinging pain. In desperation, they plopped jars of cold cream into our locks and we all rushed to our homes to wash it out. Bill Powell said he had to wear a hairpiece after that.

BAWDEN: From *Father* you went to *I Remember Mama* [1948]?

DUNNE: [Director] George Stevens offered it to me after Garbo passed. I said I'd take Garbo's seconds any day because the part was so rich. I added some weight on my own—just a lot of tapioca pudding—and also there was a lot of padding.

We shot so much of it in San Francisco and the cast included Oscar Homolka, who got a Supporting [Actor] Oscar nomination. Barbara Bel

Geddes was my teenaged daughter although she really was twenty-eight. I had a dialect instructor but I didn't want to go heavy on that. The war had changed George. He told me he couldn't do comedies any longer. This one was a huge hit and I really thought I'd get the Oscar this time, but Jane Wyman won it. I was nominated and lost five times, becoming the Adlai Stevenson of the Oscar races.

BAWDEN: Next came your turn as Queen Victoria.

DUNNE: In *The Mudlark* [1950]. My downfall. We thought we were doing something quite splendid. But the anecdote about a waif getting into Windsor Castle to see Queen Victoria—well, it was too slight to hold interest. Fox shot it in Britain because the Labour government had frozen British currency. I put cotton batten in my cheeks to look like the old queen, I had latex on my throat and lines all over the place. It was not an Irene Dunne part, was it? Alec Guinness came on too strong as Prime Minister Disraeli. There was no balance in his portrait. Everything was scrupulously researched. Victoria had only spoken German until she was eighteen, so I had a very faint German accent. The British press were unkind in howling that an American was to play such a beloved English monarch. But Victoria was three-quarters German, I believe. It was the House of Hanover, after all. Such an expensive production and it barely earned back its costs.

BAWDEN: Is this the big reason you retired after just one more movie?

DUNNE: The business was changing. Again. My type of comedy was out, my type of drama was gone. I made *It Grows on Trees* [1952] and it was just terrible and went out on a double bill. The next year I took over as hostess of [television's] *Schlitz Playhouse of Stars* and I didn't have control as Loretta [Young] did of her show and so I moved on. I did a TV pilot of the film *Cheaper by the Dozen* in 1956 but it, thankfully, did not sell.

I never formally retired. That would have been presumptuous. But an awful lot of the girls my age soldiered on in bad vehicles. I'd do a TV half-hour drama every year just to keep my hand in it. But I couldn't run around with an axe in my hand like Bette and Joan did to keep things going. The difference was I had a family and they didn't have one—only the all-mighty career.

And I did get movie offers. MGM wanted me to play Grace Kelly's mother in *The Swan* [1956], which, ironically, would be her last movie, although nobody knew that. The part was choice, but I'd have to settle for fourth billing and my husband said to forget that. "Go out number one," was his advice. Well, Jessie Royce Landis finally took the part and was very funny. And then MGM wanted me as Leslie Caron's dotty aunt in *Gigi* [1958], but the subject matter was distasteful. The family was raising their precious to be a courtesan. If they'd offered me one great song I might have reconsidered.

The latest offer was to be in one of those *Airplane* movies—Universal said they'd donate six figures to a Catholic charity, but I didn't want to be stuck inside a crippled airplane for several months of shooting. But I still haven't retired. At least not from life.

Afterword

Though Irene Dunne starred in her last feature film in 1952, she remained very active in her charity work and efforts on behalf of the arts. She was appointed as an alternative United Nations delegate by President Dwight D. Eisenhower and served on a statewide California arts commission during Ronald Reagan's years as governor there. She died in 1990 at age ninety-one.

Joan Fontaine

Interview by James Bawden

Joan Fontaine was one of the great Hollywood leading ladies of the 1940s, Her performance in Alfred Hitchcock's *Rebecca,* the Oscar-winning 1940 film, lifted her into the top ranks of dramatic actresses. She followed up that success in 1941 with Hitchcock's *Suspicion,* for which she won the Best Actress Academy Award.

She was married four times—to actor Brian Aherne (1939–1945), producer William Dozier (1946–1951), writer-producer Collier Young (1952–1961), and golf writer Alfred Wright Jr. (1964–1969). All four marriages ended in divorce. Fontaine had a daughter by Dozier and an adopted daughter. She was estranged from both children.

Setting the Scene

I first met Joan Fontaine at a Toronto hotel where she was peddling her tell-all 1979 autobiography *No Bed of Roses.* I interviewed her a second time in 1987 in an L.A. screening room when Fontaine was promoting her appearance in the TV documentary *The RKO Story.* And a few years later she appeared on a panel with Tommy Tune and Stanley Kramer for the Movie Channel and we lunched afterward.

The Interview

BAWDEN: Why did you decide to become an actress?

FONTAINE: I needed a job. My sister [Olivia de Havilland] was doing nicely at Warners, so I became Joan Burfield for RKO and had a bit part in Katharine Hepburn's movie *Quality Street* [1937].

BAWDEN: What happened?

FONTAINE: I bombed at RKO. They made me Fred Astaire's leading

Joan Fontaine with Orson Welles in *Jane Eyre* (1944). Courtesy of 20th Century-Fox.

lady in *Damsel in Distress* [1937] only because first choice Jessie Matthews had to bow out due to schedule changes. I remember walking along a path and Fred dancing around me. I was truly awful!

BAWDEN: But you managed to get into some big pictures.

Joan Fontaine (*right*) shies away from Judith Anderson in *Rebecca,* the Oscar-winning Best Picture of 1940. Courtesy of Selznick International and United Artists.

Fontaine: In bit roles. George Cukor hired me as the insignificant ninny who is part of *The Women* [1939]. I really only had a telephone scene to strut my stuff and George lit it as carefully as Norma Shearer's close-ups. And I met Joan Crawford on that set and I continued to get Xmas cards from her until she passed. Both Paulette Goddard and I had tiny parts. When MGM rereleased it in 1946, we were elevated to top star billing! And I had a bit as Doug Fairbanks Jr.'s sweetheart in *Gunga Din* [1939]. I remember, after a day of shooting, I looked out the window and saw Doug and his current flame, Marlene Dietrich, off to some grand soirée all dressed up and I sighed. Because that kind of glamour always eluded me.

BAWDEN: What do you remember of the making of *Rebecca*?

FONTAINE: How miserable I was. Larry Olivier had tested with his wife, Viv Leigh, but [producer] David Selznick said it was too early after [his] *Gone with the Wind.* In fact, scenes from *Gone with the Wind* were being done at the same time as we started. I also know Loretta Young and Maggie Sullavan had tested, but both were considered too American. Finally David said, "I guess it will have to be you," which is hardly a ringing endorsement.

The best thing is that David was so busy with the last-minute details of *Gone with the Wind* that he stayed away for long periods of time, which was unusual for him. Hitch [director Alfred Hitchcock] simply refused to discuss characterization. Occasionally they'd meet for a great blowup. One of the scenes had the young lovers meeting in the hotel lift. David came on set and told Hitch to do it again because he'd paid for the construction of a great breakfast room and he wanted to show it off. Hitch did as told—this was his first movie [in America] and he had no clout.

Larry and Judith Anderson were very mean to me, but I now see this only increased my performance because I had nothing else to fall back on, no technique.

Oscar night I was in a hissy fit. I didn't want to win; I was only twenty-three. David insisted I would, but he was wrong. Ginger Rogers walked away with it that year. And as it turned out, *Rebecca* was the only David Selznick movie I would ever star in.

BAWDEN: But he promptly loaned you and Hitch out to RKO for *Suspicion* and you won the Oscar.

FONTAINE: Hitch was angry David demanded so much off the top for us that there wasn't an adequate budget for production. At the time I was very contemptuous of Cary Grant. I thought he was only interested in himself. Rewatching the film, I see how he threw whole scenes to me. He seemed aloof at the time, but he never was the gregarious sort. I loved knowing Nigel Bruce—so warm, so winning. Hitch kept mumbling all the time it didn't look at all like England. But neither did *Rebecca,* really! This

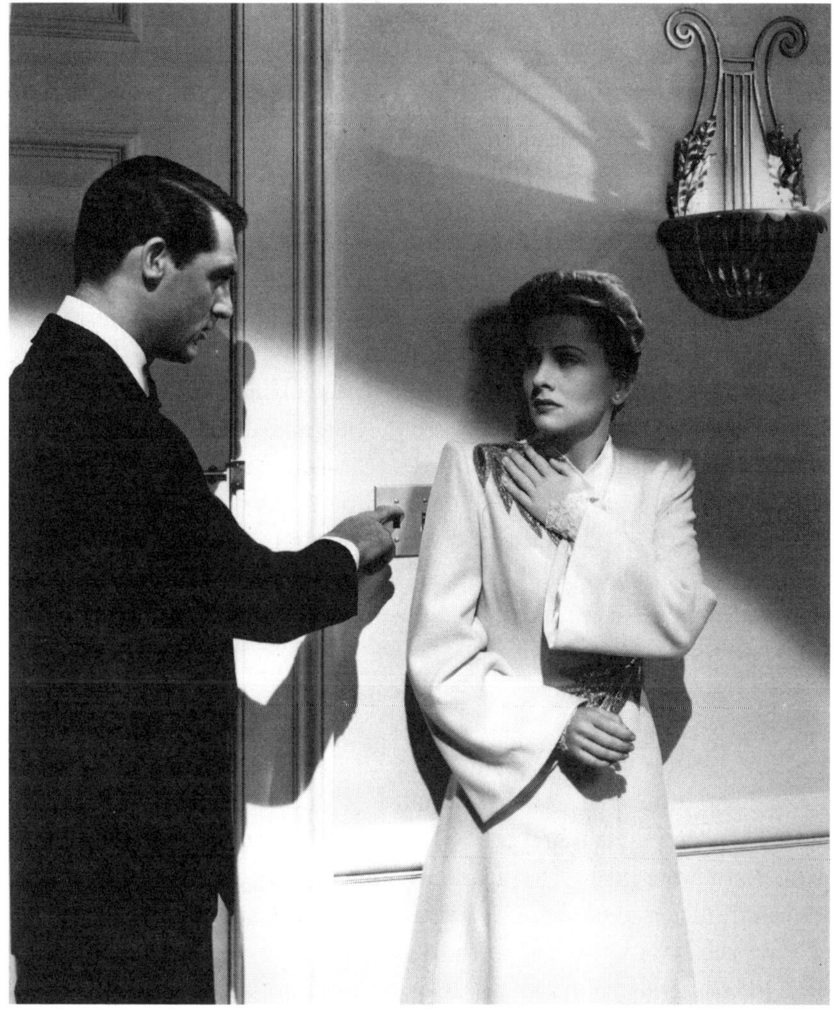

Joan Fontaine suspects husband Cary Grant is trying to kill her in Alfred Hitchcock's *Suspicion.* She won the 1941 Best Actress Oscar for her performance. Courtesy of RKO and United Artists Television.

time I got the Oscar. It changed my life. It changed my relationship with David, too.

BAWDEN: Explain.

FONTAINE: After *Rebecca,* he went out of production for three whole years. He started a lavish remake of *Jane Eyre* [1944]. I'd be Jane. Another Selznick director, Bob Stevenson, would direct it. Orson Welles was signed.

David did all sorts of market tests and finally concluded the public would confuse it with *Rebecca,* so he sold the whole thing—sets, scripts, cast, crew—to Darryl Zanuck, who had a huge success. People always ask me, did Orson interfere? Well, he certainly tried to! But Bob was a guy who knew movies inside out. And there was our cinematographer George Barnes, who had trained Gregg Toland.

BAWDEN: But you are too pretty to play Jane!

FONTAINE: Kind sir! This was Hollywood, after all. I first met little Elizabeth Taylor on that set, all about ten years old, Dresden china features. It's one of my faves to this day.

BAWDEN: How did your relationship with Selznick evolve?

FONTAINE: He sold my services to the biggest bidder and pocketed the profits. I wanted to only do a picture a year. David needed money to pay for all his failed ventures. I think he'd pay me $2,000 weekly for ten weeks and get up to $150,000 for my services. You do the math. I didn't much want to do *This Above All* [1942], but it was with Ty Power, who was the biggest leading man around at the time and it was a good picture to make for wartime audiences.

BAWDEN: Then you played a twelve-year-old in *The Constant Nymph* [1943].

FONTAINE: A few years back, Turner Classic Movies arranged a screening for me. I watched in awe. I was really good and then I staggered into the sunlight in desperate search of a gin and tonic. This was the movie that really started the Joan-Olivia feud. I was at Olivie's home studio. I'd gotten the assignment after director Teddy Goulding had turned her down as too mature. I did not know that at the time. Teddy was a magician. He drew from me emotions I never knew I had and also from Alexis Smith, who was only twenty-four at the time and playing a frosty beauty of thirty-five.

BAWDEN: You brought it up, so I have to ask about your famous feud with your sister.

FONTAINE: It takes two to feud. I know how Livvie was shocked the night in 1942 I won an Oscar over her. But I've always tried to make amends. She was shocked when our mother [Lillian Fontaine] started acting—she played Ray Milland's landlady in *The Lost Weekend* [1945]. I'm always shocking her, but she doesn't ever shock me. We're so close in birth terms, we're more like twins, and twins do quarrel on occasion, right?

BAWDEN: Eventually Selznick drew tired of trying to recast you in another mold.

FONTAINE: He discovered Jennifer Jones and she was very pliable. He managed every phase of her life. I was not so malleable and I was not about to divorce my husband to marry him as Jennifer did. Eventually it drove both of them crazy. I was still under contract to him until 1947 and we often battled about the parts he wanted me to play for other producers.

BAWDEN: I know you hated *Frenchman's Creek* [1944].

FONTAINE: Awful leading man! I told [director] Mitch Leisen to fire him—Arturo de Córdova. Eventually Mitch agreed with me and asked Paramount to substitute Ray Milland, but we were too far along in filming. All Mitch cared about was the decor. So his assistant, Phyllis Seaton, really directed it.

BAWDEN: You once said *Ivy* [1947] was your favorite film.

FONTAINE: Why not? I get to poison the cast, which is an actress's dream. Bill Cameron Menzies, who designed *Gone with the Wind,* designed it, and the sets are fantastic. And we later did a sort of modern-day version called *Born to Be Bad* [1950], which is another favorite.

BAWDEN: What do you remember about *Letter from an Unknown Woman* [1948]?

FONTAINE: Max Ophuls [the director] was such a pleasure to work with. He'd take his time, then only shoot a take or two. He was convinced this would be his big hit, but it really is an odd tale of obsession. Her romance with the conductor is all in her head. No wonder moviegoers were confused. The layers of European society are beautifully shown off. It was so expensive to make. When it bombed, Max's heart was broken and, like so many other European directors, he left Hollywood in some disgrace. I just love its perversity, the way nothing is overdone. It was a forgotten film for a long time; now is being revived to acclaim.

BAWDEN: Why sign with Paramount in 1948?

FONTAINE: Why not? The business was changing and independents like David were right out of it. My first Paramount was the only Bing Crosby film to lose money—*The Emperor Waltz* [1948], which Billy Wilder misdirected. Bing would stroll in every morning with his writers and announce, "Billy, we've changed the dialogue a bit." Billy would rage, but there was nothing he could do. Bing was Paramount's leading star. Later on, I worked [in 1954's *Casanova's Big Night*] with Bob Hope, who had the same technique. He told me I was the straight man. My job was to feed him lines and he'd react accordingly. I did so, and we had a big hit.

Then I did *September Affair* [1950] for Hal Wallis and it was a huge hit.

Joan Fontaine as Queen Ludmilla in the TV movie *Good King Wenceslas,* her final screen role. Courtesy of the Family Channel.

But *Something to Live For* [1951] was a real misfire from George Stevens. He never talks about this one!

BAWDEN: At MGM you were the loveliest Rowena in *Ivanhoe* [1952].

FONTAINE: That got me going at MGM and I later made *Until They Sail*

[1957]. I was forty by then, playing the frumpy sister who never married. Paul Newman told me he'd grown up on my movies, but Paul was only eight years younger! And I had a 20th Century-Fox period with *Island in the Sun* [1957], *Voyage to the Bottom of the Sea* [1961], and *Tender Is the Night* [1962].

BAWDEN: I remember *Island in the Sun* was considered highly controversial.

FONTAINE: I played Harry Belafonte's lover but we were not allowed to touch hands, let alone kiss. One day I casually brushed against his arm and alarm bells went off with the censor, who considered it racial, and we had to reshoot the scene. But I much preferred *Voyage* because I fell into the fish tank and got eaten by Peter Lorre's shark. I was the older wife in *A Certain Smile* [1958], and everybody at 20th said how big a star Christine Carere was going to be. Nobody ever heard from her again!

BAWDEN: You have an amusing story to tell about *Tender Is the Night*?

FONTAINE: One day around lunch I picked up my phone in my dressing room and, through a crossed wire, heard David [Selznick] instructing Jennifer Jones on what exactly to do in the scene. The bells rang, we reassembled, and Jennifer did exactly what David had said! The director, Henry King, was beside himself, but the picture flopped because, King told me, "I shall never permit the bedroom antics of the story to sully the reputations of my stars." Also, no top male star would work with Jennifer, who got more and more skittish. [William] Holden and [Gregory] Peck both said they'd done their duty and didn't want another bad experience.

BAWDEN: Then came your horror outing.

FONTAINE: In 1966: *The Devil's Own* [aka *The Witches*] was actually as literate as a horror yarn can be and stocked with all sorts of wonderful British scene-stealers.

BAWDEN: Compare all this with acting on TV.

FONTAINE: As a guest star, they give you a dowdy trailer and throw a few sandwiches your way at lunch. But that's where the audience is. But after I did *Cannon* [1975], I got tons of mail. Same reaction when I did *The Users* [1978]. Much reaction and offers to do more. I've replaced Deborah Kerr on Broadway and also Julie Harris, but it's hard to get anything established these days on the stage. I replaced Loretta Young in the TV pilot for *Dark Mansions* [1986], which was fun to do, but I knew it wouldn't be series bound, despite all [producer] Aaron Spelling told me. So far I've even appeared on *Love Boat* [1981]. I have no shame! So I guess I'm drifting these days. When I'm bored, I do the game shows for pure fun.

Afterword

Joan Fontaine's final screen appearance was in a made-for-TV movie, *Good King Wenceslas* [1994] for cable's the Family Channel. She died in her sleep in her home in Carmel, California, on December 15, 2013. She was ninety-six.

Dorothy Lamour

Interview by James Bawden and Ron Miller

Dorothy Lamour is too often unjustly overlooked by movie fans who seem to remember her only for her subordinate role in the *Road* pictures with Bing Crosby and Bob Hope. Though Lamour was certainly a vital presence as "the girl" in those zany comedies, she was a genuine star in her own right before Hope and Crosby started chasing her across the screen. She was also a very capable dramatic actress and a singer of exceptional quality.

If you want a demonstration of the latter claim, check out that still glorious wartime musical *The Fleet's In* (1942), in which Lamour was the top-billed star and sings one of her greatest songs, "I'll Remember You," with the Jimmy Dorsey band. She was billed over two future superstars—William Holden and Betty Hutton. Lamour was beautiful, sexy, and every bit the star. To see her in good form as a dramatic actress, try *Last Train from Madrid* (1937) or *Johnny Apollo* (1940) or *The Greatest Show on Earth* (1952), the Oscar-winning Best Picture in which director C. B. DeMille required her to learn how to hang by her teeth on a circus high wire.

Lamour was a shapely, dark-haired beauty with a sultry voice. She was the ideal comic foil for Hope and Crosby, starting first with Hope in his first feature film, *The Big Broadcast of 1938* (1938), then joining both stars in *Road to Singapore* (1940).

But if you want to see why Paramount studios first pushed her as a star attraction, look at her first starring role, in *The Jungle Princess* (1936). This is still a very entertaining movie and Lamour was simply stunning in the sarong that became her trademark wardrobe item. Director John Ford followed that up by casting her as a South Sea island beauty in *The Hurricane* (1937), a sensational romantic epic, opposite the virile Jon Hall.

When her movie stardom faded in the 1950s, Lamour turned to stage and club dates and for years toured in musicals like *Hello Dolly* and *Mame.*

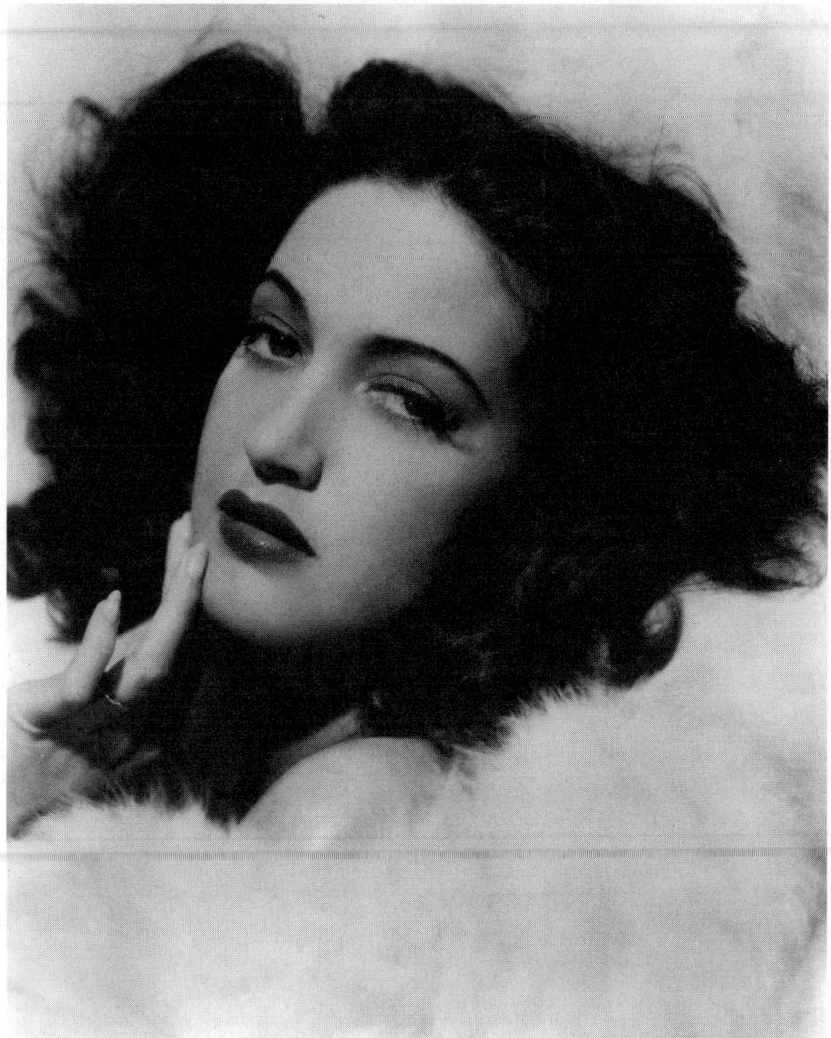

Dorothy Lamour. Courtesy of Paramount Pictures.

Setting the Scene

Both of us conducted our own interviews with Dorothy Lamour over the years. We have combined them for this presentation but offer our individual memories of the circumstances of those interviews.

BAWDEN: I first noticed Dorothy Lamour on TV's *The Late Show.* It was watching those wonderful *Road* pictures she made with Bing Crosby and Bob Hope that made me a fan. The adjective "orchidaceous" seemed meant for her. She was a beauty, but she didn't play femme fatales. Instead, she gave an intriguing comedy take. And then I saw her in *Swing High, Swing Low* (1937), *Manhandled* (1949), and *A Medal for Benny* (1945), which gave proof positive that she could resist type casting when a part was demanding.

In 1984 I got my one chance to meet her in person when she gave me an interview in Toronto to promote her appearance in a dinner theater presentation of *Barefoot in the Park.* Fans her own age filled the theater, but there were also college students who simply adored the *Road* pictures.

She was nervous about being photographed, so I booked the best *Toronto Star* photographer, Boris Spremo, who spent an hour carefully composing the lights and applying her makeup. The result was so astonishingly beautiful Lamour used the shot as her PR photo for the rest of her career.

Miller: When I met her in 1991, Lamour was seventy-seven. She smoked one cigarette after another during our chat. However, smoke clouds aside, she was an engaging lady and I liked her instantly. She enjoyed talking about her grand days of the late 1930s and early 1940s.

Lamour had agreed to the interview to help promote an upcoming TV special on the American Movie Classics (AMC) cable network about the war-bond rallies and other home-front activities in which she had been involved during World War II. Over lunch near her San Fernando Valley home, Lamour talked about her many national war-bond tours, in which she reportedly helped raise more than $300 million for the war effort.

Lamour and her husband were married for thirty-five years until his death in 1978. She admitted to me that she had been very lonely ever since and was grateful for the fact that she still received lots of fan mail from moviegoers who had been writing her since the 1940s. Many of them had become her friends.

The Interview

Bawden: How did you get to Hollywood?

Lamour: Well, I was Miss New Orleans of 1931! I then headed to Chicago, determined to be a big-band singer. Instead I wound up as an elevator operator at Marshall Fields department store. By 1933, I was in L.A.

Dorothy Lamour with Ray Milland in her first "sarong" film, the 1936 *Jungle Princess.* Courtesy of Paramount Pictures.

and my first bit was in *Footlight Parade.* I did have gigs with Rudy Vallee and Eddie Duchin, and in 1936 I signed with Paramount.

BAWDEN: One moment you have an uncredited bit in *College Holiday* [1936] and the next movie it's first star billing in *The Jungle Princess.* Explain, please.

LAMOUR: It was a small-budgeted thing, not even in Technicolor. No big stars, really. Ray Milland had just come over from Universal. He badmouthed it and me in his book, but who cares? It wasn't meant to be taken seriously. One of the natives was Ray Mala, who was in the movie *Eskimo.* Talk about ethnic diversity! We had a pool scene in a pool constructed on the studio lot and just before a take, we're already in the water and Ray Milland whispers, "Dottie, I just tinkled in your water." Well, I got so hot and bothered I ran out screaming and wouldn't return until all the water was taken out, disinfectant added to clean the sides, and new water added. That took several days and brass were so angry at Ray they threatened to dock his pay.

Bawden: But it was your first time in a sarong.

Lamour: Well, the film really took off and made a mint. And as far as the sarong goes, decades later I finally went to Polynesia to check for myself and found all the girls used only the bottom. They were all going around bare-breasted!

My next sarong flick was *The Hurricane* [1937], which had an awfully big budget, except at the last moment ol' Sam Goldwyn [the producer] decided to shoot everything inside his studio. We'd been promised a trip to Hawaii. Well, Jack Ford [the director] was as mad as a hatter. But when you look at it today, you can't tell the difference. And it was another roaring hit and I had my "gimmick." Every gal has to have one to become a big attraction. And I've had the sarong ever since. Heck, it's better than being known as the sweater girl.

Miller: Though you never made any of those movies in Polynesia, you took a cruise there in your later years. Did you feel at home there?

Lamour: You know, you go to these places that look like Bali Hai and you see these little waitresses in sarongs, wearing flowers in their hair like I did. It looks like a whole bunch of Lamours running around.

Miller: Do you think you could break into movies today the same way you did back in your *Jungle Princess* days?

Lamour: In my day, the films were romantic. Now they're all raw sex. I don't know what I'd be doing in pictures if I were starting out today. I certainly wouldn't be doing what most of them are doing. As for my sarong, that would be like wearing long underwear today.

Bawden: You got to work with some top female stars in those early days.

Lamour: With Irene Dunne [in 1937's *High, Wide, and Handsome*], I only remember her supreme kindness. She'd say, "Oh, no, Dottie. Turn that way. It's your better side." With Carole Lombard [*Swing High, Swing Low*], there was a lot of laughter on set, but then she'd settle down and do an immaculate and very sad take. And right afterward, Carole left Paramount forever. All the big stars left that studio as soon as possible because of the lingering Depression. They could get bigger salaries freelance.

Bawden: You first worked with Bob Hope in *The Big Broadcast of 1938.*

Lamour: Well, we both were in the picture and I was cast as his fiancée but his leading lady was Shirley Ross. I sang my one song—"You Took the Words Right out of My Heart"—to Leif Erickson. I still kid Bob he got fifth billing behind W. C. Fields, Martha Raye, me, and Shirley! It was very definitely a Bill Fields vehicle. He'd been off for a year drying out and he left the studio after this one for Universal. Boy, was he ornery—and he stank so, if one got too close. That Kirsten Flagstad number? She filmed that in New York. I've never met her to this day. [Director] Mitch Leisen told me he wasn't so much a director as a traffic cop. Bill did exactly what he wanted and got away with it. I was still learning my way in comedy. I don't think I was particularly effective.

BAWDEN: Why do you think jungle movies were so popular during the war years?

LAMOUR: Because it was the war, that's all. People had to get out of their homes or go crazy. And so many boys never came back. My popularity soared; so did Veronica Lake and Paulette Goddard. And the studio got to know how to make effective jungle pictures like *Typhoon* [1940], *Moon over Burma* [1940], *Aloma of the South Seas* [1941], and *Beyond the Blue Horizon* [1942]. But that's a relatively small quota of my entire pictures. The color was dazzling; I always felt I looked better in Technicolor than black and white. I really did.

BAWDEN: You say Paramount was not the happy family it was portrayed in the press.

LAMOUR: Not al all! People left all the time because of the atmosphere. One of my best buds was Lynne Overman—I'm sure you know his work in pictures like *Northwest Mounted Police* [1940], *Reap the Wild Wind* [1942]. He had a certain kind of nasally delivery, so effective others stole his act. A damned great friend. He could save any scene with his antics. I first met him in *Big Broadcast of 1938,* then *Her Jungle Love* [1938], *Spawn of the North* [1938], *Typhoon, Caught in the Draft* [1941], *Dixie* [1943]. Then one day in 1943 he comes into my dressing room and cries his eyes out. As part of an economy move, Paramount was dropping him. I said, "Lynne, with your talents you can go anywhere. You'll have a fine freelancing career." But no, he couldn't see it that way. He only made one freelance picture—*The Desert Song* [1943] and then dropped dead of a heart attack at fifty-five. It was really a broken heart. The bottom line got him and killed him. Paramount did that to him. I never forgot that!

MILLER: Since you were more or less a "sex goddess" at Paramount, did the men treat you with respect?

LAMOUR: I used to walk on the set in the morning and the guys would come up, put their arms around me, and kiss me. I thought that was wonderful. If they got vulgar, I'd just tell them to get lost. But there was no big thing made out of it.

Bawden: Why did Paramount loan you out for two movies in 1940?

Lamour: Said they needed the money I could command by then. I did three movies for them that year and two for Fox. I was a busy girl, I was. I absolutely adored Tyrone Power [her costar in Fox's *Johnny Apollo*]. He was a great male beauty, but also a poet, a philosopher. I replaced Linda Darnell on short notice; I think she quit because of [director] Henry Hathaway. He was a yeller. Yelled all over the place when he got ticked off. I shouted back, "Yell as loud as you want, kind sir, and then we can start making a picture." He loved that, and he made sure I was photographed to perfection. It was a great part and I came to adore Henry Hathaway. In fact, when I get back to my home in L.A., I'll drive by his pad and give the old dear flowers. Ty asked for more challenging roles and he got it. When I saw the first cut I had tears in my eyes. I was actually acting!

I had another Henry—King, that is—as director of *Chad Hanna* [1940]. I loved my name in that one—Albany Yates. I didn't love working with Henry Fonda, who was a worrywart. He really was a bit too old as the boy joining the circus. The color was wonderful. Fox led in the development of color. But the film didn't really work and that was that.

Bawden: How did you get to costar with Bing Crosby and Bob Hope in *Road to Singapore* [1940]?

Lamour: It was prepared as a George Burns-Gracie Allen vehicle. With Charlie Ruggles as the third wheel. Then Burns and Allen left for MGM to make *Honolulu* and never came back. So Fred MacMurray and I were substituted. Charlie couldn't make it and Bob Hope was substituted. Then Fred left to be replaced by Bing. Bing and Bob had been in vaudeville, not together, but they knew each other. They had a history.

I knew Bob. At first it was all tentative until Bob brought in his radio writers to add gags. Then Bing brought in his writers. So I hired a few myself. My biggest memory is looking up one day after I'd done a scene with Bob and our director, Victor Schertzinger, was madly thumbing through the script looking for a line, any line that was in the script.

One day Bob got silly waiting for a take and threw soapsuds all over me, which took the rest of the day to clean up. By the way, look closely at the credits. I'm billed over Bob. That was the first and last time in any *Road* picture.

Bawden: What did you think about those pictures, which made you a big star?

Dorothy Lamour with Bing Crosby (*left*) and Bob Hope in the 1945 *Road to Utopia.* Courtesy of Paramount Pictures.

LAMOUR: *Road to Zanzibar* [1941] was much better than *Singapore.* Victor was again director and he just stepped back this time and let the boys go at it. Bob came to my dressing room and apologized for taking second billing. I wasn't complaining. In fact, I hadn't noticed at that stage. This wasn't a sequel in any way. It was a script that was already rewritten and they tweaked it to make it a *Road* picture. We played completely different characters.

Victor did four movies in '41, the reason he died at fifty-three in October. It was overwork and Paramount said that might be the end. But then they came with *Road to Morocco* [1942], which is considered the best of the bunch. David Butler stepped in [as director] and he knew when to get out of the way. We were at our wacky best and this one was a monster hit. I remember the talking camel.

And I had my favorite-ever song, "Moonlight Becomes You So." It hit a nerve with wartime audiences, I'm guessing. We then went on a three-year break. We were so busy touring army camps and making [non-*Road*] films. And Bing always considered *Road to Utopia* [1945] the best one. My song "Personality" occasioned a brush with the censors, but I love it. It's right up there as a personal favorite.

Miller: Was it uncomfortable being "the girl in the middle" between those two wisecracking characters?

Lamour: When the ad-libbing started, I tried to get one in whenever I could, but it was impossible—just impossible!

Miller: Let's talk a bit about your work in the war effort. They still talk about how effective you were at selling war bonds on the home front.

Lamour: I kept saying to myself, "What can I do to help the war effort?" I could have enlisted in the WAVES, the WACS, or whatever, but I didn't think I'd do as much good that way as I could if I found a way to use my name value to do something constructive.

My mother had told me what a great job Mary Pickford had done selling war bonds in World War I and I remembered that. The next day I called Y. Frank Freeman, who ran Paramount, and asked him what he thought of the idea. He liked it and called his friend Henry Morganthau, who was President Roosevelt's treasury secretary. Mr. Morganthau asked me to come to Washington for a meeting and next thing I knew, I was the first Hollywood star to go on tour selling war bonds.

Before I started my first tour in 1941, I met with a group of influential bankers to let them know our plans. I wore a conservative dark suit for that meeting, which was a good thing, because they told me, "Miss Lamour, you know you won't be able to wear that sarong whatchamacallit when you're out there selling bonds for America."

"I hadn't planned on it," I told them.

Miller: So how did it go when you finally hit the road?

Lamour: I began by reading from a prepared speech written for me by the Treasury Department, but before I got more than a few words out, the crowd started yelling, "Dotty, take it off!" So from then on, I winged it with my own words. The government wanted me to accept only cash, not pledges. I collected $9 million in cash in the first six days—and $31 million by the end of my first New England tour.

Miller: I know you toured in your own railroad car, but what kind of security did you have, with those huge crowds you were drawing?

Lamour: We had no armed guards, no plastic bubble over my car. People were very respectful then. They were my friends. They saw you on the screen and thought of you as a friend. I don't know what they think you are now, but I don't think you'd dare go around like that today.

Bawden: When you were back at work, you continued with Hope, even when there wasn't a new *Road* picture. For instance, you did a Bob Hope comedy—*They Got Me Covered*—at Goldwyn in 1943.

LAMOUR: Bob had a two-picture deal and got Sam Goldwyn to buy my services on a loan-out. David Butler directed. He'd done another Hope comedy, *My Favorite Blonde* [1942]. It could have been made at Paramount, really. Otto Preminger was the nasty villain—I'm not sure he was acting.

BAWDEN: Your take on the Bing-Bob relationship?

LAMOUR: It was all studio publicity stuff. They were not best friends. Never! There was a string of rivalry that made their adventures all the more fun. Bing wanted to be as funny as Bob. Bob just wanted Bing's studio clout, his absolute authority, that's it. They'd golf together on the front lawn but only to an audience.

Bob was growing ever more popular during the war, but Bing already was an institution. He never was carefree like his image. He was tightly coiled. His poor wife, Dixie Lee, slipped into alcoholism because of his indifference. His brother, Everett, was always around as his business manager. He had his finger in all kinds of enterprises. And Bob envied that great fame and wealth.

Look, I never found Bing anything but coolly controlled. He was nice but distant, whereas Bob wore his feelings on his sleeve. But Bob's wife suffered through some serious bouts of womanizing. I admire Dolores completely, but she had to put up with a lot. And sometimes Bing and Bob would switch girlfriends, which kept studio tongues crackling. If a girl starred with both Bing and Bob, then something was going on. But not with me, mind you. I would have cuffed either guy if they attempted anything, so they knew to proceed with caution.

MILLER: One day I was at Hope's house and he showed me where you lived, just a block away in Toluca Lake. What kind of a neighbor was he?

LAMOUR: Well, one night he came by real late with five reporters who wanted to meet me. He knocked on the door and said, "Don't you recognize my nose?" My husband and I were already in bed, but we had to bring everybody in for drinks.

MILLER: Did you ever needle him about his womanizing ways?

LAMOUR: Once he drove by my house to show me his new car, so I went for a ride with him. When we came back, he gave me a little good-bye kiss. I told him, "Not that way! The neighbors are watching!" So I put my arms around him and gave him a really long kiss just so the neighbors would think he was sneaking around.

Bawden: Did you feel equal to Bob and Bing in your *Road* pictures?

Lamour: We were a team—the three of us. When they made that terrible road adventure almost without me [1962's *The Road to Hong Kong*], it never worked out. I like to think I was as essential as the boys were.

Bawden: One of your best movies, *Dixie,* is seldom seen on TV.

Lamour: For an obvious reason. It was the one time I saw Bing really enthusiastic about a picture. He really believed in this one. But it's a fictionalized saga of Daniel Decatur Emmett, who virtually invented the minstrel shows that roamed the old South and he wrote "Dixie." Bing was convinced this would do for him what *Yankee Doodle Dandy* [1942] did for Cagney. Didn't happen. They added new songs rather than the standards Emmett had written. And even in 1943 the racial element was a bit touchy. Blacks found it offensive. I found it offensive, but Bing said not to worry because we were portraying slavery as it was. He said his earlier hit *Mississippi* [1935] had fared well. Paramount was so enthusiastic they gave him Technicolor for the first time. It didn't bomb, but it was one of his lesser hits.

Bawden: I've never seen *Riding High* [1943].

Lamour: Lucky man! You didn't miss much. George Marshall directed it and it certainly moved. It was wartime and it made a barrel of dough. It might have been Dick Powell's last musical. He was bitter about having to do it. We had fun making it but nobody ever asks me about that one.

Bawden: How did you get along with Betty Hutton in *And the Angels Sing* [1944]?

Lamour: As well as anybody could. Betty was bigger than life. She sucked all the energy out of a scene, she was so brash. George [Marshall] directed again. His method was to shoot a scene and maybe do a second take for insurance. Sometimes he'd shoot the rehearsals. Very funny old guy who was just glad to still be working. And that's why there's never been a festival of his movies. He had no distinct style. I mean, can you imagine me, Betty, and Diana Lynn as sisters? Fred MacMurray was the guy and he was getting ready to leave Paramount for all that lush freelancing money. It didn't happen because movie revenues crashed after the war.

Bawden: Why is *Road to Rio* [1947] your favorite *Road* picture?

Lamour: Because it was the last one of the original bunch. And we got it so right. Paramount then told us receipts were less than expected and our salaries so high that this was it. And we only did one more on the lot, but that was five years later and it was lousy. Receipts in 1947 plunged across the boards, and some critics suggested Bing and Bob were, at forty-four, a bit leathery to play those good ol' boys. But I got to sing one of my favorite Paramount tunes, "Experience." A lot of Bob's best lines were interpolated by his radio gag writers. And those Wiere Brothers! They made me laugh out loud, ruining many takes. Gale Sondergaard told me she never had as much fun. We didn't know it at the time, but Paramount's golden age was running out of steam.

BAWDEN: But you were very busy that year. You also made one with Alan Ladd.

LAMOUR: *Wild Harvest!* We made that one with pickets on the streets outside the Paramount lot. [Some of the Hollywood craft unions were on strike.] So [director] Tay Garnett had us all bunking down at the lot so we wouldn't cross over a picket line. I had a nice dressing room, but some of those extras really balked about bunking on empty soundstages in cots.

A darling guy, Lloyd Nolan, also was the narrator. Very handsome, a swell actor. Why he never became a top star beats me. Gosh, he was great with me in *Disputed Passage* [1939].

Laddie by this time was striving to break free of Veronica Lake. She'd become quite an alcoholic. But we were neighbors in Toluca Lake. My kids played with his kids. You know, Laddie was dead serious, never fooled around—in fact, he once found Bing and Grace Kelly fooling around in his pool cabana and angrily ordered them off his property. Kissing him was strange. He got red faced. After all, I'd have to go home and wave to his wife, Sue Carol, out on the porch.

Wild Harvest was about harvesters who travel. This wasn't enough for a movie. I was awkward and it showed, and the movie was a big bomb. Bob Preston was about to jump from Paramount after seven years. They told him he'd always be a second stringer. To think that Bob wound up in *The Music Man* [1962]! Hurray!

BAWDEN: Then there was your last non-*Road* picture with Hope, *My Favorite Brunette* [1947].

LAMOUR: Alan [Ladd] has a gag cameo in it that, I remember. Rights reverted to Hope Enterprises and the lug forgot to renew it, so it's now in public domain. It was a spoof of private eye movies. Bob played a baby photographer who stands in for a real private eye, played by Alan Ladd. His name was McCloud! Not bad, as I recall. The preview audience really laughed. Peter Lorre was so tiny, I'd pat him on the head as I walked by. Bing did his cameo in one take and walked off with a $5,000 check, which really ticked Bob off. He said for his cameos on Crosby films he had to do take after take.

BAWDEN: It seems you were treated badly after 1947.

LAMOUR: So what? Who wasn't? The studio system crashed first at Paramount, which was one of the first studios to be required to sell off its theater chain. Then TV came along and, well, profits went thataway. So as soon as a star's contract was up, out they went! Veronica Lake left first in '48. Macdonald Carey left in '50. Diana Lynn, Mona Freeman, John Lund, Ray Milland—all disappeared around the same time. Nobody new was being hired. And even Bing and Bob were complaining about how they were being treated. And in 1948 Paramount sold me to Benedict Bogeaus for three consecutive pictures, all stinkers.

BAWDEN: What happened with *On Our Merry Way* [1948]?

LAMOUR: Benedict Bogeaus made it for UA [United Artists] and it was quite a mess. It was an idea of Burgess Meredith, who was then married to Paulette Goddard. Jimmy Stewart and Henry Fonda had a [story line]; so did Fred MacMurray and Bill Demarest years before they were on TV's *My Three Sons*. I was a gal who had to don a sarong in a musical revue—Victor Moore was my sidekick. After I did my scenes, Charles Laughton's scenes as a minister were cut completely. I really felt bad about it! King Vidor and Leslie Fenton were the directors, but John Huston and George Stevens were also around.

BAWDEN: Then came *Lulu Belle* [1948].

LAMOUR: Ouch! Another Bogeaus stinker. It was sort of a period musical. George Montgomery was the male lead. Nice guy, couldn't act. It did absolutely no business. Then I did another with George called *The Girl from Manhattan* [1948] and Laughton was in that one, too. It was my third and last for Mr. B., who really knew how to churn them out. So I limped back to Paramount with my career in tatters.

BAWDEN: But back at Paramount you finally made a film noir, *Manhandled*, which I quite like.

LAMOUR: No, I made it for Pine-Thomas, which was situated across the street and only released through Paramount. It was shot very quickly by Lew Foster, and Dan Duryea was a sleazy private eye investigating a murder and Sterling Hayden was an insurance investigator. I didn't like playing it so hard, but I got good notices. Dan, such a family man in private, could really play nasty. I remember Irene Hervey saying, "I've got the best part. I get murdered and I don't have to come back to this rat trap."

The same year I did *Slightly French* [1949] at Columbia with Don Ameche, which surprised everybody with its strong box office. So these two reminded Paramount I still had loyal fans out there.

BAWDEN: But you were inactive for the next few years?

LAMOUR: Inactive? Is that how you describe giving birth to two great sons? I remarried in 1943 and stayed married to the greatest guy in the world, Bill Howard, until his death in 1978. And we had Ridge Howard in 1946 and Tommy Howard in 1949. So what you call inactivity, I call maternity.

But seriously, folks, I remained under Paramount contract, and in late 1950 I started training for *The Greatest Show on Earth* [1952]. Cecil B. DeMille had always eluded me and I got the part of Phyllis only because he was out of sorts with Paulette Goddard. I'd actually talked to him about the gal in *North West Mounted Police* [1940], but even though I'm part French, he chose Paulette and used her again in *Reap the Wild Wind* and *Unconquered* [1947]. That's where she fell afoul of him by refusing to be tossed into a cold, fast-running mountain stream. A stunt double was used and C. B. thereafter refused to even talk to her.

For *Greatest Show*, she bombarded him with presents. No response. Paulette had made one of the greatest-ever bombs at Paramount in 1949—*Bride of Vengeance*. Paramount was paying her not to make movies there! And C. B. commanded me to appear at his office and told me I'd be Phyllis. Now, her circus trick is to twirl in the air [hanging by her teeth], and for a civilian to try this would break anybody's neck. So it took almost a year of training to get my jaw and neck into that shape. Plus I had to be extra skinny so the weight wouldn't be an issue. I sang "Lovely Luawanna Lady," which was a great hit for me. I reluctantly did it in a sarong and that made ol' C. B. beam.

I thought it terrible hokum when I watched the first assembled print. Boy, was I wrong! It cost $4 million, made $14 million, and certainly showed C. B. was the master showman of the movies. [The film won the 1952 Best Picture Oscar, too.]

BAWDEN: Then you made your last Paramount, *Road to Bali* [1952].

LAMOUR: It was a coproduction between Bing Crosby Productions and Hope Enterprises. I thought it the worst one so far. We'd stopped making them five years earlier. They stuck a shot of Bogey from *The African Queen* [1951] in there. Now that was funny. It was the only one made in Technicolor, and we all looked our age. In real life, I was a contented matron with kids and walking around in a sarong now embarrassed me. After my last shot I went out the side entrance. I couldn't face driving through those famous gates one last time.

Both Bing and Bob looked downcast. Time had passed them by. Martin and Lewis were the top attraction, followed by Bill Holden. Bing decamped in 1956, but he did get to make that great film *The Country Girl* before he left. Bob left in 1957. Management was very nasty in commenting how many of his later films bombed. But hey, everything changes, right?

BAWDEN: What about *Road to Hong Kong* [1962]?

LAMOUR: What about it? Another decade had lapsed. Bing and Bob were about to hit sixty. And they were competing with their younger selves on the *Late Show.* I didn't know anything about it until I read the announcement in the trades. And it hurt to have Bing infer I was too old to be the leading lady, although he was more than ten years my senior. I just put it out of my mind until Bob phoned from London all a-tizzy. He'd been getting a lot of unpleasant publicity and the film was not going well. Joan Collins was almost thirty years younger than these boys and it showed. So after some dickering I got a hefty salary for showing up in a cameo as myself and singing one song. I remember I said, "That's the plot so far? Guess I'd better hide you—from the critics."

BAWDEN: Wasn't there going to be another *Road* picture in 1977?

LAMOUR: Bob was talking about it when Bing died suddenly on a golf course in Spain. I suggested one title: *The Road Downhill.* And later Bob revived the idea, first with George Burns and then, would you believe, John Wayne?

BAWDEN: But after *Bali* you soldiered on in TV appearances?

LAMOUR: We moved to Baltimore; I became a housewife first. And I did live TV when I could fit it in. I did *Ed Sullivan, Colgate Comedy Hour, Four Star Revue, Red Skelton, Jimmy Durante.*

BAWDEN: I saw you a lot on *Hollywood Squares.*

LAMOUR: And Bob always had me on his specials. Bing? Never! In the summer I'd go out in shows with my little boys in tow. When my husband's health got bad, we moved back to Toluca Lake and we took the home next to Bob's.

BAWDEN: There were a few more movies?

LAMOUR: Ol' Jack Ford phoned me and said, "Dottie, you're finally getting to Hawaii with me." The movie was *Donovan's Reef* [1963]. Not much, but a lot of fun to make. One thing about ol' Jack: he likes to surround himself with vets like yours truly, Duke Wayne, Mike Mazurki, Cesar Romero, Dick Foran, Edgar Buchanan, Mae Marsh. It was old home week. Then I had a guest bit in *Pajama Party* [1964], which was fun. And I've lasted ever since on TV parts—*Marcus Welby, Love Boat,* you name it, and for the seasons I went out on summer stock in *Mame,* I insisted Mitch Leisen do up all my costumes at his atelier.

BAWDEN: This year [1984] you've been busy.

LAMOUR: I did *Remington Steele* and had as costar Virginia Mayo, who was at Warners all those years. She's a real scream and we both have similar reminiscences about surviving the studio system. Then I did *Hart to Hart.* I'm still kicking.

Afterword

Lamour was married to bandleader Herbie Kay from 1935 to 1939, but they divorced. During the war, Lamour met and married Army Air Force captain Bill Howard, later an advertising executive. The marriage lasted until his death in 1978. Lamour died in 1996 from a heart ailment. She was eighty-one.

Anna Lee

Interview by James Bawden and Ron Miller

Early in 1983, a seasoned member of the cast of ABC's popular daytime soap opera *General Hospital* was ushered before Queen Elizabeth II at Buckingham Palace and presented with a signal honor by Her Majesty: she was made an MBE—a Member of the Most Excellent Order of the British Empire. Her name was Anna Lee.

If you are a lifelong fan of *General Hospital,* then you know that for decades Lee played Lila Quartermaine, the most senior female member of the enormous cast of soap opera characters in that long-running serial. But if you are a film fan, you will remember Anna Lee most for a whole slew of great roles in movies, especially as the beautiful, blond British heroine in tales of great danger and adventure. A prime example: Kathy, the plucky girl who joins Alan Quartermain (Cedric Hardwicke) in the epic search for her missing father in primitive Africa in the 1937 version of H. Rider Haggard's *King Solomon's Mines.* (We've always secretly suspected ABC figured the character she played on *General Hospital* was a distant relative of Alan Quartermain!)

Altogether, Anna Lee had a remarkable career on film, from 1930s leading lady to 1980s daytime TV icon. And her personal journey was every bit as engrossing as any of the movie plots she brought to life on the screen.

Setting the Scene

Both of us conducted separate interviews with Anna Lee over the years. We have combined them for this presentation, but offer our individual memories of the circumstances of those interviews.

Bawden: I first met Anna Lee in Toronto in 1982 when she was being feted by the Toronto Film Society with showings of two of her films: *Hang-*

Anna Lee as Bronwen in John Ford's *How Green Was My Valley,* the Oscar-winning Best Picture of 1941. Courtesy of 20th Century-Fox.

men Also Die (1943) and *Bedlam* (1946). We met again in 1984 at her English-style cottage in the L.A. hills above the Sunset Strip. Another date was arranged in 1988 when I visited her on the set of her great soap opera hit *General Hospital.* By the time of my last visit in 1995, she was confined to her bed and not able to carry on much of a conversation. After she was dropped from *General Hospital* in 2003, I phoned her. Her distress was evident: she always thought she had a lifetime contract.

Miller: I was born in 1939, the year that Anna Lee came to America with her first husband, movie director Robert Stevenson. By that time she had already made a number of films that I would savor years later when I saw them as a grown-up. One was *The Man Who Changed His Mind* (1936), also known as *The Man Who Lived Again,* in which Lee was slobbered over by Boris Karloff a decade before he locked her up in his asylum in *Bedlam.*

Yet another favorite from that period was the amazing *Non-stop New York* (1937), in which Lee plays a British girl who witnessed a murder during an earlier visit to America and is the only one who can prove the accused murder suspect innocent. In this Hitchcock-style thriller, she's targeted for death while flying to New York for the trial aboard a bizarre propeller superplane of the future that was like the HMS *Titanic* of the air!

My chance to finally meet Anna Lee came in the summer of 1983, long after her glory days in movies were over and she was a fixture in the cast of *General Hospital.* Lee was still flushed with pride over her MBE honor, and we chatted for several hours in her dressing room on the set of the soap opera at the Sunset Gower studios. Lee was sixty-nine and living in Beverly Hills with her third husband, the novelist Robert Nathan. She was a warm, gracious, and charming lady.

The Interview

Bawden: How did you get started in acting?

Lee: I was born in Kent [in 1913], the daughter of a very proper rector. My real name is Joanna Boniface Winnifrith. I loved dressing up and cavorting around. I was the town extrovert and, aged seventeen, I got Papa to enroll me in London's prestigious Central School of Speech Training, located at the Royal Albert Hall. My teacher was the famed Elsie Fogarty, who also taught Larry Olivier and Johnny Gielgud. I assumed my future would be on the London stage. And soon I was touring in productions of *Jane Eyre* and *The Constant Nymph* in 1931–1932.

A school chum told me about the "quota quickies," which paid good money and were shot out in the suburbs. I could get as much as £5 a day, and I was hooked. But that ruined me at school. I was allowed to finish out my term and I left with my new best friend, Queenie Thompson, who later changed her name to Merle Oberon. She was so poor she'd come over to my place to take a bath. Her digs had no washroom.

Bawden: I just saw you in a 1932 flick, *His Lordship.*

LEE: I had a few days' work on it. My big break came the next year with *Bitter Sweet*, starring Anna Neagle. I had a dress with a plunging neckline. Noël Coward looked at the dailies and said he could see the white cliffs of Dover and I felt devastated. If you're blind, you'll miss me in that one.

BAWDEN: *First a Girl* [1935] had your first supporting role.

LEE: A Jessie Matthews vehicle. It was later remade as *Victor/Victoria*. She'd spend weeks rehearsing for the dance numbers and was always a nervous frazzle. In 1974, she came to L.A. for a concert and was mobbed by fans. I met her for tea. [She was] older, haggard, and very bitter about the way the British business had dumped her.

BAWDEN: Why did you change your name?

LEE: I was told Joan Winnifrith was too stuffy. Orientalism was in so I changed it to Anne Lee. I should have used Leigh because when Anna May Wong came to the studio, she wanted to meet her kinsman!

MILLER: Along the way, something really important happened: You met a movie director named Robert Stevenson.

LEE: We met and fell in love while I was acting in *The Camels Are Coming* [1934], an action adventure picture he was filming on location in Egypt. We were married in 1936.

BAWDEN: Right away he moved you into a very important role.

LEE: He put me into a big hit in 1937—*King Solomon's Mines*. I stayed in London and an extra did my scenes in Africa. I acted in front of transparencies, I must confess. And of course we had the charismatic Paul Robeson.

BAWDEN: You had become a British star. Name some of the pictures you were getting as a leading lady.

LEE: I adored making *The Man Who Changed His Mind* with dear Boris Karloff. He refused to do his own stunts, the mark of a true Hollywood star. Then I made *Non-stop New York*. The title says it all. Then came *Four Just Men* [1939], a very timely film about British heroes fighting the forces of Nazism.

MILLER: Were you keen on going to Hollywood to make movies?

LEE: I hadn't the slightest desire to come to Hollywood. I was quite happy doing pictures in England. But Bob was put under contract by American producer David O. Selznick to make a series of films for him in the U.S. I'd just given birth to our daughter, Venetia Stevenson, and I'd already turned down two Hollywood contracts. But I agreed to take a three-month holiday and come over to America with Bob.

BAWDEN: England was also facing imminent war with Nazi Germany. How did that affect your plans?

LEE: Bob was a conscientious war objector. I was not. I didn't know what to do, so I phoned 10 Downing Street. I'm convinced I spoke to Prime Minister Neville Chamberlain, who said, "Little lady, there will be no war." So I sailed in August to be with my husband and war came the next month and I was stranded in America for the duration. I was given the lowest priority in getting back and I never did. The British consul advised me to stay put in L.A. to help the propaganda effort, which I did.

MILLER: How were you treated when you arrived in America?

LEE: Mr. Selznick's staff met us at the dock in New York, then escorted us on board the luxury *Super Chief* for the rail journey west. When we arrived in Hollywood, we were shown to our private apartment at the Garden of Allah Hotel. On our first night, Mr. Selznick invited us to his home, where we watched a rough cut of his new movie, *Gone with the Wind.* Clark Gable and his ladylove, Carole Lombard, were there, too. It was just a fascinating evening, a lovely way to start off.

BAWDEN: Your first American-made film was *Life with Caroline,* but the first to be shown in theaters was *Seven Sinners* [1940].

LEE: That's right. There were many problems with *Life with Caroline* [1941] and we had to do retakes. On *Seven Sinners,* Marlene Dietrich was the boss. She took one look at me on my first day and stated, "I vill not vork vit anutter blonde." So I had to go to the beauty shop and get my hair dyed mud brown. I couldn't help but like the director of *Seven Sinners,* Tay Garnett, for the way he handled her and the enormous amount of energy he put into every setup. It certainly did not hurt to start off with a box office smash.

Seven Sinners was a parody of those dreadful South Seas adventures that starred Dottie Lamour around that time. But Marlene had no humor. She'd just joined Universal and selected John Wayne as her leading man. According to [producer] Joe Pasternak, she first spotted the Duke in the commissary and shouted, "Mommy wants that for Christmas." John stayed as far away from her as possible. There were lots of characters in it, like Andy Devine, and don't forget I run off with the Duke at the end of the picture.

BAWDEN: Then *My Life with Caroline* was released.

LEE: Botched! It was a very weak comedy and I felt off kilter as this dizzy blonde. I was completely at sea, didn't understand her. It was a Jean

Arthur part. Instead they got me. Ronnie Colman was very kind and sympathetic. But the idea he'd chase after me was ridiculous. And there was a problem with director Lewis Milestone. He simply did not understand comedy. Scenes went on for too long. Ronnie was the soul of patience. He should have objected. Instead he'd whisper "Courage!" before each and every take.

BAWDEN: How did you get the plum part of Bronwen in *How Green Was My Valley* [1941]?

LEE: I tested for [director] Willie Wyler. He said I was second choice after Greer Garson. Then her MGM career took over and MGM asked too much for her. So I was in. Months went by as the Fox crews meticulously re-created the Welsh village up the hill at the Fox ranch. Finally, Willie was recalled by Sam Goldwyn to direct *The Little Foxes.* John Ford came in and I was very scared of him. A rough character. I had heard he despised the English, so I invented an Irish grandfather and told tales to him that were simply not true.

Our picture is anything but Welsh. It stars a Canadian [Walter Pidgeon], some Irish [Maureen O'Hara, Sara Allgood], English [Roddy McDowall], and Scottish [Donald Crisp]. I think Rhys Williams was the only genuine Welsh performer. What saved it was the enormous preparation time Willie had poured into it, mixed with Ford's sentimentality.

I found Ford to be a very curmudgeonly taskmaster, but always very fair. He always knew what he wanted in a scene. He never overshot. God help you if you didn't deliver what he wanted. And he liked me enough that I finally told him my Irish grandfather was fictional. He roared over that one. We've been close friends ever since. He used me a lot over the next few decades.

MILLER: Altogether, you made eight films with John Ford, so that makes you a real authority on his directing style. Could you be a little more specific about how he operated?

LEE: He didn't direct you. He never told you what to do. He would talk to you, mostly about something completely different, and you would find yourself doing the right thing. It was really very spooky—what he did.

MILLER: Your most dramatic scene in *How Green Was My Valley* is when Bronwen reacts to the news that her husband has died in a mine disaster. The scene calls for her to take a fall. Is it true that, after doing that scene, you suffered a miscarriage and lost one of the twin babies you were carrying?

LEE: Yes—and Ford was crushed. He didn't know I was pregnant. He thought it was his fault. He sent me to the doctor who had delivered his own children. He was very, very sweet to me. After that, on every picture I did with him, Ford would assemble the whole cast and crew before shooting started and ask me if I was pregnant. Seven years later, when I was filming *Fort Apache* with Ford, I collapsed in 90-plus heat. The next thing I knew, I was in John Wayne's arms, being carried down to my dressing room and Ford was leaning over me, saying, "Are you pregnant, Anna?"

BAWDEN: Despite so many fine roles, you never became a top star like Greer Garson. Any regrets?

LEE: Of course! Madeleine Carroll was reigning at Paramount, dear Greer at MGM. That left me RKO and Republic! Plus I had quite a brood to look after—five children—and she never had children. You can't play the Hollywood star to the hilt with so many egotistical youngsters. I spent much of 1943 touring with a USO troupe headed by Jack Benny. With Jack I logged fifty-six thousand miles of flying across Africa and we did a skit called *Five Jerks to Cairo*. I desperately wanted to get home but I had no priority.

BAWDEN: You were part of the Hollywood British colony and its busy wartime fund-raising movement?

LEE: We certainly hated the German colony of expats. And they hated us! Dame May Whitty and Sir C. Aubrey Smith hosted gigantic teas to raise funds. Ronnie Colman had all-star cricket in Victoria, British Columbia, to raise dough. There were more British actors in Hollywood than in England, and many were there to evade the call-up. Older stars suddenly sprouted gray sideburns! Nigel Bruce would deposit one-way tickets in their letterboxes with letters urging the quitters to return home. I certainly tried to, but the British consul said stay put, make money, send that home.

MILLER: It sounds as if you and your husband had very different attitudes about your role in the war effort.

LEE: I couldn't get a visa for returning to England. The U.S. policy then was to keep British women with children out of the war zone. I tried to evade the rules by moving to San Francisco and enlisting as a Red Cross volunteer for service in England. They told me I could only go if I obtained my husband's permission. Bob refused to give me clearance to go. Looking back, that probably was the beginning of the end for our marriage.

MILLER: I know your husband was a pacifist, although he eventually served in the U.S. armed forces, but his career also was booming in Hollywood.

Anna Lee with John Wayne in *Flying Tigers* (1942). Courtesy of Republic Pictures.

LEE: Yes, he getting some very good assignments, starting with *Tom Brown's School Days* [1940], the 1941 remake of *Back Street,* and *Jane Eyre* [1944] with Orson Welles, Joan Fontaine, and two new child stars, Margaret O'Brien and Elizabeth Taylor.

MILLER: Selznick was famous for cashing in on the stars he had under contract by loaning them out to other studios. Did that work against you after the one good loan-out to Fox for *How Green Was My Valley*?

LEE: I found myself at RKO for the next three years, mostly taking suspensions because I didn't like the things they were offering me.

BAWDEN: You made *Flying Tigers* [1942] at Republic.

LEE: Even then it was hardly considered a top feature. But I got to know the Duke, who was very resentful he couldn't go into the real war. Had a number of children and a wife. But he was making peanuts compared to Coop or Gable. He really wanted to be considered a good actor. To me Big John was terrific. I mean, did you ever see Larry Olivier in a western? He was, at thirty-five, one of the best-looking men in movies, and he knew it. The fact is he was irreplaceable.

BAWDEN: Then came a real anti-Nazi film—*Hangmen Also Die* [1943]?

LEE: It very accurately depicted life inside the Nazi regime. Director Fritz Lang was dramatizing the assassination of Gestapo head Reinhard Heydrich. Let me just say it was a horror to make. I'd been warned about Lang in advance. Behind his back the crew called him the Prussian, but he really was virulently anti-Nazi. But he made it plain from the beginning he did not want me.

One example: I had a simple piece of business where I had to smash my hand through a glass pane. Ordinarily, candy glass would have been used, but Fritz insisted on the real thing. I did it perfectly on the first take. He grimaced and asked for a second. There were mumblings from the crew. This time I cut myself rather badly and the blood just flowed. He ran over and lapped up the blood.

Another story: I wasn't there at the time, but he was punched out by

Anna Lee with Brian Donlevy in *Hangmen Also Die* (1943). Courtesy of United Artists.

one of the crew he started berating for not obeying his instructions. Cinematographer Jimmy Wong Howe said the cast and crew simply went about their business while Fritz lay unconscious on the floor. Many years later at a soiree at Joan Bennett's home, I accidentally bumped into him and he told he'd never forgive me for the way I was standoffish. In his mind I was the villain!

MILLER: You've often referred to Fritz Lang as "a sadist." Did he do other things that personally tormented you?

LEE: He would come on the set in these Prussian boots, wearing white gloves, and stamp his foot. He always made me walk barefoot because he said I was too tall. Then he would crunch down on my feet. His great object, you see, was to make me cry. But, being British, I wouldn't. He never got to me, even though he did unbelievable things.

BAWDEN: Tell me about working with the great Paul Muni in *Commandos Strike at Dawn* [1943], which you filmed in British Columbia.

LEE: He was a pain and a strain! It was supposed to be Norway. The B.C. coastal scenery was a perfect match. His wife, Bella, sat right out of camera range, and after every shot she had to wink or we'd do it again. She also did not like her Paul getting too close to his leading lady. We came back to L.A. and shot stills at Columbia in silhouette against the sky. Bella wasn't there that day and Paul suddenly became carefree and quite silly. He said at one point, "Oh, you English girls are so reserved—like ice."

BAWDEN: What about George Sanders in *Summer Storm* [1944]?

LEE: We had Linda Darnell as our leading leady. *Orchidaceous* is the right word for her. Couldn't act at all, though. George loved being nasty to every single individual. An idle comment would bring a tongue-lashing. He certainly was not nice to Linda, who desperately needed praise. When, decades later, I read the biography of him by Brian Aherne, I saw where that nastiness came from. George had been born in Russia and his whole life was a tale of make-believe. He had it in for all of us.

BAWDEN: Then came a grand reunion with Boris Karloff for *Bedlam*.

LEE: He greeted me like a long-lost friend. He certainly never regarded *Bedlam* as just another horror outing. The design was precise, the screenplay by Val Lewton exceptional. He used the pseudonym Carlos Keith. The sets were suggested by William Hogarth engravings, and this was the most expensive of Val's RKO horror outings. The studio took one look and lost heart and just released it without fanfare. It broke my heart. It lost money. The asylum was a redressed set. It had been the church in *The*

Bells of St Mary's [1945]—but we never did meet Bing [Crosby] or Ingrid [Bergman]!

BAWDEN: You had a small part in *The Ghost and Mrs. Muir* [1947].

LEE: But I took home my biggest pay packet. I was paid per week. But filming was suspended for weeks at a time because of the lingering illness of Gene Tierney. I had to be on call because my scenes had only just started. I played George Sanders's wife! But, thankfully, had no scenes with him, which was heaven. It's a film people have taken to and still ask me about. We were eighty-five days in production, compared to the next one, *High Conquest* [1947], I made at Monogram in twenty-one days!

BAWDEN: John Ford gave you a good part in *Fort Apache* [1948].

LEE: He said, "Anna, you are about to join the Jack Ford stock company. So watch yourself, girlie!" And no more phony Irish grandfathers either! I toddled on set and he bellowed, "Get rid of that blond hair. Won't do for frontier gals!" But I kept my accent because a lot of these wives were from Britain. I loved those assignments as long as Ford wasn't picking on me, as he sometimes did. I had my scenes with Shirley Temple and three decades later I met her again and asked if she remembered her Auntie Em? And she laughingly said, "You can't fool me! You're Lila Quartermaine from *General Hospital!*"

MILLER: You've described two of Hollywood's most iconic movie stars—John Wayne and Boris Karloff—who were famous for their screen images—the rough, tough cowboy for Wayne, the sinister menace for Karloff. Did either of them surprise you with behavior that rattled their screen images?

LEE: John Wayne was such a nice man, but he was always a little shy with women, particularly blondes. As for Boris, he was a lovely man. We used to have great fun reciting poetry to each other.

MILLER: Even though you were frustrated in your efforts to go back to England and help the war effort there, you did help the U.S. by raising funds for the war and entertaining the troops through the USO. Along the way, you met one of our most famous military leaders, General George S. Patton.

LEE: That was on a USO tour in Sicily. Most of the servicemen I'd met so far were dirty and disheveled, but here he was—all clean, wearing his polished pistols, and looking like he'd just stepped out of a magazine. All he wanted to talk about was the wounded men in hospitals. He became very emotional and started crying. It was very embarrassing.

MILLER: After the war ended, your marriage also hit the skids.

LEE: I discovered my husband had been cheating on me and the marriage came to an abrupt end. [Robert Stevenson found a nearly permanent home at Walt Disney Studios, where he directed some of Disney's biggest hits, including *Mary Poppins,* for which he earned an Oscar nomination, *Old Yeller, The Shaggy Dog, The Love Bug,* and *Bedknobs and Broomsticks.*]

BAWDEN: Your career changed in 1950.

LEE: To say the least! The market in pictures dried right up. I spent more of my time in New York, acting on live TV, than I did doing anything in L.A. Bob Montgomery said I could do any kind of part, and used me a lot on his series [*Robert Montgomery Presents*]. I remember the first one was *The Citadel* [1950]. Then there was *The Ford Theater Hour.* In 1951, I was in a darned good presentation of *Peter Ibbetson* opposite Richard Greene. On one of them I had Angela Lansbury as acting partner. She was always promising me something on *Murder, She Wrote,* but the show was cancelled and she never delivered. I did *Monsieur Beaucaire* in 1951 on *Pulitzer Prize Playhouse* with Vinnie Price and Audrey Meadows.

MILLER: In 1951, you also costarred in the daytime series *A Date with Judy,* the TV version of the hit radio show.

LEE: I played Judy's mom. The show went on live at 10 a.m., which meant we had to start rehearsal at 3 a.m. It was live, which was quite frightening at times.

MILLER: Can you remember any of the things that happened because you were on live TV?

LEE: I remember one *Kraft* show when I literally didn't have time to put on another shoe. So I played the whole scene with one high heel on and one off. You would just dive into the set, falling over cables and everything. It was very exciting and I adored it. I did a lot of episodes of *The Charles Farrell Show* in 1956. I kept busy. Strangest assignment was dubbing the voice of Patricia Morison in *Song without End* [1960]. She was considered to speak too American-sounding.

MILLER: Tell about your second marriage and the impact it had on your career.

LEE: My new husband was George Stafford, a B-17 pilot I met when he flew our USO troupe around Europe during the war. He had a dream of his own to fulfill when he left the service: he wanted to run a cattle ranch in Montana.

MILLER: I guess we're talking major cultural shock: a fine British lady who had become a world-famous movie star, suddenly transported to the American outback, far from civilization.

LEE: We moved to a cattle ranch that was sixteen thousand feet up and forty miles away from the nearest place where you could buy a tube of toothpaste. I'd always thought it would be fun to have a place where you could relax away from things, but this was a little too much. I mean, there were no telephones, no electricity, no nothing. When I found I was pregnant with my second child, I didn't know what to do. I drove into Butte to see a doctor, told him the roads would be impassable when winter came, and asked what I should do. So he gave me a pamphlet on how to deliver my own baby. I read it, and it said to spread old newspapers on the floor for the "birthing activity." That did it for me! I decided if my baby couldn't be delivered on the *London Times,* that was enough for me. I left the next morning and came back to California.

MILLER: You divorced Stafford in 1964 and then you tried to resume your movie career?

LEE: I had a baby boy and no child support or alimony. I hit my all-time low. There was no work for me in Hollywood, and I was forced to go to work in a shop as a salesclerk. I dreaded it any time an old Hollywood friend would come into the store and see me.

MILLER: How did you finally get out of that fix?

LEE: One of those humiliating moments turned out to be a big break for me. [Actress] Joanne Dru came into the shop and recognized me. She urged me to get back into acting and invited me to a party she was hosting at her home for John Ford's daughter. I went to the party and Ford was there. He immediately promised to put me back to work in his pictures.

MILLER: Didn't you get another "big break" from that same party?

LEE: Yes, you could say so. I met novelist Robert Nathan, who was recently widowed. We liked each other and that started a romance. [Nathan had written several popular novels, two of which had been turned into hit movies—*The Bishop's Wife* and *Portrait of Jennie.* Nathan and Lee were married in 1970. She was his seventh wife, but the marriage was a happy one that lasted until his death in 1985.]

BAWDEN: John Ford was a man of his word and put you back to work.

LEE: Indeed he did! I went back to London to make *Gideon's Day* in 1957, a day in the life of a British detective played by Jack Hawkins. And I had a glorious reunion with all my old leading men at the Dorchester hotel: John Loder, Frank Lawton, Griffith Jones. Then Mr. Ford gave me a choice character part in *The Last Hurrah* in 1958. I was Gert Minihan. I remember that name. The very next year I was Mrs. Buford in *The Horse Soldiers* [1959]. The Duke spotted me on the set my first day and picked me up and carried me around. Mr. Ford had a part for me in *Donovan's Reef* [1963], but I was busy with *Whatever Happened to Baby Jane?* so I sent my youngest son Jeffrey in my place and he was treated fine. And lastly I got a juicy bit in *Seven Women* [1967]. Days after we started, our star Pat Neal was felled by a stroke and had to be hurriedly replaced by Anne Bancroft. It never seemed the same after that.

BAWDEN: Tell me about *Whatever Happened to Baby Jane?* [1962].

LEE: I was the nosy neighbor. My dressing room was between those of Bette Davis and Joan Crawford. I could feel all those evil vibes slipping through the doors. Bette was quite nice to me because her chunky daughter, B.D., was playing my daughter. I'm never standing next to B.D. because of her girth and tallness.

With Joan there was a polite distance. Cases of Pepsi arrived daily for the crew. I had no scenes with her except for the bit where she tries to toss down a note from her bedroom window. But it is true Joan weighed herself down with jockey weights when Bette had to drag her across the floor. And later Bette did kick at Joan's face. It was all quite tense, I can tell you. I was never more shocked when B.D. wrote that tell-all book about life with Bette. That wasn't the Bette I saw cooing over her daughter's every screen move.

BAWDEN: Then came your biggest-ever movie.

LEE: *The Sound of Music* [1965]. So what if my part was tiny! I got noticed. It was heavenly. I simply wanted to be a part of a monster hit. But production dragged on for so long I had to give up another nun part on *The Singing Nun.*

BAWDEN: Then came your soap opera adventure.

LEE: I was asked in 1976 to play Lila Quartermaine. I wasn't working much, so I thought why not try it for six months? I've been there ever since. If I want to do something else, they'll write me out. It's like working in rep. There's a real family of dedicated actors. But it's ironical—my family in England have never seen it. It never played over there. There are no retakes. It's first time for everyone. The scripts are huge, but I learn them and forget the next day. When I had back problems and went into a chair, I thought, "This is it!" But they wrote it into the story and I got many letters from shut-ins, saying I gave them courage. I still get fan mail, mostly from people who think I've been dead a long time.

Anna Lee as Lila Quartermaine in ABC's *General Hospital*. Courtesy of ABC.

So I shall continue. The British Raj is dead, but I still run my Union Jack outside my cottage and I still serve crumpets and tea. I also have a life of movie memories. I'll go on until they shoot me.

Afterword

Anna Lee's beautiful daughter, Venetia Stevenson, became an actress, working in pictures from *Darby's Rangers* (1957) on, then shifting to the production side of the business. Venetia was married to actor/dancer Russ Tamblyn and then to Don Everly of rock's Everly Brothers. Anna's granddaughter, Erin Everly, is the ex-wife of rocker Axl Rose of Guns N' Roses. Her son by George Stafford also became an actor, known as Jeffrey Byron.

Anna Lee died on May 14, 2004, from pneumonia. She was ninety-one.

Dorothy McGuire

Interview by Ron Miller

Stage-trained actress Dorothy McGuire was one of the most interesting leading ladies of the 1940s and 1950s, but she didn't build a large cult following of fans despite a solid legacy of truly memorable screen performances. Perhaps that's due to her general aversion to publicity and a life lived without a breath of scandal or notoriety. (She even played the Virgin Mary in George Stevens's 1965 *The Greatest Story Ever Told.*)

Yet her work from the 1940s through the 1950s bears serious comparison to that of any other actress of her era. Any star whose credits include Elia Kazan's *A Tree Grows in Brooklyn* (1945) and *Gentleman's Agreement* (1947), Robert Siodmak's *The Spiral Staircase* (1946), Jean Negulesco's *Three Coins in the Fountain* (1954), William Wyler's *Friendly Persuasion* (1956), Robert Stevenson's *Old Yeller* (1957), Delmer Daves's *A Summer Place* (1959), and Delbert Mann's *Dark at the Top of the Stairs* (1960) surely had lots to brag about in her twilight years. Clearly, she was extremely versatile, bringing style and grace to every performance.

Setting the Scene

Dorothy McGuire's disdain for publicity always brings a smile to my face because I remember how severely I was warned about that subject when she agreed to do an interview with me in 1983 in connection with the ABC TV movie *Ghost Dancing.* The publicist insisted, "Don't ask her about anything except the new movie. She hates talking about the past. If you try asking her about the 'good old days,' she may get up and walk out on you!"

Well, I certainly didn't want that to happen, yet . . . how could I ignore those "good old days," which included so many movie classics? So here's what I resolved to do: concentrate hard on getting the bare essentials about *Ghost Dancing,* then damn the torpedoes and go full speed ahead into all

Dorothy McGuire, circa 1945. James Bawden collection.

the really good stuff. If she bolted on me, then I'd still have enough for a story on the current project, even if she dumped her soup over my head when I asked about her earlier work.

It turned out to be a pretty decent plan. McGuire issued no new rules when she arrived for our luncheon date at the Beverly Wilshire Hotel in

Beverly Hills, so I hot-footed it through the *Ghost Dancing* questions, then waltzed her right down memory lane without giving her a chance to catch her breath.

If she knew she'd been scammed, she didn't let on. McGuire turned out to be a relaxed and friendly lunch companion, still a handsome woman with genuine class. My guess is she did like to talk about the earlier days—as long as the questions were fair ones. She also seemed to appreciate the fact that I was actually knowledgeable about what she'd accomplished in her career.

The Interview

MILLER: From what I've read about the beginnings of your acting career, I'd say there was a blessing on you from the start.

MCGUIRE: Maybe so. I had such extraordinary breaks—from the moment I entered the theater. I made my stage debut at age thirteen at the Omaha Community Playhouse in James Barrie's *A Kiss of Cinderella.* My leading man was the young Henry Fonda!

MILLER: I'm guessing the breaks continued when you finally headed for New York and the Broadway stage.

MCGUIRE: I arrived on Broadway in 1938 and began as the understudy to Martha Scott for the role of Emily in the original production of Thornton Wilder's *Our Town.* When Martha was signed to star in the movie version, I took over for her.

MILLER: Getting to play the leading female role in a play destined to become an American drama classic was certainly a big career plus for a young actress. So that made you a pretty hot property in theater?

MCGUIRE: It certainly led to my getting the title role in *Claudia,* the play based on Rose Franken's novel and stories about a young woman who marries and starts learning about adult life in the 1940s. That was in 1941. The producers had rejected 208 other actresses before picking me.

MILLER: I guess their faith in you was justified when you won the New York Drama Critics Circle award for your performance.

MCGUIRE: I think it also justified Leland Hayward's faith in me. [Hayward, her agent, was the most influential Broadway agent at the time.]

MILLER: With Leland Hayward going to bat for you, you were in good shape for theater work—and you had a pretty good spokesman for your movie career, too, didn't you?

McGuire: If you mean David O. Selznick, you're right. He signed me to a movie contract after *Claudia* became a Broadway hit, and he was then the most successful producer in Hollywood after *Gone with the Wind* and *Rebecca* had won back-to-back Best Picture Oscars.

Miller: What did he have in mind for your movie debut?

McGuire: He really didn't have anything for me and, as it turned out, I never made a movie with him! But he decided to make some money off me by loaning me out to other studios, who did have things they wanted me to do. I think he needed to pay off some of the enormous sums he spent on *Gone with the Wind* and that was one way to do it.

Miller: Did you resent that?

McGuire: No. That turned out to be perfectly okay. David watched over what scripts were sent to me and things like that. He was a man of great integrity.

Miller: Where did he send you first?

McGuire: Fox and RKO. They both were making good pictures in those days. 20th Century-Fox had the movie rights to *Claudia,* so they had me reprise my stage role, playing opposite Robert Young as my husband, David.

Miller: *Claudia* [1943] turned out to be a big hit for Fox, especially among women who identified with the young wife as she learns how to grow up at the same time she's learning how to be a wife. It was such a hit that they immediately decided to continue the story in a sequel, *Claudia and David* [1946]. That was a phenomenal start for a young actress with no film experience.

McGuire: I took it all for granted, I'm sorry to say. I thought it was just the way it is.

Miller: While the sequel was being written, Fox put you into another prestige picture, the film version of Betty Smith's best seller *A Tree Grows in Brooklyn.* Your reaction?

McGuire: I was terrified. I didn't think I'd be convincing in the challenging role of teenage star Peggy Ann Garner's pregnant mother. At that exact moment in my life, I'd never had a child. I wasn't quite sure about the whole mechanism, about what really happened to you. Being a very serious-type actress, I was very upset by this.

Miller: Your director was Elia Kazan, who was making his debut as a movie director after years on the stage as an actor and director. Did you get much help from him?

McGuire: I went to him and told him I had no such experiences in life and didn't know where to get the emotions I'd need. He was very patient with me and let me ramble on about my misgivings and anxieties. What he did, in a sense, was lock up all this intensity inside me so it wouldn't be dissipated. He was marvelous. There are intangible things about actors like that which he just instinctively knew.

Miller: The film was a big success and put both you and Kazan on the map as the hot new prospects in Hollywood. James Dunn, who played your alcoholic husband, won the Supporting Actor Oscar and Peggy Ann Garner won a special Oscar as best child actress of 1945. That's when RKO stepped up with another wonderful role for you.

McGuire: They gave me the part of the mute servant girl who's menaced by a serial killer in *The Spiral Staircase.*

Miller: That was a real acting challenge because you had to play virtually the entire film in pantomime. How did that go?

McGuire: Robert Siodmak was a brilliant director and he lifted the film out of the ordinary. You know those creepy close-ups where we just see the eye of the strangler, watching me? That was Robert's eye! He was that vain!

Miller: Then Fox reteamed you with director Elia Kazan and gave you the leading lady role in *Gentleman's Agreement,* the film version of Laura Z. Hobson's best seller about a journalist [Gregory Peck] who poses as a Jew to write about anti-Semitism in America. Your role, as the girl he's planning to marry, wasn't completely likeable.

McGuire: She has to search her own soul for signs of anti-Semitism. It wasn't a cut-and-dried part. It required a lot of internalizing.

Miller: You were rewarded with a Best Actress Oscar nomination.

McGuire: But Loretta Young won it for *The Farmer's Daughter.* Kazan won the Oscar for Best Director and Celeste Holm for Supporting Actress. But it was still an honor to be the leading lady in the film that won Best Picture of 1947!

Miller: I noticed that you never were asked to play an overtly sexy or seductive woman, but instead were almost always cast as reserved, intelligent, refined women.

McGuire: There were a few exceptions. RKO cast me as a married woman who has an affair with a younger man in *Till the End of Time* [1946]. That was my first "older lady." Would you believe I was supposed to be a whole four years older than the young man? There's a comment on the period!

Dorothy McGuire with Gregory Peck in Elia Kazan's *Gentleman's Agreement,* the Oscar-winning Best Picture of 1947. Courtesy of 20th Century-Fox.

MILLER: But you did wind up playing quite a few mother roles. How did that go over with you?

MCGUIRE: I rebelled against that. I didn't want to be a mother forever.

MILLER: I guess you got your wish, getting to play a mature career girl in *Three Coins in the Fountain* on location in Rome.

MCGUIRE: That was nice. I love to work on location. My husband and I traveled a lot, so I've seen most of this world we live in—and I'm glad.

Dorothy McGuire in her most famous "mom" role, with Tommy Kirk in Disney's 1957 *Old Yeller.* Courtesy of the Walt Disney Corp. and NBC.

MILLER: But after *Friendly Persuasion,* in which you played a strong-willed Quaker mother on the frontier, and *Old Yeller,* the quintessential Disney mom role, I guess you were permanently bedded down in the world of "nice."

MCGUIRE: I'm not all that bothered by it. I prefer playing "good" women.

MILLER: I'm told that you've never been a temperamental actress and that you not only get to know all the crew people on your pictures, but you also tend to brag about their accomplishments.

McGuire: I also learn all my lines before shooting starts. It's an old work habit. If the director tells me to stand on my head, I'll be able to do it and still know my lines.

Miller: Now that you're older, you seem to be getting more variety in your roles and not always "nice" ladies. In this new TV role in *Ghost Dancing,* for instance, you play a weather-beaten, cantankerous woman who lights up a couple of dynamite sticks and blows up a city water system that's destroying her farm by draining it dry. It doesn't seem like the Dorothy McGuire we all know.

McGuire: I had to deprogram after that one. The character does sort of get inside you. My friends didn't know what I was up to, walking around saying things like, "Spit it out, honey!" I was talking like my character.

Miller: Well, I'm happy to say, sitting here with you, that you don't seem anything like that little old lady in the movie.

McGuire: Listen, honey, there are some people who probably think of me as a little old lady—and I'm afraid there's nothing you can do about it.

Afterword

Our interview finally ended when the waiter brought our lunches. "Turn off your recorder," she told me. "Now we're going to eat." Which is what we did, all right, just chatting about nothing in particular from then on. With the recorder off, Dorothy McGuire was just a handsome middle-aged lady having lunch with a friend in Beverly Hills. And, except when I play one of her films for a reminder of how good she was on-screen, that's the way I'll always remember her, too.

McGuire was married for thirty-five years to *Life* magazine photographer John Swope and had two children with him. Her last film role was in a 1990 TV movie *The Last Best Year,* and she spent the last decade of her life in retirement. She died of cardiac arrest in 2001, just a few days after the September 11 terrorist attack on the World Trade Center, so there was little news space devoted to her death. She was eighty-five.

Maureen O'Hara

Interview by Ron Miller

Maureen O'Hara was still a teenager when she came to America from her native Ireland to star in *The Hunchback of Notre Dame* (1939). She was the film's leading lady, and she almost never played a role in either movies or television during the next sixty-plus years in which she wasn't the leading lady. The tall redhead was one of the screen's strongest female personas, the equal to every male action hero with whom she ever shared the screen, including her frequent costar John Wayne.

Born Maureen FitzSimons in a suburb of Dublin, she was raised to be a stage actress and trained in drama, music, and dance from the age of six. Still, she also attended business school and became a proficient bookkeeper and typist. Though her first screen test did not immediately lead to a role in a movie, actor Charles Laughton saw it and decided she had the makings of a movie star. After playing a one-line bit in a 1938 Irish film, she was cast in *My Irish Molly,* a musical, at Laughton's suggestion, but then played her first leading role opposite Laughton in 1939's *Jamaica Inn,* director Alfred Hitchcock's last British film before he came to America.

Laughton arranged for O'Hara's voyage to America and gave her the much sought-after role of the Gypsy girl Esmeralda in *The Hunchback of Notre Dame,* in which he played the title role. Her reception was so good that she went on from there as a full-fledged movie star.

O'Hara was married in her teens to writer-producer George H. Brown, but the marriage was annulled in 1941. She married film director William Houston Price in 1941, but divorced him in 1953. Her third marriage was in 1968 to Brigadier General Charles F. Blair Jr., an aviation pioneer and former chief pilot at Pan Am Airways. He died in an air crash in 1978.

Long off the movie screen, O'Hara returned to films in 1991's *Only the Lonely* to costar with comedian John Candy. Her last screen appearance was in the 2000 TV movie *The Last Dance.*

Maureen O'Hara. Ron Miller collection.

Setting the Scene

Maureen O'Hara met with TV reporters in 1998 in connection with her TV movie *Cab to Canada.* She agreed to a private interview with me later that day. She was a warm and good-natured woman with a rich memory, brimming with anecdotes about some of her favorite people in a long movie career.

The Interview

MILLER: I can't believe the stories I've heard about what a disastrous first screen test you had.

O'HARA: Well, I thought it was absolutely awful. I was with the Abbey Theatre when I was asked to go to England for the test. I couldn't wait to get back to Ireland because I was cast in a play and was afraid I was going to lose the part. I was only a teenager, but they put me in a gold lamé gown with batwing sleeves and put Mata Hari makeup on me. I thought, "Oh, God!" The test consisted of me going into a room, picking up a phone, putting it down—and doing it over and over. I thought, if this is the movies, then I don't want anything to do with them.

MILLER: But that wasn't the end of it?

O'HARA: No, I had an agent—you had one from the time you were born!—and he told me that, before I went back home, he wanted me to meet somebody. It turned out to be Charles Laughton and Erich Pommer, the head of Ufa films in Germany. Laughton gave me a script and had me read out of it, but being a smart-assed teenager and so cocky and sure of myself, I said, "I-I-I'm terribly sorry, but I can't read something I know nothing about. I'd be happy to take the script and come back and read it for you."

"No, no, that's all right," they said.

We shook hands and I went onto the boat—my mother was with me—and by the time we arrived back at the house, there was a seven-year contract waiting for me.

MILLER: Let's talk a bit about your first two screen appearances and then *Jamaica Inn.*

O'HARA: In *Kicking the Moon Around* [1938], I just put my head around a door and said, "You're wanted on the phone." They put it in the picture, but there was really no part. I never saw *My Irish Molly* and don't know anything about it. I'd already been cast in *Jamaica Inn*, but Pommer said I had no film experience, so they loaned me to this company and it was awful. It was done under my real name—Maureen FitzSimons—so I guess they thought nobody would know it was me.

MILLER: And how about *Jamaica Inn*?

O'HARA: Hitchcock was half Irish, you know. He was a magnificent director. He taught me how to use your breath—how to hold it in, when to let it out—for dramatic purposes. His daughter [Patricia] and I were both very young, and the biggest thrill for us was to get a ride on the camera dolly. So the crew would give us a ride across the stage and back again.

MILLER: Were you actually under personal contract to Charles Laughton?

O'HARA: Yes. He's the one who changed my name to O'Hara. He said I could either be O'Mara or O'Hara. But I had a teacher at school that I couldn't stand whose name was O'Mara, so I said no way to that name.

MILLER: Hitchcock always spoke highly of you. Why didn't he use you again?

O'HARA: He wanted to use me right away in his first American film because he said he wanted to have someone he'd worked with before. [Hitchcock was going to make a film about the *Titanic* sinking, but it was never made. He went on to make *Rebecca* as his first U.S. film.] But I was making *Hunchback of Notre Dame* and the director, William Dieterle, wouldn't hurry up so I could be free to work with Hitchcock.

MILLER: In your second year in Hollywood, you starred in *Dance, Girl, Dance* [1940] as an aspiring ballerina. It was directed by one of the very few female directors of her day—Dorothy Arzner. Your reaction to her?

O'HARA: Dorothy Arzner was a charming, wonderful woman. There had been another director on the picture, but he was fired and they brought her in. We got along fine.

MILLER: The following year, you played Angharad in the Oscar-winning film of 1941, *How Green Was My Valley*. It was your first picture of many with director John Ford. Talk about him.

O'HARA [*chuckling*]: He was the meanest old devil you ever met in your life! He was a fibber. He'd rather tell a lie than the truth. And possessive! He didn't want Duke [John Wayne] or Ward Bond or me or Victor McLaglen to do anything for anybody but him. He liked to say we were nothing, that he made us what we were. He was gruff. And when we finished a picture with him and he said, "That's a wrap!" we'd say, "I wonder what he's going to do next?"

MILLER: Sounds like a love-hate relationship?

O'HARA: Certain things he used to do, I couldn't tell you. You couldn't put them in print. And he'd do them in front of the crew! He was smart, intelligent, but he'd never pay you a compliment. Duke and the rest of us used to say, "He's the meanest son of a bitch, but he's *our* son of a bitch!" We all felt the same way, but we'd never tell the truth about him. He knew he had our total loyalty.

MILLER: Keep talking. I love this.

O'HARA: Okay. Once while we were making *Wings of Eagles* [1957], he was so mean to me all day. I had a death scene to do and I'd worried all week about what to do, but he said, "Just die!" So I decided I'd do the death scene then quit, and he could get somebody else if he wanted to reshoot. I was just choking with anger! So I did the scene and when I was finished, he said, "Stop!" and made all the men come down from up above and gathered everyone around to say, "Ladies and gentlemen, if you want better acting than that, go find it!" Then he turned and walked off and I said, "Aw, isn't he sweet?"

MILLER: Over the years, you've worked with a lot of kid actors—from Roddy McDowall in *How Green Was My Valley* and Natalie Wood in *Miracle on 34th Street* [1947] up to Hayley Mills in *The Parent Trap* [1961]. How do you get along with kid stars?

O'HARA: I love kids, and I love working with children. All you have to do is understand them and know them and their imagination and you'll have them eating out of your hand. I've had over forty to work with.

Roddy was like my brother. He was about fourteen and I was nineteen. We were pals and were in contact ever since 1941. I happened to call him on the phone the week before he died. He answered the phone and sounded like the same old Roddy I'd known for fifty-seven years. We talked about how much we loved each other. Then he said, "You know, Maureen, I'm in a terminal situation." I didn't know he meant cancer. I thought he meant the sale of his house, the completion of a script, or so many other things. I was making my annual trip to Ireland and he said, "When are you coming back?" I said I'd be back in a week and he said, "The minute you get back here, call me." I arrived during the night and he died in the morning. When I got here, there was a postcard from him and it just thanked me for all the things I'd said about him and asked me to call him right away. But it was too late.

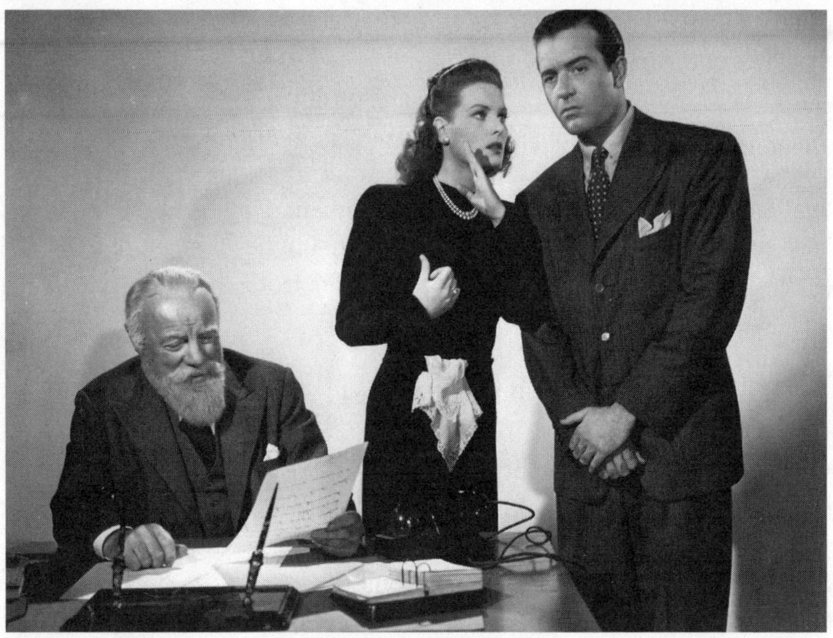

Maureen O'Hara with Edmund Gwenn (*left*) and John Payne in *Miracle on 34th Street* (1947). Courtesy of 20th Century-Fox.

As for the others, Natalie Wood was super-heaven and the Mills girls, Hayley and Juliet, too. All the kids in *Spencer's Mountain* [1963] were heaven to work with.

MILLER: You've very rarely played any woman who wasn't a strong, positive image.

O'HARA: One time I played a murderess in a film with Ray Milland called *Lisbon* [1956], and I just didn't know if the public would accept it or not. But I was so busy going from one picture to another that I didn't have time to find out. I wouldn't murder anyone anyhow. Hit them over the head maybe.

MILLER: Have you ever played a character like yourself in a movie?

O'HARA: No, but I loved the character in *The Quiet Man* [1952] and the ones in *McClintock* and *Spencer's Mountain.* I like strong people—in real life and on the screen. I don't care if they're nasty as long as they're dedicated, tough, strong, and have the courage to go out and try to do what they dream about.

MILLER: You mentioned *The Quiet Man.* Didn't it take forever to get that film before the cameras?

Maureen O'Hara gets a lift from frequent costar John Wayne in 1952's *The Quiet Man.* Courtesy of Republic Pictures and NTA.

O'HARA: There was an awful lot of time spent just trying to raise the money. Nobody would put up the money. It went to Fox, to RKO, to Metro—and they all turned it down as a silly, stupid little Irish story that wouldn't do any business. We did *Rio Grande* [1950] to raise the money to make *The Quiet Man.*

Every summer, because I took shorthand, I would take the notes and the instructions from John Ford for *The Quiet Man.* We'd go to Catalina on his boat and I'd work on it every summer. Mary Ford would take the kids—her grandchildren and my daughter—and go into the yacht club later and type up all of his notes—all that time that he was preparing the picture. Then Duke said, "Let me take this script to Old Man Yates" [Herbert J. Yates, head of Republic Pictures]. Of course, Republic studios was a letdown to Ford, but eventually he said fine. Yates read the script and said, "It'll never make a picture! But if the same cast, same director, and same producer make a western for me to make up the money I'm going to lose on this silly story, I'll finance it." And that's how we made *The Quiet Man,* by making *Rio Grande* first.

MILLER: I've always believed you were the only woman who ever really stood up to John Wayne in a movie, even though he dumped you in a water trough once and pushed you around a lot.

O'HARA: We were both big and tall. As his kids said, "You can stand toe to toe with our dad!" And I did, too, and had the bruises to prove it. In *The Quiet Man,* when I socked him in the scene in the kitchen, the pain that went up my arm was incredible. I hid it in my petticoat, but Duke came over to me and asked to see my hand because "You nearly broke my jaw!" When he looked at my hand, every finger was like a sausage, so I was sent to the hospital because I'd broken a bone in my wrist. But I'd meant to kill him, I was so mad at him that day.

MILLER: Some critics believe you were never more beautiful on-screen than you were in Technicolor in *The Black Swan* [1942].

O'HARA: *Black Swan* is still used to this day in training classes for young cinematographers to teach them about color. In the beginning, when studios couldn't make up their mind whether to stay with black and white or go to color, [color consultant Natalie] Kalmus used a close-up of me in Technicolor to sell it to the studios.

But the only time I was ever surprised at how I looked on-screen was in *Jamaica Inn.* I wasn't aware, being part of a big Irish family where you're laughed at all the time, that I was anything to look at. You're talking about Ireland, not New York or L.A. There are so many beautiful girls there.

MILLER: You worked with a lot of handsome leading men, including Errol Flynn in *Against All Flags* [1952]. He was such a notorious womanizer. Did he ever come on to you?

O'HARA: No way! He was a very charming and efficient actor, but he had a drinking problem and by about 4 in the afternoon they'd send him home and I'd do all my close-ups to an X on a black flag.

MILLER: I suppose it wouldn't be fair to our readers if I didn't ask you about playing *Lady Godiva* [1955]?

O'HARA: Frankly, I wasn't that mad about the movie. We had the Hays Office [the industry censors] and certain things were permitted and some were not. It's a shame we don't have the same rules today.

MILLER: After a long hiatus from making films, you agreed to come back to star with John Candy in *Only the Lonely.*

O'HARA: I didn't want to go back to work, but [writer-director] Chris Columbus chased after me. He wrote the part for me and my ego wouldn't let me turn it down.

Maureen O'Hara with Hayley Mills in the 1961 Disney classic *The Parent Trap.* Courtesy of the Walt Disney Corp. and NBC.

MILLER: I understand you wanted to meet John Candy before you would agree to do the picture.

O'HARA: I flew to America and he came down from Canada. I was with him five minutes and I said, "All right, I'll be your mama." He was absolutely the sweetest, kindest man you could ever meet—and a really fine actor. If God had spared him, I think you would have seen John Candy doing remakes of a lot of the Charles Laughton films. [Candy died not long after finishing the movie.]

MILLER: What plans do you have for the future?

O'HARA: I'd like to live to be a hundred. I really, really would.

Afterword

Maureen O'Hara died in her sleep at her home in Boise, Idaho, on October 24, 2015. She was ninety-five.

Luise Rainer

Interview by Ron Miller

There is a special place in Hollywood history for Luise Rainer. She was imported from Europe in the 1930s as a leading lady at MGM. More important, she became the first actor to win back-to-back Oscars: in 1936 for *The Great Ziegfeld* (only her second screen role) and in 1937 for *The Good Earth.* Rainer also made history by rejecting the whole idea of Hollywood stardom and leaving the movies just ten years later—pretty much for good. After a disastrous marriage to playwright Clifford Odets in the 1930s, Rainer left him and walked out on her studio contract after a series of disappointing movies, including *The Emperor's Candlesticks* (1937), *Big City* (1937), *The Toy Wife* (1938), and *Dramatic School* (1938), and returned to Europe, where she spent virtually the rest of her life off the screen.

Setting the Scene

In November 1983, Luise Rainer succumbed to the appeals of producer Douglas Cramer and agreed to return to the screen in an episode of TV's *The Love Boat.* She did not want to do a lot of interviews for such a miniscule "comeback" performance, but an ABC publicist persuaded her to meet me for a chat.

I was then living in Los Angeles and Rainer invited me to meet her after lunch at a popular hotel in Beverly Hills. I met her and some of her friends, including her daughter, Francesca, who lived in Los Angeles. Moments after my arrival, Rainer announced to the luncheon group, "You go on. I want to take this man up to my room now!" How could I resist such an invitation?

For the next hour, I was utterly charmed by this captivating woman. Rainer, who was then seventy-three years old, was still radiantly beautiful and quite beguiling. She was a sheer delight.

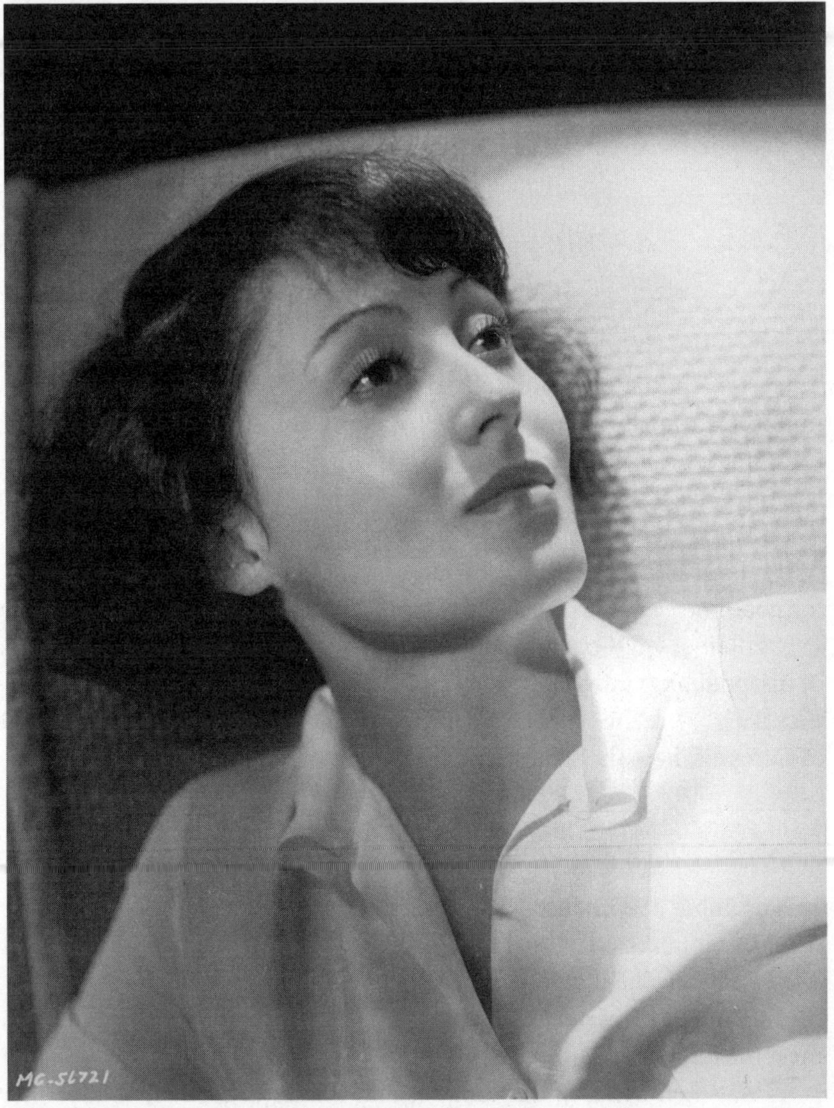

Luise Rainer, circa 1938. Courtesy of MGM.

The Interview

MILLER: Getting an interview with Luise Rainer is like getting a date with Greta Garbo. Why have you become such a recluse?

RAINER: I have the reputation of a recluse. They say Luise Rainer doesn't need to work, that she has too much money and doesn't need to work. I'm *not* a recluse. The fact of the matter is, I'm an actress. I love to work.

MILLER: Well, then, why haven't you done anything since you did an episode of *Combat!* in 1965?

RAINER: But I have worked. I do my one-woman show, in which I do a reading of Tennyson's epic poem *Enoch Arden* to music by Richard Strauss. I've performed this several times in America and I've most recently done it at UCLA while I was doing *Love Boat.*

MILLER: But why do something like *The Love Boat*?

RAINER: I didn't know what *Love Boat* was. I'd never seen it. I didn't like the script Mr. Cramer [producer Douglas Cramer] had for me, but he promised to write a new one expressly for me in which I play two roles—a wealthy woman and a simple domestic.

MILLER: How did it feel to be working in a modern TV show?

RAINER: I really enjoyed doing the show because I like to work quickly. I like one take, no more than two, if necessary. Television is quick and I must say I enjoyed it thoroughly.

MILLER: Take me back to 1935 and your arrival in Hollywood as the next big European movie star.

RAINER: I had been the protégé of impresario Max Reinhardt in Europe. I was just seventeen when I became a star onstage in Europe. I was twenty-five when I came to America to play a Viennese girl in *Escapade* [1935] with William Powell. I was totally unprepared for the idea of stardom and what it would entail.

MILLER: You were then—as you are now—a luminous beauty. Men flocked to you. One of them was America's most promising young playwright, Clifford Odets.

RAINER: We fell hopelessly in love and were married in 1937. He was handsome and recklessly brilliant. Later, I discovered he was a cruel-mouthed, mean-spirited, egotistical womanizer. [Odets's relationship with actress Frances Farmer was dramatized in the 1992 movie *Frances,* which explored her mental deterioration and death.] Offscreen, my life was turning into a nightmare.

MILLER: At the same time, your movie career was exploding. Tell me about making *The Great Ziegfeld.*

RAINER: I saw the script and noticed that there was an incredible scene in it where my character, Anna Held, makes a phone call to congratulate

Luise Rainer as Anna Held with William Powell in *The Great Ziegfeld*, the Oscar-winning Best Picture of 1936. Rainer won her first Best Actress Oscar for her performance. Courtesy of MGM and Turner Classic Movies.

her ex-husband on his marriage to Billie Burke. I knew this was a heartbreaking moment because Anna still loved him so.

MILLER: How did you do that scene, which many think was the scene that won you your first Oscar?

Luise Rainer as a Chinese peasant with Paul Muni in *The Good Earth* (1937). Rainer won her second consecutive Best Actress Oscar for her performance. Courtesy of MGM and Turner Classic Movies.

RAINER: I like a director who leaves me alone. If you have the stuff, it will come out all right.

MILLER: As I understand it, your director, Robert Z. Leonard, let you find your way through that scene alone.

RAINER: Yes, he did. And it's true what you've heard: I put myself in the mood for it by thinking about my beloved cocker spaniel who was going to have to be put to sleep. I didn't think about Flo Ziegfeld at all!

MILLER: Then, one year later, you won a second Best Actress Oscar, playing O-Lan, the Chinese peasant wife in *The Good Earth.* Your career seemed to stall after that. Was it the so-called Oscar curse?

RAINER: I don't think the Oscar was a jinx. If I had not been married to Odets at the time, I would have been the lasting kind of star I could have been.

MILLER: I know you blame the dissolving of your marriage for your decision to leave the movies, but you also were put into a series of poor-quality movies by MGM's Louis B. Mayer.

RAINER: I was put on a pedestal that was very narrow. I had nowhere to go. I decided to break my contract with MGM and go elsewhere.

MILLER: How did Mayer react to that?

RAINER: He was furious. He told me, "We made you and we can break you!" I told him he didn't buy me like a cat in a sack and he couldn't get rid of me that way either. Then what he did came over me like a hurricane.

MILLER: You were divorced in 1940 and left your career behind in Hollywood. What would have happened if you had stayed on?

RAINER: I would have cracked up.

MILLER: You made one other film after leaving MGM—Paramount's *Hostages* [1943]—and that was that?

RAINER: It was not a success. And then I was married again.

MILLER: It seems as if the second marriage—to British publisher Robert Knittel—was a great success.

RAINER: If I had been married to him in 1937, everything might have been different for me. I've suffered a great deal in my life and I've had hard times. But I've learned from everything that has happened to me. I love people. I also know that I not only have to love, but I need to be loved.

MILLER: Does your return to the screen on *The Love Boat* mean you're ready to return to movies as well?

RAINER: My eyes are closed. That's all I'll say.

Afterword

Luise Rainer made no more movies or television performances after *The Love Boat.* She came to America in subsequent years to make cameo appearances at the 1998 and 2003 Academy Awards ceremonies and was interviewed onstage by Robert Osborne at a Turner Classic Movies celebration of her career. She died December 30, 2014, at age 104.

Rosalind Russell

Interview by James Bawden

Tall, sophisticated Rosalind Russell started out in movies as a serious dramatic actress, but her gift for wisecracking comic characters soon flowered, and she is today best remembered for those roles in *His Girl Friday* (1940), the original *My Sister Eileen* (1942), *Auntie Mame* (1958), and the musical *Gypsy* (1962). Oscar nominated for dramatic roles in *Sister Kenny* and *Mourning Becomes Electra* in the 1940s, she won the Jean Hersholt Humanitarian Award at the 1972 Oscar ceremony for her charity work.

Setting the Scene

At the 1972 TV Critics meeting in Los Angeles, an ABC publicist asked if I'd mind going over to Rosalind Russell's home at 8:30 a.m. to interview the great lady in advance of her scheduled press conference. Russell was promoting what turned out to be her last acting assignment—the TV movie *The Crooked Hearts.* But she was nervous about doing a mass press conference for fear she was getting forgetful and might not remember her best stories. She'd spied my name on the list of attending critics and remembered I'd recently interviewed her on the phone for a CBC salute to all her old movies. And so I guess she thought I might serve to tune her up for the press event. Anyway, at 8:10, an ABC limousine rushed me to her home. She was waiting for me—immaculate, warm, and gracious. As we sipped black coffee, she answered questions with humor and wit.

The Interview

BAWDEN: What was your upbringing like?

RUSSELL: I had a mother and father who cared. I was the middle child in a big batch of seven children. I don't think Mother wanted me to be a

Rosalind Russell. James Bawden collection.

stay-at-home mom as she had so proudly been. My father was an affluent lawyer, but his will made news and is still listed in the law books. He wanted his children to take care of themselves, but he'd support us in any educational endeavor as long as we wanted. Then, for at least three years—nothing! We had to try to make it in the world on our own abilities. I thought I'd try acting. It had always intrigued me, which meant a lot of studying at first because that's exactly the way Dad would have wanted it.

BAWDEN: So you graduated from the American Academy of Dramatic Arts.

RUSSELL: In 1929. Hardly the best time to be a struggling actress. The Depression took until 1930–1931 to really sink in. I had an agent, Chamberlain Brown, [and] a verbal five-year agreement with Mother that I'd try something else if I wasn't a success by that time. I had never really thought about movies. The few talkers I had seen were crude, primitive, the acting laughable. But four weeks after graduation, I had an Equity contract as leading lady for a stock company run by R. F. Casey in Saranac Lake, New York. Hardly a Broadway debut, but something better. I got experience in a new Broadway play every week and I was making $25.

BAWDEN: You toured in 1930.

RUSSELL: In a production of *Garrick Gaieties*. Then I got a job in a Broadway play called *Company's Calling* with Lynne Overman. We lasted all of eight performances. I was offered a standard ingenue contract from Universal Pictures, so I thought, why not? I instantly hated the studio, which was out in the [San Fernando] valley, but was reputedly near bankruptcy. MGM told me they'd love to have me, so I went in to see "Uncle" Carl Laemmle [the Universal studio chief] and dressed as badly as I could with lots of rouge and told him I'd decided to remain onstage. He took one took at me, shuddered, and released all claims to me. I went to Metro the next day, signed on the dotted line for seven years. The same day a kid named Spangler Arlington Brugh also signed. They redid his teeth, shaved back his hairline, and a year later as Robert Taylor he was a big romantic star.

BAWDEN: How did MGM see you?

RUSSELL: [Studio chief] Louis Mayer told me I'd be a warning to Myrna Loy not to get uppity. Because of my background, they saw me as what I called a "Lady Mary" character, very high class. I first did that part in a Joan Crawford picture *Forsaking All Others* [1934]. She was awfully nice to this kid. Years later, in makeup, I was wondering out loud if there was a Roz Russell second stringer? There was a tug on my shoulder and Ruth Hussey said, "Hi, Roz! It's me!"

BAWDEN: Your first big picture was the all-star *China Seas* [1935]?

RUSSELL: Who could argue about being in such august company? There was [Clark] Gable, [Jean] Harlow, [Wallace] Beery, plus Robert

Benchley. We did all our picture out at the MGM lake. There was room there for our ship, tugs, a paddle wheeler. Jean was the first big star I truly got friendly with. With Crawford there was a certain distancing. Gable always talked to me as an equal, which I certainly was not. I'd go home with Jean, met her family. She was completely the opposite of her movie self. She'd been private schooled, was easily shocked. She craved respect, as did all of the big sex symbols. And we all cheered when she finally found happiness with Bill Powell. But it was not to be. Fate can be very cruel. The whole lot was in tears when she passed on. I know I was.

BAWDEN: Your first big lead was in *Rendezvous* [1935]. How did that happen?

RUSSELL: Well, at MGM I was always considered a second Myrna Loy. When Myrna left for Europe in a contract dispute, MGM called her bluff. The picture had been written for her and Bill Powell with lots of that comical timing audiences had expected. I was very nervous, but Bill helped. He was such an exceptional actor—the best on the lot, very methodical in rehearsals, then he'd just relax right into the part. It was all set during the Great War, and female audiences were disappointed by the dated costumes or they missed Myrna. I got nice notices that seemed to always end with a cry for her to come back. Which she did eventually.

BAWDEN: The studio started loaning you out a lot.

RUSSELL: Who could be upset by being loaned to Fox for *Under Two Flags* [1936]? It was one of those big adventure epics so popular then—absurd story, but so much action. And it was Ronnie Colman's last for Fox before he went off on his own. He kept on extolling the virtues of freelancing so much that I began to wonder what I'd do when my MGM contract was over in 1941. Claudette Colbert had the big female lead. I was cast in one of my Lady Mary outings—actually, I was called Lady Venetia.

One thing Ronnie taught me: how to kiss, movie style. I'd been doing it all wrong. It had to be not on the lips but slightly above to the left, depending on where the camera was located. I giggled a bit but watching the rushes the next day I saw he was completely right. Never kissed any man on the lips since then—in the movies, I mean.

BAWDEN: You then finished the year at Columbia in *Craig's Wife* [1936].

RUSSELL: A wonderful play. I'd never seen the silent version. [Studio chief] Harry Cohn said he'd been watching me and got me on a straight loan-out. It was the most challenging role I'd had as yet. I'd known a lot of these ladies. I based Harriet on women I'd known in my mother's circle. They became obsessive about their houses because they had no other life. We had a wonderful cast: John Boles, Tommy Mitchell in his first movie, Billie Burke as the lady next door. It was shot very quickly, economically. At MGM, they would have added a sheen that was wholly inappropriate.

BAWDEN: At MGM they tried to make you into a team with Robert Montgomery.

RUSSELL: Metro was into teams right then: Powell and Loy, MacDonald and Eddy. Trouble was Bob did not accept me as an equal; I was only a leading lady in his eyes. I hesitated on doing *Night Must Fall* [1937] until Mr. Mayer told me my character would substitute for the audience. You would see the events unfolding through my eyes and my gradual realization that Danny is a serial killer. (I don't think we used that term in those days.) I can't praise Bob's performance enough—first the boyishness, then the madness starting to seep through. When I met playwright Emlyn Williams the next year, he was full of praise for what Bob had accomplished—even using an Irish accent instead of Emlyn's Welsh one.

Dame May Whitty, as she insisted on being called at all times, had done the original play in the West End. She did lay it on a bit thick, but was mightily impressive. MGM created huge English gardens and woods on the back lot. I always wondered why this wasn't the first English production to be done at MGM's new British studios, instead of *A Yank at Oxford* [1938].

BAWDEN: Mayer came to hate the film.

RUSSELL: Oh, he loathed it! It was completely against the family-friendly Metro image. Although Bob got—and deservedly so—an Oscar nomination, Mr. Mayer campaigned behind his back, asking all Metro voters to vote for Spencer Tracy in *Captains Courageous,* who did win. I wound up making four films with Bob, but we never were much of a team.

BAWDEN: In your autobiography, you describe a tense scene where you had to go to the men's dressing rooms and tell one of your costars to lay off. Would that have been Montgomery?

RUSSELL [*irritated*]: Yes. Next question.

BAWDEN: MGM then sent you to its Denham studios [in England] as a last-minute replacement for the Robert Donat film *The Citadel* [1938].

RUSSELL: All I know is Mr. Mayer dropped the lovely British star Elizabeth Allan, and she wound up suing the studios and never worked there again. I rushed over, which took a few weeks in those days. To the crew, I was this upstart American taking over her role. But star Donat could not have been more understanding. He understood my quandary and immediately put me at ease and had the crew understanding my predicament. It was a very smooth shoot after this rocky start and director King Vidor shot the book, which was an important one about the perils of being a society doctor. My part as the wife was small but stolid. She badgers him to join the people. We had these wonderful refugees from the West End: Ralph Richardson, Emlyn Williams, Rex Harrison. The cast and crew took two tea breaks a day and I saw it helped their work and I've been taking them on almost every picture since then.

BAWDEN: How did you snag the choice role of Sylvia in *The Women* [1939]?

RUSSELL: Well, nobody else wanted it. She was a real gargoyle. I barged into [director] George Cukor's office and he said, "Roz, you are a lady!" He wanted his Broadway buddy Ilka Chase, who had done the original play. I auditioned and tested for producer Hunt Stromberg, who figured he could save money by casting an MGM contractee. Hunt produced *Night Must Fall*. He knew me inside out. At first I tried to inject some malice, but George said to go for the broadest comedy. I dressed Sylvia horridly for show with more than a little help from [chief fashion designer] Adrien. We first glimpse her at Mary's house, and I wore an awful blouse with a great big bulging Picasso-like face staring back. Norma [Shearer] took one look and protested to George, "She's not going to wear that, is she?" In my mind Sylvia was ungainly. In the department store confrontation, I fall back into a garbage bin. I also had a wonderful wrestling match with Paulette Goddard that we rehearsed a whole day. Her character stole my husband. I really got going and at the end I grab her leg and bite it. Paulette wisecracked that she was going to get hydrophobia and the line stayed in.

There was some backstage tension with Norma. She was also brawling with Joan Crawford. I was told I'd get under-the-title billing, so when enough of my part was in the can, I started phoning in sick. MGM's Benny Thau knew exactly what I was doing and eventually phoned and said I'd get star billing under Shearer and Crawford, but in smaller letters.

BAWDEN: You immediately jumped into *His Girl Friday,* the remake of *The Front Page*.

RUSSELL: *The Women* premiered in September 1939 to huge crowds. I naturally expected MGM would now be buying properties specifically for me. Nothing happened. They did not even try promoting me for an Oscar

Rosalind Russell with Cary Grant in the 1940 comedy *His Girl Friday.* Courtesy of Columbia Pictures.

nomination. The next month Harry Cohn, who'd seen *The Women,* arranged a loan-out for *His Girl Friday.* [Director] Howard Hawks had gone through [Irene] Dunne, [Ginger] Rogers, [Jean] Arthur—all of whom had turned down [the role of] Hildy. I went over to see him and my hair was still wet from the shower. That's how much effort I put into that audition. Howard told me he had this idea of changing Hildy's sex at a party and read the play with a script girl. *The Front Page,* he said, was, after all, a great love story. I left his office all enthusiastic and it remains one of my favorite parts.

There are all these wonderful character actors: Porter Hall, Ernest Truex, Gene Lockhart, John Qualen. They'd try stealing scenes like crazy. Don't forget Cary Grant, who is a smash. He just enjoyed himself so much. Howard very correctly resisted attempts to open it up, and it plays like a photographed stage play. It's true I hired a gag writer to give me some lines because Cary was ad-libbing like crazy. Most of it was so good Howard let him keep the lines in.

BAWDEN: Then what happened?

RUSSELL: Harry Cohn came on set at the end and invited me to come to Columbia when my MGM contract lapsed in 1941. At first I laughed. Columbia was the smallest of the majors. But Harry's reasoning was sound. He told me Columbia could give me one grade A picture a year with all the trimmings, meaning I would not be forgotten as I felt at Metro. And I could do a second picture elsewhere and keep all that salary.

BAWDEN: Then you went to Warners.

RUSSELL: For *No Time for Comedy* [1940] opposite another MGM star, Jimmy Stewart. We both recognized we were doing our best work at other studios and making a ton of money for MGM. Jimmy said he was going to freelance when his contract was up in 1942. We thought it crazy we'd never worked together at Metro, but here we were together crosstown. This film wasn't as well made as I'd hoped, but was still a hit.

When I got back to MGM, I summoned my courage and went in to tell Mr. Mayer I was leaving in a year's time. Oh, he pulled out all the stops, crying, singing, the whole performance. But I was steadfast. And I've never regretted it. But I never again worked at MGM after leaving. He felt betrayed, and I just understood right there I could never go back.

BAWDEN: Nineteen forty-one was then your busiest year.

RUSSELL: I had forty weeks left on my MGM contract, and I was worked every one of those days. I finally got leads at MGM, but by then it was too late. My character of woman executive was born then and it went right through the war years. I had the pinstripe suit already in *His Girl Friday.* The broad shoulders, the pattern—the secret was in the three fittings, so it never seemed mannish. Those suits had to look expensive. But I always got a pin for the label—can't look too masculine. *Hired Wife* [1940] was certainly in that vein as the hair got higher and higher. I don't know how they kept it up like that. It just went higher and higher. The story became basically the same: I'm taught that a woman cannot operate like a man and at the end I'm trying to get back with the male lead, be it Lee Bowman or Mel Douglas or Brian Aherne.

BAWDEN: You finally costarred with Clark Gable.

RUSSELL: On *They Met in Bombay* [1941]. He walked on set the first day and said, "What took you so long?" Clark was right; it had taken seven long years to become his leading lady. This started off as a very classy jewel theft yarn and then our director, Woody Van Dyke, kept looking at the papers and the Japanese became our enemies and we wound up thousands of miles from Bombay. I could have done a dozen hits with Clark. He was so virile and attractive and very much at ease in this kind of comedy.

BAWDEN: How did you fit in the Paramount comedy *Take a Letter, Darling* [1942]?

RUSSELL: I had a few months off before my Columbia contract kicked in. It was supposed to star Claudette Colbert, but she jumped to *Palm Beach Story,* replacing Carole Lombard. Well, I loved it there. [Director] Mitch Leisen was very much in the Cukor vein. Paramount made me seem more beautiful than I'd ever been at MGM. I've always had great respect for Fred MacMurray, who was the most talented light comedian in the business. I say that and people are startled, but it was true.

BAWDEN: Your first Columbia hit was *My Sister Eileen* [1942].

RUSSELL: It was a version of the Broadway play, which starred Shirley Booth. I loved the part of Ruth Sherwood so much I made it into a Broadway musical in 1953. I remember my first meeting with Leonard Bernstein and I told him I couldn't sing a note. He said everybody can sing a bit. I did one song and he said, "You're right. You can't sing a note!" Harry Cohn owned the movie rights and said he wasn't going to pay for a property he already owned and made his own musical in 1955. The best we could do was a kinescope, and it still exists. And, as far as the movie went, I finally got my first Oscar nomination.

BAWDEN: Then you signed with RKO in 1943.

RUSSELL: I usually did one for Columbia and one for RKO each year after that. First up was *Flight for Freedom* [1943] as Amelia Earhart, although the name had to be changed. Her widower, George Palmer Putnam, asked for a name change. I insisted on Fred MacMurray as the handsome guy Toni falls for over sedate Herbert Marshall. It didn't all come together as it should have because we feared Putnam's wrath. But the whole ploy of going out to map islands coveted by the Japanese made it a hit.

BAWDEN: You were then sidetracked by a major health scare.

RUSSELL: I tried doing too much. I married Freddie Brisson, who became a big producer. His nickname was the Wizard of Roz. Then, after finishing *What a Woman!* [1943], I gave birth to our son Lance and promptly collapsed. A thyroid condition. I just couldn't work. In fact, I couldn't do anything. My most depressing period, as work was everything to me. I went to Palm Springs and stayed there a year. Found out I wasn't made of iron after all. I'd been bouncing from one movie to the next, entertaining the boys [military servicemen] on weekends. I just had it.

I returned eighteen months later in a Columbia picture, but in a Warners drama, *Roughly Speaking* [1945], opposite Jack Carson, I was an emancipated woman who discovers she still needs a husband and family. I thought I was forgotten. It put me back up there, although it had more slapstick than I like. Jack could be a scream. He was very encouraging and we even did it on radio. I had another thyroid scare and then I made *She Wouldn't Say Yes* [1945] with Lee Bowman.

BAWDEN: You decided to change the course of your career.

RUSSELL: With *Sister Kenny* [1946], I took a story most studios had turned down as too depressing. I had to practically break down the door of RKO head Charlie Koerner to get it done. It took two years to get the script right and only after scriptwriter Dudley Nichols came on board. He turned our characters back into real people and got so hooked he said he had to direct it. We all knew it wasn't going to be a huge box office hit but it was my most challenging part. It did make a moderate profit and Charlie still talked to me.

BAWDEN: Then came *Mourning Becomes Electra* [1947].

RUSSELL: I was stunned when Dudley offered it to me. I thought I could get by as the mother, but he said, "Oh, no. You must play the daughter, Lavinia." Couldn't understand her or that family. We filmed and filmed and after the third time when the carriages come up to the door, I asked Dudley if that were necessary. He snapped, "How else are people going to get to the front door?" I started hating it, although I did as told. Katina Paxinou as Christine seemed to be braying all the time. Michael Redgrave was always in a snit. Ray Massey really got it right. I think I was just awful.

I was very surprised to get an Oscar nomination. [On] Oscar night the idea that I was standing up before Loretta Young's name was called is ridiculous. In fact my mother was sick and I was trying to get her home. That accomplished, I turned around and went to Loretta's victory party to congratulate her.

BAWDEN: Another dramatic picture, *The Velvet Touch* [1948], came next.

RUSSELL: It was the first of three pictures I made for Freddie's Independent Artists company. It was an excellent look at the state of Broadway and technically completely accurate. We got there well before *All about Eve.* I was a light Broadway star who wants to play Hedda Gabbler. In a fight I kill my manipulative producer, played by Leon Ames. I set things up so that an alcoholic has-been, so well played by Claire Trevor, takes the rap. We had Sydney Greenstreet as the investigating detective trying to break me down and Leo Genn as the new love interest. I loved being stalked by Sydney and Claire won her Oscar [for *Key Largo*] just as the picture opened, which really put us over the top.

BAWDEN: You then went back to comedy with *Tell It to the Judge* [1949] and *A Woman of Distinction* [1950].

RUSSELL: I get these two mixed up. Both Bob Cummings and Ray Milland are first-class farceurs. They'll do anything for a laugh. I could see the working-woman premise was wearing thin for postwar audiences.

By this time I desperately wanted to return to the stage. I'd been away too long. But I wondered if I still could make it in front of an audience. I went on a long tour of *Bell, Book and Candle* [1952] and I was pretty awful at the start because I was rusty. By the time we hit Chicago, we were roaring and made a huge profit of $600,000 on an investment of just $14,000.

BAWDEN: Your last movie for some time was *Never Wave at a Wac* [1952]?

RUSSELL: We did it live on TV, did touch-ups, and then filmed it for RKO and good profits. Then Dick Powell phoned and asked me to join Four Star Productions along with Charles Boyer, David Niven, and Joel McCrea. It would have made me a very rich girl. But I chose *Wonderful Town* [1953–1954] on Broadway and never regretted it. Eventually Joel withdrew as well and stuck to his movie westerns. I lost several million dollars, but *Wonderful Town* was a wonderful hit. There was a great opening night, but afterwards I sat in my dressing room and nobody came. Finally Marlene Dietrich popped her head around the door and whispered, "Roz, on opening night you're supposed to greet everybody onstage." It felt oh, so good to be on top again.

BAWDEN: In 1955 came *Picnic.*

RUSSELL: I was floored when [the playwright] Bill Inge phoned me up and said, "Roz, you must be Rosemary." I'd seen and loved the play but I was concerned she might be relegated to secondary status. Both Bill and Harry Cohn assured me there were five main characters and all would have equal treatment. But on location in Kansas it was evident director Josh Logan was giving Kim Novak special privileges. Hers was a dazzling beauty, but she couldn't act a bit. That kind of attention tipped the balance and then Harry suggested I take a secondary [Supporting Actor] nomination. He had just cut my big scene and I was in no mood for compromises. I refused because it would have been unfair to Rosemary.

Rosalind Russell in *Auntie Mame* (1958). Courtesy of Warner Bros. and PBS.

BAWDEN: There was nothing secondary about your part in *Auntie Mame!*

RUSSELL: She just flew into everybody's hearts. It was the Eisenhower fifties. People were desperately looking for color in their lives. She was this beautiful dame overstuffed with emotions. And yes, Morton Da Costa and I did a bit of rewriting of the script. You see, it was necessary to get Mame off the stage for a large chunk of act 2 or audiences would have become exhausted with her.

I grew so fond of little Jan Handzlik, who played my nephew. When his mother was in the hospital I went to see her with him and I ordered Warners to hire him for the movie although he was growing up fast. Then he moved to Seattle and I lost touch with my dear little boy.

For the movie I worked on getting Mame's dimensions lowered for film. I didn't want to wind up stagy and overbearing. But I now see I should have done even more. I really like the play better than the movie. Jack Warner immediately asked me to do a sequel titled *Around the World with Auntie Mame*. I refused. Bad decision. I think I should have done it, but I didn't want to repeat myself in any way.

BAWDEN: In 1961, *Time* magazine said you were the busiest movie actress—with three projects about to shoot.

RUSSELL: Mervyn LeRoy offered me the lead opposite Alec Guinness in *A Majority of One*, which Gertrude Berg had made into such a big Broadway success. Mervyn said she'd only made one movie and was not a big enough name internationally. And Mervyn said Guinness would only do it if I did it. I phoned this great actor up during intermission time—he was costarring in the West End as Lawrence of Arabia—and we briefly chatted, and I did it and I loved doing it. Yes, I'm aware I was overly flamboyant as the Jewish widow. Had to be. Alec is one of the most introverted actors I've ever met. But he had found his character and I had to pitch mine slightly higher or we would have created a snore fest. Mrs. Jacobi was just so very eager to get out of that apartment, that was the key to her character. Look, I loved doing that part and the receipts justified Mervyn's faith in us.

BAWDEN: Then came *Five Finger Exercise* [1961].

RUSSELL: A mistake. The problems started when screenwriters Frances Goodrich and Albert Hackett transferred the story from England to California. But I argue that was wrong because the family remained so British in their actions. We actors thought at first we were doing splendid work. Then one day Jack Hawkins whispered to me, "It isn't working," and it wasn't. I felt so sorry for Max Schell, who was coming off such a hit and an Oscar in *Judgment at Nuremberg*. This mess did not help his career at all.

BAWDEN: There was much controversy over *Gypsy*.

RUSSELL: It came from the [Ethel] Merman camp. Mervyn LeRoy, who directed *Majority*, convinced me to give it a try. He'd scouted Ethel Merman on Broadway but found her too clownish and he said her actual movies hadn't done well. He needed a trained movie actress who could flesh out the character. We got lovely Natalie Wood as Gypsy and Karl Malden, who was wonderful. Mervyn threw everything he had into this one. He started off as a vaudevillian, you know.

But he warned me to brace for a tide. The Merman people were mining sympathy for everything. I never complained when Columbia made a musical out of *My Sister Eileen*. I never did so when a musical of *Mame* came along later. MGM remade *The Women* as the musical *The Opposite Sex*. Then there was the singing controversy. I sang all the lines and when I first watched it put together that was me croaking each tune. I was told they revved it up on the album but I never heard it. That controversy meant I was deprived of a nomination. This I truly believe.

BAWDEN: The huge receipts for your two nun movies floored Columbia.

RUSSELL: Me, too. I thought the first was a pleasant family film. *The Trouble with Angels* [1966] was moderately budgeted. Hayley Mills didn't want to play those teens anymore, she told me. She stayed in character between takes, always sticking her mouth out at me. She refused to do the sequel, *Where Angels Go . . . Trouble Follows*, two years later. It was a road-trip thing and Stella Stevens wasn't quite right as Hayley's replacement. I joked to Bob Taylor I'd finally grabbed him as leading man. Binnie Barnes is in both of them. She was married to producer Mike Frankovich and was there to see the director finished on time every day. Watch her closely: she only has a few lines of dialogue.

BAWDEN: What about *Oh Dad, Poor Dad, Mama's Hung You in the Closet and I'm Feeling So Sad* [1967]?

RUSSELL: What about it? My worst-ever film. A disaster. When I got off the plane, I just had this feeling I should have jumped right back on. Our director [Richard Quine] was as mixed up as the characters.

BAWDEN: And *Rosie* [1968]?

RUSSELL: Ross Hunter bought it for me. It was a Ruth Gordon play she also starred in. An odd mixture of Queen Lear and Laurel and Hardy. They started introducing more farce as production proceeded. Sandra Dee was in it, Brian Aherne, too. It just didn't come together.

BAWDEN: You wrote *Mrs. Pollifax, Spy* [1971].

RUSSELL: I wrote it, so I must take the blame. Not much at all. There wasn't enough meat in the story, this I must admit.

BAWDEN: And now *The Crooked Hearts*?

RUSSELL: TV is where it's at these days. I'd never worked with Doug Fairbanks. We were at different studios, you see. Same with Kent Smith—he was at Warners when I was at MGM. I started out with Maureen O'Sullivan and there we were again. It had only taken thirty-eight years since *West Point of the Air* [1935]. They let me do makeup and hair at my house to save time, and the location work was done at Pacific Palisades.

Now I'm going back to Broadway in *Twigs*, I think. There's a TV life of Aimee Semple Macpherson I should do. I'm toiling on an autobiography. I'm as busy as ever.

Afterword

These future projects were not to be. Russell battled cancer before succumbing on November 28, 1976. She was seventy-one. Her legacy as a much-respected actress seems secure, especially after *Premiere* magazine named her Hildy Johnson one of the top one hundred movie portrayals of the twentieth century.

Fay Wray

Interview by James Bawden

There are many reasons why movie fans of the twenty-first century should remember Fay Wray: she was a fine actress, a dazzling beauty, and a very classy lady all through her life. Yet to most people she's a screen immortal because she was the girl in the paw of the giant gorilla atop the Empire State building in the 1933 film classic *King Kong*. It's important to remember that she left behind a great many other memorable performances both before and after *King Kong*.

Setting the Scene

I first met Fay Wray in the checkout counter at Gelson's Supermarket in Century City in June 1972. There I was, buying supplies to take back to my room at the Century Plaza Hotel—I was attending a TV critics' convention there—when she tapped me on the shoulder and said, "I just love your coat pin. It's my Maple Leaf flag, too." We sat outside in the sunlight for an hour, talking old movies, and she joined me for lunch the next day.

We met again in 1974 for high tea, and in 1977 I phoned her to talk about the new version of *King Kong* (the awful one with Jessica Lange in the Fay Wray role), which she positively hated.

After many telephone chats, we met again in 1989 when she roared up in her roadster to take me out to lunch in L.A. She was then promoting her autobiography—*On the Other Hand*. At eighty-two, she was dazzlingly handsome. No, make that beautiful—poised and chic. And she was filled with stories.

The Interview

BAWDEN: You are among the most famous of Canadian movie stars. How many others did you meet?

Fay Wray in *Not a Ladies Man* (1942). Courtesy of Columbia Pictures.

Wray: I actually did meet Mary Pickford when I was first in L.A.—late twenties. And she was very sweet, gracious. Walter Pidgeon somewhere along the way. These days the Canadian consul general is always inviting me to Canada Day parties at the Canadian offices here. I know Ann Rutherford is Canadian; Yvonne De Carlo, too; Jane Russell lived in Manitoba for years growing up. But I've never been asked to make a movie there. I was eligible to make three movies in England in 1935–1936 because I was Canadian, of the empire.

BAWDEN: Describe your beginnings.

WRAY: I was born near Cardston, Alberta, on a ranch known as Wrayland. Lived there until I was almost four and we had to move to Salt Lake City. The Alberta winters were just too rough for Mother. We'd be snowed in for weeks. I know what cabin fever is! My parents emigrated from England at the turn of the century. Dad didn't really know that much about farming. Mother was too genteel to be a country wife. I had four brothers and sisters. We were miles from the nearest town. I came back for the centenary and the house was gone, only the gigantic rock with "Wrayland" carved on it had survived, and I arranged for it to be transported to L.A. We left in 1911—June, very hot.

BAWDEN: From there you go to L.A.

WRAY: My parents divorced, which was a scandal at the time. And we were very poor, desperately so. As soon as I could, I searched for work and decided to apply at the Hal Roach Studios, and I got a six months' contract just like that! And at $60 a week, heavenly for those days. I got to do a lead in a two-reeler with Charley Chase, directed by Leo McCarey, and I played the ingenue in a Stan Laurel short. I photographed okay, I guess, and I had enough to buy a secondhand auto.

On my way to work I'd pick up a best buddy, Janet Gaynor, and drive right along Selma Avenue to the Roach Studios. My family rented a nice little house based on the money I was bringing in. That was 1925, I'm figuring. Then came two-reel westerns at Universal; Janet was there, too. Everything was shot on the Universal back lot and against flats to simulate a western town. My costars were Art Accord, Jack Hoxie, and Hoot Gibson, who was the biggest star. I learned how to ride. And in 1926 Janet and I were nominated as WAMPAS Baby Stars. It stood for Western Association of Motion Picture Advertisers. Mary Astor was also there at the gala, so were Dolores Costello, Dolores Del Rio, and a few others I can't recall offhand.

Then Janet said she was quitting westerns to do a film at Fox called *Sunrise* [1927] which, along with *7th Heaven* [1927] and *Street Angel* [1928], won her the very first Academy Award. [The first Academy Awards in 1927-1928 permitted actors to be nominated for multiple performances.] My little buddy became a superstar overnight, and I wanted to do the same thing.

Bawden: How did you get to Paramount?

Wray: I heard Erich von Stroheim needed an ingenue for a film he was making at Selig Studios called *The Wedding March* [1928]. But an agent said I was the wrong type—too big and brunette and von Stroheim wanted a petite blonde. But I persisted and he met with me. And at the end of a long interview, he simply stood up and said, "Goodbye, Mitzi." Mitzi was the character I'd be playing. The contract was for $500 a week and I was under contract to Stroheim's Celebrity Pictures. There were always musicians on set playing Viennese music to put us in the mood. Once a scene started, I just got in character and did what I'd been told in rehearsal. There was no dialogue to learn, of course. [Films were still silent.] Of course, I fell in love with him a little. It was puppy love, but he never tried to seduce me. I'm not sure what I would have done if he had tried. I was so naïve.

I watch the film today—thank goodness it has been preserved—and I'm entranced. And it is a great film. The first of two great films I'd ever make.

Bawden: How did Paramount get the film?

Wray: Celebrity Pictures ran out of money and sold the negative to Paramount, along with my contract. And production was halted and that was that. By that time von Stroheim had shot two hundred thousand feet of film and made a rough cut of fifty thousand feet and was asking to release it in two parts of three hours each! Yes, *Greed* [1925] all over again! [*Greed* originally ran eight hours in length, but was severely cut by the studio and released in a truncated form.] Joe von Sternberg took over editing and there were two films after all. *The Wedding March, Part One* [now known only as *The Wedding March*] ran fourteen reels, complete with synchronized sound effects, and was a fair hit. Part 2 was retitled *The Honeymoon* and ran only in Europe because sound had taken over Hollywood. There was one print of it left at Paris's Cinémathèque and it was destroyed in a vault fire in 1957. Now it is listed as missing. I've never seen part 2.

Bawden: You did a few sound films at Paramount. How many?

Wray: Three. *First Kiss* [1928] paired me with Gary Cooper. The studio saw us as the new young lovers, but both of us were very restrained. Gary would blush after every smooch. I didn't care. He was positively beautiful. And *First Kiss* was made so quickly it was released before Paramount got *The Wedding March* down to a commercial length. Then I made *The Legion of the Condemned* [1928]. It was written by John Monk Saunders, my first husband. Billy Wellman directed it and it was about flyers in the French Foreign Legion. Again it was love scenes with Coop. But the public couldn't have cared less. Because before long I was being featured in movies with Dick Arlen.

Then I was rushed into *Street of Sin* [1928] with Emil Jannings, who spoke atrocious English. The studio was rushing it because everyone sensed his career in America would be destroyed by sound. As it turned out, he didn't even bother to stick around and collect his Oscar [Best Actor, 1927–1928, for *The Last Command* and *The Way of All Flesh*] before departing for Germany. Mauritz Stiller directed it. He'd brought over his protégé, Greta Garbo, and she'd run off with John Gilbert and Maury could sense that he, too, was doomed in the new Hollywood.

Bawden: I've always wanted to see the 1929 version of *The Four Feathers*.

Wray: It had some sound scenes. Merian Cooper, the producer, wanted it all sound but Paramount didn't have enough equipment. I did von Sternberg's first talkie, *Thunderbolt* [1929]. It was made largely at night so the equipment for sound could also be used on another sound film by day. In *Pointed Heels* [1929], I was with Bill Powell, a villain in silents, but his great Broadway training was turning him into Paramount's first talkie star.

Around that time we were all lined up and given talking screen tests. I passed; so did Gary, despite his nervousness. Florence Vidor failed and was let go. They let Warner Baxter go around that time and he strolled over to Fox and won an Oscar for *In Old Arizona* [1929]! And they lost Richard Dix to RKO and he made *Cimarron* [1931], a huge hit. The stars they imported from Broadway were often too old for the cameras. I think only Ruth Chatterton really made it, and she was fourteen years my senior.

Bawden: Then you went to Broadway to star in *Nikki* [1931]?

Wray: I made more Paramount programmers before the studio dropped me in 1931. My husband, John Monk Saunders, wrote a beautiful play for me and I did it without stage training. I must have been pretty brave! John wrote *Wings* [1927] and then *The Dawn Patrol* [1930] and then *The Last Flight* [1931] with Dick Barthelmess. Helen Chandler played Nikki in that movie, but by the time the movie opened I was starring at the Longacre Theatre on Broadway in the musical version. I did an audition scene with the tall, dark, and handsome leading man and we fell for each other very hard. His name was Archibald Leach. Yes, Cary Grant before he became Cary Grant. The play was pretty terrible, but Archie got the most wonderful reviews. We quickly closed and he was off to Paramount with a new name. He chose Cary from his *Nikki* character's name, Cary Lockwood.

BAWDEN: You seemed to drift for awhile.

WRAY: It was the height of the Depression. Jobs were scarce. I only was in three 1932 releases. I'd just come off the only stinker Ronnie Colman made back then, a dog-awful thing called *The Unholy Garden.*

BAWDEN: How did you get to star in the most famous movie in history, *King Kong*?

WRAY: Well, I needed work and Merian Cooper phoned me up and said to come to his offices at RKO. He showed me various sketches of jungle scenes and there was one of a giant ape climbing up the Empire State building. I still hadn't a clue and when he said, "You're going to have the tallest, darkest leading man in Hollywood," I clapped my hands. I thought first of Coop, but he wasn't that dark. Maybe it would be Cary Grant or Gable? And then he showed me an eighteen-inch monkey and introduced us and I felt vastly cheated. Still, I needed work.

Then I listened in rapture as Merian wove his tale—from the primitive jungle to the heights of New York. He said he needed a great actress to put it over. I naïvely suggested Katharine Hepburn—already at RKO—and he laughed.

"I said I needed a good actress, not a great personality," he said.

At a later meeting, I got to chat up Edgar Wallace [who wrote the story line of *Kong*]. He was very pudgy and very British. Always eating sweets. Very rotund. Sweated profusely in the California warmth. At first, he seemed to think my name was Kay Fay! Which gave us all a laugh. And then, ten days later, he caught pneumonia from all that sweating and was soon dead. Merian ditched most of his script and started again with a new one by James Creelman and Ruth Schoedsak.

BAWDEN: When did production begin?

WRAY: Oh, not for months. I was on salary. I'm thinking it was less than $300 a week or so until we started actual production. I actually made about $10,000 from those ten months of work. Anyhow, we first filmed a test reel with back projection in the faux jungle that was being constructed. I was up in a tree screaming and there was a battle between prehistoric monsters. Took twenty-two hours to film that few minutes, but the moneymen in New York had to have something to raise the money. In fact,

Fay Wray is perched in a tree by the giant gorilla in 1933's *King Kong.* Courtesy of RKO Radio Pictures and Turner Classic Movies.

King Kong took ten months, but I had weeks and weeks off between setups and layoffs, so I made four other films that year. All were in the horror genre. I'd become Hollywood's scream queen without realizing it.

BAWDEN: You did *The Most Dangerous Game* [1932] in the *Kong* jungle, but why with Joel McCrea?

WRAY: Because he'd also been signed for *King Kong.* But after we filmed *Game,* which took two weeks, Joel got upset he was waiting around and not being paid much. So he left in a huff, to be replaced by Bruce Cabot. Bruce wasn't as good an actor and he was a lush so he never had that sustained career. And I later heard from Joel he felt it was the worst career mistake of his life.

BAWDEN: What do you remember about those fantastic scenes in the jungle? How much of Kong was full size?

WRAY: Only the mechanical arm that could clench me. I'd be placed in the hand and then the hand would be raised way off the floor. A wind machine gave me that tousled look. And I was scared I'd be thrown and hit that concrete, so that screaming is for real. I'd scream for eight hours up there and then I'd almost faint and they'd have to call it a day. Merian [directed] all those technical scenes and [Ernest] Schoedsack did all the scenes on the boat and the landing on the sandy beach and my imprisonment by natives on Skull Island.

BAWDEN: Describe the premiere.

WRAY: There were two of them. It first opened at Radio City Music Hall and played to packed houses for weeks. There was a lineup for the 9:45 a.m. screening! Then two weeks later it opened again, this time in L.A. at Sid Graumann's Chinese. Wonderful reviews for the film, but not much said about the human actors, for good reason. I simply thought I screamed too much. I spent a week recording screams to be interpolated through the film. But to be in such a hit was a huge plus, I guess. It literally saved RKO from bankruptcy and did so several more times over the next fifteen years. I heard the take up to 1950 was something like $7 million. And then in the late forties, when I wasn't acting anymore and was sprinting over Olympic boulevard, a very nice young chap stopped me and shouted, "Beauty! Where's your Beast?"—or something like that, and I felt I'd become part of history.

BAWDEN: Do you still watch it on TV?

WRAY: I really would watch more often if I had residuals. It cost $680,000, a huge sum in those days. Made several millions the first issue and about the same when reissued every seven years or so. Somebody got very rich off it. Not me. Not Ernest Schoedsack, who had it all figured out how much RKO owed us. But there's no RKO anymore, is there?

BAWDEN: That same year you also made *Doctor X* and *Mystery of the Wax Museum* at Warners, both starring Lionel Atwill and both directed by Michael Curtiz.

WRAY: That's right. Both were in early two-tone Technicolor. The movie cameras were immense, but the arc lights were so intense I'd get spots in my eyes. And the heat generated was something else. Lionel was a very handsome older man who'd been acting since he was a little boy. But there was a depth of depravity there. Stories of orgies at his home intrigued us all. He was married to the ex-wife of General Douglas MacArthur and to be invited to one of their so-called parties was considered a great moment. But I demurred. And later, when details were leaked out, Lionel was virtually blacklisted by the film community.

The sets in *Wax Museum* are very Germanic. I think it's better than *Doctor X*, which is far more gruesome. In *Museum,* Glenda Farrell and Stu

Erwin are so funny with their fast-talking repartee. But we shot some scenes from the two movies one after the other. I just had to scream, so who cares what movie I was in at that time? Curtiz, you know, was the nastiest of directors, concerned with lighting and shadows—ignored me most of the time. But once he lit into Glenda and she shouted right back at him and the crew applauded.

Then, because I had ten days off, I did *The Vampire Bat* [1933] with Lionel Atwill and Melvyn Douglas. I mean, Mel had just acted with Garbo. Now this? Dwight Frye from *Dracula* was in it, too, and a fellow Canadian, Maude Eburne. It was the Depression and nobody could afford to turn down work. But it's the only time I worked with Mel. Who knew two Oscars were in his future—thirty years in the future?

BAWDEN: You also acted that year with Spencer Tracy in *Shanghai Madness*?

WRAY: A strange man. Undoubtedly a great actor. But so wracked by personal problems. My apartment in Century City looks down upon the old Fox lake, which is now paved over with condominiums. And when I look down I think of Spence. He came on to me. He came on to every girl. And when he drank, look out! He went on a bender on this one that lasted for days. His wife was distraught, so I went out on a tour of Hollywood's seedy bars and I found him. Fox dried him out, but a few years later he was dropped because of his alcoholism.

I was up for the colead in *A Man's Castle* [1933], but [director] Frank Borzage chose Loretta Young and she really fell for Spence. I saw right through him, which could be the reason Spence asked that I not be chosen. When Fox fired him for alcoholism in 1935, he cried in his dressing room but moved over to MGM and became a big star. Met him decades later and he just nodded and walked on. Was he embarrassed I might have remembered his drunken antics? Or did he simply not remember?

BAWDEN: Another movie you squeezed in in 1933 was *The Bowery*.

WRAY: The first movie made by Twentieth Century. Louis Mayer put up half the funds for that company and loaned two of his biggest stars, Wally Beery and Jackie Cooper, fresh from *The Champ*. It wasn't much and George Raft was such a gentle man he blanched in one scene where he has to sock me. He barely touched my cheek. Director Raoul Walsh yelled, "Slug that bitch!" and George did it again just as daintily. And twelve more taps until I said, "Do it and let's move on." All those taps and I had a bigger welt than if he'd really slugged me once really hard.

Darryl Zanuck ordered me into his office and said if I'd just play along I could be a big star. He said I could star next with Clark Gable in *Call of the Wild* and after that with George Arliss in *Cardinal Richelieu.* A contract at Twentieth Century would have saved me from slavery in B pictures. I was rapidly descending because I lacked a long-term major studio contract. Then he tried to kiss me and I ran out sobbing. If I'd played along, who knows how far I would have gone?

BAWDEN: You made your last picture with Cooper in 1933, *One Sunday Afternoon*?

WRAY: Never seen these days on TV because Paramount sold remake rights to Warners, which redid it as *The Strawberry Blonde* with Jimmy Cagney. I had the "bad girl" part, that of Virgie Barnstead. It was so strange. I'd been gone, what, two years and everybody had changed. [Paramount chief Jesse] Lasky was out in a coup engineered by Adolph Zukor. Almost all the other stars of my era, with the exception of Coop, were gone. He was still Gary, never really bothering to memorize his lines, catnapping between scenes, still blushing during kissing scenes. He was attached to a lovely girl, Rocky, who can actually be seen screaming in the New York sequence of *Kong.* She was good for him and he was beginning to grow into the Coop myth. Hey, it worked a long time for him, didn't it?

BAWDEN: But you were in another big picture, MGM's *Viva Villa* [1934].

WRAY: It had been filming in Mexico, Howard Hawks directing. And one of the stars, that delicious alcoholic Lee Tracy, stood on a balcony stark naked in front of the assembled Mexican army and tinkled on them. Well, it provoked an international incident. The entire company got deported. Hawks was fired, to be replaced by Jack Conway. Mona Barry was the girl and she was changed, too—for me. Stu Erwin replaced Tracy and only Wallace Beery was left, and great gobs of the story had to be refilmed. You see, I looked Latin and I resembled Mona, who can still be glimpsed in some very long shots. David Selznick liked me after *Kong* [which he executive produced] and later had me make a test for *The Prisoner of Zenda,* but Mary Astor got that part. By that time I was hopelessly mired in the Valley of the Bs.

BAWDEN: Besides *Villa,* you made nine other movies in 1934.

WRAY: I was busy, yes, but stardom had once again eluded me. *The Affairs of Cellini* [1934] wrapped up my [Twentieth Century studio] short contract. It was artistically fine, but a bit of a bomb box office-wise, even

Fay Wray with Wallace Beery in *Viva Villa* (1934). Courtesy of MGM.

with Connie Bennett, Frank Morgan, and Freddie March in the cast. The only other A film was *The Richest Girl in the World* at RKO with Miriam Hopkins in the lead. I had the second lead and it was okay, I guess. I did a lot of Bs around then with Ralph Bellamy—and we're still friends.

BAWDEN: Why did you go to Britain for pictures?

WRAY: To escape a faltering marriage. So I get off the boat, a BBC reporter is there and we are to go to BBC headquarters for an interview. And all they want me to do is scream into the microphone. Which I do and it promptly breaks the service. And BBC is off the air for minutes until repairs can be made.

I signed with Gaumont British, and a lot of Yank stars were over there at that time: Bob Young, Connie Bennett, Eddie Robinson. First up I made *Bulldog Jack* [1934] starring Jack Hulbert and a young man named Ralph Richardson. I remember waiting around for weeks with nothing to do but see the sights. The film was funny, if you liked Jack Hulbert, but he was unknown in the U.S. and it had few play dates.

Then it was on to *The Clairvoyant* [1934] opposite the greatest actor I ever met—Claude Rains. A very tiny man. But Claude was only just starting out in movies, and it played the bottom half of double bills. Then I stayed to costar with Jack Buchanan in *Come out of the Pantry* [1935]. Another credit few have ever seen over here. But I needed money, so I signed for another Jack Buchanan starrer, *When Knights Were Bold* [1936]. This one was rather good. I hear from my Canadian cousins it was a hit in your dominion. But not in the U.S.

There was a sticky moment when it turned out I wasn't eligible, as an American, to work so long in the U.K. When the British chap heard my story about being born in Canada, he gave me a British passport. Which I still cherish, although I only used it that one time. As you know Canadian passports did not exist then. We Canadians were all citizens of the British Empire. And when I returned to Hollywood I'd been away so long I was forgotten.

Bawden: You went back to L.A and to Columbia?

Wray: Needed work, any work. The marriage floundered, I had a baby daughter. Columbia was the home of B pictures and I was a former silent actress, now thirty, and hardly a new face. Harry Cohn [studio boss] knew a good deal and offered me a five-year nonexclusive thing. I'd first met him on loan-out to do *Dirigible* in 1931. I warned him I was pregnant. Harry was very solicitous, said he'd always wanted a son. But he paid just enough to meet the bills. Columbia made its Bs in two weeks–twelve days. And one worked every minute.

My first was *Roaming Lady* [1937] with Ralph Bellamy. Then I made *They Met in a Taxi* [1936] with Ralph. Alfred E. Green directed it, he being a refugee from Warners. In *It Happened in Hollywood* [1937], I had the great Richard Dix as partner, and in *Murder in Greenwich Village* [1937], it was another Paramount refugee, Dick Arlen. We hadn't worked together since *Border Legion* in 1930, and seven years later we were industry retreads.

Bawden: Your career was winding down?

Wray: You said it! Only one movie in 1938—and a bad programmer at Universal titled *The Jury's Secret.* In 1939 I did *Navy Secrets* at Monogram and *Smashing the Spy Ring* at Columbia, again with Ralph. We were the king and queen of the B's by then. I desperately wanted to play Belle Watling in *Gone with the Wind,* but Selznick said I was too young. I don't think I even got to test on that one. I had to settle for *Wildcat Bus* [1940] at RKO. You've never seen it? Lucky you!

BAWDEN: You had one last big picture.

WRAY: Yes, *Adam Had Four Sons* [1941] at Columbia. I was plainly on my last legs and newcomer Susie Hayward was all the talk. Although Warner Baxter was the nominal star, a new Selznick contractee, Ingrid Bergman, got all the attention. I played his first wife and disappeared fairly early. One day Warner whispers in my ear just before a scene, "To think it has come to this!" I knew exactly what he was talking about.

Flash-forward a quarter of a century and a little more to an island in the Gulf of St. Lawrence beside Montreal. It's Expo '67 and I'm there showing *King Kong* to an overflow crowd. Who should pop out of the audience but my *Adam Had Four Sons* costar Ingrid Bergman? And then along comes Gloria Swanson, who takes me aside and mutters, "Isn't it sad how badly Ingrid has aged?"

BAWDEN: You only made two more Bs and then retired at the grand old age of thirty-five? You cowrote a play with Sinclair Lewis around that time.

WRAY: I was always getting involved with writers. I went to Cohasset, Massachusetts, to do summer stock, a play called *George and Margaret*. And it was there I met Sinclair Lewis. He'd been at a dinner party once in L.A., as I recall. He was getting ready to act in a play he'd written, *It Can't Happen Here*. Then he followed me on to my next stop. I mean, he was the ugliest man I'd ever met—pockmarks, teeth stained from tobacco. He started writing a play for the two of us called *Angela Is Twenty-Two*. And it was strange. By then there was also Howard Hughes in pursuit. All this did wonders for my morale. Maybe I wasn't so old after all.

BAWDEN: Your second husband was also a screenwriter.

WRAY: That's right. Bob Riskin. Got the Oscar for *It Happened One Night* [1934]. That picture made him and it made Frank Capra, who is very cruel in his memoirs to Bob. Frank wanted all the glory, but he couldn't write two sentences down and have them make sense. I met Bob in 1941 at a party hosted by Richard and Jessica Barthelmess. And we married and had two lovely children. Who wanted to act? Time to be a stay-home mom.

And then one day in 1951 Bob came home from Fox, where he'd been writing a script for Clifton Webb as "Mr. Belvedere." Said he was weak in one arm. Been having blinding headaches for weeks but didn't want to tell me. Within days he was operated on but he never quite recovered. He was paralyzed. And there was no money coming in.

BAWDEN: Is that why you returned to work?

Wray: Oh, yes. I phoned Darryl Zanuck, who was Bob's boss. And he arranged to give me a small but choice part in *The Treasure of the Golden Condor* [1952]. I'd been away from acting for just a decade, you see. Then MGM phoned. Would I mind playing Jane Powell's mom in *Small Town Girl* [1953]. Would I? She was sweet and very professional and we had a ball. And then all that summer I did a TV situation comedy for CBS called *Pride of the Family,* a kind of poor man's *Father Knows Best.* My sixteen-year-old daughter was played by Natalie Wood, desperate at that time for work. Two years later she was in *Rebel without a Cause* and had an all new career ahead of her.

Bawden: You became the mother to a whole new generation?

Wray: Oh, yes. There was little Debbie Reynolds, although I was actually the mother of the bachelor, Leslie Nielsen. And John Saxon in *Rock Pretty Baby* [1956] and Gary Clarke in *Dragstrip Riot* [1957] and John Saxon again in *Summer Love* [1958]. I was busy!

Bawden: You also had choice parts in a few big A productions.

Wray: Well, *The Cobweb* [1955] was just plain weird, but I got to know and admire Miss Lillian Gish. Then there was *Queen Bee* [1955]—a Joan Crawford soap. She wrote me a welcoming note saying how she'd always admired veterans of the silent days. And I never had the courage to inform her I was actually a year younger than she was. On every Crawford picture, she had a younger cast member to berate and on this one when she had to slap pretty little Lucy Marlowe, she did so with such fury it could be heard all over the sound stage.

With Barbara Stanwyck [in 1957's *Crime of Passion*], here was a true pro, in her last year of screen stardom. We shot mostly on locations just to save money. One day I saw her applying her own makeup beside the truck before a shoot. She looked up and just shrugged. Who could blame her? This production was cost efficient.

Bawden: After 1954 you did a ton of TV work.

Wray: Paid the bills and some of it was fun. *Alfred Hitchcock Show* always treated actors well. I was on a few of those. I did three *Perry Masons*—nice money, good working conditions—two for *Jane Wyman, Wagon Train, G.E. Theater* on multiple occasions. But I stopped acting after the Kennedy assassinations. Just lost all hope for a long spell.

Only acted once since then—in *Gideon's Trumpet* in 1980, playing Hank Fonda's landlady. A very introverted, circumspect man, the complete actor, very much at the top of his game despite physical infirmities. I did that for my daughter Susan Morgan, who produced it. But there were no more offers after that.

BAWDEN: Weren't you offered the role of the elderly survivor of the *Titanic* in the 1997 *Titanic*?

WRAY: Yes. I thought it would be too much for me and I'd disappoint too many people. [Gloria Stuart substituted.]

BAWDEN: You remarried in 1970.

WRAY: To Dr. Sandy Rothenberg, who operated on Bob in 1951. We were both free twenty years later and we live across the street from the Century City hospital where he works. He insists we dine out every night, which means I don't have to cook. And we never tire of finding new restaurants.

Occasionally I'll go out to a showing of *King Kong* or better yet *The Wedding March.* My two great films! I'm so lucky! Many of my contemporaries never had one great movie. And I've got two to my name.

Afterword

Fay Wray died of natural causes on August 8, 2004, in New York City, a month and a few days short of her ninety-seventh birthday. On August 10, the lights on the Empire State building were dimmed for fifteen minutes in her memory. She is buried at Hollywood Forever cemetery right behind Paramount Studios, where she became a star. In 2006, Canada Post honored her with her picture on a 51¢ commemorative stamp as one of four Canadians who made it in Hollywood. The others: Mary Pickford, Lorne Greene, and John Candy.

Jane Wyman

Interview by James Bawden

It's fairly easy to make the case for Jane Wyman's place among the most important movie stars of the golden age. Consider the facts: she ran the gamut from extra to bit player to supporting actress to box office superstar. She played comedies, love stories, serious dramas, and even musicals. She was a genuine movie star and a Best Actress Oscar winner. She even sang (with Bing Crosby) the Oscar-winning song of 1951, "In the Cool, Cool, Cool of the Evening" from Paramount's *Here Comes the Groom*. She was a TV star with two hit series in different eras.

And, as an interesting footnote, Wyman is the only movie actress ever to be married to a president of the United States (Ronald Reagan), although it was before he took office.

Setting the Scene

In 1974, I had lunch with Jane Wyman for the purpose of discussing a CBC-TV project that involved telecasting almost every movie she'd ever made. The luncheon venue was the Polo Lounge in Beverly Hills, and when Wyman, then semiretired, was given what she thought was an inferior table, she had a major hissy fit.

Things had improved by the time we met again in 1979. It was the same restaurant, but this time she had the best table as she was then enjoying a rebirth of her stardom after triumphing in CBS's *Falcon Crest* primetime soap opera.

Later, I also visited her twice in her palatial suite on the *Falcon Crest* location. The rumor that she had personally measured the trailer of incoming guest star Lana Turner to see whose was larger was, she said with a sparkle in her eye, "pure speculation."

Wyman always refused to talk about former husband Ronald Reagan once he became president.

Jane Wyman. James Bawden collection.

The Interview

BAWDEN: Have to admit I haven't seen many of your early movies at Warner Bros.

WYMAN: You mean you haven't seen *Here Comes Carter* [1936], *He Couldn't Say No* [1938], *Brother Rat and a Baby* [1940], *Tugboat Annie*

Jane Wyman and Ronald Reagan celebrate parenthood with child actor Peter B. Good in the 1940 *Brother Rat and a Baby.* Wyman and Reagan, who were married that year, had two children of their own but were divorced in 1948. Courtesy of Warner Bros. and United Artists Television.

Sails Again [1940]? Well, neither have I. I was so busy making these B films at the time. In 1936, I made eleven movies, always in the background and never billed.

BAWDEN: Did Carole Lombard really discover you?

WYMAN: Sort of. I'd been in Los Angeles since 1932, mainly as an extra, but also working in shops. I was in a restaurant one day in 1936 and Bill Demarest spotted me. He was then an agent and he took me to see his pal Carole Lombard, who got me a bit in *My Man Godfrey* [1936]. It was a party scene and I had one line, which was cut before release. But I got paid as support, not as an extra, because of that line and so I was on my way.

Bill shopped me to Bryan Foy, who ran the B movie unit at Warners, and he put me under contract—$65 a week with options for renewal every six months. I was still being unbilled, but occasionally I'd say something. I was a secretary in *Cain and Mabel* [1936] and I have a line or two. And in *Stage Struck* [1936], I stick my head out of the chorus and say to Dick Powell, "My name is Bessie Fuffnick. I swim, dive, imitate wild birds, and play the trombone." And Dick, twelve years later, on Oscar night, sends me this telegram: "Dear Miss Fuffnick, forget the trombone, you also win Oscars."

BAWDEN: Then you were home free?

WYMAN: Not exactly. Every six months I was petrified I'd get dropped as so many girls were. But Bryan Foy took me under his wing and kept me working. I never turned down an assignment, although sometimes I'd be in two pictures at the same time. From eleven movies in 1936 I was only in nine in 1937. Almost had time on my hands.

BAWDEN: Give me your first impression of the studio. Did you meet the great stars?

WYMAN: Never worked with most of them. There were two studios—one was the old Warners lot in downtown Hollywood where Bryan made a lot of his B fodder. The other was the former First National lot in Burbank. I was there a lot, too. Jimmy Cagney knew me and was always shouting, "Hang in there, kid! Fight for every part!" And Kay Francis was very nice to the youngsters, as we were called. In 1937, Ann Sheridan was part of our gang, Marie Wilson, too, and Jane Bryan joined the company that year. Priscilla Lane was to join in 1938. By 1939, Kay Francis was leaving, as was Joan Blondell. Glenda Farrell had left, and I took over her role in the *Torchy Blane* series [in] *Torchy Plays with Fire* [1939]. Those Bs were turned out in twelve days or two weeks (because we always worked Saturdays) and used existing sets. I'd be fitted in wardrobe—dresses were never made for me. Somehow I kept going. Foy ordered me to go to elocution classes. He said my voice was too high pitched.

BAWDEN: Gradually, you were working your way up.

WYMAN: Gradually! Yeah! "Gradually" is the word. By the time of

Flight Angels [1940], I had the second female lead to Virginia Bruce and that was my first picture with Dennis Morgan. We went on to make three more pictures together. And the studio also tried to make me and Jack Carson into a team. In 1940, I was only in six features—I was going up the ladder. My first A picture where I was the leading lady was *Larceny, Inc.* [1942] with Eddie Robinson, who was so supportive. Jackie Gleason was in that as a soda jerk.

If Warners had nothing for me, they'd lend me out. I did *My Favorite Spy* [1942] with Kay Kyser at RKO and *Footlight Serenade* [1942] at Fox with Betty Grable. I remember my name was Flo La Verne. It was typical Grable stuff except for some reason it wasn't in color. It made so much money that Darryl Zanuck officially declared every Grable picture would henceforth be in Technicolor. We became big buds. I recognized her in me. We'd both graduated from the school of hard knocks and both were grateful for every job that came our way.

BAWDEN: But in 1943 you only did one movie.

WYMAN: I was pregnant at the time! And *Princess O'Rourke* was the turning point for me. It was another Livvie de Havilland vehicle, actually just about the last under her contract. I think *Deception* might have been in there, too. At picture's end she was Livvie-izing and said she was glad to be free of Jack Warner, but he surprised her by tacking another six months onto her contract to cover all her suspensions. She sued and three years later broke the power of the old studio system.

Our film was quite cute. I'm convinced parts of the story were "borrowed" for *Roman Holiday* [1953] with Audrey Hepburn. Livvie was nicely cast as a timid princess who goes AWOL during an American tour and Bob Cummings was the ordinary bloke who shows her the country. I was married to Jack Carson [in the picture]. This was a serious part for me and I tackled it with relish. The scenes at the White House were shot there and we even see FDR's little dog, Fala. It was shot in wartime so there was ample opportunity to praise our wonderful country.

BAWDEN: Wasn't it a surprise when you were offered the female lead in Billy Wilder's *The Lost Weekend* [1945]?

WYMAN: It saved my career, really changed it. I was on a promotion tour in New York, tub-thumping the Warners product to exhibitors, when I got a long-distance call from producer Charles Brackett at Paramount. He said he'd arranged to borrow me for the movie version of this best-selling book and was sending over a copy and could I please read it right away.

So I squirreled up in my hotel room and read it one evening, but I couldn't see anything for me.

I was so conditioned to think of myself in comedy. But the part of Helen St. James was mine, and how I worked on it! Billy shot many scenes on the streets of New York, which was considered a novelty at the time. He could be abrasive, cutting, and several times Ray Milland threatened to quit. I thought Phil Terry as the brother quite good, too, and Ray's landlady was played by Joan Fontaine's mother. It opened to tremendous notices and Ray won the Oscar and it was named Best Picture. And I was on my way.

BAWDEN: How did this affect you at Warners?

WYMAN: My next picture was *Night and Day* [1946], the biopic about Cole Porter. It starred Cary Grant and Alexis Smith. My part was subsidiary, that of a blond gold digger who, when she gets her big chance, says she hasn't the pipes and drags out Mary Martin to sing "My Heart Belongs to Daddy." I hated every minute, and halfway through filming the roof on our sound stage collapsed. It was the hottest summer and they put gigantic blocks of ice up there and it was a real mess.

Right at that time MGM borrowed me to play Ma Baxter in *The Yearling* [1946] because the original girl wasn't up to it. They had to start right away, said the director, Clarence Brown, because if they waited the fawns would all grow up. We had a flock of them. So every morning I was Ma bawling to Greg Peck, and when *Night and Day* resumed filming I was silly Gracie Harris every afternoon. But Greg and I both took Oscar nominations, although these days Greg tends to downplay the movie as too pretty. I disagree. He should watch it with a family audience. And it made me realize I was going places at other studios but not at Warners.

BAWDEN: You also made *And Now Tomorrow* that year, a remake of *The Animal Kingdom.*

WYMAN: Oh, pooh! It was made at least three years earlier and shelved during the war. The billing says it all: Ann Sheridan and Dennis Morgan were the stars, and Jack Carson and I were the comic relief.

BAWDEN: In 1947 you made two more pictures: one okay, one very bad.

WYMAN: *Cheyenne* was the very bad one, another western with Dennis Morgan. [Director] Raoul Walsh later told me it was the worst picture he ever did at Warners. Then I also did Billy Wellman's *Magic Town* for RKO opposite Jimmy Stewart. It was a Frank Capra movie without Frank

Jane Wyman, playing a deaf girl in *Johnny Belinda* (1948), "feels" music for the first time when Lew Ayres places her hand on a violin. Wyman won the Best Actress Oscar for her performance. Courtesy of Warner Bros. and the Thalia Theatre.

Capra. The script by Bob Riskin was quite charming, all about pollster Jimmy finding an ideal average town to gauge all sorts of opinions about everything. But Bill lacked the light touch. Every time a scene faltered, Ned Sparks would be popped in to chatter on in that irritating voice of his. But there is one great scene: in a deserted schoolroom. Jimmy tried to recite *The Charge of the Light Brigade* while I'm reciting *Hiawatha.* Now that scene really worked!

BAWDEN: Finally, *Johnny Belinda* [1948] made you a superstar.

WYMAN: Producer Jerry Wald went to bat for me; Jack Warner couldn't see me doing it. For one thing, I had to play a teenager. And she's deaf. First I studied with deaf students for months. But I couldn't get that right until I plugged my ears with beeswax. We shot in northern California to simulate Nova Scotia, so we were away from the studio executives, who would have wanted changes. When Jack started getting the dailies, he'd roar about the numerous shots of seagulls. I think the supporting cast really makes it work—Charles Bickford, Aggie Moorehead, Lew Ayres as the doctor. I poured all my soul into it, but when we finished Jack just shelved it, called the picture a clinker. There was a studio strike on and he finally needed product and it just caught on. But he'd already fired our great director, Jean Negulesco, who promptly marched over to Fox!

BAWDEN: And you got your second Oscar nomination—and won!

WYMAN: In 1946 I was up against Livvie de Havilland and she won, and two years later we're both at it again and she was expected to win again. I mean her performance in *The Snake Pit* was amazing. The other contenders were Irene Dunne, who had never won and certainly had a lot of supporters; Barbara Stanwyck, another nonwinner; and Ingrid Bergman. I think I partly won because of the anti-studio feelings that year as the strike lengthened. I had stood up to Jack. I made him take out full-page ads in *Variety* thanking everyone, including Jean. And our film had heart, which is always a pleasing ingredient, I think.

BAWDEN: Then you went back to comedies.

WYMAN: Jack Warner didn't know what to do with me. Was this all a fluke or what? So he played it safe. Remember, I didn't win until March 1949. So I made two very average films [before winning the Oscar]. *The Lady Takes a Sailor* [1949] plopped me back into comedy, and again Dennis Morgan was there and Eve Arden did her stuff. I like the original title much better: *The Octopus and Miss Smith.* And I did a very pleasant comedy with David Niven, *A Kiss in the Dark* [1949]. Both made money, so Jack became convinced I really could carry bigger-budgeted films.

BAWDEN: You became *the* big female star at Warners.

WYMAN: Bette Davis left the studio in a snit in 1949. I got her dressing room, which was completely redone. Ann Sheridan had already left; Alexis Smith went in 1950. Among the guys, Dennis Morgan and Jack Carson were about to leave. Errol Flynn got dumped a year later and Humphrey Bogart left to freelance. Joan Crawford said she'd stay until they dragged her out by her hair, but she left in 1952. John Wayne and Gary Cooper came on board as independent producers and actors. The studio just changed. Doris Day was as big a star as I was by 1950.

Jack announced my new contract and it gave me right of refusal. I [made] more movies away from the WB lot after 1950.

BAWDEN: What do you think of *The Glass Menagerie* [1950]?

WYMAN: Charlie Feldman was the producer. I tried, I really tried. Jack told me if I didn't do it he wouldn't make it because it needed a big box office star. Irving Rapper came back to the lot to direct it. Irving went off to New York looking for the right actress to play Amanda, the mother. He tested Ruth Chatterton, Miriam Hopkins, Tallulah Bankhead—all turned down by Warner. I did a test with Ethel Barrymore who was wonderful but she admitted, "I'm twenty years too old." Finally Gertrude Lawrence was cast and she didn't have that fire. She was a musical comedy star and the camera simply frightened her. I remember her long, teary accusations every time we had to redo a scene. It was awful. Tennessee Williams was always around and he'd voluntarily rewrite chunks to emphasize farcical elements that better suited Gertrude's moods. But I agree it just didn't come across. However, Kirk Douglas made a fine gentleman caller and Arthur Kennedy was just wonderful as the narrator, Tom.

BAWDEN: And you also made *Stage Fright* [1950] for WB in England.

WYMAN: Hitch [director Alfred Hitchcock] specifically asked me to do it. Now I'm reading he says he had troubles with me, but that's Hitch. He very clearly had problems with Marlene Dietrich. She took me under her wing and tried to glamorize me, but that wasn't the part. Eve was a dedicated RADA student. I had wonderful scenes when I don a disguise to play the maid's odd cousin. And what fun acting with Alastair Sim and Dame Sybil Thorndike as my parents! My favorite scene? I'm at a carnival and Sim gives a little boy a doll he's bloodied to walk up the aisle and give to Marlene, who is singing. All this must be registered on my face without dialogue—and I did it!

BAWDEN: Did you like working with Bing Crosby in Frank Capra's 1951 comedy *Here Comes the Groom*?

WYMAN: Bing is the supreme professional, always accommodating, but he's the big star, so you watch and listen when he's speaking. Frank was complaining about the rushed schedule and felt the staff were relaying stories back to management to hurt him. When I got to sing with Bing, it was a dream come true. And a year later he asked for me again in *Just for You* because Judy Garland's health wasn't up to it. I was lucky I was available so I came on board very quickly. It was pure escapism and little Natalie Wood was so sweet. Ethel Barrymore kept complaining of the number of takes required. She preferred one take and that was it.

BAWDEN: You took your third Oscar nomination for *The Blue Veil* [1951] at RKO.

WYMAN: Once again it was Jerry Wald. I hated that term "Wyman weepies," which some fan magazine dreamed up. For one thing I did not parade my emotions. I may have suffered but I rarely wept out loud. [Director] Curtis Bernhardt understood that. Everything was very restrained. I was shaking in my boots when Charles Laughton came on board but he said he was equally shaking. He claimed he was afraid of me. You know Joan Blondell got a Supporting [Actor] Oscar nomination; she's very good. The picture made a lot of money for RKO, and I'm proud of it. But I didn't want to go to the Oscars that time. I was up against Vivien Leigh as Blanche DuBois. How could li'l ol' me compete against that brilliance? And she, predictably, won.

BAWDEN: Let's not forget *Three Guys Named Mike* [1951].

WYMAN: I did it to show I could still do comedy. And it was a popular theme at MGM. Janet Gaynor made the original as *Three Loves Has Nancy,* and then there was Ann Sothern's *Three Hearts for Julia.* It was basically a commercial for the flying industry. I went to hostess school to make sure it was all realistic. The guys in order of billing were Van Johnson, Howard Keel, and Barry Sullivan. Which one do you think I picked? The top-rated male costar, of course!

BAWDEN: I was disappointed in *The Will Rogers Story* [1952] back at WB.

WYMAN: Blame that on *The Jolson Story.* Everybody was getting biopics by then. I argued that Will Rogers Jr. looked like his dad, but he lacked acting skills and I was right. But I did it to accommodate Jack Warner. Then I remade *So Big* [1953] for him, a classic soaper and it still worked.

BAWDEN: This was the era of remakes. You then remade two Irene Dunne classics.

WYMAN: She stopped me at a party once and said comically, "Will you and Deborah Kerr please stop remaking my old films?" I said, "Irene, you emerged as the winner because our retake on *The Awful Truth*—called fittingly, *Let's Do It Again* [1953]—is a ripe stinker." But I think *Magnificent Obsession* [1954] came out just right; I got producer Ross Hunter to do it, although he argued it was plain hokum. I had to choose which leading man at U-I [Universal-International] to have—Jeff Chandler and George Nader were the other contenders—and I went for Rock Hudson, who was mired in B movies as once I had been. The director was Douglas Sirk and he caught Rock's basic humanity and this one made him a truly big star and it was my biggest box office hit.

BAWDEN: But you had already decided to jump to TV. Why?

WYMAN: Well, *All That Heaven Allows* [1955], again with Rock, wasn't as big a hit at the time, although now everyone says it's a grand picture. And I had a Paramount commitment and they put me in *Lucy Gallant* [1955], which was made by Pine-Thomas, which operated across the street. I also made my favorite-ever movie, *Miracle in the Rain* [1956], with Van Johnson. We shot in New York City using hidden cameras—but Warners held on to it for more than a year. Jack Warner was readying *Giant* [1956], and he put all the publicity money into that one and I could see that the era of simple movies that say something was over. Blockbusters were the new rage. So I got out of movies while the going was good.

BAWDEN: Do you remember your last day at Warners?

WYMAN: Do I! I scrubbed that dressing room and vacuumed it. Actually, there were three rooms. But I wanted to say good-bye to the people who had helped me, and they had already left the lot before me. I was the last actor from the thirties still there. Jimmy Cagney had left months earlier after completing *Mister Roberts* [1955]. From the forties only Virginia Mayo was still around. Annie [Sheridan], Alexis [Smith], Eve Arden had all departed and even Doris Day had left [in 1954]. Crawford lasted until 1952. Dennis Morgan, Jack Carson—all gone to other studios or TV. The crews were mostly gone, although some were working on TV. I'd been there since 1937, and now it was 1955. Every lot was affected and some studios, like Republic and RKO, had virtually disappeared. Different times. The last time I talked to Jack he was all puffed up about Jimmy Dean—and weeks later Jimmy was dead. You go figure it all out.

BAWDEN: How did the TV deal come about?

WYMAN: My agent was Lew Wasserman—end of story. He did it all, yeah. The guy who helped dismantle the old studio system wound up as owner of Universal. My deal with NBC through Lewman Productions was a three-year no-cut contract for $3 million to be spent as hostess, producer, and occasional star of *Jane Wyman Presents the Fireside Theater.* We shot at Revue Studios. Aaron Spelling sold his first TV script to me. Rod Serling wrote the third or fourth episode we ever ran. He won the Emmy that year for his script of *Patterns* [1955]. Of course, it was similar to Loretta Young's show. She got there first and later Junie Allyson and Barbara Stanwyck had similar anthology series. One day I stopped to get gas and the attendant gave me a script which I used and it got an Emmy nomination. And Loretta and I used to swap scripts. I'd say, "Here's one that better suits you. Now give me one of yours!"

I used stars I could trust to work fast yet deliver big—Everett Sloane,

Fernando Lamas, Mercedes McCambridge, Paul Henreid. When Fernando was costarring with me he shouted, "Janie, I'm leaving the set. Gonna have a baby. I mean, Arlene [Dahl] is." And he just left. That baby is now Lorenzo Lamas and I've told him never to leave the set because your father used up all the excuses. We shot in 3.5 days. The half day was rehearsal time and for costume fittings. But what I did not factor into the equation was the rise every year in costs. Consequently, the third season there were only twenty-three episodes and NBC then cancelled us, although ratings were still strong.

I sold the package of ninety-three episodes to ABC and that network ran them in daily reruns every afternoon for years. And that made me well off for the first time, so I didn't have to attempt any of those terrible horror movies featuring some of the other old girls. Honestly, I could never run around with an axe in my hand and I can't scream very well. It's the Belinda in me. [Her character in *Johnny Belinda* was a deaf-mute.]

BAWDEN: But you did jump back into movies very quickly.

WYMAN: Well, in the middle of the night Clifton Webb phones me in a panic and says Gene Tierney can't play his wife in *Holiday for Lovers* [1959] because she was still too fragile. He said, "Janie, you owe me one." This was true because I'd left *Three Coins in the Fountain* [1954] for the TV series. So I went back to movies too quickly and it was terrible. All done against rear projection, although set in South America. Then I did two for Walt Disney. *Pollyanna* [1960] didn't do as well as Walt figured. He later told me the title scared a lot of people off because they thought it would be sugary sweet, and it was full of mischief. *Bon Voyage* [1962] with Fred MacMurray was a popular family picture. And that was it until *How to Commit Marriage* [1969]. Mickey Mouse time with Bob Hope and stuff about gurus. It did make money because of Bob's popularity.

BAWDEN: And you did make attempts to get into another series.

WYMAN: *Dr. Kay* [1962] was a TV pilot that Desi Arnaz had high hopes for. CBS passed. I was told a family doctor was not an exciting premise. Ha! Along came something similar in *Marcus Welby*. Then I made several pilots as Amanda Fallon [1972–1973] that ran on *The Bold Ones*. In one I had a marvelous reunion with Pat O'Brien. It was very moving for me. And I did a presentation with Dennis Weaver that cast us as high school vice principals, but it never went to pilot stage.

BAWDEN: So what were your reactions when Earl Hamner phoned and offered you the lead in *Falcon Crest* in 1979?

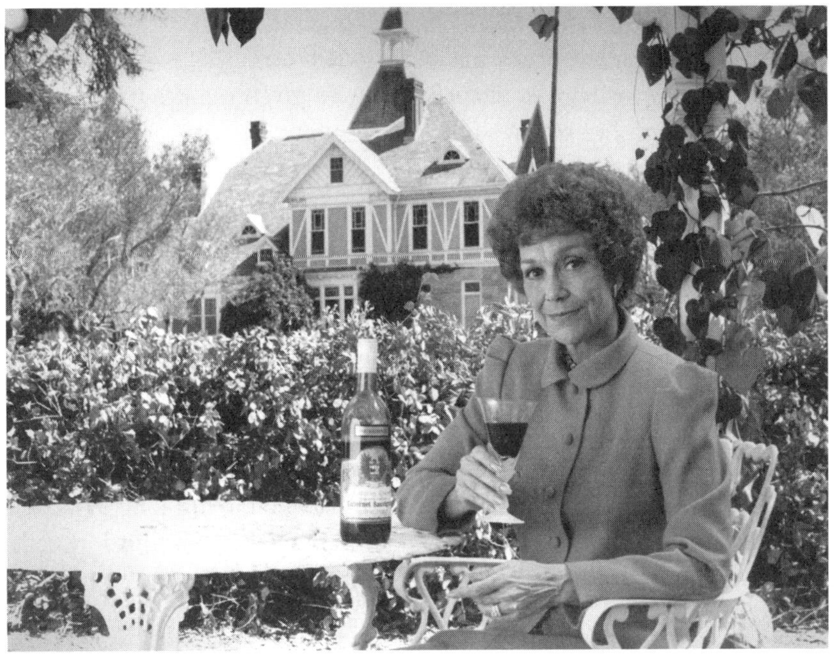

Jane Wyman as Angela Channing in her hit TV drama *Falcon Crest,* circa 1981. Courtesy of CBS.

WYMAN: I told him I'd heard Barbara Stanwyck had turned it down. And he said that was an untrue rumor. It had never been offered to her. He said he was looking for a sympathetic actress and warned me I'd be typed in the press as a female J. R. [The J. R. Ewing character in TV's prime-time soap opera *Dallas* was an amoral power broker.] He said he was dramatizing the flip side of *The Waltons*—this family was infected by wealth, whereas poverty had threatened his Depression story. The pilot was tagged "The Vintage Years" because of the grape-growing story, and I had to sport a white fright wig which I positively hated. And I had a crazy daughter up in the attic. It was dreadful, but Lorimar had a contract with CBS for the hour after their hit *Dallas.* So we soldiered on. I virtually produced the second pilot. Some of the regulars, like Clu Gulager and Samantha Eggar, were replaced. I remade my character, Angie Channing. She now wore only the best. Story lines were hardened.

[Later, at a 1990 party, I spoke with Wyman again about the upcoming finale of *Falcon Crest.*]

BAWDEN: Here you are at the end of this huge hit. Comments?

WYMAN: Only pure pleasure I made it this far. I've been off for a lot of the season [due to late-onset diabetes]. But I'm roaring back in for the grand finale, and what a final speech they've given me. It's been a huge undertaking. And I've gotten some knocks along the way. Mel Ferrer says I had him replaced. Nonsense. His story line was over and the producers wanted him out. Lana Turner? I could never figure that one out. She was never prepared and you must know your lines on episodic TV. And after we had Leslie Caron around and then Gina Lollobrigida I told the producers, "No more international harlots. Do you understand me?"

Oh, there was the day Lorimar bought MGM studios based on profits from our show and said they'd be relocating it to Metro for the next season. I just put my foot down. MGM was by then a real dump. So we stayed on the Warners back lot.

The other day I'm talking to a young thing who has just joined the cast and she chirps, "I hear you've made some movies, too." And I sweetly smiled and said, "Kiddo, I've been at it for sixty years. You should be as fortunate, I dearly hope."

Afterword

Jane Wyman died in Palm Springs on September 10, 2007, aged ninety-three.

Loretta Young

Interview by James Bawden

Loretta Young was a motion picture icon whose presence on the movie screen stretched from her debut as a child in 1916's *Sweet Kitty Bellairs* until her final appearance more than seventy years later as the leading lady of the 1989 TV movie *Lady in the Corner.* Young achieved stardom very early—she was Lon Chaney Sr.'s leading lady in his silent classic *Laugh, Clown, Laugh* (1928)—because of her great wistful beauty. But she soon proved she could dazzle audiences in serious dramatic roles and subtle comedies as well as romantic matchups with Hollywood's top male stars. In her twenties, she starred in a long string of Warner Bros. films in a variety of roles—she even played a Chinese girl who tempts then betrays Chinese Tong assassin Edward G. Robinson in *The Hatchet Man* (1932)—before moving to Fox, where she starred in many big-budget films.

Though never ranked with the screen's great dramatic actresses, Young was adored by filmgoers and won the Best Actress Academy Award for 1947's *The Farmer's Daughter,* an engaging comedy that later became a popular television series.

Young concentrated on television in the 1950s, starring in her own anthology series, *The Loretta Young Show,* which started in 1953 and ran for nine years. After a long absence from the screen, Young returned as the star of *Christmas Eve,* a 1986 made-for-TV movie.

Young was born Gretchen Michaela Young, and two of her sisters were also movie stars in silent screen days—Sally Blane and Polly Ann Young. Another sister, Georgiana, was the wife of actor Ricardo Montalban.

Young was married briefly to actor Grant Withers, but they were divorced and she later married producer Tom Lewis, who supervised her TV series. Throughout her career, Young was always a pillar of the Hollywood community, much admired for her charity work.

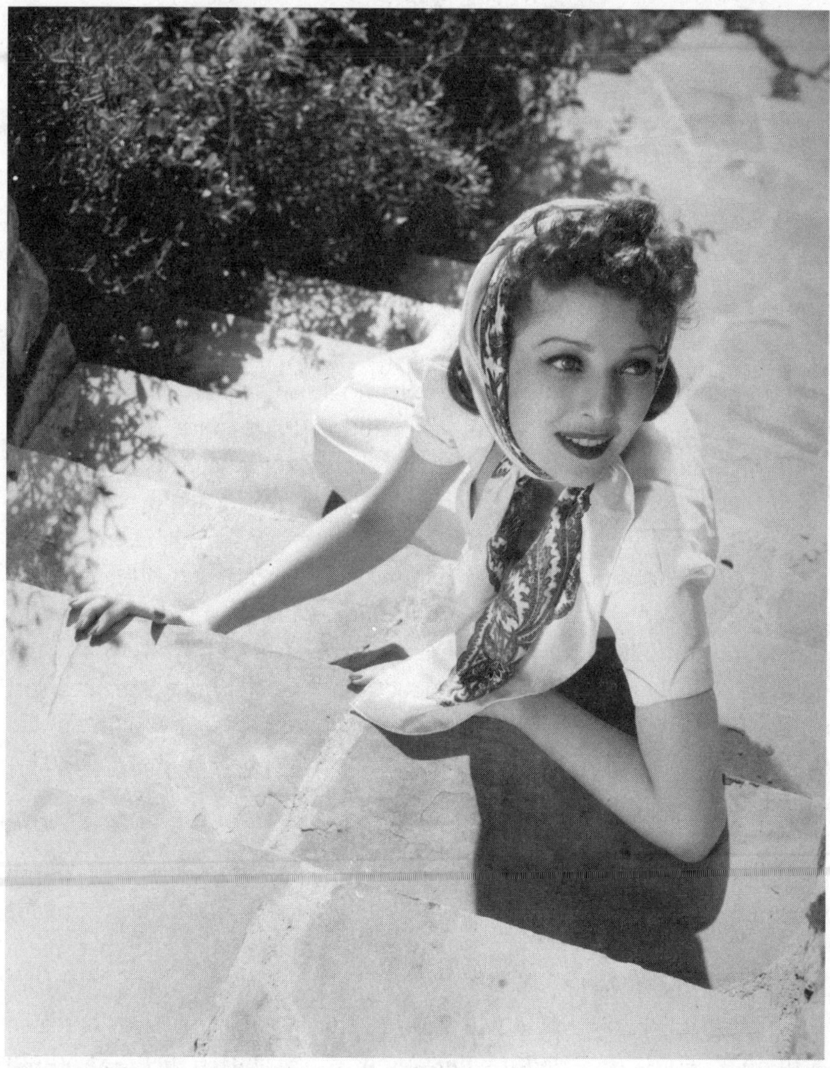

Loretta Young, circa 1947. Ron Miller collection.

Setting the Scene

One blustery Saturday morning in November 1986, I ventured down to Toronto's University Avenue courthouse to meet Loretta Young. The famous TV and movie actress had been retired for twenty-three years, and it was the last day of shooting on her comeback effort, the TV movie *Christmas Eve.*

For weeks I'd been trying to get on the set, without success. Then the president of NBC International made a personal plea for one interview because, as he bluntly told Young, "You have a financial stake in this movie and it hasn't been sold to Canadian TV as yet because nobody knows who you are anymore."

Young complied, but specified the interview could last only fifteen minutes, and then I would have to go. But in her trailer she was annoyed at being unneeded on the set—the cast and crew were doing mundane pickup shots—so I cajoled her with my questions, and that short interview stretched into a marathon session of more than seven hours.

The Interview

BAWDEN: Now that you're almost finished making *Christmas Eve,* what changes do you notice in making films?

YOUNG: Thank you for not calling it a comeback. Because I never retired from life. We're shooting this one almost entirely on location [in Toronto]. In the bad old days, we'd do everything on the back lot and in front of transparency screens. We've finished a scene where Trevor Howard as my chauffeur drives me around the city at night. No process screens! They put the car on a gigantic truck and photographed us that way. It was sheer fun.

Differences? The role of women, certainly. I see women carrying things all over the set. I guess it's called equality. I just hope they don't break their backs.

BAWDEN: I don't see your famous "swear box" anywhere.

YOUNG: Oh, Canadians are very polite. I started that not to make money for charity but to remind my crew that they were taking the Lord's name in vain. Oh, I know all the words. But my box was to restore decorum. Once Joe Mankiewicz, who was very full of himself, waltzed by on the set of *Come to the Stable* [1949], stuffed $5 in the box, and said, "Now, Loretta, I can really tell you where to go." It didn't faze me—I had his money for my latest cause.

BAWDEN: Why pick this particular project?

YOUNG: I was going to return in a TV movie called *Dark Mansions* [1986] for Aaron Spelling who, when he was acting, used to rehearse in my garage with my daughter, Judy Lewis. Just before filming started, he told me ABC could change the script even during production. I left, and dear

Joan Fontaine took over. Then I was offered *The Two Mrs. Grenvilles* [1987] and I thought it needed a top producer to put it over, but there are no Sam Goldwyns today. I refused it, and Claudette Colbert took the mother-in-law role. If I'd accepted either of those, I couldn't have done *Christmas Eve,* which is a wonderful family story I predict will become a seasonal favorite.

BAWDEN: Did you ever miss acting?

YOUNG: You mean, was I sitting at home dusting my trophies? Hardly! I was always working at my charities. I had a youth project in Phoenix. Back in L.A., I worked at a hospice. One day I was rubbing the feet of a man named Ernie as he watched me in *Along Came Jones* [1945] on his TV set. He glanced up, startled, then said I looked much better these days. So he got an extra ten minutes of massage for that!

I visit old friends. I live in the smallest home in Beverly Hills. I'm not a clotheshorse. I can wear a Jean Louis dress from twenty years ago or something new. I'm into other things. I never considered myself a beauty. I think I lasted because I was the hardest worker at the studio.

BAWDEN: But your reputation is . . .

YOUNG: As a holy roller? My son took me to see *The Killing Fields* [1984], and it was so powerful. I loved *Greystoke* [1984], *Tootsie* [1982], *Places in the Heart* [1984]. I kept thinking of all the strange things we couldn't do back then. It was foolish to show married couples in twin beds. I did sue Fox for interpolating scenes of me into that trash [*Myra Breckenridge,* 1970]. But I've never been divorced from life. I love Benny Hill. Yes, I really do. I love a good laugh!

BAWDEN: Is the story of your first big role in movies true?

YOUNG: Oh, yes, I answered the phone when I was all of thirteen-fourteen, and it was a nice man, Mervyn LeRoy, at First National, looking for my older sister Sally Blane. I'd been in the flickers since I was four, but as an extra. The first one was with Fanny Ward. Then, at thirteen, I did *Orchids and Ermine* [1927] with the great star Colleen Moore and she got FN [First National] to put me under contract—$150 a week for forty weeks a year. We were very poor. Mother ran a boardinghouse and we could feed the whole family on that.

BAWDEN: When did you join Warners?

YOUNG: Never joined. In 1927–1928, First National was purchased by Warners. FN's huge Burbank lot was my home for seven years. Warners picked me up along with Colleen, Dick Barthelmess, lots of others. Colleen recently saw me at LeRoy's eightieth birthday party and hollered over the din, "Hey, Gretch!"

BAWDEN: Do you remember many of your silents?

YOUNG: No, because I never saw them when first released. I was too young and my parts were as the young girl. In 1928, I was loaned to MGM for *Laugh, Clown, Laugh,* one of Lon Chaney's last silents. He was a magnificent actor, very soft spoken, a pantomime genius. The director was Herbert Brenon and he hated me and screamed a lot. Then Mr. Chaney would come over, dry my tears, and say, "I think you should do it this way" and act out my part for me. He got this little girl through it and I was noticed for the first time, and I went back to Warners in triumph. Then in 1931 I made *Beau Ideal* and Brenon was the director, sinking fast because he couldn't adapt to talkies. And he yelled at me just as much as before!

BAWDEN: You were kept busy!

YOUNG: In 1929, I made six pictures; in 1930, I made eight pictures. In 1931, I made eight and collapsed and had to be hospitalized for physical exhaustion. We worked six days a week then. So Jack Warner said he'd modify that pace. I only did six pictures that year [1932]. Always as "the girl." I never had much personality in those days.

Remember, we worked forty weeks with twelve weeks of unpaid layoff. If I wasn't engaged, Jack would loan me out, and gradually it occurred to me the loan-outs always turned out better. In *The Devil to Pay* [1930], I was opposite the great Ronald Colman. I was all of seventeen—he was thirty-seven, and I thought him impossibly old. But before every take he'd whisper, "Courage, my dear!" Myrna Loy was the bad girl. And ten years later I'm driving down Sunset and there's a billboard of its rerelease: Ronald Colman and Myrna Loy with Loretta Young. I was downsized! Had to stop the car because I was laughing so hard. But Myrna had just been named queen of Hollywood and I was temporarily blackballed by the studios.

Another great loan-out was to Columbia for *Platinum Blonde* [1931], directed by Frank Capra, a tiny little Italian, and opposite Jean Harlow in her slinky period. And Capra guided me so smoothly, I got attention I'd never received at Warners. I remember one tough speech; we did it ten times. I was in tears and I shouted, "I don't know what you want!" And Frank whispered, "I just think you can do better." What a great line to toss to an eighteen-year-old desperate for recognition, approval.

Also on loan-out, I did *Zoo in Budapest* [1933] at Fox. The photography is shimmering. I just saw it—for the first time! And at Columbia *A*

Man's Castle [1933], directed by Frank Borzage, with Spencer Tracy. It really came off, made me very hot in the business.

Oh, and over at MGM I did *Midnight Mary* [1933] with [director] Wild Bill Wellman. We were both in the Warners doghouse right then. Intended as a three-week B, it became one of Metro's biggest grossers of the year. Every scene crackled with tension, and Bill never directed a dud in his career. So yes, my biggest hits were away from the home lot.

BAWDEN: You missed acting with most of the big Warners stars.

YOUNG: I played the girl in *Heroes for Sale* [1933]. I was twenty, Dick Barthelmess forty, and I considered him so old. I'd already done *Taxi* [1932] with [James] Cagney. Completely forgot about it until a friend loaned me a tape. I remembered in one scene director Roy Del Ruth told me to slap Jimmy hard on the face and run up the stairs as fast as I could because he wasn't expecting it. The look of surprise on his face is supreme. I slapped Jimmy Cagney and got away with it!

BAWDEN: You left Warners in 1934.

YOUNG: The studio was run by Darryl Zanuck and he left to found Twentieth Century Pictures, releasing through UA [United Artists]. He got Connie Bennett and George Arliss to follow him and when he asked me, I thought that was just fine. Jack [Warner] offered another seven years at the price tag of $1 million, a fortune in the Depression. But I felt another seven years of mediocre pictures and I'd be through for good.

BAWDEN: Your first movie at Twentieth was *House of Rothschild* [1934]?

YOUNG: I had forgotten I made a movie with Mr. George Arliss, as he insisted on being billed. I thought him pompous until one day he called me over and said if I wanted a long career I'd have to acquire knowledge of the basics, including lighting and lenses. He said to stick closely to the cinematographer, who can make or break any actor. He was a strict disciplinarian where ingenues were concerned. Insisted on a code of listening and learning. I'd never worked with him at Warners. I wound up as an ardent admirer. I'd always been my best on the first take, but he drummed into me that many retakes were needed to get that perfect pitch. He insisted raw emotion wasn't enough, that what I needed was rehearsal and more rehearsal. Both Bob Young and I were worked furiously and loved it that we were being taken seriously.

BAWDEN: You were telling me over lunch about your worst-ever picture.

Loretta Young with Jack Oakie (*left*) and Clark Gable in 1935's *Call of the Wild.* Young and Gable had a love affair during the filming, which resulted in the birth of Young's daughter, Judy. Courtesy of 20th Century-Fox.

YOUNG: *Born to Be Bad* [1934]. One critic simply wrote, "It is." That was the entire review. Made that at Twentieth and it was a rich, ripe stinker. I was an unwed mother, Cary Grant a pig farmer from Wisconsin. Then the Production Code weighed in and nobody could figure what was happening after those guys got through with it. One ten-page directive concerned the provocative clothes I was to wear. We made it and it was rejected and Sidney Lanfield came in and redid about half the scenes. But that made things worse. It seemed really dirty and then whole chunks were cut out. The first director was Lowell Sherman, who'd guided Kate Hepburn to an Oscar, so expectations were big. But I didn't know how to play heartless and nasty. It was against my better judgment. I only wanted to play good girls. Thirteen years later Cary and I were reunited [in *The Bishop's Wife*], and he comes on set the first day and says, "Loretta, you owe me one good picture." And he was right.

BAWDEN: Your first 20th Century-Fox film was the all-star *Ladies in Love* [1936].

YOUNG: Oh, they remade it many times. It was about three girls in the big city. Think *How to Marry a Millionaire.* That was one of the remakes. Budapest was re-created on the back lot. Even pieces of the set from *Sunrise* [1927] were still up and usable. I watched as Darryl systematically cut down Janet Gaynor's part, although she had first billing rights. He was convinced her huge salary—$400,000 a year—was a drag on studio expenses and, after all, she was all of thirty! Janet was so disheartened she asked for her contract terminated and got it. Second billed was Connie Bennett, no longer the box office sensation of a few years back, just glad to get a job. And I got third star billing. Unknowns in the cast included Ty Power and Don Ameche and a little French number, Simone Simon, Darryl was determined to make into a star. She never took with American audiences but it wasn't for [lack of] trying.

BAWDEN: You said some of your Zanuck films you positively hated. Which ones?

YOUNG: Well, *Suez* [1938] was right up there. Firstly, it was all wildly inaccurate. Zanuck was trying to promote the career of Annabella, another French import. At the time Ty and I were dating. We'd dart into the Westwood movie palace after work and eat popcorn and hot dogs. Then he stopped asking me out. He'd fallen for her! He was twenty-three and she was twenty-seven. Oh, it was a scandal in all the movie magazines.

A lot of dough was spent on costumes, sets, but there was no story. They had Disraeli [played by Miles Mander] getting involved, and that never happened until the British coup to take over the whole thing. Director Allan Dwan said it was about a guy who digs a ditch. I hated being Eugenie so much I ordered the costumer to make really big hoop skirts, so large I couldn't get through most doors or even sit down. If I didn't have the lines, at least I'd have the audience's attention. Then Ty married Annabella in real life and Zanuck was so angry he virtually blackballed her!

BAWDEN: How do you remember Tyrone Power?

YOUNG: Originally, as a dreamy youth. We grew up together. He was completely committed to the theater but wound up this amazing box office attraction. At one point he was the only true superstar under contract at

Twentieth. He was so beautiful. He hated that. We confided in each other. We looked good together, so we made a succession of romps which all made money: *Love Is News* [1937], *Hotel Metropole* [1937]. He hated them all, wanted to tackle the classics. But that was the fad then—beautiful people. After all, it was the Depression. I did two with Franchot Tone, who was just as pretty. So was Bob Taylor. People didn't need realism then. They had it on the bread lines.

BAWDEN: Describe life at Twentieth.

YOUNG: I'd get up at the crack of dawn. I lived in Bel Air and I'd drive down—no entourage for me—and through the back gates. The lot was a beehive of preparation for the upcoming day's shoot. As a teenager, I'd go home, put the Victrola on, and dance for an hour, driving my mother crazy. I never was a clotheshorse. That was Connie Bennett, who used to joke about the lines on her neck, which she called her necklaces. I hated my swan's neck, and my ribs stuck out in front. When I stopped acting, I stopped smoking—and promptly put on ten pounds. The cameramen liked photographing bones. I hated being reviewed for my beauty. To me Dietrich and Lamarr were the beautiful ones. I couldn't do drama like Bette Davis or comedy like Carole Lombard, but I could do both passably and that's why I had a strong female fan base. I was average enough to appeal to all those shopgirls, you see.

BAWDEN: Some of your movies from this period are disappointing to watch today.

YOUNG: Like *Four Men and a Prayer* [1938], which Jack Ford says he did under duress. I had no idea why I was making this thing, I just exchanged wardrobes a lot. It was definitely a make-work project for us all. *Kentucky* [1938] was passable because in was in Technicolor, but my part was negligible. Walter Brennan got a Supporting [Actor] Oscar for that one. At the time Zanuck was promoting the career of Richard Greene, a very pleasant boy. Zanuck said Richard would go farther than David Niven, who was also in *Four Men and a Prayer,* which shows nobody can predict screen stardom.

But the movie that wrecked it all for me at Twentieth was *The Story of Alexander Graham Bell* [1939]. I blame Mrs. Mabel Bell for ruining my career there. Oh, Hank Fonda hated that one—third billed as the second male lead to Don Ameche. In real life, she was a deaf mute, as they were then called, but Zanuck would have none of that. I told him I intended to sign in the early part of the film as Mabel had done, and he blew up and stormed off the set. I loved it when Charlie Coburn piped up one day and said to Gene Lockhart, "We had much more fun on the set of *Edison the Man*." As far as it goes, I wasn't even to suggest the strange atonal speech a deaf girl would use since she couldn't ever hear herself speaking. Everything was fake in this one, right down to the soap chips as snow, and I was sick of that.

BAWDEN: Is that why you left Twentieth at the end of 1939?

YOUNG: My contract was up and I decided to freelance as my pals Irene Dunne and Roz Russell were doing. Zanuck was floored. He just assumed I'd automatically renew, based on the money offered. I said, "I'm leaving because he never sent flowers," which was a joke and a dig at him for ignoring me. But Louella [Parsons] heard it and made a big fuss about what a spoiled child I was. Child? I was twenty-seven with fourteen years of being under contract. Time to strike out on my own.

BAWDEN: But at first there was no work.

YOUNG: Month after month there were no offers. I had an agent, Mr. Townsend, but I never really needed him when under long-term contract. But he said he could do nothing. Then I was testing for *Rebecca* [1940] for David Selznick and I told him my predicament and he said, "Why, you have been blackballed!" Got in touch with his brother, who was an agent—Myron Selznick. And Myron threatened a lawsuit—restraint of trade. And he cagily got Harry Cohn at Columbia to break the blacklist by hiring me for two pictures for the price of one—$80,000—and I was back at it as both pictures were successful. Then the offers flowed in and I could pick and choose as I wanted. I made two or three picture deals after that.

BAWDEN: How was Cohn?

YOUNG: I rather liked the old coot. Very vulgar, but he loved making movies. Our first, *The Doctor Takes a Wife* [1940], was amiable, and I had Ray Milland as costar and he brought in the women in the audience and it was a big hit. Then for *Bedtime Story* [1941], Harry got so mad he yanked the film back at the last moment and switched billing—Freddie March was now number one—and that cost a lot of money. In our final scene I needed a party dress and costumes couldn't supply one, so Harry said to go down to Bullock's and get an appropriate long dress and I picked one with a huge price tag, charged it to him, and he literally blew his top. I guess I should have checked, but we went at each other for the next decade before I finally apologized. Another Columbia comedy, *A Night to Remember* [1943], was already in the can or nearly finished, I think.

Loretta Young in *The Bishop's Wife* (1947). Courtesy of Samuel Goldwyn Productions, RKO Pictures, and TV station KTVU, Oakland, CA.

BAWDEN: Did freelancing work out?

YOUNG: I started making the films people remember me for. My first for Paramount was a wartime thing, *China* [1943], that was popular because of the conflict. The studio asked if Alan Ladd could be my leading man. They were trying to wean him off gangster roles. I liked him and his sense of family, but he was very wooden. By the way, he was shorter than me, so I'd stand in a foxhole for romantic moments. But the public response was so strong we were immediately reteamed in another, *And Now Tomorrow* [1944], and he was a doctor trying to cure me of deafness. But he was smoother, obviously learning as he went along. Imagine my surprise at the premiere when our names were switched and I got second billing. I learned why when I went outside after it was over and there was a huge crowd of bobbysoxers calling his name.

BAWDEN: You also worked with Gary Cooper and Orson Welles in that period.

YOUNG: *Along Came Jones* with Gary Cooper was a comedy western that slowed right down every time Coop ambled on-screen. It underperformed at the box office. Watching Orson direct and star in *The Stranger* [1946] was a lesson in cinema making. Did you know his original choice of the war crimes commissioner was going to be Aggie Moorehead and she'd been promised the part, but our intrepid producer said no, there'd only be suspense building with somebody like Eddie Robinson doing the tracking.

BAWDEN: Did you expect to win an Oscar for *The Farmer's Daughter*?

YOUNG: I'd been officially an actress for two decades. At thirty-four, I'm suddenly nominated and it wasn't that difficult, my performance. Remember I told you I tested for David Selznick for *Rebecca* and was turned down because I was considered too American? David promised he'd use me someday, and it only took seven years. And it only came about because Ingrid Bergman turned down the role of the Swedish maid. She said no more Swedes. Our little picture was no masterwork, but it affirmed American values. And there was such a wonderful cast of scene-stealers: Ethel Barrymore, Charlie Bickford, Rhys Williams. The director was Hank Potter, who never gets his due. And there were three unknowns as my brothers: Jim Arness, Lex Barker, Keith Andes. Whatever happened to them? See, it wasn't just a comedy, it was about something without being a flag waver.

On Oscar night I felt queasy. At the subsequent banquet RKO had bought two tables side by side: one for us, supposedly the losers, the other for the winning team of *Mourning Becomes Electra*. When my name was announced, all I heard was this gush of surprise from the audience. I sat there stunned. Then my sister, Georgiana, sitting right behind me, said, "Oh, Gretch!" and poked me and I ran up sobbing to accept. Felt awfully sad my best bud Roz Russell didn't get it, but she was so strong she drove her mom home to bed and then came back to party. RKO changed the nameplates and we got the larger winners' table!

BAWDEN: Did it advance your career?

YOUNG: Not much. I only had one film out in 1948, a good one, *Rachel and the Stranger,* casting me as a colonial bondswoman, and I had two big leading men: Bill Holden and Bob Mitchum. At the beginning of 1949, *The Accused* came out and it was the true story of a college prof accused of murdering a student who comes on to her. A real film noir, and I liked that it was almost entirely shot out on the streets of Los Angeles.

BAWDEN: And you also came back to Twentieth.

YOUNG: Darryl phones up after the Oscar win and offers me a three-picture deal. Never mentions his blazing indictment that I'd never again work in this town! I said I'd do *Mother Is a Freshman* [1949] only if I could also do a script he'd had in the closet about Belgian nuns in New England: *Come to the Stable.* He started roaring on the phone: "Religious pictures don't sell!" Me: "That's funny coming from the producer of *The Song of Bernadette.*" A truce was called. I did *Mother Is a Freshman* and it was a cute comedy and made a few bucks. But *Come to the Stable* was a huge grosser and is shown on TV every Christmas.

The third picture was *Half Angel* [1951], back with Joe Cotten. We were too old to play these cute parts and both of us knew that. We started with Julie Dassin. After ten days of laborious overdirecting, we didn't have a single funny scene. I called Zanuck at home that night. He watched all the takes over the weekend and replaced Julie with Dick Sale Monday morning. But the picture still flopped. It was a comedy about sleepwalking that put everybody to sleep, cast included.

BAWDEN: Did you feel your career was slipping? Is that why you jumped to TV?

YOUNG: Nuts! *Key to the City* [1950] with Clark Gable was a hit. My husband [Tom Lewis] and I made *Cause for Alarm!* [1951] on the streets of L.A. in three weeks and it made money. *Paula* [1952] was a hit. Ditto *Because of You* [1952] with Jeff Chandler. [It] was as big a hit as there was in 1952. The girls loved seeing me in Jeff's arms. And by the time I finished *It Happens Every Thursday* [1953], I'd already signed with NBC.

You see, I'd seen the sense of wonderment on the faces of my three little kids as they watched TV. It was a revolution even bigger than talkies, and I wanted to be the first movie star to try it. I naïvely thought there'd be time every summer for a movie. When it was announced, L. B. Mayer phoned up and said, "You'll never make another picture, dear." In Beverly Hills, I was considered a traitor. There were no TV antennas there. He was absolutely right! I never did! But when we geared up [for *The Loretta Young Show*], we rented space from old Sam Goldwyn at his studio—old Sam recognized a bargain when he received it.

BAWDEN: How did it all come about?

YOUNG: My husband and I formed a company and decided to make presentations and NBC immediately wanted it. CBS offered me one where I'd play the same character every week, a housewife, and I even visited with Lucy Ball to see how she did it in front of a studio audience.

From the get-go we saw it as a filmed anthology series titled *Letter to Loretta,* and I would introduce every episode and star in many shows. Half hour. And NBC gave us a wonderful slot—Sundays at 10 p.m. We used great movie directors: Rudy Mate, my brother-in-law Norman Foster. George Nader was my first costar and we got him back a lot, and for casts I used all the wonderful character actors then floating around: Ellen Corby, Mae Clark, Frank Ferguson, Bruce Bennett, Burt Mustin—I knew them all and the fact they were looking for work because the picture business was slowing down. Dick Arlen said he'd come back as often as he could because our cinematographer made him look ten years younger. We treated them royally and they delivered. Every twenty-five-minute episode was shot in three days, which meant no multiple retakes. But these veterans could do everything in one perfect take.

An early director told me to swirl my skirt during an introduction and it became a staple. But you see, as long as I showed myself I could go on and become any kind of character I wished: a dumb blonde, a Hiroshima survivor, nuns, wicked women—every permutation. Hard work never frightened me. You see, in my long career I never complained about the long hours.

We got more popular by the year. I'd naïvely thought I could make a movie every summer during hiatus. That never happened! We started off with thirty-six episodes, which was far too many. By season 5, we were down to twenty-nine, which was too few, said NBC. We ended with season 8 and thirty-one new shows.

The reruns were repackaged by NBC as a summer series, and my old pal Anita Louise came in and provided new introductions. We sold first rerun rights to NBC for millions and the network reran them for years in the afternoon. Yes, it's true I did successfully sue NBC years later because our deal said they couldn't use the introductions because people would naturally assume I was wearing outdated fashions.

Bawden: You made 216 episodes in eight years but immediately were offered and took a second series. Why?

Young: *The New Loretta Young Show* [1962–1963]. I was playing the same part every week and my boredom showed. My fans hated it. I hated it and it lasted twenty-six weeks. Did it to satisfy the old ego, and I flopped.

Then I spent six months sleeping, then I traveled around the world. My pal and I enter this nightclub in Tokyo, the orchestra leader spots me and the band starts playing, "Ramona, when day is done I hear your call" [from her 1936 film *Ramona.*]. Stardom! Couldn't even escape it in Japan!

BAWDEN: You were offered other movie roles but refused. Why?

YOUNG: Nothing seemed to work. They offered me the lead in what became *The Innocents* [1961] with Deborah Kerr, and I thought about it. And then when Joan Crawford got sick on the set of *Hush . . . Hush, Sweet Charlotte,* I was asked to substitute. Couldn't do that to my old pal. Besides I'd look silly running around with a saw in my hand. It would have disappointed my fans. I'm not passing judgment on those old gals who do this sort of thing—they really need the money.

BAWDEN: Now what?

YOUNG: There's room for more acting. I have three adult children I'm proud of. Judy used to be a TV producer and is now studying to be a psychologist. Peter is back studying at university and painting houses to make it through. Chris makes horror movies direct to video. They must be powerful because he won't let me see them. I'm divorced from my husband, but under church law cannot remarry and for that I'm grateful because it has prevented me making another mistake. From my vantage point I now see that God has had it all planned out for me. He has really been very, very good to me and I'm grateful.

Afterword

Loretta Young's daughter, Judy Lewis, wrote a shocking tell-all book, *Uncommon Knowledge,* which reported that Young and Clark Gable had an affair during the making of *Call of the Wild* [1935], which resulted in a pregnancy and the birth of an illegitimate child, Judy, who was subsequently adopted by Young. The star had covered up the fact she was adopting her own child, and the book's publication caused a rift in their relationship, although the two later reconciled.

In 1993, despite her protestations in our interview, Young married for a third time; her husband, dress designer Jean Louis, died in 1997. Young died August 12, 2000, aged eighty-seven, at the residence of her sister Georgiana and her brother-in-law, Ricardo Montalban.

IV

The Queens of the Bs

Jane Greer

Interview by James Bawden

There are some fans who doubt that film noir could have existed properly if there had never been a Jane Greer. Though she was a beautiful woman under any kind of lighting, Greer was exceptional as the ice-blooded temptress of that dark, mystery-shrouded genre of movies, especially in her greatest role as the sleek beauty who drives both Robert Mitchum and Kirk Douglas wild in the classic *Out of the Past* (1947). When they rank Hollywood's best "bad girls," Greer will surely be at the top of the list.

Setting the Scene

I was only vaguely aware of Jane Greer until I saw her on a TV *Late Show* in the early 1960s starring in *Out of the Past.* I guess I was an impressionable teenager because she made quite an impact as the thoroughly amoral Kathie Moffett. A little bit later I caught her on the big screen in *Where Love Has Gone* (1964), and later still in *The Outfit* (1973). She always made an impression, even in limited roles. I vowed I would try to talk with her someday. So in the summer of 1984, while I was in Los Angeles, I arranged a lunch with her. She had the choice of venue and, oddly, she picked Hamburger Hamlet in Century City.

The Interview

Bawden: Why did you laugh when I phoned to ask for an interview for a career article in the *Toronto Star*?

Greer: Because I thought, "What career?" I've only been an actress off and on. Then you asked about *Out of the Past* and, well, I thought, "Why not?"

Bawden: Where did you come from?

Greer: I grew up in Washington, D.C. It's not only the U.S. capital, it

Jane Greer. James Bawden collection.

also has very poor sections, which is where we always lived. I was born September 9, 1924, and I have a twin brother, Donne. He wanted to act, too, but a funny little thing called World War II intervened. Dad was an inventor of household gadgets like an onion peeler. We weren't exactly poor; destitute [was] more like it. Mother had had her career ambitions thwarted by the times. She went all out for me until that day tragedy struck.

BAWDEN: Meaning?

GREER: I was seventeen, going out to the pictures with my boyfriend. I opened the door, he took one look and shrieked. I looked in the mirror and shrieked, too. One eye was bloodshot and flowing heavily. My mouth was horribly contorted and gaped open. I couldn't close it. My entire left side was distorted in an ugly grin that would not go away. When I went to sleep that night, I had to manually close my left eye. One half of my face was completely paralyzed.

I had Bell's palsy. It comes from a virus. Many people never get over it. Mom rented a heat lamp to put on my face. I slept with a hot water bottle up to it. It took months before there was a muscle flicker. The doctor had warned me I might never get better. I did, but gradually. I had to go for arduous physical therapy sessions. When I went back to school months later, I'd twist that face into a smile before setting off. People came to think I had a Mona Lisa expression. Even in my movies, I don't smile or frown very much. It's the way I am.

BAWDEN: How did you get into show business?

GREER: I could always sing. A little. Had to drop out of high school in my last year because we had no money. I was hired to sing for Enric Madriguera's orchestra, which played at Washington's Club Del Rio. The salary was $100 weekly, more than Dad made in a month. An agent saw me and hired me to model the new uniforms for the newly created Women's Army Auxiliary Corp. I was on their official poster and *Life* picked up some of the shots and then I appeared in a Paramount newsreel with my hair up in a bun. Paramount signed me—and dropped me within one month, saying they had many girls of my type already.

BAWDEN: But Rudy Vallee saw the ads!

GREER: He phoned the army, got my address and Washington telephone number, and phoned me. I know what you're going to say. He's crazy! But he was only forty-one then and a big singing star. He invited me to Hollywood and my mother said no.

I next did a test for David Selznick in New York City, photographed by Stanley Cortez, that Mr. Selznick said was fine. Freddie Schuessler was casting director for both Selznick and Howard Hughes and he told Howard about me. Howard was just then getting back into movies. He was about to make *The Outlaw* [1943], but had already cast Jane Russell. Of the two offers, Howard promised more money and I signed, something I regret to this day.

BAWDEN: He pursued you?

GREER: That's putting it mildly. Mom and I arrived in early 1943. Howard sent two [train] drawing room tickets, which I cashed in for some clothes, and we had [much cheaper] upper berths. When Howard learned of my ruse, he was angry! But he started me with coaches. He then had a dozen girls under contract. He was kind and considerate at first. I was under a sort of house arrest, forbidden to go anywhere. But Rudy persisted. He was my only friend out there and we eloped on December 2, 1943. We divorced the next year. Cheap? That's too nice a word to describe him. Howard found out and hit the roof. He never used me and that hurt and finally I bought my way out of the contract and in 1944 I signed with RKO. I thought I was through with him.

BAWDEN: When did you make your first movie?

GREER: In spring 1944, *Two o'Clock Courage.* A B thing with Ann Rutherford. Then I was in RKO's *Pan-Americana* in the fall, 1944. Then I made *George White's Scandals* [1945] with Joan Davis and Jack Haley. I was then in *Dick Tracy* [1945], and my first name was shortened from Bettejane to just plain Jane. George Raft tested me for *Nocturne* [1946], but he wanted a name and hired Lynn Bari. So I made *The Falcon's Alibi,* which we made in 1946. I was a nightclub singer and sang in my own voice. And then I was in Frances Langford's movie *Bamboo Blonde* [1946]. And I was in a bad western called *Sunset Pass* [1946]. I was working, but in trash.

BAWDEN: Then what happened?

GREER: RKO went into a big shakedown. I thought I'd be dumped. Dore Schary came in [as head of production] and he liked me and put me into this A production, *Sinbad the Sailor* [1947], starring Douglas Fairbanks Jr. and Maureen O'Hara. I was Maureen's slave gal servant, but on her orders had such a huge veil that you only saw my eyes. Some days makeup would only do the top of my face to save time and money! But it was great to be in such a mammoth production. I was finally on my way.

BAWDEN: Your first A film lead was in *They Won't Believe Me* [1947]?

GREER: I got the second female lead because the director, Irving Pichel, was told he had to use a studio contractee. He'd already hired Susan Hayward from Walter Wanger for this picture. The title was prophetic. Nobody could believe nice Bob Young as a killer and the movie bombed. I'm not

Jane Greer with Robert Mitchum in the 1947 film noir classic *Out of the Past*. Courtesy of RKO Radio Pictures.

saying it's terrific, but it works for me. I got great reviews for my very nasty turn; Susan was out of sorts at not being noticed. RKO told me from now on I'd get star billing.

BAWDEN: How did you get the female lead in *Out of the Past*?

GREER: I was the only one available! No, I'm being serious. They had tried to get MGM's Audrey Totter, but she was already booked. Jacques Tourneur [the film's director] asked me to do it and said he'd guide me every step of the way.

It was also Bob Mitchum's first A feature as star. We got along beautifully. Still do. He's an unbelievably sincere guy, not at all like his tough image. After every scene Bob would rip those pages out of his script until there was nothing left. The real star was our cameraman, Nicholas Musuraca, who shot everything at dark because he said the sets were so shoddy. People are always asking me to explain the plot, but we never understood it then, when it was being filmed. We'd beg Tourneur to explain a scene, but he was more interested in lighting and creating all those darkened sets. That's why it's so popular these days on TV: people are endlessly trying to dissect it.

There was real tension between Bob and Kirk Douglas, who had the third role and really resented Bob's ascendancy. Bob was always letter perfect; he rarely flubbed a line. Kirk slapped people around, including me, and I wound up with bruises on my arm after he manhandled me in one scene.

I was told by Jacques to appear as aloof as possible. To wash away all emotions from my face. Be a blank screen because she never felt anything. I was the baddie here. Audiences were startled by this and also I wasn't the conventional cheap blonde. I died in a wonderful hail of bullets—it was juicy. Audiences didn't know what to make of all of this. They promptly assumed I was like that in real life! Wish I was. I was still so nice, eager to please.

BAWDEN: You did a second movie with Mitchum, *The Big Steal* [1949].

GREER: Bob had just been arrested on charges of smoking marijuana. He always believed the charges were rigged by the studio to make him behave. It really made him a bigger star than ever! But Liz Scott, who was scheduled to costar in it, refused to be seen with a jailbird and left for her home lot, Paramount. RKO asked me to step in, which I did even though I didn't much like the script. It was really a B plot. Bill Bendix was in it and Patric Knowles and even old-timer Ramon Novarro. During filming Bob had to serve a sixty-day sentence at the L.A. County [jail] farm. He complained they fed him potatoes every meal to fatten him up. We all sat around for two months getting paid and waiting for our leading man to reappear. Don't be fooled by what Bob said about it. He was mortified by the whole experience. He was really hurting. He had expected his career to evaporate, which it certainly did not do. He was forever typed as a bad boy.

BAWDEN: In between, you made a western I very much like—*Station West* [1948].

GREER: As Marlene Dietrich's replacement! Director Sidney Lanfield had asked for Marlene, but her salary demands were considered steep. And I was twenty years her junior, which made Dick Powell [the film's star] pick me. Dore Schary stepped in and made the final decision. He'd just become RKO's new production chief. I rather liked it and the cast, which includes Agnes Moorehead and Burl Ives, was fine. I sang a song called "Sometime Remind Me to Tell You," which had been written for Marlene so I did it in her style. Dick wanted to make it to get away from the tough private eyes he'd been playing. But at the preview in Chicago he told me it had turned out to be a film noir western. It does have a certain style, and it helped establish my "above the title" status.

BAWDEN: After that you didn't seem to work much.

GREER: I had married [attorney Edward Lasker] in 1947. We had a son in 1948 and a second boy the next year. That made Howard Hughes furious. He had bought RKO and I figured I was through. But he was still fixated with me. When I was well enough to work, he simply stopped sending scripts. Had to pay me or the contract would have blown up. But just to get at me, he sent the checks and no work offers. Refused to loan me out. He was going to punish me for marrying someone else. He was going to make me suffer.

Then at the end of '50 he put me into *The Company She Keeps* with Liz Scott. On the first day we sat down and exchanged parts. This time I'd be the nasty bitch and she was my probation officer. Howard was told and loved it! A more genteel girl I never met. Quiet. Sweet. Loved playing the parole officer in her trench coat. I was the jailbird she's trying to help go straight. John Cromwell directed and he was superfine. One day he gives direction to Liz and she interrupts, "You're asking me to open that door and say lines at the same time?" But she did it—beautifully, too. I got all the nasty lines, the slutty glamour outfits; Dennis O'Keefe was my boyfriend. Liz later told me it was one of her favorites. Because John Cromwell directed, a real gentleman. Do I see her these days? Nope. She's just so timid and sweet a creature.

BAWDEN: How did you get to Fox to make *You're in the Navy Now* [1951]?

GREER: Howard loaned me out. Never told me. A Fox script landed on my doorstep. If I'd refused, I would have been suspended without pay. And Gary Cooper was in it. My hero from all those Saturday matinees in the thirties. But it was one of Gary's few flops. It was a service comedy directed by gruff Henry Hathaway, who was born without a funny bone. A lot of huffing and puffing around, guys banging into each other. Gary looked embarrassed by it all. I didn't know how to handle this material. If a scene wasn't working, Henry would bark to everybody to exaggerate as much as possible. We had Ray Collins, Eddie Albert, Jack Webb, and nothing was working. They released it as *U.S.S. Teakettle* and when it bombed put a new title on it—*You're in the Navy Now*—and it bombed again.

Fox paid Howard for a second movie—before the first was out. Now it was truly foul: *Down among the Sheltering Palms.* It was Fox's answer to *South Pacific.* We were all in the South Pacific via the back lot and it really stank. Old Eddie Goulding directed it and he didn't know how to make a musical. I remember Jack Paar was in it. Imagine! And Bill Lundigan, Gloria DeHaven, Mitzi Gaynor. June Haver retired rather than do it. Good for you, June! Goulding and [Fox studio boss] Darryl Zanuck ended up not speaking to each other. I was the niece of the local missionary played by Gene Lockhart. Gloria was a busybody reporter. The island's king was Billy Gilbert. I got to sing two songs in my own voice. Great gobs of plot were cut out. I have never seen this one on TV. Not that I'm actually looking for it! It was finally released in late 1953.

BAWDEN: Then how did you get to MGM?

GREER: Dore Schary [who had become head of MGM by then] had liked me at RKO. He told me as soon as my RKO contract expired I'd be asked on board. Howard did offer another contract, but I had to be careful. If I told him about Metro's offer he might sue me for breach of contract. So I just let the RKO deal peter out and then I jumped to MGM. But it wasn't the MGM I'd grown up loving. First up, I did a lame comedy with Peter Lawford—the studio was trying to build him up into a heartthrob. It was called *You for Me* [1952] and nothing worked. I was very uneasy and it went out as the bottom of a double bill. The story had Peter shot in the bottom with birdshot and I'm the very sarcastic nurse. Gig Young was the third wheel and he thought it was very bad and he was right. I've never met a soul who ever saw it. So MGM put Peter into a TV series version of *The Thin Man* and I kept getting bad movies.

Next up there was a quickie remake of *The Prisoner of Zenda* [1952]. We all sat around watching a movieola of the 1937 classic with Ronald Colman. I had the Mary Astor part and I played it as seriously as Mary had. But Stewart Granger, James Mason, and Deborah Kerr mocked the material and it seemed as if I'd wandered in from another movie set.

Then when Betsy Drake walked from *Desperate Search* [1952], I got her part as the wife of a bush pilot, played by Howard Keel. There was a lot of action stuff, but again the budget was very tiny and nobody noticed me in it. I wanted to play the silly silent star in *Singin' in the Rain,* but Dore refused to even test me, saying Jean Hagen had been promised the part and she really was great in it.

Then I did a quickie remake of *The Champ* called *The Clown* [1953] with Red Skelton trying to prove he could do drama—only he couldn't, and that one was a real mess. There was a lot of shouting on the set and I retreated into my shell. I just couldn't get any traction, so MGM dropped me just like that and I was out of movies for three years.

I left MGM without working with any of the truly greats. Don't get me wrong. I liked Howard [Keel] and Red [Skelton] and Peter [Lawford], but first stringers they were not.

BAWDEN: You did TV work instead?

GREER: I did series like *Revlon Mirror Theater* and *Celebrity Playhouse* and a whole bunch of *Ford Television Theater* just to show I was still around. Live TV frightened me to death but at least when it was over nobody could see it again and I never had to look at myself to see how awful I'm sure I was.

BAWDEN: You were off the screen for three years and then returned.

GREER: I had no offers at all. Then Bob Waterfield at UA—he was married to Jane Russell, who remained a pal—offered me a month in Mexico for a remake of an old flicker called *The Most Dangerous Game* called *Run for the Sun* [1956]. I was a magazine journalist trying to find adventure writer Dick Widmark. Well, I do find him and as he's ferrying me back to Mexico City our plane crashes into the jungle lair of Nazi madman Peter Van Eyck. Dudley Nichols, of all people, did the screenplay. Most scenes it was just Dick and me running around the jungle. That was tough work, considering the humidity and the various critters who'd pop out.

I just adored Dick. And to my surprise, this one was popular on double action bills—Roy Boulting, an Englishman, was our intrepid director. We got off the return plane in Los Angeles and I see my children running to me and they run right past. Sheena, queen of the jungle, who was hot on TV at the time, was right behind me. What a letdown that was!

BAWDEN: Next came *Man of a Thousand Faces* [1957]?

GREER: Jimmy Cagney loved it and ordered that I be hired as his second wife, Hazel, in the biography of Lon Chaney. Dorothy Malone had the juicier role of first wife Cleva Creighton, who was crazy. She'd just won the Supporting [Actor] Oscar and was very demanding. Jimmy preferred to do everything on the first take, but Dottie would demand take after take and drive him to distraction. You know, Jimmy did not resemble Lon in any way but he was such a mesmerizing actor you just had to believe. We had Marjorie Rambeau, Jim Backus, and Bob Evans played Irving Thalberg. He'd been picked by Thalberg's widow, Norma Shearer. It wasn't historically correct and at that time Chaney had been dead for twenty-five years and nobody was familiar with most of his pictures.

BAWDEN: Then there was another big break.

GREER: Well, I had three nibblets to look after by then. And as they grew older they became more demanding. And then in '63 I had a delicate heart operation. The lining of the heart—the pericardium—had to be surgically removed. I was very weak, thin, very depressed for weeks. Then out of the blue Frank London, who was casting for [director] Eddie Dmytryk, remembered me and said to come in to read for *Where Love Has Gone* [1964]. I'd known both these guys twenty years earlier at RKO. And it was a small but juicy role as the probation officer for Susan Hayward's daughter, played by Joey Heatherton. And I got through it okay, although I was so very tired.

My first day on set I'm sitting there and Susan breezes in. She stops and says, "Oh, it's you!" and walks back to her dressing room and slams the door shut. Still my antisocial Susie! Her later fights with Bette Davis were said to be epic, but I was off the picture by then.

Then Peter Lawford heard I was back and hired me for a Patty Duke vehicle, *Billie* [1965]. It was based on the Broadway success *Time out for Ginger.* Patty was the rage then with her TV series. I was the long-suffering mom married to Jim Backus, who was an old friend. Billy DeWolfe was in it. It was very cute rather than funny. And it got me some more work.

BAWDEN: What do you remember about *The Outfit* [1973]?

GREER: Ouch! I'm trying to forget that one. Look, we all know Bobby Duvall is a master actor and here he was trapped in junk along with Karen Black and Joe Don Baker. Robert Ryan whispers to me, "How do you spell *shit?*" I couldn't stop laughing. Marie Windsor was around and so was Elisha Cook Jr. MGM was stumbling badly and this one was barely released.

BAWDEN: Now you're back again in *Against All Odds* [1984].

GREER: It's a remake of *Out of the Past*—well, sort of suggested by it. Rachel Ward has my part, Jeff Bridges is Bob Mitchum, and James Woods is Kirk Douglas. I play the mother, who did not appear in our first version. So I'm reduced to playing my mother! [Director] Taylor Hackford is a big booster of the first film and he asked me and got Dick Widmark for my scenes.

And I've also joined the cast of *Falcon Crest* [in 1984]. It should be called *The Jane Wyman Show.* She dominates everything. She lines the players up the way she wants for a scene. She questions the cameraman

Jane Greer (*center*) in *Against All Odds*, the 1984 remake of her classic *Out of the Past*. Rachel Ward (*left*) played Greer's role from the earlier film and Greer played her mother. With them is Richard Widmark, who was Greer's leading man in *Run for the Sun* in 1956. Courtesy of Columbia Pictures.

about lenses he may use that day. Very distant, but a commanding presence and ten years my senior, which makes me feel young again. And all us old broads get to wear nice duds, which is refreshing. So yes, I'm back in business once more.

Afterword

Jane Greer turned up in a total of six episodes of *Falcon Crest*. And the next year she telephoned to say she'd be on *Murder, She Wrote* at Angela Lansbury's request. In 1990, she had her last extended TV role, on *Twin Peaks* as Vivian Smythe Niles.

Although we never talked about it, she had been the companion of Frank London since he hired her for *Where Love Has Gone*. She died of cancer in Los Angeles on August 24, 2001.

Audrey Totter

Interview by James Bawden

Audrey Totter was signed to an MGM contract in 1944 when the studio was still considered the biggest and best in Hollywood. Then twenty-six, she already was an experienced and versatile radio actress, but her new studio defined her future career for her by plunging her into a series of "tough girl" roles in the dark, sinister noir thrillers then becoming a vogue in wartime Hollywood. Today Totter is best remembered for those classic noir films and holds a cherished place among the leading ladies of that genre.

Setting the Scene

Audrey Totter was fifty-six when I met her for lunch at the Beverly Hilton in Westwood, California, just a few miles from the old MGM studio where she began her long Hollywood journey. I talked with her a second time at her apartment when she was a frail widow, aged eighty-one.

The Interview

BAWDEN: What was your first reaction when you arrived at MGM in 1944?

TOTTER: I came from radio, where I'd had some very busy years. But when I was first taken around the MGM lot in 1944 I couldn't quite believe it. There were twenty-five huge soundstages, all working at complete capacity, and thousands of people, all under exclusive contract. I'm not talking of the hundred or more actors, but directors, writers, and musicians, too. The studio system was based on the assumption everybody had to go to the movies at least once a week. I think attendance was up to 90 million people weekly and business was really booming despite the closing

Audrey Totter, circa 1946. James Bawden collection.

of foreign markets because of the war. It was the cheapest and most efficient way to make movies. The back lot with its false front streets and villages was huge. We almost never went off the lot to make pictures in those days.

I was so lucky to get there at a time when MGM was still MGM. A few years later, TV came in and movie attendance slid and the whole system just melted away in a few short years. But in 1944, MGM was still the quality lot. My mentor was talent head Billy Grady, who said the studio wanted to build me slowly and give me lots of publicity and practical experience in moviemaking.

I played the bad gal in a little B called *Main Street After Dark* [1944] starring Edward Arnold. Then, because of my radio experience, I was the evil voice taunting Phyllis Thaxter in *Bewitched* [1945]. Phyllis later told me she thought she could have done the voice herself. But I wasn't seen. This was a "radio assignment" for the movies.

BAWDEN: How did the studio system work for a contract player?

TOTTER: You were paid for forty weeks, on turnaround for twelve weeks without pay. You couldn't take a vacation without the studio's permission! All the print ads you might do—that money went to the studio. They arranged for the radio appearances and kept most of the money. My father told me to put aside 10 percent of my salary and invest it! And I was twenty-six when I got there, with years of acting experience in radio behind me, so my head was not easily turned. But some of the girls came from very poor backgrounds and were making their first big money. It went to their heads and they got into debt. The studio would lend them money to buy cars or houses and then had complete control, meaning they couldn't turn down parts. Because that meant suspension without pay and they couldn't afford this.

And there were times the studio had nothing for you but didn't want to pay you, so they'd deliberately send over a lousy script, knowing you had to turn it down. Then it was suspension without pay until they needed you again. The suspended time was tacked onto the end of your contract until Olivia de Havilland took Warners to court in 1944 and, after a bitter two-year court battle, that tactic was ruled illegal because of existing anti-peonage laws. So it was Olivia who broke the back of the old studio system.

BAWDEN: Your first A picture must have been *The Postman Always Rings Twice* [1946]?

TOTTER: No, it was *Adventure* [1945], but if you blink you'll miss me, and that was deliberate. I'd had some small speaking roles when director Victor Fleming spotted me on the lot and requested me. It was a walk-on without lines. I was a bit distraught, but the star, Clark Gable, came to my rescue. He told me to turn slightly when the scene started and nobody would see my face! And it worked: nobody saw me. The picture was a huge bomb and later, when I met him in the commissary, Fleming joked, "Did you know something about the picture I didn't?"

Audrey Totter with Robert Montgomery in *Lady in the Lake* (1946). Courtesy of MGM.

I was a voice again in *Ziegfeld Follies* [1946]. Remember the skit where Keenan Wynn is trying to use the phone? I was the unseen operator.

With *The Postman Always Rings Twice* I got a small part in a big-time movie. I was the trampy blonde John Garfield picks up. I was in a train station and I say, "It's a hot day and I've got on a thin skirt and that's a leather seat." How that passed the censors, I'll never know. We shot it out of the studio but there was a lion in a cage in the background and it peed and the scene was useless. So we did the retake back at the studio. [John] Garfield was very cool, quite a cutup. But Lana Turner was in her blond goddess mode and what struck me was how tiny and petite she was.

Bawden: Then came *Lady in the Lake* [1946]?

Totter: Bob Montgomery had come back from the war and the studio was desperate to keep him because they'd lost Jimmy Stewart, who simply said his contract was up and left. Gable had come back and made the horrid *Adventure.* So Bob got carte blanche to direct and star in *Lady in the Lake,* using the subjective camera. That meant that for the whole picture the camera took the perspective of Montgomery as detective Philip

Marlowe. Bob could occasionally be glimpsed in mirrors. The other actors had to look directly at the lens and Bob couldn't find a leading lady who could do that. He tested everybody at MGM, including Lana, but it was no go. Then somebody slipped in a shot of me from *The Hidden Eye* [1945] when he was running tests and he jumped up and shouted, "I've got my girl!"

Billy Grady protested that I needed more experience, but Bob said it had to be me, particularly after he learned about my radio training. On radio I'd always looked at the mike. Studio head Louis Mayer watched the daily rushes and remained unconvinced the perspective change would work. Mr. Mayer was very conscious of the look of MGM. There's one scene where I'm awakened in the night and rush to the door. My hair was quite properly all askew. Mr. Mayer stood up in the screening room and ordered that the scene be reshot with my hair combed and the makeup just so. He said, "A Metro star must look her best, even asleep." He was peddling dreams. Reality never interested him.

The film came out to great critical attention, but audiences were puzzled. Finally, MGM ordered us back to shoot a conventional ending where Bob steps into view and we kiss. He told me he was going on to the new Greer Garson picture, *Desire Me* [1947], but it was such a shambles he left. I mean he left MGM for good. It's the only MGM film ever released without a director's credit. So MGM lost Bob after all.

BAWDEN: It seems MGM loaned you out as much as they used you?

TOTTER: They were making fewer pictures by war's end and could make a lot of money out of loaning out their talent. I was loaned to Warners for *The Unsuspected* [1947] because the director, Michael Curtiz, was big on me. He was making his first picture for his own company to be released through Warners and he publicly said he wanted to buy out my contract as well as the contracts of the star Michael North and Joan Caulfield, who was borrowed from Paramount. It was a wonderfully noir mystery starring that ace actor Claude Rains as a radio personality who plots the incredibly complicated murder of his niece [Caulfield]. I was the trampy niece, Althea Keane. Hurd Hatfield, also borrowed from MGM, was my alcoholic husband. Curtiz was a dazzler with the camera work and the complicated setups.

I absolutely adored Claude Rains. I think he was my favorite actor. I met him many years later when I was at Columbia and he was doing a TV thing and reminded him of the times I'd come over to have dinner with him and his wife. There were tears in his eyes. I did not know she had left him. And he said, "Oh, my dear, that was a hundred years ago."

BAWDEN: Is it true you were the original choice for the female lead in *The Killers* [1946]?

TOTTER: We were so long making *Lady in the Lake* that they had to start without me. So Billy Grady said to Universal, "I'll send you over this brunette as compensation. She can't act but she has a certain look." And Ava Gardner's superstardom was launched. I went on at MGM to do *The High Wall* [1947], another noir thing with Bob Taylor, another MGM returning veteran who'd been emotionally scarred by the war. By the way, he was very solid as a distraught man who thinks he's killed his wife.

Then I made *The Saxon Charm* [1948] at Universal. Bob Montgomery was a ruthless Broadway producer patterned after Jed Harris. You should catch it—it's splendidly bitchy and it was made before *All about Eve* [1950]. Bob borrowed me from MGM. Susan Hayward played the solid wife of playwright John Payne. There was this certain air about Susie. You knew she'd go to the top and she'd wring the neck of anybody in her way!

Then there was another loan-out to Paramount in 1949. Ray Milland was [playing] the devil and it was a wonderfully dark fantasy and I thought it would be a smash. Just before release, Paramount changed the title to *Alias Nick Beal.* Get the devil connection? And the film just died because it seemed a bit obvious, that title. Ray was very big right then. And very protective. Late one night I told him I had to go and meet a Paramount producer about another offer. And Ray said the man had a terrible reputation with ladies and drove me home instead!

BAWDEN: *The Set-up* [1949] is considered to be just about the finest boxing picture. Any memories?

TOTTER: I didn't want to do another loan-out, but director Bob Wise sent over a script. I looked at a few of his films and knew he was a talent. It was photographed in real time. The story took exactly sixty-nine minutes—the same time on the screen. Bob Ryan had a real character part as this washed-up fighter—and he ran with it. He was magnificent. It was shot on real locations instead of false studio fronts. Did you know it was based on a poem [by Joseph Moncure]? We thought we had a winner, then RKO head Howard Hughes panicked. He heard there was another boxing picture, *Champion,* with Kirk Douglas, going to open. He was determined to beat it so we opened with no press publicity and we just died. But I did go to last year's American Film Institute tribute to Bob Wise just to say thank you for such a great part. People are always mentioning that one to me.

BAWDEN: Some people assumed you'd marry Clark Gable because the two of you used to go out together.

TOTTER: I never did. I knew him since *Adventure.* Then we made *Any Number Can Play* [1949]. Yes, we dated. He was a tremendous guy, very witty, with a huge romantic aura. But all the girls he dated looked a little like his late wife Carole Lombard. He was still in love with her. So we settled for being great friends.

I never thought I'd marry. I dated Ross Hunter at one time—then he realized he was gay and I later met his sweet boyfriend. I dated John Payne, who was a control freak. He phoned me one night and said, "I can't make dinner. I'm getting back with my wife." That was Gloria DeHaven, but they eventually did divorce. I ran into her recently and told her how controlling John was. And she said, "Tell me about it."

Like I said, I thought I'd never marry. And then one day I was shopping at Bullock's for cuff links. And I met a man who was buying the very same ones I'd bought. He was a doctor, Leo Fred, and he was assistant dean of medicine at UCLA and he asked me out. Normally, I would have turned him down, but you see I knew we would marry. And from that moment I lost all my ambition. I lived for my family and not my career.

BAWDEN: Were you shocked to be dropped by MGM?

TOTTER: I could see it coming. I'd been out at Dore Schary's home for dinners, but his concept for MGM was so different from Mr. Mayer's. [Schary succeeded Mayer as head of production.] Dore wanted message pictures. And the studio output was dwindling. I did one last great MGM picture, *Tension* [1949] and got mostly loan-outs after that. Mr. Mayer was a confidant, a dear older uncle. Dore was brash and completely wrong about MGM's future. The way he went on, you'd think the studio was called Metro-Goldwyn-Schary! When Mr. Mayer was deposed, it seemed like the end of an era. But I think the studio really died the day Dore let Gable go [in 1953]. Yes, they thought the king was over the hill. But he had one final Metro picture awaiting release and it was *Mogambo,* his biggest postwar hit, so he walked out a true king. So yes, I left [in 1951]. So did Angela Lansbury at about the same time. So I was in good company.

BAWDEN: Then you went to Columbia?

TOTTER: A very different studio! Harry Cohn, the head, was something else. I told him I was going to get married. There was no reaction. I said my fiancé was a doctor and Harry brightened up.

"Audrey, I've always wanted to be a doctor," Harry said.

"Oh, Mr. Cohn, that's so noble of you," I gushed.

"Yeah, that way I could screw all my female patients and the wife would never suspect anything," he cackled.

The pictures I made at Columbia included *Man in the Dark* [1953], *Cruisin' Down the River* [1953], *Massacre Canyon* [1954], *Women's Prison* [1955]. Do those sound like MGM titles to you? Of course not! But, like I said, I was now focused on my family. I didn't care and I think that showed. I did a terrible one called *Assignment Paris* [1953], and George Sanders was so mean he never talked to me or the costar, Marta Toren, between takes. We're both Swedish so we'd babble on in Swedish until he blew up, thinking we were making fun of him. I remember he finally said something strange: "My dear, whatever are we doing in such tripe?"

BAWDEN: Then you went into TV.

TOTTER: No, I'd been doing live TV right through the fifties and loving it as a kind of theater. I also liked doing those half-hour dramatic series because you'd shoot one in three-four days and get home in time to have dinner with your family. But in 1958 I signed for my first series, *Cimarron City,* and I was told I'd star in every third episode. George Montgomery was the other star. But it turned into shots of me waving from the balcony, and when the producers changed I asked them to pay me off and the series died right after that anyway. Then in 1962 I did the pilot for a comedy series, *Our Man Higgins.* ABC was so very high on it. Stanley Holloway had just experienced a great late-life success in *My Fair Lady* and he was an English butler who found himself sent to America to serve a family and I was the suburban mom. We debuted against a new CBS sitcom, *The Dick Van Dyke Show,* and the rest is history.

Then, in 1972, the producer of *Medical Center,* Frank Glicksman, was having dinner in L.A. at a Hamburger Hamlet. He told his wife Jayne Meadows was leaving the series and he needed a replacement, saying, "I need a feisty woman as head nurse, somebody like Audrey Totter." Just at that moment I walked by with my husband. And Frank hired me on the spot as Nurse Wilcox and I was on from 1972 through 1976. I'd do all my scenes in one day for every episode and it was very eerie walking around the MGM back lot as all the old streets were being torn down. I thought it was such a waste.

They asked me to go to the premiere of *That's Entertainment* [1974], and we all lined up afterwards for one last group shot. I've got that shot and a lot of the greats have since passed on: Gloria Swanson, Marjorie Main, even Alexis Smith. And Ava Gardner walked up to me and said, "Audrey, I have always admired you. Because you got the two things I never had: a loving, supportive husband and a child." And she's right. Try sleeping with a career!

I didn't act after that series because my husband needed taking care of. He died four years ago and I'm only just beginning to date a bit now. And the man I'm currently dating I met on the MGM lot in 1944: Turhan Bey! But it's only for dinner. I don't want to be married again.

Acting? The critics said I acted best with a gun in my hand. And I recently did an hour interview special, *The Women of Film Noir,* on AMC with Jane Greer, Marie Windsor, and Colleen Gray. And I think we still look great. Marie had the best line. She said, "We didn't call it film noir in our day. We called it B picture making." But those are the movies people remember. Strange, isn't it?

Afterword

Audrey Totter's last screen role was in a 1987 episode of TV's *Murder, She Wrote* with old MGM pal Angela Lansbury. She died in 2013 in Woodland Hills, California. She was ninety-five.

Marie Windsor

Interview by Ron Miller

I've often wondered what Emily Marie Bertelson might have said if some soothsayer in her hometown of Marysvale, Utah, had accosted her at the age of five and told her she was going to grow up to be Marie Windsor, the best darn cheap thrill ever given to the hoodlums, thugs, informers, and two-timing dirty rats of Hollywood's B-movie world. It's nice to think she would have taken the cigarette out of her mouth and told the soothsayer, "Beat it, buster. You're standing in my light!"

But most assumptions about our favorite stars are baloney, and that one certainly is. The truth is Emily was a pretty nice little girl—and stayed that way long after Hollywood turned her into Marie Windsor and made her queen of the Bs, if not the empress of noir.

The tall, stunning brunette was a blossoming beauty when she won the Miss Utah title in 1939. She was studying at Brigham Young University, but her heart had been set on being an actress from childhood. The Miss Utah contest included a trip to Hollywood, which she took and contacted famed Russian actress Maria Ouspenskaya, who accepted her as a student.

Once in Hollywood, she learned how long it can sometimes take for a star to rise. Before 1949, she had appeared, uncredited, in twenty-eight films. Her first screen credit was for *Smart Alecks,* a 1942 East Side Kids comedy in which she played an unnamed nurse. She did hundreds of radio programs and some stage plays while gradually learning her way around lights and cameras.

Finally, she began to get noticed, mostly in westerns like *Hellfire* (1949), *The Fighting Kentuckian* (1949), and *Dakota Lil* (1950). But the films that really put her on the map were *Force of Evil* (1948) with John Garfield and Richard Fleischer's *The Narrow Margin* (1952), the classic film noir that gave her an extraordinary opportunity to play a sultry "bad girl" (even though she was really an undercover cop).

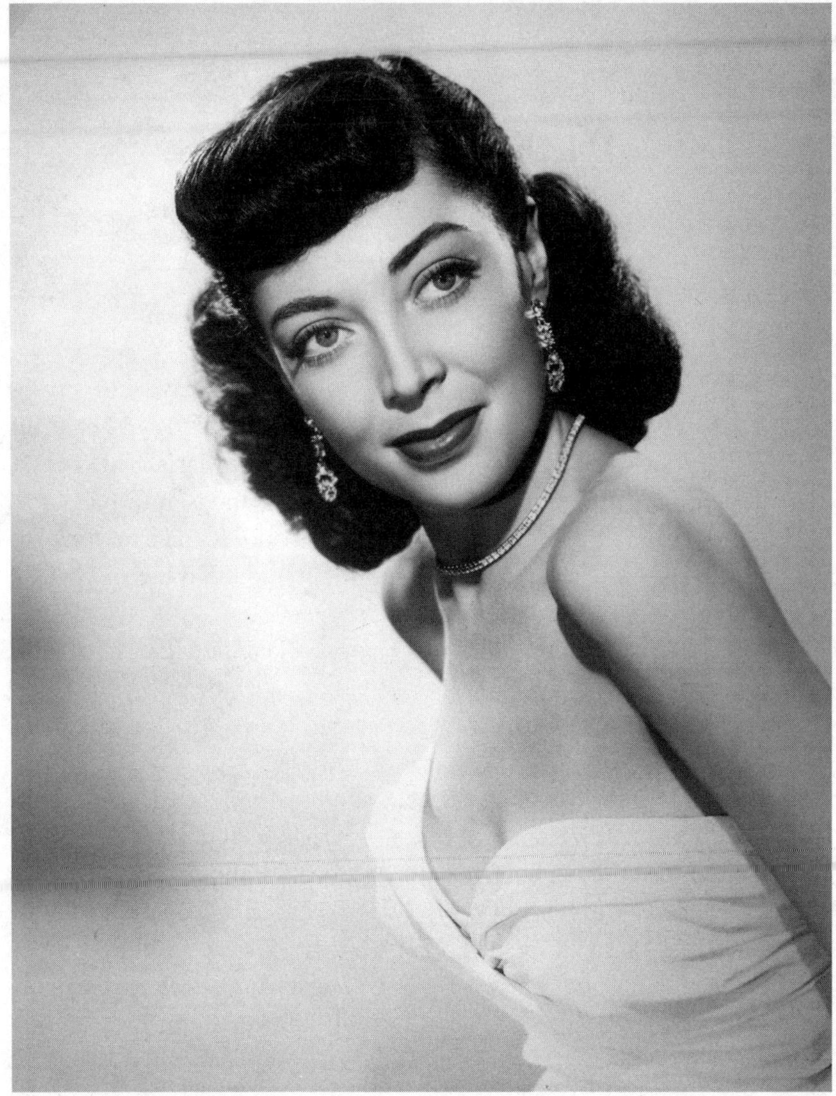

Marie Windsor. Ron Miller collection.

By the time Windsor had appeared in several more grim thrillers like *The Sniper* (1952), *The City That Never Sleeps* (1953), and especially Stanley Kubrick's *The Killing* (1956), she was beginning to be widely anointed as the queen of the Bs.

From the late 1950s on, Windsor appeared in nearly every western and crime TV series on the air, usually playing the hard-as-nails saloon girl that had become her specialty.

Windsor was married to bandleader Ted Steele in 1946, but the marriage broke up quickly. Eight years later (1954), she married Jack Hupp, a businessman and member of the 1936 U.S. Olympic basketball team. They remained together until her death.

Setting the Scene

Marie Windsor was one of the nicest people I ever met in Hollywood, far removed from her "bad girl" image. I'll never forget sitting with Windsor in the kitchen of her Beverly Hills home in 1988, surrounded by framed photos of her with John Wayne, Robert Mitchum, James Garner, and lots more of the roughest, toughest leading men of her era, drinking coffee and laughing about the good times she remembered from her long film career.

Windsor had gradually withdrawn from the entertainment world to concentrate on her business activities, which made her very successful off the screen. She'd just begun doing a small regular role in the new ABC dramatic series *Supercarrier,* which never got as hot as the coffee we were drinking and was gone within just a few weeks after our interview. I don't think she had any illusions about where that show was going, but figured it was as good an excuse as any to talk about her career with somebody who obviously loved her work and appreciated what she'd done over the past forty-seven years.

The Interview

Miller: How did the acting bug bite you in the first place?

Windsor: When I was a little girl, I saw Clara Bow in the movies and decided I wanted to be a movie actress. Even though I grew up in this little town of two hundred to three hundred people, my family never said I couldn't do it.

Miller: Did anybody in your family have any show business background?

Windsor: No. I don't think they even sang in the choir. But they found a way for me to go to drama school after I'd had two years of college. There was never any idea that I wasn't going to make it. I expected to be a superstar, but I never made it. Still, it's been a nice career.

MILLER: You studied with Maria Ouspenskaya?

WINDSOR: Yes, but I also studied with Stella Adler every summer until just the last few years. She taught pure technique. They didn't call it the Method back then, but she was working from the Stanislavski theories. I had a very thick Utah twang. That's part of the reason why I speak so deliberately. I worked on physical movement, body language, and how to use your imagination. Not drawing on your own memories, which I consider unhealthy. Just using your imagination is limitless, where using just your own experience isn't.

MILLER: What do you remember from your first movie role in *American Co-ed* [1941] with Frances Langford?

WINDSOR: All I remember is that I got my Guild [Screen Actors Guild] card with that. I was very young.

MILLER: Almost from the start, they seemed to see you as a bad girl. Why do you think that happened?

WINDSOR: I think it was physical. All the women were small in those days. The men were smaller, too, so taller women didn't get much of a chance. It was my looks and my voice, and I played menace very well. That's the way they saw me, and it was easy to do.

MILLER: But how did you envision yourself on-screen?

WINDSOR: I was always a little girl in my heart. As I grew older, I really felt like Greer Garson inside. But outside it didn't come out like that.

MILLER: Did it ever get frustrating to you?

WINDSOR: It seemed very natural to me to be slinky and sexy. The June Allysons can't be slinky and sexy. I've sort of given up and just accept it.

MILLER: I understand you had plastic surgery early in your career to take a bump off your nose.

WINDSOR: That was about twenty-five years ago. But the moment I did it, bumps on noses became very fashionable My timing was just not right.

MILLER: Many of the male actors I've talked with who wound up playing heavies in movies all seem to think those are the better parts. Do you feel the same way about your saloon girls and hookers?

WINDSOR: Some of the leading ladies I know—the wispy ones—feel they're missing something. They want to do the parts I'm doing. And I've played a lot of good-hearted madams. They started seeing there could be something nice in this kind of a character, so I started getting parts where I was full of a little more love and understanding rather than stealing

Marie Windsor spent lots of time in frontier saloons and dance halls. Here she is in a 1964 episode of TV's *Destry.* Courtesy of ABC.

somebody's husband. And by the way, I don't think fixing my nose made any difference whatsoever.

Miller: Who were the nastiest bad girls you ever played?

Windsor: God, the woman I played in *Japanese War Bride* [1952].

What a bitch I was in that! And of course *The Killing.* God, what a horrible woman I was in that, jerking that little Elisha Cook around, sleeping with Vince Edwards, and trying to make it with Sterling Hayden. Then shooting him on top of it!

MILLER: Ah, now you're talking about some of my favorite films. I mean, *The Killing* is a masterpiece and made Stanley Kubrick the hottest director in town. Did you have any idea that was going to turn out like it did?

WINDSOR: I don't think any of us knew. I was very excited about it. Kubrick had seen me in *Narrow Margin.* The minute he picked up the paperback that became *The Killing* [Lionel White's *Clean Break*], he told Jim Harris [his producing partner] that he wanted me for Sherry. But my agent did a terrible thing and booked me for a terrible picture called *Swamp Women* [1956] in the Louisiana swamps and overlapped the schedules. But I loved the script of *The Killing* and didn't want to lose it. So Kubrick started his picture two days late and Roger Corman let me out of *Swamp Women* two days early. I got off the plane from Louisiana and went right to work on *The Killing.*

MILLER: How long did it take to make the film?

WINDSOR: It was only something like twenty-one working days. But boy, was [Kubrick] organized. His wife at the time was not only a ballerina but a very fine artist. She'd done charcoal drawings, under his direction, of every scene the way it should be shot. Everybody was excited about it. And I certainly got a lot more work after that.

MILLER: How did Kubrick work with actors?

WINDSOR: His partner, Harris, was always well dressed, the tailored look. Kubrick always wore what I refer to as khaki work pants. I think he got them at a war surplus store or something. He never quite wore the right length and they certainly weren't fitted. He came up to the house a couple of times and wore those same work pants. They were characteristic, like Howard Hughes's sneakers.

He had a great authority about him in a very quiet way. He never yelled at actors or spoke in a loud voice. He would call you behind the set and whisper a suggestion or two. He was very calm and easygoing. Some directors want to move you around like puppets, but I think he was so pleased with that cast that a mere suggestion with all of us seemed to work very well.

MILLER: I guess this would be a nice time to ask you about a film that won its place in cinema history for an entirely different reason: Robert L. Lippert's *Cat-Women of the Moon* [1954].

WINDSOR: My agent just told me there's a commercial being made that uses a clip from *Cat-Women of the Moon*. God, I can't stand the thought of it! That has to be the worst picture ever made! Did you see that? We're going out into space and I'm one of the scientists, but it was such a cheap production that they've got me rolling around the spaceship in a deck chair! We still had four pages of dialogue to do on the final day of the picture and Mr. Lippert pulled the rug out from under us. Told us to figure it out in the editing room.

I did a lot of pictures for Mr. Lippert. All my memories of Mr. Lippert don't reflect my feelings about *Cat-Women*. He sent me to India to be in *The Jungle* [1952], and that certainly was one of my most memorable experiences. But yes, I don't have a lot of A pictures in my repertoire.

MILLER: Before we leave that area, I need to ask you about working with Bud Abbott and Lou Costello in *Abbott and Costello Meet the Mummy* [1955].

WINDSOR: They weren't getting along very well. They were having a little tiff over something and would invite their little cliques to lunch, but you'd never be invited if both of them were there. Working on the set, though, you'd never know anything was wrong.

MILLER: Some might wonder why you didn't turn down some of the really cheap pictures you did.

WINDSOR: I love to work. I never turned down a job unless I was asked to undress.

MILLER: For a girl who dreamed of being a movie superstar, was it hard to accept the fact that you were going to be remembered as the queen of the Bs?

WINDSOR: I used to be offended by it when they called me that. Then I began to enjoy it. It's better to be the queen of something than nothing. One of the things that's kept me mentally healthy during many heartbreaking periods in my career is that I have a very strong direction about facing reality. If something's wrong, I try not to blame somebody else or the situation. Since I seem to be a rather content individual, I guess it's working.

MILLER: You worked with some genuine superstars many times. For example, you did *Cahill, U.S. Marshal* [1973] with John Wayne. You seemed to go well with such big, rugged leading men.

WINDSOR: I think I'm more comfortable with the Duke type. He developed his own acting technique, which was splendid. He had extraordinary timing and was a great listener. He was the kind of actor who shared with the other actor. Very often those people [superstars] are so wrapped up in their subtext that you're not getting anything from them and there becomes a wall there.

MILLER: Did you find yourself competing for roles with the same actresses all the time?

WINDSOR: Yes, because there are so few good roles for us old broads these days. There are several of us who have survived and we all seem to be going out on the same interviews. I'm very dedicated, but I thank God for Jack [her husband], who pays the rent and loves for me to have a career. I feel so sorry for some of these actresses who come in for an interview and you know they have to get it to pay their rent or buy a new dress.

MILLER: Though I'm a great admirer of your work, do you think most moviegoers are familiar with your career?

WINDSOR: I think I've built up this good reputation with film buffs who have glommed on to those few classics. I also made twenty-two westerns and there are a lot of western film buffs. But frankly, I don't think three-quarters of them [moviegoers] know who I am.

Afterword

Marie Windsor did no more movies after our interview and appeared in only a few more TV episodes. Her last credit was in a 1991 episode of *Murder, She Wrote.* She died in 2000 at age eighty in Beverly Hills, California.

V

The Singing Cowboys

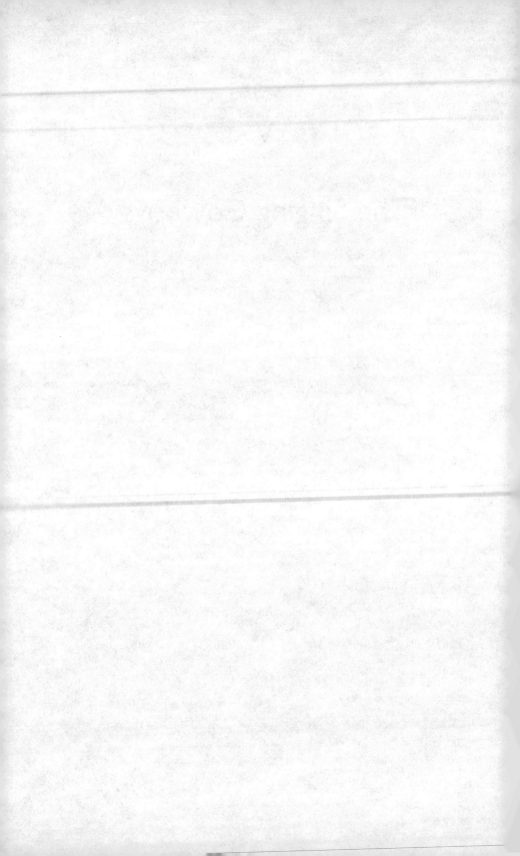

Gene Autry

Interview by James Bawden

Though he never claimed to be the screen's first "singing cowboy," Gene Autry certainly started the boom in musical western movies that swept through Hollywood in the 1930s and created a popular genre that lasted two decades. A radio singer from *The National Barn Dance* in Chicago, Autry made his screen debut in 1934's *In Old Santa Fe* with actor Ken Maynard, who had starred in westerns since the silent movie era and whom Autry always credited with being the first cowboy to sing onscreen. Because he was already an immensely popular singing star on radio and on recordings, Autry got the chance to star in a movie, the 1935 Mascot serial *The Phantom Empire,* which led to his development as the singing hero in a long series of musical westerns at Republic Pictures. In just a few years, Autry became a top 10 box office star in the movies, while his *Melody Ranch* radio series was a smash hit and his recordings sold in the millions. Even his performing horse, Champion, became a celebrity.

When Autry returned from service in World War II, he found studio rival Roy Rogers enshrined as Hollywood's "king of the cowboys," so he left Republic and went to Columbia, where he once again became a top box office performer.

In the late 1940s, the musical western began to fade in popularity, but Autry and Rogers followed William "Hopalong Cassidy" Boyd into television, where they continued their popular run well into the 1950s.

Meanwhile, Autry had invested wisely, buying many broadcast properties and the Los Angeles Angels baseball team, becoming one of the wealthiest men in Hollywood. Additionally, his recording of "Rudolph, the Red-Nosed Reindeer" became one of the all-time best-selling tunes, a holiday standard that's still heard widely today.

Though Autry was never greatly esteemed as an actor, he was one of

Gene Autry, circa 1948. Courtesy of Gene Autry's *Melody Ranch Theater* and the Nashville Network.

America's most popular entertainers for more than three decades, earning a place in movie history that has stood the test of time.

Setting the Scene

One night in July 1988, I was among the scores of TV critics who visited the magnificent new Gene Autry Museum of the West in the San Fernando Valley. We were to be given dinner, with a tour of the fantastic museum to follow, and it was rumored that Mr. Autry himself would make an appearance. He did indeed show up at dinnertime with his wife. He looked quite resplendent in his western finery. I persuaded the TV public relations people to seat him beside me, and we talked at length.

The Interview

BAWDEN: Mr. Autry—

AUTRY: Oh, call me Gene. Everybody does. It's not my real name, but nobody would dare call me Orvon to my face. [He was born Orvon Grover Autry.]

BAWDEN: I remember my mom braved a terrible February blizzard in 1953 to take me to see your traveling show in Toronto. Do you remember that date?

AUTRY: I remember that blizzard. We were playing in Erie one night before and we had twenty-four hours to pack up everything, including the horses, and get those tractor-trailers off to Toronto, but we got stuck in a blizzard and we weren't sure we would make it. A few hours we traveled by inches. Then we got there with just an hour to spare—no sleep, no food. The horses were angry but as soon as we got in the arena they just perked up. They were real hams and Champion came through with a tremendous performance. He always did. We were a great team.

BAWDEN: Speaking of Champion . . .

AUTRY: No, he is not stuffed. I asked Roy [Rogers] why he'd stuff Trigger and he said he was going to stuff Dale [Evans, his wife] when her time came. I'm sure he was only joking, but nobody is going to stuff me, and Champion is not stuffed. He's laid to rest standing up because that was his preferred position in life. One reporter said I did it to save ground because a smaller grave would be less expensive. Nonsense!

BAWDEN: How real was that feud with Roy Rogers?

AUTRY: There never was a feud. I was king of the cowboys at Republic until the war broke out. And when I signed up, Republic still had Roy and Dale and they soared in popularity. Why Roy did not join up is none of my business. He has a very big family. Maybe he couldn't afford to. But when I returned, the lot was too small for two big cowboy stars. Columbia made me a deal and that was that. And it worked out great for me because Columbia was a richer studio and I made better pictures that made bigger profits.

Gene Autry and his faithful horse, Champion, in *South of the Border* (1939). Courtesy of Gene Autry's *Melody Ranch Theater* and the Nashville Network.

Bawden: Can you guess my favorite?

Autry: Well, you're Canadian, so it would be *Blue Canadian Skies* [1952]. It's a pretty fair oater, I must say. George Archainbaud directed it. We filmed for twelve days or so. Gail Davis, who I discovered, was a great leading lady, so blond and perky. A great rider and a great shot. Pat Buttram was the sidekick, the best laugh getter in the business. I had to screen it recently for our Nashville TV series [*Melody Ranch Theater* on the Nashville Network], and unbilled I could spot Don Beddoe, Cactus Mack, Chick Hannan, Gene Roth, dozens of familiar faces I had almost forgotten. We shot at Big Bear Lake to make it seem Canadian like. And then there was *Gene Autry and the Mounties* [1951], which we shot right before that.

BAWDEN: Why do you think you became such a big western star?

AUTRY: Because I was needed. If I hadn't come along, somebody else would have. I loved the big silent stars like Tom Mix and Buck Jones, but they had trouble with sound. And I had a novelty: I sang. So that attracted people who normally would pass on watching a western. If I'd come a few years later, there would have been no movie career like the one I had.

BAWDEN: What leading ladies do you remember most fondly?

AUTRY: Well, Annie Rutherford now tells me she was only thirteen when we worked together in 1936. I thought she was an old lady of seventeen. But Virginia Grey was real cute. So were Mary Carlisle, Elena Verdugo. We had perky heroines, not gals who just sat around drinking tea.

BAWDEN: What did you enjoy best about making westerns?

AUTRY: We were out in the fresh air all day. The lunches were always great. We'd break around 6 p.m. unless there specifically was a night scene. Same crew right along, many of the same supporting players, like Onslow Stevens. They always delivered on time. Later, I bought the old Monogram ranch and named it as Melody Ranch and we'd film there.

BAWDEN: As I remember, there was a code.

AUTRY: There certainly was. We were teaching life lessons. Then I saw *Butch Cassidy and the Sundance Kid* [1969], and there's one scene where the antihero kicked the other antihero in the nuts. Then there was *True Grit* [1969], where fat old John Wayne with a patch on one eye kept falling off his horse. And that's when I finally realized the western was dead.

BAWDEN: Why jump to TV?

AUTRY: Those kids' matinees where my pictures played were being discontinued. So I did *The Gene Autry Show* on TV for CBS for five seasons [1950–1955], and I produced *Annie Oakley* with Gail Davis for my company. And don't forget my spinoff *The Adventures of Champion* [1955].

BAWDEN: You're now back on TV with *Melody Ranch Theater* [1987]?

AUTRY: Introducing, with Pat [Buttram], the old films—and they get huge ratings. So now I'm on cable! And the response from young viewers who cannot have been around when the films were made is amazing and gratifying.

BAWDEN: Christmas will always be yours.

AUTRY: Well, add Bing Crosby in there, too, will ya? I knew "Santa Claus Is Coming to Town" would be a hit the moment I finished recording it. Those residuals still keep coming in. But "Rudolph, the Red-Nosed Reindeer"? I thought it a fun novelty item. Never guessed it would outperform the other one. One night I was going into a lavish dinner affair and the waiter nudged me and said, "Gene, they're playing your song." The little kids sing it to me when they recognize me. It's goofy but it says something about being considered an outcast but still pulling ahead of the pack.

BAWDEN: Is the story about you and Will Rogers true?

AUTRY: Oh, sure. I was working as a telegraph operator, making $150 a month, and to break the monotony on the graveyard shift in Chelsea [Oklahoma] I was singing some of my own songs. A stranger came in to file a telegram and listened a bit and then told me he thought with a little work I just might make it singing. That stranger was Will Rogers and years later, after my first movie, he walked up to me at a party and said, "I see you made it." True story. He was dead later that year in a plane crash in Alaska.

BAWDEN: When did you cut your first record?

AUTRY: In 1929. It was called "My Dreaming of You." But I had no success until 1931 with "That Silver-Haired Daddy of Mine," which sold half a million copies the first year and I was on my way.

BAWDEN: You were big in country western circles well before the movies came a-callin'?

AUTRY: Yup. I came out to Hollywood along with Smiley Burnette for a Ken Maynard western where I sang a song during a break in the action. And then I made the serial *Mystery Mountain* [1934] as costar with Ken. Then I was hired for the twelve-part serial *The Phantom Empire*. I was paid $15 a week and was on my way.

BAWDEN: How did you get to Republic?

AUTRY: Hold on there! Mascot merged into Republic and my first for [studio boss] Herbert Yates was *Tumbling Tumbleweeds* [1935]. We made one every six to eight weeks. Had to be about an hour to fit into the double part of a double bill. And by 1937 I was one of the top ten movie stars in little movies kids and families loved and those big-city critics rarely bothered to even review.

BAWDEN: You began feeling used by Republic's Herbert Yates?

AUTRY: I was naïve. Took me a whole long time to realize Republic was block booking us. Theaters could only get Autry pictures by buying other Republic titles they didn't really want. And brother, that made me mad. Republic even had a share of my personal appearances, which really rankled. I walked out and Yates hired a new guy to replace me—Roy Rogers.

BAWDEN: But one of your biggest hit songs—"Back in the Saddle Again"—came from a George O'Brien western?

AUTRY: I needed a signature tune for my radio show. My pal Ray Whitley had written it and we made a deal and it's been paying off for us ever since.

BAWDEN: You were so unsure of "Rudolph, the Red-Nosed Reindeer" that—

AUTRY: I agreed to record it at the end of a session in a single take with no retakes and it made me millions.

BAWDEN: It seems everything you touched made millions for you.

AUTRY [*chuckling*]: You're forgetting the Angels [baseball team], aren't you? Did you know I was once drafted for the minor leagues? Yes, I was an okay baseball player in the twenties. But in 1960 I made a bid for my TV stations to cover the new Los Angeles team that was going to be set up by the expansion and the baseball owners were so impressed by my presentation they asked me to make my own bid and I got the Angels, which started up in 1961. And I'm still a vice president of the American League. I thought we'd get a pennant when I signed Reggie Jackson for more money than I'd ever heard of. But no—not yet, anyway.

BAWDEN: Here we are in your magnificent Museum of the West. Tell me how it started.

AUTRY: For decades I was collecting memorabilia, which I stored in warehouses. There are three floors—one for the American West, one for the Spanish West, one for the Canadian West. I have original Northwest Mounted Police uniforms nobody in Canada has. You Canadians had an entirely different experience. The Mounties led, civilizing the West far ahead of the settlers. So the law and order issues never arose. Plus you treated the Indians far better and more humanely.

BAWDEN: I see your wife is waving for you to leave.

AUTRY [*yelling*]: I'll leave when I'm good and ready, honey. I'm talking to an Autry fan from 1953 and somebody I might have missed altogether during that danged blizzard. So farewell to you, sir, farewell.

Afterword

Gene Autry died from lymphoma on October 2, 1998, at his home in Studio City, California. He was ninety-one. He had no children from his two marriages. He is the only performer to have five stars on the Hollywood Walk of Fame—one each for movies, television, radio, recordings, and live theater.

Roy Rogers

Interview by Ron Miller

From the early 1940s on, Roy Rogers was known simply as "the king of the cowboys." More properly, that should have been "king of the singing cowboys," since Rogers was the number one singing cowboy in the movies, nudging Gene Autry out of that spot while Autry served in World War II.

Born Leonard Slye in 1911, he grew up in rural Ohio and first began to sing in public in his early teens while working as a square dance caller. He moved to California, where one of his sisters lived, in 1930 and got his first gig singing on radio amateur shows. He was then invited to join a radio singing group called the Rocky Mountaineers, where he met Bob Nolan, who would later join with Roy in forming one of the most successful western singing groups of all time, the Sons of the Pioneers.

As a member of the Sons of the Pioneers, Roy made his screen debut in the 1935 B western *The Old Homestead.* He and the boys also appeared in several Gene Autry and Charles Starrett westerns. Their most notable screen appearance came in the Bing Crosby musical *Rhythm on the Range* (1936), in which Roy Rogers can be plainly seen stepping out to sing a chorus of "I'm an Old Cowhand" with Crosby and the boys. In most of those films, Roy was known by the name Dick Weston.

In 1937, Republic Pictures signed him to a contract to star in a new series of singing cowboy westerns—he'd already been rejected at rival Universal after a screen test—and in 1938 he made his first film as the leading star, *Under Western Stars.*

Republic tried only once to use Rogers as a nonsinging actor, not playing himself—in the big-budget 1940 western *Dark Command* with John Wayne. Though Rogers did well in the film, his singing westerns were so popular that there was no need to do anything else with him. (He appeared in two popular Bob Hope comedies much later—*Son of Paleface* in 1952 and *Alias Jesse James* in 1959.)

Roy Rogers, Republic Pictures' king of the cowboys, circa 1944. Courtesy of the Nashville Network.

Leonard Slye became Roy Rogers during a meeting with Republic studio executives who insisted he have a new screen name. Roy had always admired humorist/actor Will Rogers so chose that surname, and Roy sounded best of all the short first names they considered.

Rogers's famed horse, Trigger, was originally a studio horse named Golden Cloud that Roy chose as his regular mount—and then legally acquired. The new name Trigger was suggested by one of Roy's frequent costars, singer-composer Smiley Burnette.

Roy was married twice. His first wife was Arlene Wilkins, who died in 1946 not long after giving birth to their son, Dusty. The couple also had two daughters. He married his frequent leading lady, Dale Evans, in 1947. They had first worked together in *The Cowboy and the Senorita* in 1944.

Not only did Roy Rogers become a top box office star in movies, he sold many hit records, had his own radio show (and later a television series), and toured frequently with live shows in which he performed tricks while riding Trigger.

Roy and Dale sold their large ranch property near L.A. in the 1960s after the tragic death of their eleven-year-old daughter, Debbie, in a bus accident. They wanted to get away from the setting that reminded them constantly of her. They settled on a golf course property in Victorville on the road to Nevada, and Roy built his museum of items from his storied career near there. The stuffed and mounted Trigger was a primary exhibit at the Roy Rogers-Dale Evans Museum. After Roy and Dale died, the museum was moved to the resort community of Branson, Missouri, but declining attendance caused it to shut down in 2009.

Setting the Scene

I didn't much care for Roy Rogers when I was a kid, although you were supposed to like him because he was the king of the cowboys. The woman I married says she had a crush on him in her youth, which most girls did, I guess, especially the ones who dreamed of riding horses like real cowgirls.

Well, I'm grown up now, and somewhere along the line I became a fan of Roy Rogers. I started to look at some of those early westerns he made in black and white and decided they were pretty darn good, and he was a lot more capable as a cowboy than I had given him credit for. Moreover, I started to realize those energetic, lively little musical westerns he made at Republic in the 1940s were a heck of a lot of fun.

Then there was my belated discovery of Dale Evans as a legitimate sex object. Hey, she was a very sexy gal in her youth—and had lots of attitude that got lost somewhere along the way, probably because of all that churchgoing she got into in the late 1940s. When I started to turn up some of her glamour shots from that period, I was convinced Roy knew what he was doing when he went after her with a certain zeal.

Finally, I wound up spending the better part of an afternoon with Roy at his cowboy museum (when it was still located in Victorville, California) and decided he was a down-to-earth, regular guy who was loaded with interesting stories. He was also a very gracious host and answered every question I put to him with apparent sincerity. That was in 1992 when Roy was still pretty fit and healthy, healthy enough to hop on a motorcycle and storm off into the sunset after our interview,

Today I regard Roy Rogers as a phenomenal character who represented the very best side of American success. He was not a big, imposing man like John Wayne, but he was a very handsome fellow, maybe a shade better looking than his ultimate rival, Gene Autry. And he had been riding horses since his youth, so he was not one of those make-believe cowboys you always hear Hollywood was full of back in the days when westerns ruled the box office.

What kind of an actor was he? Well, I think he was a lot better than we all gave him credit for. His movies didn't demand an awful lot of him beyond charm, but sixteen years after what everybody thought was his last feature film—the Bob Hope comedy *Alias Jesse James*—Roy came back to play a straight, nonsinging dramatic role in the independent feature film *Mackintosh and T.J.* (1975). Roy plays a drifting modern cowboy who encounters a wandering teenage boy (Clay O'Brien) and becomes his mentor after they both secure jobs with a Texas rancher. Roy's character is accused by a jealous husband of bothering his wife (Joan Hackett) and then is nearly beaten to death by friends of the woman's husband when the man is found murdered. It's far from your typical Roy Rogers movie, but Rogers is absolutely superb playing a real dramatic role—a sure sign that he might have had an entirely different career as a serious actor if he hadn't struck it rich with his musical gifts.

For me, the chance to wander alone with Roy Rogers through his museum, listening to him explain each item in his own words, was a precious moment with a genuine American folk hero and Hollywood icon.

The Interview

Miller: Roy, it's not possible to walk past the taxidermy display featuring Trigger without asking you about your depth of feeling about the horse that was your costar throughout your career. How did he come to be your horse?

Roy Rogers and Trigger in 1949's *The Golden Stallion.* Courtesy of Republic Pictures, Roy Rogers's *Happy Trails Theatre,* and the Nashville Network.

Rogers: They had about seven or eight horses to show me that morning and were going to pick out one of them for me. But it wound up being my choice. I think Trigger was the third horse I got on, and I never looked at the rest. We just fit each other like a glove.

Miller: How much cowboy stuff did you have to learn before you could get up on a horse and ride like you were more than a Hollywood dude?

ROGERS: I had to learn a lot of rope tricks and stuff like that, but I never used one of them in all ninety pictures. I did all my own running mounts and that stuff, but not for the movies. I did all those personal appearances. You don't want to miss a running mount when you're in front of twenty thousand people at Madison Square Garden. That would be a little embarrassing.

MILLER: What about learning acting? How did you step into the leading role in a movie without any prior acting experience?

ROGERS: I didn't know anything about acting. Never had any lessons or anything. I just went in there cold and said, "How am I gonna do that?" When I had to play the bad guy in *Billy the Kid Returns,* I didn't know what to do, so I just frowned. [In his second starring film, made in 1938, he had to play a dual role—the outlaw Billy the Kid and an innocent man who's mistaken for him.]

MILLER: I know you played the bad guy in one of Gene Autry's westerns back when you were working as Dick Weston and he beat you up in a fight scene. A lot has been written about how you finally had your revenge when the studio built you up as the star of your own movies. Do you think the studio was using you to keep Gene in line?

ROGERS: I'm sure they did. The PR people made it sound like we hated each other, but that wasn't true. We hardly knew one another. Gene was under contract there and when I came along you heard a lot about that. It wasn't jealousy or anything like that, but we were competitors. They gave me a job making $75 a week and man, I was just thrilled to death about that.

MILLER: Though your career boomed overnight after your first starring feature, *Under Western Stars,* in 1938, you were far from an overnight sensation because you'd been around Hollywood, trying to make a living, for quite a few years already. Was that a rough time for you?

ROGERS: When I look back, I wouldn't take back anything. Our family went through the Depression. We didn't have much, but we had food. I'm just thankful I came along at that time, hard times and all. If you don't have hard times, you don't know how to enjoy the good times. I didn't think about going into show business when I first came out here to visit my older sister. That was the last thing on my mind. I stayed out here four months, then went back home, but when I got there winter was coming on, so I turned around, hitchhiked back to California, and I've been here ever since.

MILLER: When you look in the mirror today, do you see Roy Rogers or Leonard Slye?

ROGERS: I say, that's me—Leonard Slye. My mom never could call me Roy. She'd always call me Leonard. I finally had to change it legally when the kids started coming along. But I guess I'm like Popeye. I yam what I yam and that's what I yam.

MILLER: What was it like to work for an old Hollywood studio mogul like Herbert J. Yates? Was he as tight-fisted as the legends say he was?

ROGERS: Oh, Lord, yes! He wouldn't pay a nickel to see an ant eat a bale of hay. I became number one at the box office in 1943, so some people started coming after me to sign commercial tie-ins. I didn't know about stuff like that, so I went to Old Man Yates and he said: "Don't you ask for a raise! Do all the commercial tie-ins you want, but don't be asking for any raises!" So that opened the gate. I asked my lawyer to put that in my contract and Old Man Yates couldn't stop me.

MILLER: Who did you admire among the other cowboy stars of your era?

ROGERS: Bill Elliot was a good horseman, and I liked Buck Jones and Hoot Gibson. Hoot and I became good friends.

MILLER: What do you think of today's western stars?

ROGERS: I like Clint [Eastwood], but I think he gets too much killing in his films and that's not too good.

MILLER: Though you had some pretty good-looking leading ladies in your movies, including Dale, you didn't go in much for kissing them on-screen.

ROGERS: Well, I kissed Jean Porter in 1944. Then I started getting tons of letters from little boys, saying, "Leave that mushy stuff out of the pictures!" So we just never had the leading guy get into that stuff because we were trying to create a good image for the kids.

MILLER: In your later features, you had some pretty fierce fistfights and action sequences, but generally your movies also avoided violence.

ROGERS: Every once in awhile, they'd put something in a script and I'd just have to take it out. But we did have some pretty rough fights and I got banged up pretty good sometimes.

MILLER: Did you ever really clip somebody in one of those fights?

ROGERS: I only got seriously hit twice and also accidentally hit two guys. One of them was the great stuntman Yakima Canutt. [Roy clipped Canutt with an uppercut and chipped several of his teeth.]

Roy Rogers and wife Dale Evans in a 1981 TV special on *The Nashville Palace* celebrating Roy's fiftieth anniversary in show business. Courtesy of Solters/Roskin/Friedman, Inc., and NBC.

MILLER: After you had become Republic's number one box office star and earned millions for the studio, the public started growing tired of singing cowboy movies and you finally left Republic. What really happened to end your long association with the studio?

ROGERS: My contract came to a close in 1951 and so the Old Man wanted me to sign for another seven years. I'd been there fourteen years and done about ninety pictures. I said I'd be glad to do it if I could get some television rights. He went right through the ceiling. So I left.

MILLER: You had several sidekicks in your many westerns. Who do you remember most fondly?

ROGERS: Old Gabby [Hayes], bless his heart. He was like my brother, my father, and my buddy all wrapped up in one. I just loved him. He was fun to work with and we did about forty-one pictures together. I hated to see him leave. His contract ran out and the studio didn't want to pay him. We had some good boys come in, like Andy Devine and Big Boy Williams, but I missed old Gabby.

MILLER: What was the real Gabby Hayes like?

ROGERS: He drove onto the lot the first time I saw him, wearing a beautiful English tweed suit. Every hair in his beard was in place and he drove in this long, sleek Continental convertible. He went into the wardrobe department, put on his outfit and took his teeth out, and when he came back out, he was Gabby. It's people like that who made our pictures successful.

MILLER: You also battled a whole lot of villains over the years, but the one I remember most vividly is big, burly Roy Barcroft.

ROGERS: He was one of the nicest guys I ever met, but he could play a bad guy on the screen like nobody else. He lived just across the field from me in Encino. We were like family, real good friends.

MILLER: How did you get along with those studio directors like Joe Kane? Did they ever try to challenge you as an actor?

ROGERS: Joe Kane would just say, "Do this" or "Don't do that!" if he saw me do something wrong. But he never gave me any acting advice because he was about the worst actor I've ever seen. He'd try to show me how to do something and it was just awful. I depended on him to keep me being natural. That's what an actor does—just act natural.

MILLER: There's no point in asking you to pick your favorite leading lady, is there? You already did and you married her.

ROGERS: She's such a wonderful lady. We've been married forty-five years this New Year's Eve. In this business, that's unheard of. People ask us how we can be in Hollywood and stay together. We have an agreement that we believe in: give 90 percent and take only 10 percent on both sides and never go to sleep with an argument on your mind. Everybody lets it fly off the handle once in awhile, but we always apologize. If I've said anything to hurt her, I just tell her I'm sorry, and I really am.

Miller: You finally tackled a serious dramatic role as a character who wasn't named Roy Rogers in your final movie, *Mackintosh and T.J.* Did you ever consider doing something like that earlier in your career?

Rogers: I never got a chance to do anything like that before. Old Man Yates wanted me to do [a remake of] *The Front Page.* He brought the script to me and I said, "Mr. Yates, I can't do that!" He wanted me to play the stinker who drank whisky and smoked cigarettes. I told him I couldn't do it because I'm playing a clean-living guy in my cowboy series and it would screw up everything I'd done at Republic. He said, "What do you mean you can't do it? You're under contract to me. You have to do it! I'll just get another cowboy, put him on Trigger, and we'll just go on with the series without you." And I said, "No, you can't do that. I own Trigger!"

Miller: Are you sorry that the singing cowboy era finally came to an end?

Rogers: I don't miss making the movies, but I regret the fact that kids today have to have these action pictures where a lot of people are getting killed. I think we're reaping an awful lot of what we've been sowing because there's an awful lot of that going on in real life these days.

Miller: You're in your eighties now, but you still look like you're in pretty good shape.

Rogers: Well, that's what everybody says. But I get tired real easy. By noon I've had it, even though I haven't done anything but sit around talking. I always took good care of myself. I'm thankful I can get around as well as I can. I'm eighty-one now and there's nothing wrong with me that another forty years wouldn't cure.

Afterword

Roy Rogers lived to be eighty-five, dying in Apple Valley, California, in 1998. His wife, Dale Evans, died three years later.

VI

A Giant of Comedy

Bob Hope

Interview by Ron Miller

Bob Hope was the most successful American comedian of Hollywood's golden age. And he didn't even start out as an American. He was an immigrant lad from England who began his life in the United States in poor circumstances and without much promise. But he discovered the secret of making an entire nation laugh and went on to become one of the most beloved—and richest—Americans ever.

Hope was born Leslie Townes Hope in 1903 and was raised in a working-class family. His father was a stonemason, and Hope was the fifth of seven sons. Bitten early by the urge to perform, he thought at first his calling was the prize ring and he fought, without a great deal of success, under the ring name Packy East. Fortunately, his unique ski-ramp nose was not broken during his brief ring career—it survived to give him his distinctly comical playboy look.

He began his show business career in vaudeville as a song-and-dance man, originally sometimes working with a partner, but later without. He evolved into a very competent master of ceremonies, his joke telling a natural development for a man who frequently had to keep the crowd happy in between some pretty dismal acts.

By the early 1930s, he was known as Bob Hope and was ready for the big time, first on Broadway in shows like *Roberta* (1933). He appeared in a number of movie short subjects as a comic actor but was not rewarded with very good reviews—in fact, he was singled out for scorn by famed Broadway columnist and radio personality Walter Winchell.

In 1938, Hope became the star of radio's *The Pepsodent Show* and clearly had found his most promising medium to date; he became an overnight sensation with his rapid delivery of comic lines. That same year, he was signed by Paramount Pictures and made his feature film debut in *The Big Broadcast of 1938,* which starred a much more famous comedian,

Bob Hope cuddles glamorous Hedy Lamarr in the 1951 *My Favorite Spy.* Courtesy of Paramount Pictures.

W. C. Fields, but gave Hope a chance to display his own brand of comedy—and to sing the Oscar-winning song "Thanks for the Memory."

By 1939, Hope was a full-fledged movie star, costarring in *The Cat and the Canary* with the popular Paulette Goddard. Paramount saw great potential in this glib, facile comic and teamed him with the studio's great musical star, pop singer Bing Crosby, and its reigning screen goddess, Dorothy Lamour, in *Road to Singapore* (1940), which became an immortal comedy classic and launched a series of *Road* movies that were all box office champions.

In the 1940s, Hope was the single most popular comic star in the movies, but remained a radio superstar, too. When television arrived, he waited for the right moment, 1950, to begin what turned out to be an epic run as a TV star. He thus reigned supreme in every entertainment medium, including recordings—his second Oscar-winning song, "Buttons and Bows" from *The Paleface* (1948), also became a hit parade favorite. There was even a regular Bob Hope comic book.

During World War II, Hope further endeared himself to the American public with his overseas tours to combat zones (which he continued in the subsequent Korean and Vietnam wars), becoming the most popular of all USO entertainers. American troops never forgot the sensational shows he brought to them, often under the most trying of wartime conditions.

Hope's wise investments in Southern California real estate, among other things, made him a millionaire many times over, and he became one of the most generous of all Hollywood stars, donating millions to charity and much of his land for public use.

Setting the Scene

Bob Hope was always a distinct part of my life. I grew up listening to his radio shows and, like many of my pals, wrote down his funniest lines, taking them to school the next day to tell my friends. I loved the Bob Hope movies, especially the *Road* pictures, which couldn't come often enough to suit me. Bob Hope was most vividly the comedy king of my youth.

So it was with considerable delight that I learned Bob Hope was very friendly to the press and not only believed in doing frequent press conferences but enjoyed hosting press gatherings at his home in Toluca Lake. Over my twenty-two years as a TV columnist, I met Bob Hope on many occasions. The fact that I was nationally syndicated gave me a very special access to him, thanks largely to the efforts of Ken Kantor, who had been NBC's publicist for Hope. When NBC retired Kantor, Hope immediately hired him to work as his personal publicist. Ken arranged many interviews for me with Hope in his home, almost always over lunch, and set up telephone interviews almost anytime I had a question for Hope about anything.

Hope was not usually a hilariously funny man in person but rather a sincere and always interesting man whose energy seemed limitless and his enthusiasm for new ideas unabated, even in his older years. Hope's longtime gag writer, Bob Mills, once gave me this summation of Hope: "I think people like him because he's real. What you see up there is exactly what he's like. He's just like everybody's uncle, a life-of-the-party guy who loves humor and doesn't like to get too serious about things." That is exactly the Bob Hope I grew to know over the years.

One time I arrived at Hope's homey English Tudor manse for an interview while Bob Thomas from the Associated Press was still there doing his own interview. The two Bobs were old pals—Thomas had written a biography of Hope—and I had grown up reading Thomas's Hollywood column, loving every word of it. Hope invited me up to his bedroom, where he and Thomas were watching an old comedy clip featuring Will Rogers. Sitting on Hope's big round bed watching clips with Hope and Bob Thomas was to me the equivalent of being invited into the Oval Office to watch the president at work.

Speaking of presidents, no visitor to Hope's house could possibly fail to be impressed entering his special "den" of presidential memorabilia. In that room, the walls were covered with photos of Bob with every president from FDR to Clinton and the awards they'd given him.

One of my most significant meetings with Hope came on the evening NBC was taping a special commemorating his fiftieth anniversary with the network. The setting was a soundstage at NBC's Burbank lot that had been converted into a huge nightclub. Literally scores of famous people were there, including his old vaudeville colleague George Burns and America's former first lady Nancy Reagan.

During that evening, I got to see Hope exert his own control over the show, even though others were producing and directing it. For instance, he stopped Nancy Reagan in mid-chorus of "Thanks for the Memory," which she was singing to him with special lyrics, and told her she was off-key and would have to begin again. Later, when his own wife, Dolores, was singing a number—perfectly on pitch—Hope also stopped her and made her start again. I felt then that he did it just to make Mrs. Reagan feel better about what had happened to her.

The last time I saw Bob Hope in person was on the occasion of his ninetieth birthday. I noticed that day a very profound deterioration in both his health and his mood. He was having a great deal of trouble hearing and seemed especially hard on the poor fellow who was preparing and serving our lunch. It was the only time I was ever with Bob Hope that I felt a bit uncomfortable. Nevertheless, I will remember him always as a most generous and affable man, though I know from talking with many who worked with him that he could be quite demanding because he was a "hands-on" sort of entertainer who wanted to hold the reins of his career tightly. In my dealings with him, however, he was the most amiable and likeable of men.

For the segment that follows, I have distilled Hope's words from my many different interviews with him over the years.

The Interview

MILLER: You're such an iconic symbol of America around the world that it's often hard to believe you came here as an immigrant from England. Tell me about it.

HOPE: My uncle, Frank Hope, came over first. Then we all got on the boat—in steerage—and took off. I was four years old. They wanted to vaccinate me at Ellis Island, but I wouldn't let them. I ran all over the place. I think I was a little mischievous.

MILLER: Your dad was a stonemason. Was he a good one?

HOPE: There's a bridge in Cleveland with a sign saying, "Built by Harry Hope." It connects the east side with the west side. It's still standing, so I guess he was good enough.

MILLER: I've read a good deal about how tough it was at first for you becoming a success in show business. What was the turning point for you?

HOPE: I always go back to 1928 when I was standing in front of the Woods Theater building in Chicago. I couldn't book a date. I was getting $10 a show in those days and stood there looking over at Henrisi's Restaurant, which had an open window. I could see them eating in there and I'm starving. And I was thinking, "I've got to go back to Cleveland, get my laundry done, and get a fresh start."

That's when a guy I knew, Charlie Cooley, says, "Hey, what're you doing?" He took me upstairs to a booker who got me one day at the West Inglewood Theater for $25, which was more money than I'd ever made. From that booking, I got a booking at the Stratford, where they were using a permanent emcee for shows and pictures. I stayed there six months. When I came out of there, I could do anything.

MILLER: By then you were working as a single act, but what about before that when you had a partner?

HOPE: I worked in vaudeville in what they called tabloid theater, which were small troupes of sixteen entertainers who put on musicals. I was half of a dance act with George Byrne. We danced with the Siamese twins Daisy and Violet Hilton. That's the only reason they booked us—so we could come back after our act and dance with these Siamese twins, who were darling gals.

MILLER: You and Byrne went into a Broadway show called *Sidewalks of New York* at the Knickerbocker Theater in 1927, which allowed you to display your dance act in the big time. What happened?

HOPE: It was so bad that we were advised to go back to Chicago and start all over again. We stopped in Newcastle, just to break the jump. The manager asked me to introduce the next show, which was Marshall Walker, a Scottish comic, and his Whizbang Review. I knew Walker, so I kidded around about him to the crowd, saying he was so cheap that he got married in his backyard so the chickens could have the rice. Every time I introduced Walker, I added more jokes. So by the time I finished the nine shows there, I was doing a whole monologue and they just kept laughing.

MILLER: Going from bad reviews for your dance act and raves for your introductions of Walker must have been a wakeup call for Bob Hope.

HOPE: I decided to break up the act and go out as a single comic. George settled in Columbus, Ohio, and went to work in a drugstore. He was a marvelous guy, but he never went into show business again. [One of Hope's brothers married Byrne's sister, so the families stayed close.]

MILLER: Did that make a big difference?

HOPE: Sure, but I still came up slow. I played all these little towns. I opened in East Palestine, Ohio, then went up to Ottawa, then Jackson, Michigan, then back to do every small town in Indiana. It was character building.

MILLER: You've always seemed to the public like a constant optimist. Were you that way on the way up, too?

HOPE: I think a pessimistic man couldn't have stood the routine. Pessimism gets into your head and stomach and everything else. I've known some pessimists and they get sicker faster than everybody else. I tried to enjoy myself. I think when you get around theatrical people there's always a sort of camaraderie and fun. You're laughing and telling jokes even when you're starving.

MILLER: People who've known you a long time say you were always a guy who gave your time to help others, even in those salad days.

HOPE: How it started with me was in New York around 1932 to 1937. You were off on Sunday and they always booked benefits so the performers in [Broadway] shows could play them. We used to play maybe two benefits every Sunday night.

MILLER: Your biggest break up to then came when you were signed to play one of the leading roles in the Broadway show *Roberta* by Jerome Kern. I imagine you were doing pretty well with the ladies by that time, too.

HOPE: I felt like I had every girl in New York. I was running around with every girl in the chorus, all these beautiful dames. But one night, my pal George Murphy talked me into catching the act of what he called "a real good-looking singer" over at the Vogue Club. Her name was Dolores Reade. It was love at first sight. I just kept going back again and again to see her act.

MILLER: So you started going out?

HOPE: Pretty soon I was just sitting in the car with her in front of her hotel and talking. That was fatal. One night she finally had time off and attended a performance of *Roberta*. I was shocked to see her walk right by my dressing room after the show, completely ignoring me. She wouldn't even stop and talk to me.

MILLER: What was that about?

HOPE: She was so embarrassed because she didn't know I was one of the stars of the show. She thought I was just a chorus boy.

MILLER: I guess she got over it.

HOPE: Well, we were married soon afterward.

MILLER: Between 1934 and 1938, you made eight movie short subjects, but things didn't really boom for you until you were signed by Paramount. Your first feature was *The Big Broadcast of 1938* and it gave you your signature song, "Thanks for the Memory," which won the Best Song Oscar. Tell me about that.

HOPE: The whole thing was an accident. Paramount wanted Jack Benny for the part in the movie, but he was forty-three and thought he was too old to play the juvenile lead in a picture. And I don't think he wanted to be second billed to W. C. Fields. So he turned down the part and Paramount had to find somebody else.

Bob Hope (*right*) seems a bit jealous of Bing Crosby, who's busy romancing Dorothy Lamour in their third *Road* picture, the 1942 *Road to Morocco.* Courtesy of Paramount Pictures.

I was then working on Broadway in *The Ziegfeld Follies.* In that show, I introduced the song "I Can't Get Started." Everybody thinks it was Bunny Berrigan's song because he cut the record. But I introduced it, singing it to a beautiful redhead who turned out to be Eve Arden. Anyway, the movie director Mitch Leisen saw me in the show and was impressed that I could sing as well as do light comedy.

Miller: Are you telling me Jack Benny might have wound up singing "Thanks for the Memory" instead of you?

Hope: I don't think they intended him to sing anything because Jack didn't sing much. I think Leisen probably decided to add the song for the two juvenile leads to sing once they signed Shirley Ross and me.

Miller: When did you learn you were going to sing it?

Hope: When I arrived at Paramount on September 7, 1937, I went over to the music department and they asked if I wanted to hear the new song I was going to sing. I said, "Sure," and they played me "Thanks for the Memory." I loved it right away, but I took it home and played it for

Dolores and she said, "I don't think that's much!" I think she was a little hasty.

MILLER: When the song won the Oscar, it went to the composers, Ralph Rainger and Leo Robin, but it became your theme song. How did that come about?

HOPE: I began my radio show for Pepsodent [toothpaste] in September of 1938 and I needed a theme song. It hadn't won the Oscar yet, but it was the automatic choice for me.

MILLER: You've told me before that you've sung it on every radio show since, every TV show, in just about every live performance, and even in another movie [*Thanks for the Memory*, 1938]. But you've almost always changed the lyrics to suit the times. How did the composers react to that?

HOPE: They loved it. After all, they got royalties every time it was played—and still do.

MILLER: How about you? Ever get tired of singing that same old tune?

HOPE: No, I don't. I'm very sentimental about it. It's a beautiful thing, that "Thanks for the Memory."

MILLER: I'm wondering, after your great success with so many songs, if you ever thought about becoming primarily a singer.

HOPE: Back in 1928 when I was on the Keith-Western [vaudeville] circuit, I finished playing six months as a master of ceremonies who sang in every show. They wanted me to go on to do another act with a piano player and just stand there and sing. I said, "No way!" I'm so glad I didn't get hooked on that. I wanted to do jokes.

MILLER: Starting with *The Cat and the Canary* in 1939, you've costarred with some of the screen's most beautiful women. How about some capsule reviews of them? Like your costar that year, Paulette Goddard?

HOPE: I'd call her "society sex."

MILLER: Dorothy Lamour?

HOPE: She was sure fun in the jungle.

MILLER: Hedy Lamarr?

HOPE: She was sweet ecstasy. [Lamarr's famous nude scene was in the 1933 film *Ecstasy*.]

MILLER: Your costar in *The Paleface* and *Son of Paleface* [1952], Jane Russell?

HOPE: Oh, God. Now you're talking. She's handsomer than I am!

MILLER: How about Katharine Hepburn?

Hope: I call her "iron petticoats." [They costarred in 1956's *The Iron Petticoat.*]

Miller: How about Marilyn Monroe and Jayne Mansfield?

Hope: Marilyn Monroe was very kittenish and cute and pretty. She was very nice offstage. Jayne Mansfield was another one that came on like gangbusters and lived it right on through in her personal life. She was very sexy offstage and always had a funny line ready to throw at you. She was marvelous.

Miller: Where did your wolfish image get going?

Hope: That image originated in my radio show when I used to do all those jokes like, "I went to the football game. Madeleine Carroll sat in front of me and I want to tell you that all the passes weren't made on the field." Then there were all those *Road* pictures where we used to growl at the girls and act like hoodlums.

[Hope's private life was rather wolfish, too. He was a notorious skirt chaser and in the 1950s had a long affair with actress Barbara Payton, who later became a prostitute. In his chats with me, he professed to be scandal-free and, in truth, most of the revelations about his womanizing have come out since his death.]

Miller: I've always been blown away by your "presidents' room" and all the honors they've awarded you despite the fun you've poked at them all. Tell me about your relationship with them. Didn't they ever get ticked off at you?

Hope: Carter complained about one joke. I had said the only difference between him and Billy [Carter's brother] was the fact that Billy had a foreign policy.

Miller: I know you came out in support for Ronald Reagan and yet you certainly needled him with your jokes from time to time. Did he consider you a turncoat?

Hope: Reagan is a fooler himself and a casual sort of guy who loves being needled by comics. I've known him since he first came to Hollywood in 1937 and I started telling jokes about him as soon as he went into politics. Anyway, we had something in common: he once played Las Vegas as a master of ceremonies and comedian.

Miller: But you've gotten along pretty well with most of the Democrats who held the office, too, haven't you?

Hope: Sure. Harry Truman was a great friend of mine. When he upset Tom Dewey in 1948, I sent him a one-word telegram: "Unpack." Harry kept that telegram and displayed it for years. After he left office, I visited him and Bess Truman quite often. They were great people, yes, sir. Average Americans, you know?

MILLER: The first was FDR?

HOPE: Yes, Roosevelt was the first to lay something [an award] on me. I'll never forget doing that show in Washington that the newspaper guys put on with Roosevelt sitting there going, "Ha-ha-ha-ha."

MILLER: And Dwight Eisenhower?

HOPE: I was decorated by Eisenhower and he said, "Drop in anytime, will you?" Like he was lonesome.

MILLER: How about President Kennedy?

HOPE: He presented me with a Congressional Medal and reminded me that he'd sat in the rain to watch one of my shows when he was a young naval officer in the South Pacific during World War II. I was really touched by that and I remember him very fondly. I did a couple of jokes about him and first thing you know his man Pierre [press secretary Pierre Salinger] calls and says the boss wants to see me. From that time on, until he went to Dallas [where he was assassinated], I was in the White House six times. I had more fun with Jack Kennedy because he loved jokes. He used to send for me.

MILLER: But the only time you actually campaigned for a presidential candidate was for George H. W. Bush in 1992.

HOPE: I liked him so much that I just stepped in and did it. I flew to Houston and introduced him at his last appearance before the election. [Bush lost to Bill Clinton, but Hope told me he thought Clinton would "do just fine."]

MILLER: The *Road* pictures were so phenomenally popular that they keep being enjoyed generation after generation.

HOPE: I think they appeal to the younger people. They show them over and over on TV. When they get worn out, they send 'em back for new sprocket holes and run them again.

MILLER: Walter Winchell was very hard on your first movie appearances in those comedy short subjects, yet you keep trying to play him in a movie about his life story. Are you after revenge?

HOPE: No, I'm an admirer. On the radio, he had this mile-a-minute style of talking and it impressed me. I didn't really get going on radio until I adopted that high-speed monologue. I go so fast that it gets ahead of my brain sometimes.

Bob Hope with Jane Russell in *Son of Paleface* (1952), the sequel to their 1948 hit. Courtesy of Paramount Pictures and TV station KTVU, Oakland, CA.

MILLER: Do you think you could have been as successful if you hadn't had so many long years on the road, perfecting your style?

HOPE: In the old days of vaudeville, we could polish a routine week after week. We did the same routine for twenty years. Now you see these kids come along and it's real tough for them. Right after the first TV show, they've got to get another routine ready for the next one.

MILLER: One of the primary reasons why you're so widely loved today must be the tremendous time you put in entertaining the troops. But you did take some flak for doing it during the really unpopular war in Vietnam and defending our being there.

HOPE: If I hadn't gone over there, I'd have felt pretty awful. Those kids needed shows more than anyone else because they were just sitting around wondering what the hell was going on. It was a miserable, miserable situation. There was nothing different about Vietnam when it came to entertaining troops. I was doing the same thing there I was doing in other places. I wasn't running for office or anything.

MILLER: Lots of people thought the Academy Awards would have to shut down once you stopped hosting the ceremony. Do you miss that job?

HOPE: No, not really. I did it for so long. I mean, twenty-seven of them.

MILLER: From what I've read, you must have been one of the all-time most talented investors in real estate. How did that get going?

HOPE: My older brother, Jim, became a real estate agent. He used to call me and say he'd found a couple hundred acres for sale for $100 an acre and I'd tell him to go ahead and buy it. I kept buying it. I have a hell of a lot of it now.

MILLER: Did you ever make a mistake on land?

HOPE: Well, I've been at this place for going on fifty years. I started out by buying three acres of the site here from an outfit, then offered another guy something like $12 million for the other four acres I needed. I made the mistake of going away after making the offer. When I came back, it had been sold and the new owner wanted $15 million for it. And I had to give it to him because I really needed the other four acres.

MILLER: Of all the pictures you've made, which is your favorite?

HOPE: If *The Paleface* is on, I'll take a look at it. And I really like *The Seven Little Foys* [1955].

MILLER: This may sound like a really stupid question, but what does Dolores get you for a birthday present? It must be tough shopping for one of the richest men in the world.

HOPE: Oh, that's not so hard. She'll get me another sweater. I only have 350 of them.

MILLER: Right now the rumor is your network, NBC, is shopping for a buyer. Have you ever thought of buying it?

Bob Hope with the juvenile ensemble in one of his favorite movies, *The Seven Little Foys* (1955). Courtesy of Paramount Pictures.

HOPE: I've considered it, but what would I do with a network?

MILLER: At this stage of your life, it must be very rewarding to feel the genuine love the public has for you.

HOPE: I sure do appreciate that. I feel that from people I meet. I imagine it comes from the things we did like entertaining the troops all those years. Most people had relatives or knew someone who was over there. I've had some wonderful things happen that make me feel good about my life. Like the time when I had this bad eye problem and it looked as if I might have to lose an eye. And this young Marine said, "I'll give him one of my eyes."

MILLER: If you had it to do all over again, would you do anything differently?

HOPE: No. I couldn't be that lucky all over again.

Afterword

Bob Hope had a lot of projects on the burner in his final years, including a final *Road* movie with Bing Crosby that was cancelled when Crosby died.

He never got his Walter Winchell movie made. His final starring role in a feature film was in 1972's *Cancel My Reservation,* but he did star in a final made-for-TV movie, 1986's *A Masterpiece of Murder,* playing an over-the-hill private eye, supported by a cast of old-timers, including Don Ameche, Jayne Meadows, Yvonne DeCarlo, Anne Francis, Stella Stevens, Kevin McCarthy, and Frank Gorshin. It was not well received.

Though Hope continued to entertain even into his nineties, failing health finally removed him from the public eye. Hope had wanted to live to be a hundred—and he did. He died at his home in Toluca Lake on July 27, 2003, his legacy as one of the all-time great comedy talents assured.

VII

Four Very Special Stars

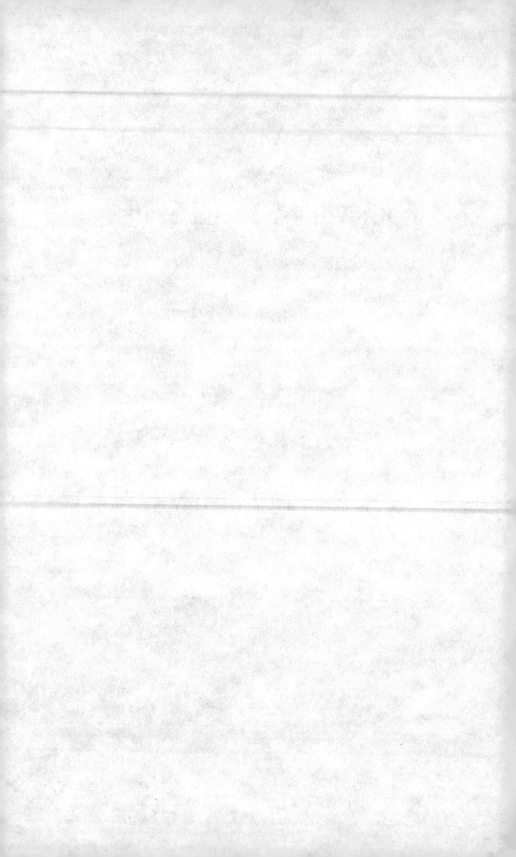

Margaret Hamilton

Interview by James Bawden

If ever an actor was defined by a single role—and loved for it through the ages—it was Margaret Hamilton, whose cackling voice and sharp features are vivid memories to generations of movie fans who remember her as the Wicked Witch of the 1939 movie classic, *The Wizard of Oz.* Hamilton was a veteran of Broadway theater, radio, and television as well as the movies, where she specialized in character roles. She might even have been remembered, if for nothing else, as Cora from the Maxwell House coffee TV ads she did in the late 1970s.

Setting the Scene

Meeting Margaret Hamilton was a real thrill for an old *Wizard of Oz* fan. It happened in January 1972. Hamilton was busy stealing scenes from Jean Simmons in the road company of *A Little Night Music* in Toronto, and I arranged an interview with her between shows. When I walked into the lobby of the King Edward Hotel for lunch with her, I suppose I was expecting someone who cackled and had a broom waiting in her parking space. Instead, I was greeted by a beautifully coiffed matron in a Chanel suit. Not once was she recognized by the other diners as one of cinema's best-ever villainesses.

The Interview

Bawden: I know you're costarring with Jean Simmons in *A Little Night Music* here in Toronto. But the other actors arc staying at the more upscale Royal York Hotel. And here you are . . .

Hamilton: At this old hotel? There's a story there. I was born in Cleveland in 1902. This wonderful King Edward Hotel opened in 1907.

Margaret Hamilton, circa 1951. James Bawden collection.

Every summer my family would travel through Toronto when I was just a little girl and stay at this hotel in its glory days. I've grown old along with this hotel. And so I asked to be booked here and, in my mind, it's still the same. But between you and me, both our facades are a bit cracked these days.

BAWDEN: Does it bother you that everywhere you go you're—

HAMILTON: The Wicked Witch of the West? Well, I wouldn't get any work at my age if I didn't have that great movie as my signature piece. I mean nobody asks me about *Mountain Justice* [1937], *The Gay Vagabond* [1941], or *Breaking the Ice* [1938]. Why would they? But to have one film that's still seen more than thirty years later? Well, it's astounding.

BAWDEN: I keep hearing you were not first choice for the role.

HAMILTON: Mervyn LeRoy, who produced it, asked me to come in and test in full makeup. I worked with the designers on what I thought was a particularly foul-looking costume. I just thought of Halloween. I suggested the pointed hat and I found an old broomstick in a corner. Then I read in the trades a week later Gale Sondergaard had waltzed in and wowed them with a particularly glamorous interpretation. And she even announced she'd gotten it. I just shrugged and kept on working on my character studies. Then I was at a football game with my little son and Mervyn spotted me and ran over and said, "We've been looking for you everywhere. You got it! Report Monday for costume and makeup tests." He offered me six weeks at $1,000 a week, which was manna for me. It eventually stretched out to twenty-three weeks. I asked him what had happened to Gale and Mervyn said, "Too pretty. We needed somebody who could scare the pants off children."

BAWDEN: But the making of that movie wasn't your fondest experience, was it?

HAMILTON: Working on it almost killed me. Buddy Ebsen, who was the original Tin Man, was rushed to the hospital and replaced by Jack Haley. The cause was paint poisoning and he was there for an awfully long time.

Supporting actors were not well regarded in those days. In one scene, I had to drop six feet through a trapdoor with the colored smoke all around me, and it was a close-up so there was no double. I was told to bend my knees and I'd land simply, but suddenly I was in flames. Somebody had prematurely touched the fire button. I was on fire! My broomstick went right up! My hat was on fire! I had to be hospitalized for second-degree burns for a month. MGM grudgingly paid the bills, but my face was seared, I had third-degree burns on one hand. I was in agony. My agent said if I sued I'd never work in this town again.

When I returned, I was told I'd be suspended in the air with a long pipe emitting smoke below me. I said no and they said I was a sissy and brought in the stand-in and she saddled up and the whole gadget exploded. She was badly wounded and spent months in the hospital.

BAWDEN: But surely there must be happy moments?

HAMILTON: Well, working with Jack Haley, Bert Lahr, Ray Bolger was heavenly. They kidded Judy [Garland] like crazy to keep her perky. Those Munchkins were something else—a bad lot, I say, but they were afraid of me and kept their distance.

Watching Judy Garland perform was lovely. She had such energy. I didn't realize it was all the Benzedrine she was being force-fed. They worked Judy to the bone. Saturdays, too, right up to the dawn breaking on Sunday morning. You know Judy was only sixteen and she was about to graduate from Hollywood High and I helped her pick the dress, but she had to do a cross-promotional *Oz* tour and only got back the day before her last day at high school.

I had my lovely little son, Meserve, with me one day in the commissary and [MGM studio boss] Louis B. Mayer waddles over and offered him a kiddie contract. "Don't you dare!" I shouted and he ran off. I'd seen, up front, the awful things Hollywood did to little children.

Take a stopwatch and you'll see I'm only around for less than fifteen minutes. It took an awful lot of effort to get those fifteen minutes. I became the real star of it because children always love to be frightened nearly to death. And little tots still recognize me on the street today. They point at me and shiver and laugh. It's quite a compliment to think I still look a bit like that.

BAWDEN: To backtrack, how did you get into movies?

HAMILTON: I was brought up in Cleveland in a Euclid Avenue brownstone. Originally I was a kindergarten teacher. [Two of her kindergarten students grew up to be actors: William Windom and Jim Backus.] I eventually had my own nursery in Cleveland Heights. I acted at the Cleveland Playhouse just for fun until I realized this should be my profession.

I was visiting in New York and saw Gertrude Lawrence in *Oh, Kay* on Broadway and it tore me up. I thought I should be up there singing and dancing. A friend was a cousin of Maude Eburne and when she was touring in Cleveland in the play *When Ladies Meet,* I met her and she told me to be persistent. And in 1931 I got a small part in a summer tour of a new play called *Another Language* [1932]. I was then twenty-nine, [but] my character was over forty. A new young juvenile, John Beal, was the star, and at the end of the summer we both got deals to follow the play to Broadway.

And an MGM scout spotted us and when Metro bought the play for Helen Hayes and Bob Montgomery, we both got deals to go to Hollywood and re-create our parts. RKO then signed me to a three-picture-a-year deal at the heavenly salary of $30 weekly. I never went back to kindergarten teaching again.

BAWDEN: Then what?

HAMILTON: [Director] Frank Capra saw *Another Language* and hired me for *Broadway Bill* [1934]. "Crinkle your nose more!" he'd shout at me. I never realized I was even doing that, but it seemed to work. And then I went back to Broadway in another play called *The Farmer Takes a Wife* [1934] starring June Walker and another promising juvenile, Henry Fonda. And both of us were picked up to be in the [1935] movie version, directed by Vic Fleming.

Janet Gaynor [who played the leading female role in the movie] was so truly sweet and petite, and this one was about the Erie Canal and it just worked. Who could have thought Hank would soar and John Beal fade into smaller roles? Then the three of us were reunited in *Way Down East,* the 1935 talkie version, but on the first day little Janet was being pursued down a hill, fell, and cracked her skull on a rock. We all heard the crack and she was out [of filming] for months. Rochelle Hudson replaced her. She was prettier than Janet, but hard, not at all the petite heroine type, and the movie didn't do well at all. Janet got dropped next year by Fox. Had *Way Down East* been the hit she needed, she would have survived under the new Darryl Zanuck regime.

BAWDEN: How did you live in Hollywood?

HAMILTON: I got on okay. Not great money, but enough to live simply in a nice boarding establishment. I just worked all the time, but in small roles. I was typecast and that kept me going. My first friend in L.A. was the wonderful old character actress Louise Closser Hale. She'd saved enough for retirement, she told me, and then made her final movie, *Dinner at Eight* [1933]. One day she told me she was going to the doctor's to get a nodule clipped from her nose. And she never returned. It was on a Saturday morning and the nodule was clipped in the office and she bled to death. It was quite a scandal. The medical building was shut down and the body removed down the back stairs. I cried buckets, but the doctor was never charged. And I lost a good friend.

BAWDEN: How did you get jobs?

HAMILTON: Often by word of mouth. I made a very winning comedy,

Chatterbox [1936], with Anne Shirley, and the director George Nicholls Jr. then asked for me again for *The Witness Chair* [1936]. I remember I played an accountant in that one. Vic Fleming was a fan and told Jack Conway to hire me for *Saratoga* [1937]. That was Jean Harlow's last film. She died during production. I was a train passenger and we shot all those sequences together. When Jean [died] a double named Mary Dees was used for long shots and another actress, Paula Winslow, did her voice. And then, in the last scene on the train, it's the real Jean again because we'd shot that part earlier.

BAWDEN: The characters you played could be stern but rarely were outright nasty.

HAMILTON: Oh, yes, in *These Three* [1936] I was the maid to the grandmother, played by Alma Kruger, and I can see right through her nasty little granddaughter, wonderfully done by little Bonita Granville. I remember when she lies to me she's had a bath. I snap, "Well, go take another!" I ran a boardinghouse in *You Only Live Once* [1937]. There was real tension on the set when the nasty director went right after Henry Fonda. It's a superb picture, you know, but the atmosphere on set was toxic. I think Fritz [Lang] just resented Hank's popularity and good looks.

BAWDEN: One British publication wrongly lists you as an extra in *Trail of the Lonesome Pine* [1936].

HAMILTON: Goodness! I never had to do extra work in my life. I know what you're talking about, but it's a mistake. I got billing in every movie I made. The shortest part I ever did was in *The Ox-Bow Incident* [1943], again with Hank Fonda. The director, Billy Wellman, phoned me up and apologized, but my sizeable part got cut to the bone. If you hiccup you'll miss me. I'm seen walking through a door. But I got paid for six weeks' work and I got billing. And it happens to us all. Beulah Bondi was dumped from *The Grapes of Wrath* [1940] for Jane Darwell. I got bumped from *And Now Tomorrow* [1937] because the director told me he wanted an actress more unsympathetic and blowsy and he recast with Minna Gombell. But Leo [McCarey] saw I got six weeks' pay for staying at home, which is nice work if you can get it. You just pick yourself up and go on in this business.

BAWDEN: Were there any of the big stars you truly enjoyed working with?

HAMILTON: Oh, Carole Lombard would be right at the top of any list. I have to explain the star pecking order in those days. The stars had huge dressing rooms—many were suites complete with kitchens and even bedrooms—and portable ones on location. They were insulated from the rest of us. We were ensconced in a holding pen. I'd read, study my lines. But interaction was rare. With Carole, she came over and sat with us. She would be taking the lay of the land. She'd get her makeup done right there. An all right dame. And her mastery of screwball comedy was supreme. She was so lithe with a comedy line even Freddie March had trouble keeping up. I ran the drugstore in Warsaw, Vermont, in that one.

Eddie Robinson was the same way in *A Slight Case of Murder* [1938]. A sheer delight, very erudite. Bespectacled between the scenes. On camera, a whirling dervish, very competitive.

The year I did *Wizard of Oz* I also had a part in *Babes in Arms* with Judy Garland. The way Busby Berkeley mistreated her was awful. And Judy's mom let him get away with this abuse. I was the aunt of one of the kids, name of Martha Steele, whom I loved. Judy asked me to sit with her in her dressing room. That way the mom couldn't have a temper tantrum. I smuggled her in cookies because she was kept on a starvation diet. I told Busby off once about his foul language. He couldn't really direct people. He could only devise those geometric shapes.

Years later during Judy's Carnegie Hall triumphs I went backstage and she didn't recognize me or Ray Bolger. He was in tears, saying she was on something. I did a *Merv Griffin Show* with her and her speech was slurred. I realized the sweet little teenager I'd known was long gone.

My first scene with Wally Beery [in 1938's *Stablemates*], I was at a loss for words. He didn't use a single line of the script. Director Sam Wood bawls, "Cut" and asks me what's wrong. Wally sidles up and whispers, "When I finish talking, just say anything that comes into your head." That was the only way to survive with all those "aw shucks" he was adding to every scene. This one was an uncredited remake of *The Champ,* which got Wally an Oscar. Only this time Mickey Rooney was a very able scene-stealer and gave Wally a run for the money.

Bawden: In *My Little Chickadee* [1940] you had to contend with W. C. Fields *and* Mae West. How did that go?

Hamilton: Bill Fields walked in the first day, reeking of liquor. He came over and apologized to me. Understand, I was in awe of his talents. I said, "Mr. Fields, on you it smells like eau de cologne," and he brightened up. A very sweet egomaniac. Ditto Mae West, who looked like an over-stuffed mannequin. She said to me, "Margaret, can I help it if every man on

Margaret Hamilton as the Wicked Witch of the West in *The Wizard of Oz* (1939). Courtesy of MGM.

this set is crazy in love with me?" Well, the love was one-sided, I can tell you. She was forty-eight and needed special lighting to wash out her creases. And Bill was constantly changing lines and she'd protest to director Eddie Cline, who told me he now knew how a wrestling referee felt.

Margaret Hamilton (*left*) with Mae West in *My Little Chickadee* (1940). Courtesy of Universal Pictures.

Everyone seems to have seen this one, but it was considered a disappointment when first released. Mr. Fields never used bad language, although he was sorely tried when Miss West was in one of her moods. She kept saying, "I'm a solo performer. Please tell Bill that next time you find him awake." Like all comics he'd try out a bit of business and then spend days refining it. He simply tried to add to his performance and she to hers. Mae would say, "Bill! Enough!" and waddle away and he'd mope for the rest of the afternoon. Thinking of that scene where he gets into bed with a billy goat still makes me laugh. But Mae wanted it out as being unrefined.

BAWDEN: A few years later you did *Mad Wednesday* [1946] with Harold Lloyd. How did that go?

HAMILTON: It was directed by madcap Preston Sturges. He had glasses made for me that were replicates of what Harold wore. And presto, we really did look like brother and sister. Look, I don't know where the money was coming from, but we'd do every scene six different ways. It was my own master class in comedy, with Harold and Preston trying to top each other. The company was owned by Howard Hughes, who was an obsessive-compulsive. Costs shot up so high it will never make back its money. Never! But I like to point out Harold was like Bill Fields, a comic who couldn't stop. That scene with the lion in the bank is funny. Then he tried to take the lion all over the place in subsequent scenes and audience interest frittered away. Because it made no sense. The film wound up with dozens of scenes shot that never made the final cut.

Preston made a fortune off it and then asked me to join *The Beautiful Blonde from Bashful Bend* [1949]. It's on the Fox books as the only Betty Grable vehicle that did not make money. Because she never showed her legs. Now that's perverse, if you ask me. Audiences didn't pay to see her in Victorian gowns! And Betty couldn't understand Preston's comedy style. All the Sturges regulars were in it, but Betty looked mighty uncomfortable. But Betty was a sweetie. She asked for me to be in her next, *Wabash Avenue* [1950]. My first day on set she lifts her gown and shouts, "See? Legs!" And this one was a huge hit.

Bawden: You once said your favorite forties film was a little B called what?

Hamilton: *Driftwood,* made in 1947. With that fine character actor Walter Brennan working his magic. And Natalie Wood at the start of her career. Allan Dwan directed it for Republic, and it just clicked with audiences. Walter is a very complete actor. He likes one take and when you've acted with him you realize what screen acting is all about. One day when he asked for a second take because he felt he could do better, my jaw dropped open. But he aced it on the second take, so he knew what he was doing.

Bawden: Van Johnson once told me you'd saved his career. I think you know what I'm talking about.

Hamilton: Yes! On the set of *State of the Union* [1948]. Van would come to my dressing room—I had one, for a change—for tea and cookies. And he was very depressed. Moaned on and on about why was he in a movie with Tracy, Hepburn, Lansbury, etc. And he was just a bobbysoxer idol. I told Frank Capra [the film's director], who roared with laughter and said, "Go tell Van Kate Hepburn has just been complaining about him and claiming he stole a scene with her by underacting." And Frank was quite correct. Van could hold his own with the best of them.

The next year Frank offered me my old *Broadway Bill* role back in his remake, *Riding High.* I wondered why. Turns out Paramount had bought the negative from Columbia and he had me and others dress exactly as we had seventeen years before. That way long shots and action scenes from the original could be interpolated at no charge. Also present were originals Douglass Dumbrille, Ray Walburn, Frankie Darro, Clarence Muse. It was a strange sort of cannibalism and Frank's movie career was crashing, I could tell that.

BAWDEN: You left movies in 1951 for nine years. Explain.

HAMILTON: Had to. Movie roles were drying up. I wanted to get back to stage acting and was based out of New York City. I had an apartment near Gramercy Park and one night I get on the elevator really late and somebody taps me on the shoulder and says, "Pardon me, Miss Hamilton, but we were once in a movie together." I look over at my neighbor and it's Jimmy Cagney. And he remembered me from *Johnny Come Lately* [1943].

Truth was I had a whole new career in live TV. I remember a live version of *The Man Who Came to Dinner* [1954] with Monty Woolley and Merle Oberon that was fun. The very next year I was in *The Guardsman* [1955] with Claudette Colbert and Franchot Tone. Best of that bunch was *The Devil's Disciple* [1955] with Maurice Evans for Hallmark Hall of Fame. It was live, and the Shaw estate [the production was an adaptation of George Bernard Shaw's play] insisted the kinescope be subsequently burned because rights for a movie had been sold to Burt Lancaster.

I did a whole stack of Studio One live dramas, and I did all the series of the time, like *The Phil Silvers Show.* My best TV time was on *The Secret Storm,* the afternoon CBS soaper, for four years [1953–1957] as the maid. My employer was Marjorie Gateson, that great old-timer from my Hollywood era. We'd acted together in *Stablemates,* and here we were on live afternoon TV! I toured in *The Wizard of Oz* a few times and went back to Broadway. And I got some movie roles in between. The last so far was *Rosie* [1968] with Roz Russell. Once again I was the comic maid. Why fight it?

One casting agent said I looked like I was wearing a steel corset. I can't think of many parts where I've been truly nasty outside of *Wizard.* Wait a minute! The teacher in *The Red Pony* [1949] was very bitchy.

What I want to explain is how grateful I've been. I could have spent all these years teaching kindergarten. I used to go out to junior grades to say hello, and all the kids would ask me to cackle. Which I always did at full throttle, and the little nippers would be cowering in their seats. We even had a few moist accidents. I've played hundreds of characters and I'm still up for more. Preston Sturges called me a "miniaturist" and that's pretty wonderful as far as I'm concerned.

Afterword

Margaret Hamilton acted until 1982, when she played guest roles on two CBS series—*Nurse* and *Lou Grant.* She died of a heart attack, aged eighty-two, in Salisbury, Connecticut, on May 16, 1985. Predictably, the obituaries' headlines all mentioned *The Wizard of Oz.*

Keye Luke

Interview by James Bawden and Ron Miller

Hollywood's golden age was never a very hospitable time for Asian American actors, who seldom were called upon to play the main character in any movie, not even those about Asian characters. But Keye Luke, a native of China who came to America as a child, had a long, long run of success as a movie actor in Hollywood, then carried his good fortune over into the TV medium He even broke the convention against Chinese leading men once and played the starring role in *The Phantom of Chinatown* (1941), taking over the detective role from Caucasian actor Boris Karloff for the final film in the Mr. Wong series of mysteries.

Best known as detective Charlie Chan's "number one son" in the popular Chan series of the 1930s, Luke also had a running role as the assistant to Dr. Gillespie (Lionel Barrymore) in the follow-up to the *Dr. Kildare* series of movies at MGM. Then, in the TV series *Kung Fu* (1972–1975), Luke was the memorable Master Po, mentor to David Carradine's Kwai Chong Caine.

Luke's career spanned more than five decades, and he's remembered fondly by his many fans today.

Setting the Scene

Both of us conducted separate interviews with Keye Luke over the years. We have combined them for this presentation, but we offer our individual memories of the circumstances of those interviews.

BAWDEN: Keye Luke was one of my first interviewees during one of my early forays to Hollywood. In those days, the U.S. TV networks discouraged Canadian journalists from participating in the mass press conferences American columnists conducted with the stars of new TV shows. That meant I was dependent on private one-on-one chats with the actors—

Keye Luke in TV's *Anna and the King* (1972). Courtesy of CBS.

if I could get them. Often I was relegated to talking with the supporting players rather than the stars. In the case of Keye Luke, that turned out to be a great break for me because he had a very special insight into the workings of the movie business over a whole lot of years.

Keye Luke was then (1972) working in a new CBS sitcom called *Anna and the King,* inspired by the success of the Broadway musical *The King and I* and the 1956 movie of the same title, both starring Yul Brynner as the king of Siam. Brynner was the star of the short-lived TV series, and Samantha Eggar was his leading lady. Keye Luke had the principal supporting role.

CBS arranged for me to meet Luke at the old Brown Derby restaurant at Hollywood and Vine. Luke arrived dressed in a dark business suit, personifying the kind of Hollywood professionalism that was quickly disappearing in 1972.

MILLER: My interview with Keye Luke was arranged to coincide with his appearance in the CBS TV movie *Blade in Hong Kong* (1985), in which he played the elderly and exceptionally wise father of the hero. We had a late lunch at a rich old Ventura Boulevard restaurant in Studio City. Luke was an especially warm and impressive man with a rich, sonorous baritone voice that rattled the glassware on the table every now and then.

The Interview

BAWDEN: How did you get to Hollywood?

LUKE: I was born in 1904 in Guangzhou, China, near Canton, and my dad owned an art shop. Growing up, I was always painting away, but we moved to Seattle when I was very young. I started out as a local Seattle artist, specializing in murals. I helped on some of the original murals in Grauman's Chinese Theatre, working on faux Chinese murals. And I had a gig drawing the art for the *King Kong* press book in 1933.

MILLER: While you were working in the publicity department at RKO in the early 1930s, I understand you almost had a chance to play a romantic lead in a big new musical. True or false?

LUKE: True. The producers of *Flying Down to Rio* [1933] wanted to follow it up with a new musical teaming Fred Astaire and Ginger Rogers, to be set in Shanghai. Anna May Wong was set as the second female lead, but they couldn't find a Chinese leading man for her. Then they remembered this guy who was working in the publicity department: me. They called me to their office and told me I would be costarring with Anna May Wong. It was like a bolt out of the blue. I was planning to go to New York to study at the Art Students League, then go to Paris and complete my art education. I knew nothing about being an actor.

MILLER: So what happened?

LUKE: The film was cancelled when the producer was fired. But I was given a consolation prize: I made my "acting" debut in a Leon Errol comedy short subject. I played his Japanese gardener in a scene where I mowed his rug with a lawn mower. I considered it a silly whim and returned to my artwork without any regrets.

MILLER: Why did you move from RKO to MGM right after that?

LUKE: Frank Whitbeck, my former boss at Fox, had moved to MGM as advertising director and he asked me to come in for a job interview. That's when I learned MGM wasn't interested in my portfolio. They had heard about my near miss at RKO and asked me to test for a role at MGM. Fortunately, it turned out all right. I got the part—and I started right out at the top.

BAWDEN: So you wound up making your feature film debut in *The Painted Veil* with the legendary Greta Garbo in 1934.

LUKE: I had the small part of Shay Key Fong [a young Chinese doctor who assisted Herbert Marshall, playing a doctor battling a cholera epidemic]. But I didn't get billing.

MILLER: Was your test so good that you beat out the real professional actors who were trying for the part?

LUKE: There were very few Chinese actors in Hollywood in those days, so I was practically a pioneer. I don't think I had any competition for the part.

BAWDEN: What was Garbo like?

LUKE: As if I really met her! She was a true beauty from the neck up. But her body was stocky, her feet long. We rehearsed our dialogue scene [together]. She was very kind to me and just moved on. The camera was her best friend. In close-ups, she was exquisite. George Brent [one of the two male leads] was after her from the beginning.

BAWDEN: Describe L.A. in 1934.

LUKE: Very racist. On my art assignments I'd enter by the service trades door and not the main gate. MGM did have Asians and blacks on staff, but working in the laundry and in the cafeteria as waiters. For me, as an actor, to have ventured into the MGM commissary would have caused a commotion. Besides, I couldn't afford it.

I never went into the big department stores. L.A. was segregated, but not formally. One never saw blacks on Wilshire Boulevard. Parts of the city I avoided—all-white areas like Beverly Hills.

Even after working with somebody like a big Caucasian actor, I'd be ignored if we met on the street. Asians were invisible, you see. We knew our place: one step back. That's why the Charlie Chan films were so important. They deflated a lot of the current racial myths. But even the Chan

Keye Luke *(left)* with Warner Oland in *Charlie Chan at the Race Track* (1936). Courtesy of 20th Century-Fox.

films had rules. Charlie never touched a white woman except as a handshake. I'd never have a white girlfriend, not that I wanted one in pictures. Whenever a young, personable "Chinaman" was needed, I'd get the job. But in films like *The Casino Murder Case* [1935], *Oil for the Lamps of China* [1935], *King of Burlesque* [1935], I'm very much in the background and often not listed in credits.

BAWDEN: How did you get into the Charlie Chan movies?

LUKE: The Fox casting director saw my work in *The Painted Veil* and was looking for a nonthreatening Asian actor. At first they wanted to hire a Caucasian, but nobody knew how to act the part, which was of a callow teenager trying to learn the detective business from his dad. I did a test with Warner Oland [who had acted with Luke in *The Painted Veil*] and he said, "Hire the kid," and I eventually did a slew of them. In 1935, I did *Charlie Chan in Paris* and *Charlie Chan in Shanghai.* In 1936 I was in *Charlie Chan at the Circus, Charlie Chan at the Race Track,* and *Charlie Chan at the Opera,* which I think is the best one of them all. In 1937, I did *Charlie*

Chan at the Olympics, *Charlie Chan on Broadway*, and *Charlie Chan at Monte Carlo*.

BAWDEN: How did Warner Oland treat you?

LUKE: Like a son. He was the greatest actor I've ever worked with. Meticulous in his use of props, the way he'd do a brilliant first take and then go downhill from there. He used no makeup, no slit-eye makeup—did it all by combing his beard and eyebrows. Refused to talk in a phony accent. Used those fortune cookie aphorisms to demonstrate Charlie's character. Was Swedish, as you know. And as long as he was in good health, he was a joy to work with.

These films ran about seventy minutes and were intended to run at the top of double bills. They were not B pictures but "programmers." We'd work for about four weeks. We did everything on the Fox lot or the Fox ranch. Lots of back projection conjured up Paris or Egypt or whatever. Lots of familiar character actors. I remember my first had John Qualen, John Miljan, Mary Brian, and they were all paid well, as was I. The directors included Lewis Seiler, Bruce Humberstone, Eugene Ford, all conscientious workers who'd toil away with little recognition.

MILLER: In today's world, the Chan movies are controversial because a Caucasian actor portrayed a Chinese character. Many Asian critics have complained about that. How did you feel about it?

LUKE: Let's be realistic. The theater is make-believe, and the people in it are artists who create characters. If an actor can create a character of another race and make him believable, then the part belongs to him. Regardless of his race, creed, or color.

BAWDEN: How did the series end for you?

LUKE: Warner always had a drinking problem and it finally caught up with him. On the set of *Charlie Chan at Ringside* [1937], he couldn't remember lines, his speech was slurred. His wife of thirty years had left him, and he became hysterical and stormed off. Production was halted, and he booked passage for his home in Stockholm, where he died after a bender. The Fox people had half a film, so they changed it into a "Mr. Moto" vehicle called *Mr. Moto's Gamble*. Star Peter Lorre protested he was being forced to utter Charlie Chan-isms, but we got through it. I was still Charlie's son, cast here as a student in Moto's detective lectures. You know, I can't hate this one, it's so damned loopy.

BAWDEN: The Chan films continued to be made, with Sidney Toler replacing Oland, but they left you out.

Luke: I just couldn't do it and they wisely recast the assistant as the second son, nicely played by Victor Sen Yung as Jimmy Chan. The first was *Charlie Chan in Honolulu* [1938]. Sidney did use makeup. I much preferred Warner, but the series kept humming along until Fox sold it in 1942 to Monogram. I had some lean years, I can tell you, but emotionally I was a wreck [because] I was so devoted to Warner. I was in such movies as *No, No, Nanette* [1940] and *Comrade X* [1940] but was uncredited.

Miller: You also were in the great MGM epic film about China, *The Good Earth* [1937], which starred two Caucasians—Paul Muni and Luise Rainer—as Chinese peasants. Your reaction?

Luke: It was an honor to work alongside Paul Muni. He was an acknowledged master and I had the opportunity to observe him and learn.

Bawden: And Luise Rainer, who won her second Best Actress Oscar playing a Chinese woman?

Luke: Luise neither acted nor looked Chinese. I thought it grotesque even in 1937. The contrast in the film between the Occidentals and the Chinese makes it hard for me to look at. But it did move the bar—it showed Chinese as human beings, struggling to keep family together. It was another blow against the Yellow Peril.

Bawden: You also played Kato in two 1940 *Green Hornet* serials?

Luke: I was the chauffeur and they asked me to adopt a Filipino accent, which I obliged, but it was awful. The [first] serial was made super quickly and Universal decided on a second, which was equally popular. But they only had rights to these two stories. Gordon Jones had the lead, a nice guy who wound up in Abbott and Costello stuff.

Bawden: In 1941's *Phantom of Chinatown,* you were the first Asian actor to play an Asian detective in a Hollywood film.

Luke: Boris Karloff's career really took off and he didn't want to do any more Monogram Wongs. So they called me in, not as a replacement but as a bustling new character, Jimmy Lee Wong, a generation younger than Boris's character. Grant Withers was still the detective and he was mad as a hornet that they didn't make his character the new lead. The girl was the wonderfully named Lotus Long, who acted under several names. She played Tokyo Rose in that Bogey movie [1949's *Tokyo Joe*] and suffered from that. She was part Hawaiian and Chinese. The story we had was written by George Waggner, who later directed the first *Wolf Man* [1941] film, but the production values were lower than low and the series was discontinued.

BAWDEN: You also went back to Chan in 1948.

LUKE: By that time I really needed the money. Toler died in 1947 and Monogram recast with Roland Winters and I was back as a middle-aged number one son. The films were both awful: *The Feathered Serpent* [1948] and *The Sky Dragon* [1949]. And Winters was five months younger than me! How about that?

MILLER: I'm one of the many who grew up watching Charlie Chan movies and always considered him a very heroic guy. How do you view those films today from the modern perspective?

LUKE: We thought we were making the best darn mysteries in Hollywood. We were proud of them. But in the late 1970s, we started to hear those films accused of being demeaning to the Chinese character. How crazy can you get? When I was in Hong Kong making *Blade in Hong Kong,* I noticed three of my Chan films were playing there. Obviously they still like them over there.

BAWDEN: Along the way you also played in MGM's continuation of the *Dr. Kildare* series as Dr. Gillespie's new resident in *Dr. Gillespie's New Assistant* [1942].

LUKE: Right. And I got a short-term MGM contract because of that. Lew Ayres [who had played Dr. Kildare] was a conscientious objector. He and Lionel Barrymore were the stars of all those popular Dr Kildare features. Then, when war came, MGM dropped Lew like a hot potato because he was a conscientious objector. MGM wanted the series to continue with Lionel and they needed a new intern that could bounce ideas off the old guy. And at that moment China was our war ally, so the character of Dr. Lee Wong How was created. MGM thought of me because I was just finishing an unbilled bit in *Somewhere I'll Find You,* a Clark Gable war thing.

I was initially nervous about meeting Mr. Barrymore. For one thing he wasn't wheelchair bound in real life. He limped around with a cane. Then he'd settle into the chair for a scene, bellow on cue, and all other actors beware! A real scene-stealer! But he made me right welcome from the beginning. Here: I'll do my impersonation of him.[Luke got up and bellowed just like Barrymore. This caused a surprised hush among the other diners.]

BAWDEN: How many of these features did you make?

LUKE: *Dr. Gillespie's New Assistant* was the first. Then *Dr. Gillespie's Criminal Case* [1943]. Then *Three Men in White* [1944]. Then *Between Two Women* [1944]. Then *Dark Delusion* [1947]. When the Communists took over China, that was the end of Dr. How. I mean, all of a sudden to be Chinese and an actor made one an object of suspicion. It also was the end of the Gillespie pictures as MGM cancelled all its series that same year. [Even] *The Thin Man* and *Maisie* features were out.

BAWDEN: You also appeared as Dr. Lee How in an Andy Hardy feature, *Andy Hardy's Blonde Trouble* [1944]?

LUKE: I was aiming for a *Maisie* credit, too. I'm just kidding! But seriously, in one scene I tell Lewis Stone as Judge Hardy I was born in a great center of learning—Brooklyn! The judge had laryngitis and I am dispatched to help him out. When the door is opened, the Hardys are scared: it's an Asian. Me! And that I think sums up my MGM career: I was a soothing, nonthreatening presence.

BAWDEN: Assess the impact of the *Dr. Gillespie* flicks.

LUKE: Well, it was a launching pad for young talent. Van Johnson was tried out in a few of them. In *Three Men in White,* Ava Gardner and Marilyn Maxwell were being tried out. In *Between Two Women,* Marilyn Maxwell and Gloria DeHaven were the up-and-comers. They would go on to top stardom at the studio.

I couldn't. The idea of romancing a white girl would have started a boycott of MGM product in more than the Deep South. I was the peaceable Asian. I had to perform this service in many an MGMer, pacifying the whites that an Asian boy wasn't all that scary. Boy? I was forty at the time.

BAWDEN: How did the series end?

LUKE: Well, Dr. Gillespie's name had disappeared from thc titles, meaning people were staying away. And Lionel was upset. Did you know he had a lifetime contract? He just hated staying at home, wanted to act every day, if he could. Much of it took place in a small town where Jimmy Craig was the doctor and I arrived and I'd talk to Gillespie on the phone. Lionel wasn't in it much and he hated that. But right after he got a top job in *Key Largo* [1948] and he was wonderful in it.

BAWDEN: In some movies in the late forties your parts were so small you were unbilled.

LUKE: Right. In *Manhandled* [1949] I was the owner of a Chinese laundry. In *Young Man with a Horn* [1950] I was Lauren Bacall's housekeeper and I wake up Kirk Douglas in the morning. He's still in bed and I'm vacuuming. I had one line of dialogue and was a day player. The director, Mike Curtiz, was nice enough to postpone the shot several times, so I got paid for a few days' work—and getting that $200 was heavenly.

MILLER: Correct me if I'm wrong, but I seem to remember you and some other Chinese American actors playing Japanese characters during World War II.

LUKE: That's true. The best for me was the part of a Japanese spy in *Across the Pacific* [1942] with Humphrey Bogart. Of course he found me out, we had a fight, and he threw me overboard!

BAWDEN: But after the war, I guess parts were scarce and you did what you had to do to survive.

LUKE: That meant TV. I was in multiple episodes of *Terry and the Pirates* [1953] and *The New Adventures of China Smith* [1953], not as a regular, but different characters. I even played a Japanese in *South Sea Woman* [1953]—had to, needed that paycheck, which was $100. I'm uncredited. I was uncredited in *Love Is a Many Splendored Thing* [1955]. The Chinese acting community in L.A. was still tiny. I'm also unbilled in *Around the World in 80 Days* [1956]. I'm an older man at the Yokohama Travel Office. I was a waiter on *December Bride* [1954] and a professor on *Meet Mr. McNutley* [1954]. Gale Storm remembered me from a day job on *My Little Margie* [1952–1955] and got me on *The Gale Storm Show* [1957] several times. I was a suspect [twice] on *Perry Mason* [1962, 1965] and several times as the same character on *Kentucky Jones* [1964]. With a little help from my friends, I kept going.

BAWDEN: You finally hit Broadway with *Flower Drum Song* [1958], which you played for almost two years in New York and two years on the road.

LUKE: I remember being in Toronto in the road show of that one. Oscar Hammerstein, who was very nice, auditioned and picked me. Dick Rodgers was not quite so nice. I didn't get the role in the movie. [Producer] Ross Hunter picked Benson Fong! In a way I felt relieved. There was now a growing community of Chinese actors. We started competing with each other. Previously Philip Ahn and I had divided up the work.

BAWDEN: How do you do it? You're in *Anna and the King* and also doing two other series: *Kung Fu* and the cartoon series *The Amazing Chan and the Chan-Klan*.

LUKE: Well, I finally got to play Charlie, so how could I turn that down? I'm only voicing the cartoon, so I do that on weekends. Then I split my time between *Anna* and *Kung Fu*. I don't have big parts. On *Anna*, I'm Siamese, but what the heck! It's a good-paying job. My only concern is we have no music rights so Yul Brynner will not burst into song. The first day he bellowed, "That's not my throne!" And he was right. They sold his golden throne during the great movie auction. They really had to rummage and they discovered Rex Harrison's throne from the 1946 movie and Yul has to do with that.

On *Kung Fu,* I'm in scenes with David Carradine. Knew his dad [John Carradine] at Fox. I think the son eccentric, but has great possibilities as an actor. So I think I'll continue a little longer at the game.

[The remainder of the interview took place years later.]

MILLER: You've had some juicy roles lately, like the old shopkeeper who sells the "mogwai" in Joe Dante's *Gremlins* [1984] and a Chinese crime boss on TV's *Miami Vice* [1985]. And I'm happy to discover you still have one of the most imposing voices in Hollywood. How do you maintain that quality?

LUKE: I practice opera to keep my voice in shape—and I'm currently memorizing all the great Shakespearean roles as a mental exercise.

MILLER: You have such a rich history in Hollywood, do you often look back on those years as almost a fantasy life?

LUKE: I don't live in the past, but I glory in the past. I think it's beautiful and the memories are golden and fragrant. But I'm more interested in life today. I find it's still miraculous and full of wonders.

Afterword

Keye Luke continued to work busily in both television and films until the end of his life. He appeared in such TV shows as *Quincy, Hunter, Vega$,* and *How the West Was Won;* his movie credits include *Won Ton Ton, the Dog Who Saved Hollywood* (1976), *Just You and Me, Kid* (1979), and his final, Woody Allen's *Alice* (1990). He died January 12, 1991, aged eighty-six, at his daughter's home in Whittier, California.

Harold Russell

Interview by Ron Miller

Harold Russell occupies a unique place in movie history. He was the first nonactor to win an Academy Award for acting and remains the only one ever to win two Oscars for the same performance. It all came about on March 13, 1947, when the Oscars for 1946 were awarded. Russell, who was then a student at Boston University, had played Homer Parrish, a World War II veteran returning home to face an uncertain future as a double amputee in the film *The Best Years of Our Lives.* (Russell lost his hands when an explosive he was handling in a training film in 1944 accidentally exploded.)

Russell, who really was a double amputee, had been nominated for the Best Supporting Actor award, even though he had never acted in a film before. (His only prior screen appearance was in the 1945 documentary film *Diary of a Sergeant,* which told the story of his rehabilitation.] He was up against four of the very best character actors in Hollywood: Charles Coburn (a previous Supporting Actor winner), William Demarest, Claude Rains and Clifton Webb.

Recognizing that a win for this untutored actor seemed highly unlikely, the board of the Motion Picture Academy had voted Russell a special Oscar to honor his achievement in portraying a character with such severe handicaps. But the academy membership loved his performance—and awarded him the Oscar anyway. Consequently, he ended up carrying home two of the prized statuettes with the hooks he employed in place of hands.

Setting the Scene

I've long believed that William Wyler's *The Best Years of Our Lives* is one of the all-time great Hollywood movies and that the performance of Harold

Harold Russell with his two Academy Awards for *The Best Years of Our Lives* in 1946. James Bawden collection.

Russell in that film is an indelible one. The pluck he shows as Homer Parrish, who's determined not to let his lack of hands keep him from a meaningful, enjoyable, and useful life, is one of the most inspiring things ever captured on film—because it represents the truth about the real man who's playing Homer on the screen.

So it was with great enthusiasm that I accepted a 1989 invitation to talk with Harold Russell in conjunction with his appearance in a two-part episode of ABC's TV series *China Beach,* the weekly series about nurses working at a military evacuation hospital in Da Nang during the Vietnam War. Russell was then hospitalized with some heart issues and had to speak with me on the phone from his hospital bed. He was a lively, witty man, and I am convinced that Russell injected much of his own persona into the character of Homer Parrish.

The Interview

MILLER: How did you get the role of Homer Parrish?

RUSSELL: William Wyler saw me in *Diary of a Sergeant* and told the film's producer, Samuel Goldwyn, he wanted to hire me to play Homer.

MILLER: How did he approach you about playing the part?

RUSSELL: He said, "We're not looking for a professional actor. We're looking for a soldier who lost both hands and came back from the war. We want someone who's playing his own life."

MILLER: Did he assign someone to teach you a few tricks of the trade before putting you in front of a camera?

RUSSELL: Goldwyn sent me to acting school to learn under the tutelage of a professional actor, but Wyler found out about it a day later and told me, "Stay away from those people! All I want you to do is play yourself. You feel it as you see it."

MILLER: Had that ever been done before? I mean, casting a real-life handicapped person to play one in a movie?

RUSSELL: I don't think so. Before World War II, I think it was always the case where handicapped people were put out of sight in institutions and care homes and kept away from the mainstream of life. I think putting me in the movie started it and they've been doing it a little more every year ever since.

MILLER: Would it be offensive to you to see an actor without a handicap play a character like Homer?

Harold Russell (*left*) as the handless veteran Homer Parrish in 1946's *The Best Years of Our Lives.* Pictured with him, from left: Teresa Wright, Dana Andrews, Myrna Loy, and Fredric March. Courtesy of Samuel Goldwyn Productions and RKO.

RUSSELL: I think if you can find an actor who actually has the disability, it's fine to have an actor in the role. But it's very difficult even for a great actor to portray a handicapped person when he hasn't been handicapped himself.

MILLER: What should an actor do who doesn't have the disability if offered such a role?

RUSSELL: Well, Jon Voight played a paraplegic in *Coming Home* [1978] and I hear he spent about six months in a cast in order to get accustomed to it.

MILLER: What was your thinking when you accepted the role of Homer?

RUSSELL: Homer is a role model to people like us and I wanted a chance to show how much we can do when given the chance.

MILLER: But after winning your Academy Awards, didn't you feel like pursuing an acting career?

RUSSELL: I love the business and I love the people in it. But to be a professional? No way. I've never seriously thought about it. I'd accept a part if I thought it was right, like I did with *Inside Moves* [1980], but I would never want to be a professional actor.

MILLER: What do you think became of Homer Parrish if we went back to see how he turned out?

RUSSELL: I don't know, but maybe he became a million-dollar insurance salesman.

MILLER: I can tell you have the same wicked sense of humor that Homer has in the movie.

RUSSELL: Humor is the best thing in the world. This world would be a lot better off if more people looked at it with a little humor, in spite of all the tragedies we face every day.

MILLER: And what about you? Besides these very infrequent acting jobs, what have you been up to?

RUSSELL: I've been working with handicapped people in employment training, housing, transportation, and all that stuff. I have what's called the Harold Russell Association. It's based in Winchester, Massachusetts. I live in Hyannis, near the Kennedy compound. Before that, I served three terms as national commander of AMVETS and served as chairman of the President's Commission on Employment of the Handicapped.

Afterword

Russell was involved in controversy when he sold his Best Supporting Actor Oscar in 1992, through an auction house, for $60,000 in order to raise funds for his wife's medical expenses. (Oscars awarded since 1950 cannot legally be sold, but Russell's award fell outside that rule, passed by the Motion Picture Academy in 1950.)

Russell suffered a heart attack in January 2002 and died at age eighty-eight.

Diane Varsi

Interview by Ron Miller

One of the genuine curiosities of the 1950s movie scene was the ethereal, elusive, and enigmatic Diane Varsi, the teenager who, without any real acting experience, landed one of the era's most coveted ingénue roles in the 1957 screen version of the notorious best seller *Peyton Place,* earned an Oscar nomination for her performance, but feuded with her studio, broke her contract, and seriously damaged what promised to be a significant acting career.

At the time, the accepted rationale was that Varsi was a beatnik-type bohemian, drifting like so many young Americans toward the dropout mentality of the so-called Beat Generation. That made a certain amount of sense if you casually examined Varsi's background. Born in 1938 in the San Francisco suburb of San Mateo, she was a rebel from the start, considered a "nutcase" by her high school classmates, and dropped out in her junior year at age fifteen. She hung out in San Francisco, where the beatnik culture was cooking, and wound up in a hasty marriage to another teenager. The marriage was annulled, but she gave birth to a son and was a single mom before she was old enough to vote.

Varsi was slim and graceful, so she joined a San Francisco ballet company, thinking she might be a dancer—or, if that didn't work out, a folk singer, a model, or maybe a hostess at a restaurant. By the time she was eighteen, she began to think of an acting career. She hitchhiked to Los Angeles, where she gained her only experience as an actress in a stage production of *Gigi.*

Varsi wanted to break into the movies and had an agent working on her behalf. Nobody seemed the least bit interested, and her agent finally dropped her in 1956 because she wasn't generating any action. Then the right people finally saw her. At that time, Hollywood talent scouts were scouring local theater companies, looking for a newcomer who could play

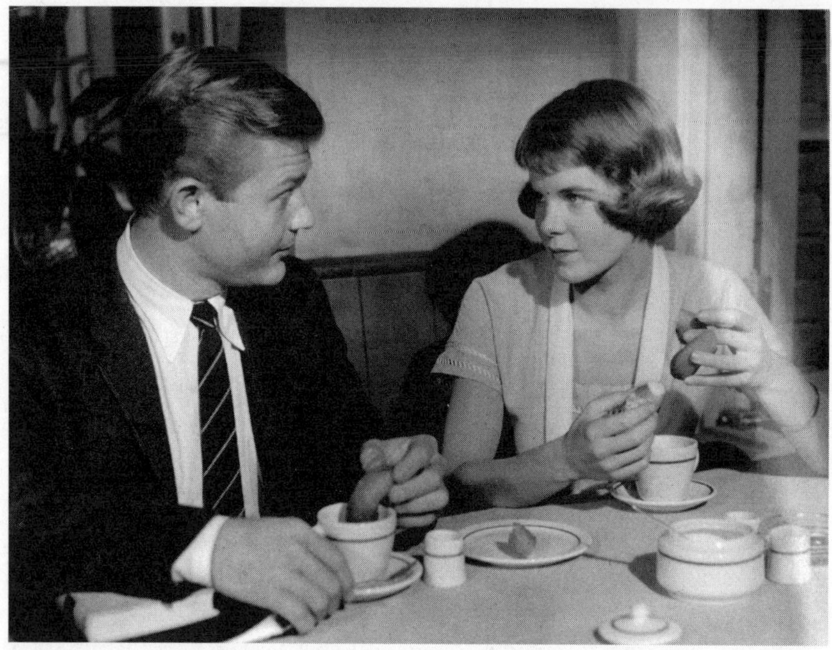

Diane Varsi with Martin Milner in 1959's *Compulsion.* Courtesy of 20th Century-Fox.

the key role of young Allison Mackenzie in the 20th Century-Fox production *Peyton Place,* based on the sex-drenched best seller by Grace Metalious. Producers had tested several well-known young actresses for the role, but when the attractive but slightly spacey Varsi auditioned, they decided she had the special "dreamy" quality they'd been looking for all along.

Though Lana Turner had the starring role as Allison's mother, Constance, the role of her daughter was a central one, counted on by the studio to attract the crucial youth audience. It was considered a star-making showcase for the unknown Varsi.

Varsi's performance in *Peyton Place* was sensitive and nuanced and she exhibited a shy, winsome appeal that suggested she was a natural actress with a bright future. Even before *Peyton Place* was released and became a huge box office hit, she had been signed to a studio contract and was quickly moved into other roles. Fox gave her second billing under two-time Oscar-winner Gary Cooper in the screen version of John O'Hara's best seller *Ten North Frederick* (1958), and she was teamed with another rising young star, Don Murray, in the routine western *From Hell to Texas* (1958), again with costar billing. The following year she was the female lead in *Compulsion,* a grim drama inspired by the Loeb-Leopold murder trial, starring Orson Welles in a role patterned after Clarence Darrow.

Varsi seemed on her way to stardom, but soon her career started collapsing. During the filming of *Ten North Frederick,* Varsi suffered what was called a nervous breakdown and was hospitalized. Rumors of her fragile health began to circulate. She also was developing a distinct anti-studio attitude. By 1959, she began turning down roles the studio lined up for her—including a leading role in *The Best of Everything.* She was already set to reprise her Allison Mackenzie role in the sequel *Return to Peyton Place* (1961) but, before filming could start, she abruptly refused to continue work under her studio contract.

Fox reminded her that she was under contract until 1965 and could not make movies elsewhere while her contract was in force. (She was replaced by other actresses in the films Fox had planned for her.) She returned to the San Francisco Bay Area and worked in a few stage productions there. She briefly stayed at the famed Actors Studio in New York. In 1961, she married Michael Hausman, who fathered her daughter, Willo.

When her contract finally expired, Varsi tried to resume her career on her own terms, but the bloom was clearly off her rose. Of the films she made in subsequent years, only a few were widely seen, among them *Wild in the Streets* (1968) and *Bloody Mama* (1970).

Her final screen appearance was a small role in the 1977 film *I Never Promised You a Rose Garden,* a title that might have summed up Hollywood's attitude to her when she started out in 1957 with little experience and a rather naïve notion of what stardom would involve.

Setting the Scene

The first time I saw Diane Varsi in person was in 1958. I was a junior at UCLA and had read that director Richard Fleischer was going to film some exteriors near Royce Hall on campus for his new film *Compulsion.* Naturally, I turned up to check it out and found myself in a small circle of students standing out of camera range while the crew filmed a scene that included Varsi, Bradford Dillman, and several others in the cast.

To be honest, Varsi could have slipped to the other side of the camera and joined us and it would have seemed appropriate. She didn't look like a movie star. She didn't wear much makeup, even on camera, and she looked like any normal college girl of 1958. Although I already thought of her as a star of tomorrow, I concluded she looked approachable.

When I was finally introduced to her, it was a little more than twenty years later, and I was a syndicated TV columnist. Varsi had not been seen in a prominently featured movie role since the 1971 independent film *Johnny Got His Gun,* the morbid screen version of screenwriter Dalton Trumbo's novel about an American soldier turned into a quadruple amputee during World War I. Trumbo directed the film himself and featured a number of players who were no longer on the Hollywood A list, including Marsha Hunt (who, like Trumbo himself, had been blacklisted during the McCarthy era) and the nearly forgotten Varsi. Varsi played a nurse caring for the title character and earned some decent reviews, though the film generally was considered a failure and did nothing at the box office.

KTVU-TV in Oakland, California, had scheduled a prime-time telecast of *Johnny Got His Gun* and, in order to stir up viewer interest, had brought in Diane Varsi to appear as the host. I was invited to lunch with Varsi in hopes an interview with the elusive star might provoke some beneficial publicity.

Varsi, who was then forty-one, turned out to be a likeable eccentric who seemed to accept her persona as a sort of bargain-basement Garbo, a star who abandoned stardom for reasons that had never really been made clear to the moviegoing public. We met at a popular restaurant near the TV station in Oakland's busy Jack London Square. I noticed that hardly anyone paid any attention to her, even though she looked pretty much like Allison Mackenzie might have at the Peyton Place high school reunion. It was obvious the other diners didn't recognize her.

She smoked cigarettes during the interview and looked, I thought, a little frail and unhealthy, though still quite attractive.

The Interview

MILLER: Do you like the fact that you can walk among us these days without anybody gawking at you?

VARSI: I never think about my identity. You might even say there's almost a refusal to have an identity.

Miller: It's never been clear to me how you managed to land the role of Allison Mackenzie in *Peyton Place* without any screen experience.

Varsi: I had enrolled in a small acting workshop run by actor Jeff Corey. He seemed to think I had talent. So when they were looking for someone to play Allison, Jeff suggested me. They called me in and I read for the part—along with eight hundred other people.

Miller: So it was as simple as that?

Varsi: Well, not everybody at the studio liked what they saw. Some thought I was too tall and not pretty enough. Some were bothered by the fact that I'd been married before and had a child. But the producer, Jerry Wald, and the director, Mark Robson, thought I was the perfect Allison—and they prevailed. They signed me to a seven-year contract. Overall, though, I think my antiestablishment lifestyle irritated the studio brass. I think they saw me as a risky investment.

Miller: But this was the era of James Dean and Marlon Brando, so I guess I kind of assumed the studios wouldn't be surprised to come across a young actor with "attitude."

Varsi: I was a woman, so I suppose they weren't quite ready for that. Anyway, I wasn't temperamental. I never walked off the job or kept people waiting.

Miller: But something began to bother you or you never would have ended your studio-directed march to stardom?

Varsi: I developed real contempt for their efforts to manufacture a movie star out of me. I didn't want to be sent on phony dates and I didn't like the whole publicity thing. And they kept trying to interfere with my private life. I lived in a cottage in Topanga Canyon and they felt that was unseemly for such a valuable property as one of their stars. The more the studio pushed me, the more I shoved back.

Miller: What about your breakdown while filming *Ten North Frederick*?

Varsi: The pressures had been mounting too high. I finally began to see a psychiatrist. I didn't want to run away from my problems, but inside, I really wanted to escape. The psychiatrist told me my feelings were perfectly natural, considering the circumstances. I mean, the studio acted like it owned me and I had nothing to say about the roles they wanted me to play.

Miller: Did the money you were making make you pause when you wanted to leave?

VARSI: Are you kidding? They were paying me $125 a week.

MILLER: What finally convinced you it was time to go?

VARSI: I was doing a TV drama on loan-out from the studio and I was injured on the set. I was forced up against a nail that was protruding from a ladder. It punctured my forehead, right between the eyes. But they didn't want to hold up production, so they patched me up at the infirmary, plastered over the wound, and sent me back to work.

MILLER: How did they react when you told them you wanted out of your contract?

VARSI: They told me they would blacklist me for the rest of my life—and they did.

MILLER: So you sat out your contract, then made some exploitation pictures at American-International. Had the market for you dried up by 1965?

VARSI: The momentum was certainly gone. I refused to be treated like a cinematic curiosity, so I held out for better roles and there weren't many being offered until *Johnny Got His Gun.*

MILLER: How did that come to you?

VARSI: Dalton Trumbo called me to his home to discuss playing the role of the nurse. Nobody had wanted to make the film for years, but anti-Vietnam War sentiment was running high and it finally got made. The nurse is the first person to find a way to communicate with the damaged Johnny, so it was a pivotal part in the movie.

MILLER: Did Trumbo have you read for him, or what convinced him you would be right for it?

VARSI: He arranged a very strange audition for me. He showed me tapes of some angry antiwar speeches and made me watch the violent reaction of the crowd. I started to get very faint, almost ill. I had to excuse myself and go outside. I thought sure I had lost the part. But it was the sensitivity he was after all along.

MILLER: What is life like for you today?

VARSI: I live in Larkspur in Marin County [north of San Francisco]. I'm not retired, no matter what you've heard. I would like to work again. I have lots of respect for my profession, despite the trouble I had with the studio.

MILLER: What about your health? I've heard that you were very ill not long ago.

VARSI: I had Lyme disease, which left me with residual nerve damage and almost constant headaches. I've played the victim very much in real life. There seems to be something I lack. I haven't been able to insulate myself against attack. But I don't feel defeated, not at all.

MILLER: Do you ever regret walking away from stardom at the peak of your fame? Don't you miss something from that glorious few years in the big time?

VARSI: I miss absolutely nothing about it, except the work.

Afterword

Diane Varsi died from respiratory failure in 1992 at age fifty-four in Los Angeles. She's buried in San Rafael, California.

Acknowledgments

All the interviews in this collection have been rewritten or revised and updated from earlier versions first published in other media. None are reprints of previously published articles.

An earlier version of James Bawden's interview with Irene Dunne appeared in *Classic American Screen* magazine. An earlier version of his Fay Wray interview appeared in *Film Fan Monthly.* Earlier versions of the Van Johnson and Rosalind Russell interviews appeared in *Classic Images: Films of the Golden Age* magazine. Earlier versions of the following interviews appeared in the *Hamilton Spectator:* Ralph Bellamy, Joan Blondell, Joan Fontaine, Cary Grant, Margaret Hamilton, and Rosalind Russell. Portions of the following interviews appeared in the *Toronto Star:* Gene Autry, Anne Baxter, Joseph Cotten, Melvyn Douglas, Douglas Fairbanks Jr., Jane Greer, Dorothy Lamour, Anna Lee, Keye Luke, Gloria Swanson, Audrey Totter, Jane Wyman, and Loretta Young.

Ron Miller's interviews with Anne Baxter, Rory Calhoun, Jackie Coogan, Kirk Douglas, Glenn Ford, Bob Hope, Dorothy Lamour, Anna Lee, Keye Luke, Dorothy McGuire, Maureen O'Hara, Luise Rainer, Roy Rogers, Harold Russell, Diane Varsi, and Marie Windsor were originally done for the *San Jose Mercury News,* and most of the resulting columns were syndicated to other newspapers in the United States and Canada.

Portions of interviews by both authors also were used in obituaries of the celebrities published on the website www.thecolumnists.com.

About the Authors

James Bawden and Ron Miller first met in 1977 at a convention of newspaper television critics in Los Angeles and discovered their common interest in the movies of Hollywood's golden age. They have been friends ever since and, after their retirement from their newspapers, worked together on the website www.thecolumnists.com.

Bawden is the former TV columnist for Canada's largest newspaper, the *Toronto Star,* where he was one of the country's most widely read entertainment writers. Bawden is renowned for his profiles of movie stars and directors. He has written for *Films in Review* and numerous cinema magazines. He lives in Toronto. This is his first book.

Miller was TV editor of the *San Jose Mercury News* from 1977 to 1999, a syndicated columnist for the Knight Ridder News Service, and the former TV columnist for *Mystery Scene* magazine. He is a former national president of the Television Critics Association and winner of a 1994 National Headliner Award for his columns. He is coauthor of *Masterpiece Theatre* (1995) and author of *Mystery! A Celebration* (1996), both official companion books to PBS television series. He's currently an instructor with the Academy for Lifelong Learning at Western Washington University in Bellingham. He and his wife, Darla, live in Blaine, Washington.

Index

Page numbers in italics refer to photographs.

Screen Classics

Screen Classics is a series of critical biographies, film histories, and analytical studies focusing on neglected filmmakers and important screen artists and subjects, from the era of silent cinema to the golden age of Hollywood to the international generation of today. Books in the Screen Classics series are intended for scholars and general readers alike. The contributing authors are established figures in their respective fields. This series also serves the purpose of advancing scholarship on film personalities and themes with ties to Kentucky.

Series Editor

Patrick McGilligan

Books in the Series

Mae Murray: The Girl with the Bee-Stung Lips
Michael G. Ankerich
Hedy Lamarr: The Most Beautiful Woman in Film
Ruth Barton
Rex Ingram: Visionary Director of the Silent Screen
Ruth Barton
Conversations with Classic Film Stars: Interviews from Hollywood's Golden Era
James Bawden and Ron Miller
Von Sternberg
John Baxter
Hitchcock's Partner in Suspense: The Life of Screenwriter Charles Bennett
Charles Bennett, edited by John Charles Bennett
Ziegfeld and His Follies: A Biography of Broadway's Greatest Producer
Cynthia Brideson and Sara Brideson
The Marxist and the Movies: A Biography of Paul Jarrico
Larry Ceplair
Dalton Trumbo: Blacklisted Hollywood Radical
Larry Ceplair and Christopher Trumbo
Warren Oates: A Wild Life
Susan Compo
Crane: Sex, Celebrity, and My Father's Unsolved Murder
Robert Crane and Christopher Fryer
Jack Nicholson: The Early Years
Robert Crane and Christopher Fryer
Being Hal Ashby: Life of a Hollywood Rebel
Nick Dawson
Bruce Dern: A Memoir
Bruce Dern with Christopher Fryer and Robert Crane
Intrepid Laughter: Preston Sturges and the Movies
Andrew Dickos
John Gilbert: The Last of the Silent Film Stars
Eve Golden
Stuntwomen: The Untold Hollywood Story
Mollie Gregory

Saul Bass: Anatomy of Film Design
Jan-Christopher Horak
Hitchcock Lost and Found: The Forgotten Films
Alain Kerzoncuf and Charles Barr
Pola Negri: Hollywood's First Femme Fatale
Mariusz Kotowski
Sidney J. Furie: Life and Films
Daniel Kremer
Albert Capellani: Pioneer of the Silent Screen
Christine Leteux
Mamoulian: Life on Stage and Screen
David Luhrssen
Maureen O'Hara: The Biography
Aubrey Malone
My Life as a Mankiewicz: An Insider's Journey through Hollywood
Tom Mankiewicz and Robert Crane
Hawks on Hawks
Joseph McBride
William Wyler: The Life and Films of Hollywood's Most Celebrated Director
Gabriel Miller
Raoul Walsh: The True Adventures of Hollywood's Legendary Director
Marilyn Ann Moss
Veit Harlan: The Life and Work of a Nazi Filmmaker
Frank Noack
Charles Walters: The Director Who Made Hollywood Dance
Brent Phillips
Some Like It Wilder: The Life and Controversial Films of Billy Wilder
Gene D. Phillips
Ann Dvorak: Hollywood's Forgotten Rebel
Christina Rice
Arthur Penn: American Director
Nat Segaloff
Claude Rains: An Actor's Voice
David J. Skal with Jessica Rains
Buzz: The Life and Art of Busby Berkeley
Jeffrey Spivak
Victor Fleming: An American Movie Master
Michael Sragow
Hollywood Presents Jules Verne: The Father of Science Fiction on Screen
Brian Taves
Thomas Ince: Hollywood's Independent Pioneer
Brian Taves
Carl Theodor Dreyer and Ordet: *My Summer with the Danish Filmmaker*
Jan Wahl